Fundamentals of Forensic Practice
Mental Health and Criminal Law

Fundamentals of Forensic Practice

Mental Health and Criminal Law

Richard Rogers, Ph.D., ABPP

University of North Texas, Denton, TX

and

Daniel W. Shuman, J.D.

Southern Methodist University, Dallas, TX

 Springer

Richard Rogers
Department of Psychology
University of North Texas
Denton, TX 76203-1280
USA
rogers@unt.edu.

Daniel W. Shuman
School of Law
Southern Methodist University
Dallas, TX 75275
USA
dshuman@mail.smu.edu

Library of Congress Control Number: 2005923617

ISBN 10: 0-387-25226-6   e-ISBN 0-38725227-4
ISBN 13: 978-0387-25226-1

Printed on acid-free paper.

Printed in the United States of America.   (TB/MVY)

9 8 7 6 5 4 3 2 1

springeronline.com

Contents

*Specifically for use as court exhibits, copies of Appendices A through I are permitted for this explicit purpose.

*Specifically for use as court exhibits, copies of Appendices A through I are permitted for this
explicit purpose.

I

Foundations of Practice

1

Clinical and Legal Framework

Mental health and legal professionals face formidable challenges in applying their knowledge and expertise to the criminal justice system. This book addresses psycholegal issues from both law (e.g., statutes, case law, and legal theory) and clinical-forensic (e.g., empirically based knowledge and specialized methods) perspectives. Within the criminal justice system, it considers the major legal, empirical, and forensic issues found in the law–mental health interface.

Psycholegal issues arise at each major phase (i.e., pretrial, trial, sentencing, and postconviction) of the criminal trial process. *Pretrial issues* include (1) the initial processing of defendants, such as their diversion from the criminal justice system; (2) psychological factors affecting the determination of bail; and (3) competencies as they relate to *Miranda* warnings and warrantless searches. *Trial issues* address several psycholegal standards most familiar to forensic clinicians, specifically competency to stand trial and insanity. Less common issues involve other matters of criminal responsibility, such as mens rea and guilty-but-mentally ill. *Sentencing issues* consider both noncapital and capital domains. In noncapital cases, sentencing examines psychological issues as they relate to rehabilitation and incapacitation. In capital cases, aggravating and mitigating factors plus other constitutionally required issues (e.g., *Estelle* warnings and *Atkins* exclusion of the mentally retarded) must be considered. *Postconviction issues* address such capacities as the competency to waive appeals and competency to be executed. As a matter of convenience, standards for sexually violent predators are also considered at this point because civil issues are raised in the postconviction, postpunishment phase.

HISTORICAL PERSPECTIVE ON FORENSIC PSYCHOLOGY AND PSYCHIATRY

Modern forensic psychiatry and psychology can be traced to several crucial developments during the 1960s that shaped and refined these closely related specialties. Early forensic practice provided a colorful, if unscientific, chronicle of infamous cases and notorious trials that often centered on the sanity of a criminal defendant (Prosono, 2003; Quen, 1981). Developments starting in the 1960s involve (a) early efforts at standardizing forensic evaluations, (b) judicial decisions on admissibility that opened the door to forensic psychology with an equivalent expert status to forensic psychiatry (*Jenkins v. United States*, 1962), and (c) a widespread acknowledgment of law as the general framework for forensic practice. The growing stature of these specialties was marked by the formation of prominent professional societies, the American Academy of Psychiatry and Law in 1968 and the American Board of Forensic Psychology in 1969. The maturation of these forensic specialties is noted by the development of sophisticated training programs at the doctoral and postdoctoral levels (Brigham & Grisso, 2003). Modern forensic psychology and psychiatry are distinguished by their sophisticated understanding of legal issues and the empirical underpinnings of their practice.

Robey's (1965) seminal research on competency to stand trial provides a simple yet elegant demarcation between early and modern practice. Robey observed that early practitioners routinely applied their customary clinical skills without appearing cognizant of the specific forensic issues. His straightforward analysis has far-reaching implications. It suggested that traditional insularity be replaced by professional accountability. In presaging empirical validation, it recommended that idiosyncratic approaches be replaced by standardized methods. Though largely unheralded, Robey (1965) easily could be considered the beginning of modern forensic practice.

CONCEPTUAL MODELS OF FORENSIC PSYCHOLOGY AND PSYCHIATRY

OVERVIEW OF THE MODELS

Conceptual models of forensic practice have evolved from the early *clinical-only* perspective to incorporate legal underpinnings and empirical validation. As a major departure from the *clinical-only* tradition, Melton, Petrila, Poythress, and Slobogin (1987) emphasized the *legal–clinical* model with statutes, case law, and legal theory providing the primary framework for forensic practice. In contrast, clinical skills were considered of secondary importance, often de-emphasized and occasionally denigrated (see Rogers & Ewing, 2003). In standardizing insanity evaluations, Rogers (1984, 1986) exemplified the current model of forensic practice: the *legal-empirical-forensic* perspective that balances the legal framework with empirical validation. Grisso (1986, 2002) has championed this legal-empirical-forensic model and is largely responsible for its widespread acceptance.

The foundational paradigm for this book is the *legal-empirical-forensic* perspective. It provides the core structure implicitly in Part I, *Foundations of Practice*, and explicitly in Part II, *Specific Criminal Issues*. Its integral elements are the following:

- The *legal* framework provides the essential template in generally defining legal standards and broadly addressing their interpretations. The law also attempts to determine the parameters of expert knowledge. However, the legal framework cannot establish the underlying science and theory of forensic psychology and psychiatry.
- *Empirical* validation is equally essential to forensic specialties. With rare exception, the law provides only nonspecific constructs. Specialties, such as forensic psychology and psychiatry, bear the responsibility of operationalizing these constructs and developing empirically validated methods for their assessment. Such methods should be theoretically driven and consonant with scientific principles. The Supreme Court in *Daubert* and its progeny demand evidentiary reliability grounded in more than self-proclamation (i.e., ipse dixitism of the expert).
- The legal and empirical components are insufficient by themselves for forensic practice. While providing broad conceptualizations, tested theory, and nomothetic knowledge, these components do not capture the singular challenges found in evaluations of individual defendants. The final component, *forensic*, is the application of legal

interpretation and specialized methods to a particular case. Forensic expertise requires more than customary clinical practice in its rigorous implementation of forensic principles, ethics, and decision-making.

Relevance to Forensic Practice

Many criminal attorneys may begin to question the relevance of the foregoing discussion to their practices. Why does it matter that forensic psychology and psychiatry embrace the *legal-empirical-forensic* paradigm? It matters because more than a few forensic experts lack the requisite understanding of one or more these essential components for forensic competence. The basis for their "expertise" is sciolism, a smattering of superficial knowledge. For each component, Box 1-1 illustrates general avenues for cross-examination. These components will be examined closely in subsequent chapters as they relate to specific legal standards.

It is surprising that cross-examining attorneys routinely allow unprepared experts to testify without rigorously questioning their competence. The illustrative questions in Box 1-1 are not intended to be antagonistic or demeaning. Rather, the expertise of experts should be calmly explored in criminal trials. For example, cross-examinations about legal understanding may uncover a substantive misconstrual of the relevant criteria. Nearly all experts will be able to recall the gist of legal standard. Of greater relevance is their understanding of the standard and their ability to articulate its meaning in their own words. Although the rules of evidence permit experts to offer non-opinion testimony (i.e., scientific or technical data), most often it is the expert's opinion that is offered. To be helpful, the expert's opinion must be based on a firm and accurate understanding of the relevant standard. This understanding provides the necessary framework for subsequent opinions. The expert's expertise (i.e., both qualifications and the accuracy of the methods employed), and the relevance of the resulting opinion to the pertinent legal issue in the case are central issues for cross as well as direct examination. Expert opinions require more than a superficial understanding of the relevant legal standard. In addition their expert application to the facts of the case necessitates empirically grounded methods and procedures.

A substantial minority of experts is unknowledgeable of the science and theory undergirding their opinions. For the criminal attorney, the essential question to be asked of experts is simply, "*How do you know what you claim to know?*" Consider for a moment three illustrative examples of knowledge that should be possessed by forensic clinicians involved in criminal cases:

BOX 1-1   ARE EXPERTS ADEQUATELY PREPARED? ILLUSTRATIVE
CROSS-EXAMINATION QUESTIONS

Legal Understanding

1. *Doctor, you were retained in this case to address* __ (i.e., a specific legal standard), *is that correct?*
2. *Why is it important to correctly understand* __ (i.e., a specific legal standard), *before rendering an opinion?*
3. *What sources of information did you use to ensure a correct understanding?* [Look for limited or potentially biased sources]
4. *You just testified about* __ (i.e., a specific legal standard). *Please tell us* in your own words *what that means to you.*... [If hesitates or stumbles] *Doctor, you appear to be unsure of yourself, wouldn't you agree?*
5. *You mentioned* __ (i.e., a component of the standard), *please tell us what that means to you.*... [If incomplete] *Anything else you would like to add?*... [If inaccurate] *How confident are you in this description?*
6. [#5 can be repeated for each major component of the standard]

Empirically Validated Knowledge and Methods

1. *Please define forensic* (select: psychology/psychiatry). *Is this a legitimate specialty with its own empirically validated knowledge and assessment methods?*
2. *Are you qualified to describe yourself as a forensic* (select: psychologist/psychiatrist)?
3. *Regarding* __ (i.e., a specific legal standard), *does forensic psychology and psychiatry have any empirically validated knowledge?*... [if unclear] *Any specialized knowledge base in scientific research that would qualify you as an expert?*
4. *Are you competent to describe this empirically validated knowledge of* __ (i.e., a specific legal standard)? [If "no," pursue further the obvious limits of expertise]
5. *Who are the most prominent researchers in establishing this empirically validated knowledge?*
6. *You mentioned* __ (i.e., a prominent researcher), *tell us about his or her research methodology?*... [If the answer addresses the major findings] *Please don't duck my question, I asked about* the research methodology.
7. [#6 can be repeated for other prominent researchers]

Forensic Practice

1. *Does forensic* (select: psychology/psychiatry) *have its own ethical guidelines?*
2. *Please be specific, which ethical guidelines are particularly relevant to this case?*... [If uncertain] *Doctor, how many months, or even years, has it been since you carefully reviewed the forensic ethical guidelines?*
3. *Doctor, did you have your mind made up before you saw the defendant is this case?*... *Please tell the court why it is important to have an open mind and consider different hypotheses.*
4. *What were the competing hypotheses in this case?*... *Where in your report did you discuss the competing hypotheses?*

(Continued)

5. [for psychologists only] *Isn't it part of your specialty guidelines to actively consider competing hypotheses?*
6. *Yes or no, doctor, is it just a coincidence that you only described the hypothesis that* (select: favors/goes against) *the defendant?...* [optional] *Can you understand why* (select: judge/jury) *might see you as biased and untrustworthy?*

1. *Determination of malingering.* What specific detection strategies for malingering were used? How were these strategies validated?
2. *Competency to stand trial.* What are the advantages of using standardized competency measures? If shunning such measures, can the expert offer a detailed explanation concerning the development and validation of each competency measure? If not, isn't this shunning simply an act of ignorance?
3. *Risk assessment.* What are the underlying assumptions in the development of risk assessment measures? What are the important roles of protective factors and moderating effects in determinations of risk assessment?

Rightly or wrongly, the onus falls directly on criminal attorneys to ensure that experts understand the science of their profession. In many areas, the amount of empirically validated knowledge has more than doubled in the last decade. As a specific example, Salekin, Rogers, and Sewell (1996) found only 18 studies addressing Hare's (1991) psychopathy and recidivism. Less than a decade later, Salekin, Leistico, Rogers, and Schrum (2003) compiled 53 studies on the same topic. Regrettably, many experts have fallen substantially behind in the requisite knowledge of their own specialty.

As the question is framed in Box 1-1, does the expert have a sophisticated understanding of the specialized expertise for his or her discipline and specialty? In Chapter 3, we examine more closely the relationship between experts and their expertise. If the forensic expert cannot name several prominent researchers and describe their major contributions (i.e., methods and results), then two possibilities must be considered by criminal attorneys:

1. *Beyond the specialty.* Forensic psychology and psychiatry do not have expertise to offer the courts on this particular question.
2. *Beyond the expert.* This particular witness is not sufficiently expert on this particular issue given the expertise available in forensic psychology and psychiatry.

Forensic practice is also informed by professional and ethical standards. Experts should be aware of their specialty standards, such as *Specialty Guidelines for Forensic Psychologists* (Committee on Ethical Guidelines for Forensic Psychologists, 1991) and *Ethical Guidelines for the Practice of Forensic Psychiatry* (American Academy of Psychiatry and Law, 1991, 1995). While these criteria are aspirational rather than enforceable, they provide official guidelines for conducting forensic consultations, court reports, and subsequent testimony. Surprising numbers of forensic experts are unfamiliar with their own specialty guidelines. For illustrative purposes, Box 1-1 provides a sample of cross-examination inquiries about forensic guidelines as well as potential issues of confirmatory biases.

CONCEPTUAL MODELS OF ATTORNEYS AND MENTAL HEALTH ISSUES

Before considering how lawyers and both psychologists and psychiatrists best collaborate effectively in forensic practice it is worthwhile to acknowledge some of the professional differences that affect those relationships. Consider first issues of process and outcome. Lacking a metric for assessing the correctness of the outcome of any case (e.g., did the jury correctly find that the defendant did it?), the law is driven by concerns with process (e.g., right to counsel). These concerns are constitutionally grounded in specific rights recognized in the Bill of Rights (e.g., right to counsel, trial by jury, confrontation of adverse witnesses) as well as the Fifth and Fourteenth Amendment of the U.S. Constitution's language that forbids the federal and state governments from depriving a person of life, liberty, or property "without due process of law." Thus, while the law is concerned with reaching the right outcome, its only certainty in doing so is to ensure that the right process was followed. In contrast, forensic psychology and psychiatry operate from a very different paradigm that is based on principles of science rather than law. These specialties are concerned with measurement and theory. Focusing on the former, measurement is *unscientific* unless it is standardized and can be reliably and accurately ascertained. For this reason, the reliable assessment of diagnoses and key symptoms is a paramount issue to forensic clinicians. Evidencing substantial differences in epistemology (see Rogers & Shuman, 2000), law seeks a fair outcome through advocacy within an adversarial system whereas forensic psychology seeks objectivity through its methods and consensus in its knowledge[1] (Constanzo, 2004). Moreover, the law is much more pragmatic than forensic psychology and psychiatry often seeking a negotiated solution (e.g., plea bargaining or a settlement) rather than a strict inquiry into truth.

Haney (1980) outlined the fundamental differences between the assumptions of law and psychology. Narrowing this focus to individual accountability helps to illustrate these fundamental differences (Melton, Petrila, Poythress, & Slobogin, 1997). The law proceeds from the assumption that it is appropriate to hold people accountable for their behavior because they exercise a sufficient degree of control over it (i.e., free will). Seeking an ordered society in which people are entitled to expect that those with whom they come in contact will follow the rules, the law is skeptical of behavioral control excuses for unlawful choices. In contrast, psychology and psychiatry propose different theories of behavior based largely on determinism. Rather than trying to fit behavioral choices into the law's moral dichotomy, psychology and psychiatry are more likely to view behavior as multidetermined and unique to each person.

SCIENTIFIC STATUS OF FORENSIC PSYCHOLOGY AND PSYCHIATRY

Faust and Ziskin's (1988) scathing critique of forensic expertise found the entire enterprise almost completely lacking in sound science. They found wanting (1) the scientific underpinning of forensic psychology and psychiatry, (2) the adequacy of their theories, and (3) the validity of their assessment methods (see also Ziskin, 1995). While unduly negative, these intense criticisms identified certain tradition-bound complacencies in forensic psychology and psychiatry. They also underscored the need for systematic research in validating measures and methods used in forensic practice.

As a major objective of this book, subsequent chapters examine the *science* of forensic psychology and psychiatry in relationship to specific legal standards. Despite considerable advances, the scientific underpinnings of forensic psychology and psychiatry have developed unevenly. This current section briefly summarizes three major achievements in forensic assessment during the last decade. They are (a) diagnostic advances,

---

[1]This statement is especially true for those doctoral programs in psychology that espouse a scientist–practitioner model. It is comparatively less true for practitioner-only models that are found with a minority of doctoral level training programs, but most psychiatric residency programs.

(b) advances in defining and understanding legal standards, and (c) advances in the specialized assessment of legal constructs.

DIAGNOSTIC ADVANCES

Accurate diagnoses of mental disorders play a central though rarely pivotal role in forensic determinations. Legal standards addressing psycholegal issues seldom specify individual diagnoses as a formal component of these standards. One rare exception is the *Atkins* exclusion from capital sentencing of persons diagnosed with mental retardation. In most other cases, the diagnoses should not be equated with component of legal standards. This misequation is often observed in personal injury cases in which posttraumatic stress disorders (PTSD) are facilely assumed to demonstrate proximate cause (Greenberg, Shuman, & Meyer, 2004). Instead, diagnoses serve the valuable function of assessing the onset, course, and severity of Axis I and Axis II disorders. These diagnostic data can then be used to address the defendant's relevant capacities and overall impairment.

A major advance in the last decade is the emergence of structured interviews with demonstrable reliability and validity. Rogers (2001) provides a comprehensive review of Axis I and Axis II interviews emphasizing their reliability and clinical applications. Several structured interviews allow forensic experts to demonstrate to the courts that their diagnoses are highly reliable across qualified evaluators (i.e., interrater reliability) and time intervals (i.e., test–retest reliability). The demonstration of reliable diagnoses is unmistakably a major advance for forensic practice. It substantively addresses a key criticism of forensic psychology and psychiatry, namely diagnostic subjectivity (i.e., the "soft science" argument; Ziskin, 1995). Simply put, reliable measurement is the *sine qua non* of science.

Structured interviews are most often used in clinical research because of its requirements for scientifically rigorous methods. Given the far-reaching consequences to criminal defendants and the community, we recommend that forensic evaluations be held to the same rigorous standards as clinical research. *As a standard for forensic practice, criminal attorneys should request, if not demand, that all diagnoses have demonstrable reliability.* The alternative is likely to be unacceptable: idiosyncratic diagnoses with unknown reliability that are prone to clinician biases.

Beyond reliability, structured interviews provide systematic data that can examine comprehensively Axis I and Axis II diagnoses and symptoms.

Box 1-2   ILLUSTRATIVE QUESTIONS FOR IDIOSYNCRATIC[a] DIAGNOSES

1. *Doctor, do you believe that forensic evaluations should be held to a high standard of practice, equaling or exceeding those used in clinical research?*
2. *Isn't it true that high quality* [select: psychology/psychiatry] *journals do not accept research with* <u>*unreliable diagnoses?*</u>
3. *How is interrater reliability established?... Why is it impossible for you to establish interrater reliability in this case?*
4. *If you were sufficiently trained in structured interviews, how might these methods have been useful in demonstrating interrater reliability?* [answer: Research has established their reliability for trained clinicians.]
5. *You relied on your own* [select: subjective/unstandardized] *interviews in rendering your diagnosis. Were you aware at the time that such interviews often miss diagnoses?... Would you be surprised to learn that such interviews miss more than half the Axis I diagnoses?*
6. [if applicable] *Doctor, did you write a complete and unbiased report?... Does your report accurately reflect your evaluation including its strengths and limitations?... [If "yes"] Please show me in your report where you acknowledged that your diagnoses may be unreliable and incomplete.*

[a] This term is applied to diagnoses rendered solely by unstandardized methods, such as a traditional interview.

Recently, Rogers (2003) reviewed clinical research that underscored the importance of structured interviews in rendering comprehensive Axis I and Axis II diagnoses. Extrapolating from Zimmerman and Mattia's (1999) review and research, traditional (unstructured) interviews conservatively miss more than 50% of Axis I diagnoses[2] (see also Chapter 12). Missed diagnoses commonly occur for Axis II disorders as well (Blashfield, 1992). Most attorneys would be alarmed to know that forensic experts relying solely on traditional interviews only "get it half right."

Many forensic experts have not kept pace with the advances in structured interviews for rendering reliable and comprehensive diagnoses. To assist criminal attorneys, Box 1-2 provides illustrative questions for undercovering the weaknesses of tradition-bound idiosyncratic diagnoses. Importantly, exclusive reliance on either method (structured or idiosyncratic) interviews may lead to diagnostic errors. However, the inclusion of structured interviews standardizes the diagnostic process, systematizes the symptom ratings, and can provide convincing evidence of diagnostic reliability.

---

[2]Combining across studies of nearly 10,000 patients, they found that most clinician-only assessments (75.1%) stopped after the first Axis I diagnosis. In stark contrast, diagnoses based on structured interviews resulted in "comorbidity rates are two to three times higher" (Zimmerman & Mattia, 1999, p. 183).

Forensic clinicians not trained in structured interviews are likely to resist strongly any inference that their diagnostic methods are not rigorous and empirically validated. Attorneys should be prepared and not deterred by the spirited responses put forth by forensic clinicians defending their traditional practices. As illustrated in Box 1-2, the crucial issue is that science not tradition should constitute the basis of clinical-forensic testimony. We recommend that attorneys be prepared for a sustained cross-examination on this pivotal issue. Otherwise, they implicitly accept the validity of tradition-bound, inherently subjective assessment methods.

Advances in Defining and Understanding Legal Standards

Roesch and Golding (1980) were among the first researchers to recognize the legal concepts were typically "open-textured constructs" that cannot simply be reduced to a single set of operationalized characteristics. Early attempts to define the key or representative characteristics were often informal processes. For example, Wildman, Batchelor, Thompson, Nelson, Moore, et al.'s (1979) early work on the Georgia Court Competency Test (GCCT) was simply a compilation of cardinal characteristics drawn from the legal and forensic literature. Even Hare's (see Hare, 1991) early work in defining the characteristics for the 20 items of the Psychopathy Checklist—Revised (PCL-R) appears to be a nonsystematic process. While defining characteristics are described as *prototypical*, no formal analyses are provided.

A major advance in the last decade is the formal use of prototypical analyses to evaluate systematically the representative criteria of ill-defined or "fuzzy" constructs. Developed by Rosch (1973, 1978), prototypical analysis rates the centrality of characteristics in defining what constitutes and does not constitute a specific construct. An early application of prototypical analysis to forensic populations sought to examine the representative characteristics of antisocial personality disorder and psychopathy (Rogers, Dion, & Lynett, 1992; Rogers, Duncan, & Sewell, 1994; Rogers, Salekin, Sewell, & Cruise, 2000). In the criminal domain, prototypical analysis has been successfully used with competency to stand trial, especially in the development of the Evaluation of Competency to Stand Trial—Revised (ECST-R; Rogers, Tillbrook, & Sewell, 2004).

Both legal and clinical constructs are typically composed of several related components or dimensions. Through the use of factor analysis, and more recently confirmatory factor analysis (CFA), researchers have added greatly to our understanding of these constructs and their underlying dimensions. For example, the construct of psychopathy has been intensively studied. Factor analytic results of psychopathy have supported the traditional two-factor model (Hare, 1991) and subsequently a three-factor (Cooke & Michie, 1997) and a four-factor (Hare, 2003) model. These later analyses are refinements of the basic two dimensions and further our understanding of this important construct.

The refinement and validation of legal constructs via CFA represents a major advance for the science of forensic psychology and psychiatry. As an example from Chapter 6, factor analysis was used to test whether the *Dusky* standard for competency to stand trial is best conceptualized as two or three related dimensions. Results from a large multisite study strongly supported a three-factor model for the *Dusky* standard (Rogers, Jackson, Tillbrook, Sewell, & Martin, 2003). In summary, theory-driven empirical research on the relevant dimensions of legal constructs undergirds forensic psychology and psychiatry with a solid scientific foundation.

ADVANCES IN THE SPECIALIZED ASSESSMENT OF LEGAL CONSTRUCTS

Heilbrun, Rogers, and Otto (2002) highlighted the major advances in the development of forensic assessment instruments (FAI) and forensically relevant instruments (FRI). In particular, FAIs are standardized measures for evaluating elements of legal constructs. In contrast, FRIs assess clinical constructs (e.g., malingering and psychopathy) that are often applicable to legal constructs. Regarding FAIs, Grisso (2003) provides an incisive yet scholarly review of most measures and the forensic applications.

The major advances in forensic measures (FAIs and FRIs) are well documented. Because these measures are reviewed extensively in subsequent chapters, this section simply highlights the more salient accomplishments. These accomplishments include the following:

1. *Standardizing the scope of the forensic evaluation.* FAIs ensure that critical issues are addressed in each forensic assessment. Most FAIs provide forensic clinicians with well-tested inquiries that cover the relevant domains.
2. *Standardizing clinical-forensic ratings.* Much of the subjectivity in forensic evaluations can be minimized by the systematic use of standardized ratings. Such ratings identify relevant criteria and provide an orderly means for quantifying responses.
3. *Establishing the interrater reliability of forensic ratings and conclusions.* With the standardization of issues, criteria, and ratings, forensic clinicians can formally test their level of agreement.

Diagnostic disagreements, and presumably disagreements about forensic conclusions, are largely the result of unstandardized inquiries (see #1) and their concomitant ratings (see #2). A classic study by Ward et al. (1962) found that 32.5% of diagnostic disagreements resulted from differences in scope and inquiries used in evaluations (referred to as "information variance"). Differences in how clinicians recorded and used diagnostic standards (referred to as "criterion variance") accounted for 62.5% of the disagreements. Therefore, the standardization of forensic-related inquiries (information variance) and legally relevant criteria (criterion variance) should markedly reduce the subjectivity of forensic conclusions and establish theoretically sound and empirically validated bases for such conclusions.

The use of FAIs allows clinical researchers to establish the reliability of forensic evaluations. For each FAI, consistent results can be tested and potentially established at three levels: individual items, scales/dimensions, and overall conclusions. Historically, researchers have been content merely to evaluate agreement regarding overall conclusions. This cursory approach may overlook major disagreements about important elements of forensic decision-making at the item and scale levels. By systematically evaluating items, scales, and conclusions, experts can convincingly demonstrate to the courts the reliability of their methods.

CONCLUSIONS ABOUT SCIENTIFIC STATUS

Substantial progress on the scientific underpinnings of forensic psychology and psychiatry during the last decade is well documented. With the establishment of structured interviews, highly reliable *DSM-IV* diagnoses are now feasible for both Axis I and Axis II disorders. Legal standards can be defined and their relevant dimensions established. One ultimate test of these empirically validated measures and scales would be their formal acceptance in appellate rulings. Given the doctrine of *stare decisis* and narrowly focused court rulings, we do not expect any specific ruling regarding the appropriateness of particular measures. Therefore, scientific advances will need to seek other forms of validation, such as construct validity. Overall, the validation of forensic measures is an exciting development that is likely to increase the scientific rigor of forensic consultations.

The challenge for forensic psychology and psychiatry is the substantial lag between research and practice. Frequently, practitioners do not stay abreast with new developments in diagnostic and forensic measures. Like all professional disciplines, practitioners often gravitate to the "tried-and-true" methods and may even disparage new developments that may require further training. Optimally, forensic psychology and psychiatry should discipline their respective professions in ensuring that current practices reflect the best science. As a practical matter, criminal attorneys are accorded this responsibility for both their own and opposing experts.

LEGAL STATUS OF FORENSIC PSYCHOLOGY
AND PSYCHIATRY

Two important themes have dominated the legal status of forensic psychiatry and psychology, the qualifications necessary to be admitted as an expert witness and the evidentiary reliability of the methods and procedures that the expert applies. Because of the historical dominance of the medical model, physicians specializing in psychiatry have long been recognized as qualified to testify as experts on the mental health issues. This same recognition has accorded gradually for psychologists over the last four decades. The watershed case in recognizing the expertise of psychologists is *Jenkins v. United States* (1962). At its time, this case was ground breaking:

> The determination of a psychologist's competence to render an expert opinion based on his findings as to the presence or absence of mental disease or defect must depend upon the nature and extent of his knowledge. It does not depend upon his claim to the title 'psychologist.' And that determination, after hearing, must be left in each case to the traditional discretion of the trial court subject to appellate review. Although there are no statutory criteria for licensing psychologists in the District of Columbia to assist trial courts, the American Psychological Association's list of approved graduate training programs provides some guidance. When completion of such training is followed by actual experience in the treatment and diagnosis of disease in association with psychiatrists or neurologists, the opinion of the psychologist may properly be received in evidence. (p. 645)

Judicial preferences for forensic experts have not been adequately studied. We suspect that substantial differences might be observed on the basis of the past experiences with certain experts, particular psycholegal issues, and financial considerations. Beyond these preferences, the trial court judge is expected to rule whether an individual psychologist or psychiatrist has *sufficient* expertise to assist the factfinder. Toward this end, voire dire can be used to inquire about the proposed expert's education, training, experience relevant to the issue on which the expert's testimony is offered. In our experience, judges have not established unduly stringent standards for determining the expert status of forensic psychologists and psychiatrists.

Besides qualifications, the expert's methods and procedures must also pass judicial muster. Although the adoption of the Federal Rules of Evidence in 1974 signaled a liberalization of the admissibility rules, recent decisions by the Supreme Court place increased demands for the trial judge as gatekeeper. In this role, judges must impose minimum threshold requirements to address the evidentiary reliability of the methods and procedures employed by proposed experts. These demands are reflected in three

Supreme Court decisions: *Daubert v. Merrell Dow Pharmaceuticals Inc.* (1993); *General Electric Company v. Joiner* (1997); *Kumho Tire Company v. Carmichael* (1999). With these decisions, expert testimony is only admissible if it is both relevant and reliable. To address these requirements the Court enunciated four separate factors that should be considered; whether the method (1) can and has been tested, (2) has been subjected to peer review, (3) has known or potential error rates, and (4) has achieved acceptance in the relevant scientific community. These components are also addressed generally in Chapter 3 with their specific applications noted throughout the text.

The application of these criteria varies in federal courts and the state courts that have adopted. Nonetheless, they represent a paradigm shift in which evidentiary reliability is not simply a matter for the jury to consider, but rather it is a preliminary issue that should be addressed as a condition of admissibility. Importantly, the standard of review imposed by the appellate courts is *abuse of discretion*. This standard provides the trial courts with broad latitude; it signals that the decisions regarding the admissibility of expert testimony will largely be left to the trial judges. Given this latitude, a lack of consistency across trial courts regarding the same evidence may be tolerated on appellate review. The key issue at the trial level will be to persuade the court judge regarding the relevance and reliability of the expert testimony.

LOOKING FORWARD AT THE CHAPTERS AND THEIR GOALS

STRUCTURE OF THE CHAPTERS

Chapters in Part I, *Foundations of Practice*, have a flexible structure to enable sufficient coverage of broad topics. Like all chapters, however, they share three common elements: conceptual issues, forensic research, and practical applications. Given the breadth of chapters, conceptual issues are emphasized in Part I with contributions from both legal and clinical domains. Forensic research is addressed very selectively because empirical studies could easily overshadow the important ideas and principles that are crucial to establishing the *Foundations of Practice*. Practical applications vary across chapters but always include specific guidelines related to testimony and sample cross-examination. While immediately beneficial to criminal attorneys, practical applications should also be useful to forensic clinicians in preparing their cases and planning for expert testimony.

Chapters in Part II, *Specific Criminal Issues*, follow a standardized format to increase the ease of use across individual chapters. Following a brief introduction, most chapters are organized into four major sections as outlined:

1. *Relevant legal standard.* Each chapter begins with clear distillation of the specific legal standard with a focus on pivotal cases and statutes/rules that address the substantive issues. Where debates occur, this section provides the differing perspectives (e.g., majority and minority opinions).
2. *Clinical operationalization of the legal standard.* Legal scholars and forensic researchers offer valuable insights into the components of each standard. Combining contributions from law and forensic research, this section integrates the theoretical and empirical basis for each legal standard.
3. *Forensic issues and methods.* The crux of this section is the understanding and application of clinical methods for addressing the legal standard. It typically includes (a) the use of standard measures (e.g., traditional tests and structured interviews) and (b) specific applications of specialized measures (i.e., FAIs and FRIs).
4. *Courtroom Issues and Cross-Examination.* The section focuses on the potential limitations of expert testimony. It features illustrative cross-examination to provide attorneys with a general template for limiting the persuasiveness of opposing experts. While obstensively geared for trial attorneys, the questions and commentary also assist forensic clinicians in their preparation for trial.

The purpose of these chapters is to provide in-depth knowledge to both experts and attorneys. The early sections of each chapter familiarize both professions with valuable insights into how legal standards can be clinically operationalized and which clinical methods are useful to the assessment process. The overriding goals are twofold: first, to provide rigorous standards of practice for forensic psychologists and psychiatrists, and second, to enable criminal attorneys to understand the principles and practices of forensic psychology and psychiatry.

STRUCTURE OF THE BOOK

Part I, *Foundations of Forensic Practice*, addresses the issues fundamental to the science and practice of forensic psychology and psychiatry. These issues are relevant to every forensic consultation and are given the highest priority in this text. Chapter 1 provides the clinical and legal framework for forensic practice and introduces the remaining chapters. Chapter 2 examines the potential for malingering and other response styles, which are complex yet integral components of all forensic evaluations. Chapter 3 offers insights into the final step in forensic consultations, namely court-room testimony. By focusing on the outcome, both attorneys and experts can better appreciate how to proceed in addressing mental health issues in criminal cases.

Part II, *Specific Forensic Issues*, parallels the criminal justice system. Chapters 4 and 5 address pretrial issues, including (1) diversions to the mental health system, (2) psychological factors affecting bail determinations, (3) waiver of *Miranda* rights, and (4) waiver of search-and-seizure rights. The next three chapters are devoted to trial issues. They include (a) Chapter 6, examining competency to stand trial and other trial competencies, (2) Chapters 7 and 8, addressing the insanity defense and other issues of criminal responsibility. Sentencing issues, both noncapital and capital, are covered in Chapter 9. The final two chapters address posttrial issues, such as competence to be executed or to abandon post-conviction relief (Chapter 10) and sexual predators (Chapter 11). Chapter 12 completes the book through its identification of overarching themes that integrate knowledge, theory, and methods across the specific forensic issues.

2

Malingering and Deception in Criminal Evaluations

A cornerstone of forensic evaluations is the systematic investigation of response styles, such as malingering and defensiveness (Rogers & Bender, 2003). In certain forensic settings, such as family law, some litigants may be strongly motivated to simulate good adjustment (i.e., defensiveness). The goals of defensiveness may be to gain child custody or extensive visitations. In the criminal settings, a minority of defendants may attempt to feign impairment (i.e., malingering) in an effort to improve their circumstances (e.g., hospital vs. jail) or the outcome of their legal proceedings (e.g., a lighter sentence). In addition, some mentally disordered defendants are so averse to treatment (e.g., antipsychotic medications) or the stigmatization of the mentally ill that they deliberately minimize their mental disorders (i.e., defensiveness). In criminal cases, forensic clinicians must systematically evaluate common response styles rather than rely on subjective impressions.

This chapter begins with an overview that addresses fundamental issues in the evaluation of response styles, including malingering and other forms of deception. This overview is indispensable to critical thinking about dissimulation. The next section examines detection strategies for malingering, both mental disorders and cognitive impairment. It also summarizes detection strategies for other response styles. The final section focuses entirely on standardized methods for the evaluation of malingering.

FUNDAMENTAL ISSUES WITH RESPONSE STYLES

Experts and attorneys are sometimes tempted to skip over introductory sections in favor of more applied material. While focusing on fundamental issues, we address critical issues and their relevance to forensic practice. This section addresses the following questions:

1. Why do some experts and attorneys summarily assume that defendants are not truthful?
2. What are the basic terms used in the assessment of malingering and deception?
3. How does the misuse of the *DSM-IV* can lead to tragic errors in the evaluation of malingering?
4. What are common mistakes by experts in the evaluation of response styles?

DISCOUNTING DEFENDANT'S STATEMENTS

Forensic criminal evaluations would be greatly simplified if we did not need to rely on the potentially self-serving accounts of defendants whose veracity is often questioned by both their criminal backgrounds and history of mental disorders. A simple yet erroneous conclusion is that all criminals are inveterate liars. A fundamental attribution error (Wrightsman, Greene, Nietzel, & Fortune, 2002) is the blanket assumption that dishonesty is a pervasive and enduring trait of criminals. Beyond criminality, a substantial proportion of patients with Axis I disorders are unreliable in their clinical presentations (Cunnien, 1997). Terms such as "poor historians" and "unreliable informant" are often applied. Any sweeping conclusions about the absence of veracity for criminals or unreliability of Axis I patients are both inaccurate and dangerous.

Our perceptions here are often biased toward believing that other people are deceptive. Consider for the moment politicians embroiled in scandals. Can they prove their truthfulness? Rarely. While it is relatively easy to discredit politicians by proving their falsehoods and inconsistencies, establishing honesty is an entirely different matter. The denial of wrongdoing is seldom persuasive. If this deception-bias is present for politicians, imagine its persuasiveness for criminal defendants.

Some experts and attorneys, including defense counsel, may automatically discount a defendant's statements. Expressions of cynicism (e.g., "They are all liars.") are indicative of this discounting. We recommend that mental health and legal professionals be aware of the distorting effects found with both the fundamental attribution error and the deception-bias. Objectivity requires a freedom from such biases.

Basic Terms for Malingering and Deception

Expert knowledge demands that forensic clinicians use professional terminology with precise meanings. Table 2-1 summarizes the commonly used terms for malingering and related response styles. Only "malingering" and "factitious disorders" are *DSM-IV* diagnostic terms.[1] The ability of psychologists and psychiatrists to differentiate between the types of motivation for malingering and factitious disorders, which is generally overlooked, is far from clear. Motivation cannot be (1) simply inferred from the circumstances or (2) easily obtained from deceptive persons (Rogers & Neumann, 2003). However, valuable data can often be observed in the patient's interactions with health care providers regarding possible factititous motivations.

Standardized methods for assessing feigned mental disorders are not likely ever to differentiate the complex motivations underlying a patient's dissimulation. Therefore, most standardized assessments prefer to address *feigning*, rather than attempt difficult discriminations between malingering and factitious disorders. Attorneys should be alert to overstatements by forensic experts: tests or other specialized measures typically do not address malingering per se.

Box 2-1 provides illustrative cross-examination for experts overstepping their expertise and attempting to objectify their opinions by stating that the test, not the examiner, concluded that the defendant was malingering. As previously noted, standardized assessments determine whether defendants are feigning, not their motivation for feigning (i.e., malingering or factitious disorders). In actuality, the likelihood of factitious disorders accounting for the feigned mental disorders is very small. Therefore, the purpose of these cross-examination questions is not a major retraction of testimony. Rather, it may illustrate the expert's slippery or slipshod method

---

[1]Malingering is not a formal diagnosis; it is listed as a "V code" under the heading: "Additional conditions that may be a focus of clinical attention" (American Psychiatric Association, 2000, p. 739).

TABLE 2-1. COMMON TERMS USED TO DESCRIBE MALINGERING AND RELATED
RESPONSE STYLES

Term	Definition and Source
Malingering	From *DSM-IV*, it is the deliberate fabrication or gross exaggeration of psychological or physical symptoms to achieve an external goal.
Factitious disorder	From *DSM-IV* (American Psychiatric Association, 2000, p. 513), it is an Axis I disorder characterized by a "psychological need to assume the sick role" that is satisfied by the intentional production of psychological or physical symptoms. When presenting with primarily psychological symptoms, this disorder appears to be rare.
Feigning	From the assessment literature, it is the deliberate fabrication or gross exaggeration of psychological or physical symptoms. The motivation is not determined (i.e., malingering vs. factitious disorders).
Overreporting	From psychological testing, it is an imprecise term that refers "more than expected" symptom endorsement. Overreporting (also the closely related term of "symptom magnification") should not be equated with either malingering, factitious disorder, or feigning. From psychological testing, it is an imprecise term that refers "more than expected" symptom endorsement.
Dissimulation	From the clinical literature, it is a general term for distortions in a patient's clinical presentation. It should only be used when clinicians cannot determine the specific nature of the response style (i.e., malingering, factitious disorder, or feigning).
Secondary gain	Originally from the psychodynamic literature and later applied in behavioral medicine, its use in forensic practice is unwarranted. This term refers to either internal unconscious goals (psychodynamic), external goals beyond the patient's control (behavioral medicine), or speculatively, external deliberate goals (forensic).
Suboptimal effort	From neuropsychological testing, it inaccurately equates a lack of complete effort with the likelihood of feigning. The level of effort can be affected by genuine disorders, sequelae of brain injury, and educational and situational factors. Also known as "incomplete effort," its use in forensic practice may result in grave errors.

of overstating his or her conclusions. If a pattern of overstatements can be discerned, the expert's credibility is vitiated.

Four terms in Table 2-1 lack precision and should be avoided whenever possible. Of these, *dissimulation* can be used to describe nonspecific distortions for which the defendant's motivation is unclear. To avoid grave misunderstandings, any use of the word "dissimulation" should be clarified

---

Box 2-1   Illustrative Cross-Examination for Test Results and
          Malingering: Overstepping Expertise

1. *Doctor, you testified the defendant's results on __ [specific test or measure]
   were indicative of malingering, is that correct?*
2. *Has __ [specific test or measure] ever been tested with factitious disorders?*
   [The answer should be "no," except for preliminary data on the SIRS.]
3. *Please describe factitious disorders for the court.* [The attorney should be
   prepared with DSM-IV to address misunderstandings about factitious
   disorders.]
4. *Factitious disorders are true disorders, correct? ... A patient doesn't choose
   to have a factitious disorder, isn't that so? ... In a real sense, a factitious
   disorder is involuntary, isn't that right?*
5. *Since __ [specific test or measure] has never been studied with factitious
   disorders, you don't know how patients with factitious disorders are likely
   to respond, do you? ... [if equivocates] Isn't it true that the only research
   to directly compare factitious disorders with probable malingering found
   very similar patterns?*
6. *In all honesty, doctor, when you testified that __ [specific test or measure]
   results were indicative of malingering you weren't being entirely accurate,
   were you?*
7. *Wouldn't a more accurate conclusion be that we don't know whether these
   data represent malingering or are the results of an involuntary disorder?*

---

with a cautionary statement, such as the following: "Despite this dissimulation, I found no substantial evidence of malingering or feigning." The
remaining three terms should be avoided entirely. *As a standard for forensic
practice, experts should avoid imprecise terminology that potentially misleads the
courts. Imprecise terms include "overreporting," "secondary gain," and "suboptimal effort."*

The term "secondary gain," as noted in Table 2-1, has at least three disparate meanings. It is derived primarily from theory and research based
on psychodynamic thinking and principles of behavioral medicine. More
recently, forensic speculations have been suggested that are predicated
entirely of inferred motivation. These forensic speculations have no empirical bases. They are dangerously misinformed and should be avoided
(Rogers & Reinhardt, 1998).

Finally, the term "suboptimal effort" (also described as "incomplete
effort") is sometimes used in intellectual and neuropsychological testing to
describe persons who may be faking cognitive[2] deficits. The implications
are clear to the courts; namely, the defendant is faking and the purported

---

[2]The term "cognitive" is used in this context as shorthand for intellectual and neuropsychological abilities.

impairment is fraudulent. The term "suboptimal effort" is tantamount to malingering in its negative impact on the fact finder. However, it is a flawed concept for the following two reasons:

1. It presupposes that *optimal* effort exists and can be reliably measured.
2. Based on an impermissible leap of faith, it presupposes that the motivation for suboptimal effort is a deliberate feigning of cognitive impairment. We would undertake a similar leap of faith if we concluded that "all fevers are demonstrable proof of malaria."

Box 2-2 includes illustrative cross-examination focused exclusively on #1. It attempts to expose absurdity of assuming the optimal effort is *ever achievable* for any extended period of time. The strategy of weakening the expert's conclusions is to focus on this unachievable standard (e.g., "optimal," "perfect," and "ideal"). If an expert uses the term "incomplete effort," attorneys may simply change the phrasing or ask the expert to acknowledge that this phrase is equivalent to suboptimal effort. When faced with a verbally facile expert, the illustrative questions provide a step-by-step approach in an attempt to achieve one of two goals: (1) the expert concedes that "suboptimal effort" has limited value, or (2) the expert's credibility is damaged by steadfastly maintaining an untenable position.

Box 2-2   Illustrative Cross-Examination: Expert Conclusions Based on "Suboptimal Effort"

1. *Did I understand you correctly, doctor? You stated that the defendant was likely feigning because [he/she] put forth "suboptimal effort," correct?*
2. *Please define for the court what is* <u>*optimal*</u> *effort.*
3. *During your hours of evaluating the defendant, did* <u>*you*</u> *always put forth* <u>*optimal*</u> *effort?* . . . [if affirmative response] *Come on doctor, you mean to tell me you didn't there wasn't a moment or two when you just put forth good effort?* . . . <u>*Always*</u> *a perfect effort?*
4. [If still an affirmative response, one option would be to bring up muffed responses from either direct or cross. The goal would be to question whether they were optimal or the "best that he/she could do."]
5. [If acknowledges, less-than-perfect effort] *Thank you for your candor. As you have acknowledged moments of suboptimal effort, would it be fair to say that you were "faking" at those moments?*
6. [likely to disagree] *What about* [select "the judge" or "a member of the jury"] *were to have a bad day and put forth suboptimal effort, would you accuse [him/her] of faking?*
7. *So suboptimal effort only means faking when you want it to?*

Misuse of DSM-IV Indices in Determinations of Malingering

DSM-IV indices were intended as a threshold model for establishing when malingering should be thoroughly investigated. While ineffective for the purpose of determining whether malingering has occurred, the major problem with *DSM-IV* indices occurs when experts attempt to use them for the classification of malingering. As summarized on page 739, the *DSM-IV-TR* (American Psychiatric Association, 2000) established a benchmark for when malingering should be "strongly suspected." It is based on any combination of the following four indices:

1. being involved in a forensic evaluation,
2. having an antisocial personality disorder,
3. being uncooperative with assessment or treatment, or
4. having symptoms at variance with objective findings.

Obviously, all criminal defendants referred for a forensic consultation automatically qualify for #1. Many defendants with extensive criminal histories dating from childhood will qualify for #2. Those defendants opposed to the forensic consultation or substantially impaired by a genuine disorder will likely qualify for #3. The mindless application of these indices to criminal-forensic consultations is likely to lead to very grave errors.

A California case provides a stark example of substandard practice by mistaking the *DSM-IV* screening indices for formal diagnostic criteria. A forensic psychologist had testified that a psychotic male defendant was malingering based on his antisocial history, the context (i.e., a forensic evaluation), and his uncooperation with the assessment. When treated with a new-generation antipsychotic medication (i.e., clozapine), he became cooperative. This psychologist's testimony was subsequently confuted by the absence of malingering as documented by years of inpatient forensic observations and an extensive evaluation of potential feigning. Such improper testimony likely affected the verdict (i.e., a conviction following the rejection of an insanity defense) and possibly the sentencing (i.e., imposition of the death penalty).

Static characteristics, such as the nature of the evaluation (#1) and the defendant's antisocial background (#2), are likely consequences of the fundamental attribution error, namely bad persons in bad circumstances are inevitably involved in bad conduct. Research does not support either hypothesis. Although Rogers and Cruise (2000) found many psychopaths engage in general deception (e.g., conning and manipulation), no link has been established with malingering. The sole exception is one small ($N = 18$) study (Gacono, Meloy, Sheppard, Speth, & Roske, 1995) of an atypical sample (nonpsychotic insanity acquittees). As detailed subsequently, the estimated proportion of malingerers in forensic cases (1/6 to 1/7) argues against the use of this indicator.

The matter of uncooperativeness (#3) deserves some discussion. Psychotic defendants, especially those with paranoid or grandiose delusions, are unlikely to cooperate with experts if they believe these experts are either attempting to hurt them (i.e., paranoid) and not according them their rightful status (i.e., grandiose). Uncooperativenesss is commonly observed with a variety of Axis I (e.g., bipolar disorders, substance abuse disorders, and eating disorders) and Axis II (e.g., borderline personality disorder and antisocial personality disorder) disorders. Uncooperativeness is also linked to the severity of mental disorders. All persons with mental disorders requiring involuntary hospitalization because of the severity of their disorders and concomitant lack of insight are, by definition, uncooperative. Therefore, the use of uncooperativness as an index of malingering is hopelessly confounded.

Rogers (1990) conducted the only study on the accuracy of DSM indices for the identification of potential malingerers. Although using *DSM-III*, these indices have remained unchanged and apply to the current *DSM-IV-TR* (see American Psychiatric Association, 2000). The study found (see Appendix A for a summary) that these indices were not useful, even as screens. When the *DSM-IV-TR* benchmark (i.e., any combination of indices) was met, the false-positive rate was approximately 80%.

A very disturbing trend is for forensic experts to misuse the *DSM-IV* indices as *determinants* of malingering. This unacceptable practice is not sanctioned by *DSM-IV*. As previously noted, the use of the DSM-IV indices for the classification of malingering is likely to lead to many errors, especially in criminal forensic cases. Both experts and attorneys must be prepared to address vigorously such deviations from accepted practice. Experts can prepare rebuttal testimony to demonstrate the impropriety of using *DSM-IV* indices on both conceptual and empirical grounds. Conceptually, several *DSM-IV* indices are illogical (see Rogers, 1997). Professionally and ethically, *any decision rule that is wrong 4 out of 5 times should not be used for expert testimony unless the expert is forthright with the court regarding the 80% error rate.*

Box 2-3 provides illustrative cross-examination that may be especially useful when the forensic expert relied only on the *DSM-IV* in reaching his or her clinical impressions. The key issue is that the *DSM-IV* indices have *never been validated.* In science, validity cannot simply be presumed but must be rigorously tested. The sole study of *DSM-IV* indices disproves their clinical usefulness (see Appendix A). Experts relying primarily on the *DSM-IV* indices must either frankly admit their invalidity or

---

Box 2-3   LIMITATIONS OF THE *DSM-IV* MODEL: ILLUSTRATIVE
CROSS-EXAMINATION

Summary: The DSM-IV model is biased against criminal defendants on the issue of malingering. It assumes that malingering should be "strongly suspected" for any combination of the following: (a) being involved in a forensic evaluation, (b) having an antisocial personality disorder, (c) being uncooperative, or (d) having symptoms at variance with objective findings. The majority of criminal defendants likely evidence the first two indices.

1. *Doctor, did you rely on the DSM-IV indices in reaching your conclusions that the defendant was malingering?*
2. [if not covered on direct] *What are those four indices?*
3. *Doctor, are the DSM-IV indices valid for the identification of malingerers? . . . How were they validated?* [Any explanation is inaccurate]
4. *What source describes the validation of the DSM-IV indices of malingering? . . .* [if answers "DSM-IV"] *Here is a copy of the DSM-IV, please turn to page 739. Is that the section on malingering? . . . Take your time, where does it describe the validation of the DSM-IV indices of malingering?*
5. *Isn't it true, doctor, you really don't know whether the DSM-IV indices were validated?*
6. *Are you aware of any research on the accuracy of the DSM-IV indices?* [The only study is by Rogers, see Appendix A]
7. *Are you aware of research by Dr. Richard Rogers on the accuracy on the DSM indices of malingering? . . . What was its major findings? . . .* [if obfuscates] *Isn't it true that it found the DSM indices are wrong 4 out of 5 times for identifying malingerers?*
8. [if does not acknowledge this, have copies of Appendix A available] *Let me show you Appendix A from Fundamentals of Forensic Practice: Mental Health and Criminal Law by Dr. Richard Rogers and Daniel Shuman. . . . Please read the title of the study to the court.*
9. *Take time to review this. . . . Please read to the court the conclusion at the bottom of the page that has been placed in bold.*
10. *In all fairness, doctor, can you now acknowledge to the court that these indices are inaccurate?*

---

actively obfuscate the issue. The matter of validity is central. Some attorneys may wish to become very thorough and deliberative in their questioning. Bright-line issues are rare in forensic psychology and psychiatry. The invalidity of the *DSM-IV* indices for malingering is clearly a bright-line issue.

THREE COMMON ERRORS BY FORENSIC PROFESSIONALS

Both mental health and legal professionals are susceptible to misjudgments and misconceptualizations about malingering and related response styles. Three common errors include the inconsistency trap, mutual exclusivity, and the ad hominem fallacy.

A common error is to assume that inconsistencies are evidence of deliberate distortions, such as malingering or feigning. For example, one well-established psychologist would systematically review different MMPI-2 administrations for the same forensic patient. Discrepancies were cataloged as evidence of deception, if not feigning. The fundamental problem with this approach is that many defendants with genuine mental disorders are inconsistent and even contradictory in their responding (Rogers & Vitacco, 2002). Inconsistencies on the MMPI-2 may reflect genuine impairments, problems in concentration, and even limited reading comprehension. As observed by Greene (1997), inconsistent responding *must be ruled out* before the evaluation of feigning. Likewise, research on the SIRS demonstrated that inconsistencies are poor indicators of feigning simply because a significant minority of genuine patients is highly inconsistent.

Occasionally, experts and criminal attorneys become susceptible to the "inconsistency trap." Because most mentally disordered offenders evidence some inconsistencies, an expert could erroneously conclude that these defendants are feigning. What about the occasional defendant with an Axis I disorder who is highly consistent in his or her presentation? An expert could erroneously conclude that this level of consistency is inconsistent with genuine impairment. We describe these erroneous conclusions as the *inconsistency trap*. Simply put, defendants with Axis I disorders are "trapped." Whatever their clinical presentations (inconsistent or consistent), the conclusion of malingering is likely to be the same.

Rogers and Vitacco (2002) observed that genuine mental disorders and malingering are not mutually exclusive. Neither classification provides a natural immunity to the other. On the contrary, our experience suggests that the majority of malingering cases also include genuine disorders.

Mutual exclusivity is described as a common error because many experts virtually stop the evaluation once malingering has been established. With inpatient evaluations, one variant of this stopping is the automatic invalidation of any reported or observed symptoms. If the identified malingerer complains of suicidal ideation, for example, these complaints are automatically invalidated as feigned symptoms.

The *ad hominem* fallacy occurs when forensic expert judges the person's character or likability and improperly generalizes to clinical issues, such as malingering (Rogers & Neumann, 2003). For instance, a manipulative inpatient may be characterized as a malingerer without a comprehensive evaluation. Although typically construed as negative, *ad hominem* fallacies can also lead to overly positive conclusions (i.e., "good" persons wouldn't malinger). Possibly convinced that youth would not fake, Faust, Hart, and Guilmette (1988) found that neuropsychologists missed 100% of the feigning cases involving youth.

DETECTION STRATEGIES FOR FEIGNED PRESENTATIONS

Malingering can occur in one or more of three general domains: mental disorders, cognitive impairment, and medical syndromes. Rogers, Salekin, Sewell, Goldstein, and Leonard (1998) asked 221 highly experienced forensic experts to identify their most prototypical malingering case and its respective domain(s). The majority (53.4%) of the cases centered on feigned mental disorders with smaller but still significant representations of cognitive impairment (19.5%), medical syndromes (15.8%), and multiple domains (11.2%). The malingering of medical syndromes will not be covered because of (a) lack of systematic research and (b) its assessment generally falls beyond the scope of forensic psychology and psychiatry.

Forensic psychology and psychiatry have made major advances in the development of theoretically sound and empirically validated detection strategies for feigned presentations. Conceptually, these strategies must differ by domain. For example, detection strategies for faked schizophrenia are unlikely to work with feigned amnesia. With feigned mental disorders, the malingerer must create a believable set of symptoms and make the following decisions: (1) their onset and course over time, (2) their effects on the malingerer's functioning, and (3) the malingerer's awareness and insight into his or her symptoms. With feigned cognitive impairment, the task is completely different. The malingerer must convince the examiner of his or her "honest" effort and then simply not succeed at standardized tasks intended to measure these cognitive abilities. These differences between feigned mental disorders and feigned cognitive impairment necessitate the development of domain-specific detection strategies.

DETECTION STRATEGIES FOR FEIGNED MENTAL DISORDERS

Most forensic psychologists and psychiatrists have a sound background in the assessment of malingering and specialized knowledge regarding detection strategies.[3] Table 2-2 summarizes the major detection

---

[3]As always, criminal attorneys should be alert for sciolism. When asked specifically about detection strategies, clues to sciolism include "The computerized report said ... " and "My consultant told me ... "

TABLE 2-2. DETECTION STRATEGIES FOR FEIGNED MENTAL DISORDERS

Rare Symptoms

Definition   These symptoms are only observed infrequently among genuine patients. Because malingerers often overendorse rare symptoms because they are unaware of their general infrequency.

Example   "Have you invented words which have become part of the English language?" (i.e., neologisms).

Strengths   It is a highly effective strategy used by most malingering scales.

Limitations   Current applications focus generally on psychotic and other unusual symptoms.

Improbable Symptoms

Definition   These symptoms have a preposterous or strangely fantastic quality to them. Some malingerers in attempting to demonstrate the severity of their psychopathology readily endorse these symptoms.

Example   "Do hair dryers emit heat-activated death rays?"

Strengths   Both professionals and nonprofessionals can appreciate the absurdity of these symptoms and recognize their bogus nature.

Limitations   Two limitations are that (1) only a minority of malingerers endorses improbable symptoms and (2) care must be taken with grossly impaired patients who may be responding indiscriminately.

Erroneous Stereotypes

Definition   These symptoms fit nonprofessionals' inaccurate perceptions or stereotypes about persons with mental disorders. Unaware of their misperceptions, potential malingerers are likely to these stereotypes for genuine symptoms.

Examples   Presented in a true—false format: "I have been troubled since childhood." "I have always been different from others."

Strengths   This strategy is both effective and difficult for potential malingers to foil.

Limitations   It has only been applied to the MMPI-2 dissimulation (Ds) scale; some items do not appear to be stereotypes.

Symptom Combinations

Definition   These symptoms are composed of unusual symptom pairs, which are common alone but rarely occur together. Malingerers often overendorse these symptom combinations.

Example   "Have there been periods when you lost your appetite for food?" [if an affirmative response] During these same times, were your thoughts racing?[1]

Strengths   This strategy appears to be very effective and difficult for potential malingerers to foil.

(Continued)

TABLE 2-2. (CONTINUED)

Limitations	Items must be developed with great care; presently, only the SIRS uses this strategy.

Unlikely Patterns of Psychopathology

Definition	On multiscale inventories, certain patterns are rarely observed among genuine patients. Several abnormal patterns may be indicative of malingering.
Example	On the PAI, genuine patients rarely endorse more persecutory ideas than hypervigilance.
Strengths	Given the complexity of this strategy, potential malingerers would have great difficulty in foiling it.
Limitations	Because of its complexity, it requires extensive validation. To reduce classification errors, only scales with nonoverlapping items should be used.

Obvious vs. Subtle Symptoms

Definition	Most genuine patients have comparatively fewer obvious (i.e., easily recognizable symptoms of a major mental disorder) than subtle (i.e., everyday problems or symptoms not easily recognizable) symptoms. Malingerers attempting to prove their incapacity often overreport obvious symptoms.
Example	For symptoms of major depression, attempted suicide is an obvious symptom whereas early morning awakening is subtle.
Strengths	An effective strategy tested across the SIRS and the MMPI-2.
Limitations	The obvious symptoms appear instrumental in using this strategy; the importance of the subtle symptoms has been questioned.

Symptom Severity

Definition	This strategy reviews symptoms to see what proportion is considered by the defendant to have extreme severity (e.g., unendurable). Some malingerers report many symptoms as unendurable to demonstrate the severity of their impairment.
Example	"You mentioned __ [list 3–4 symptoms]. Are any of these horribly painful [agonizing] or disabling? You also described __ [list 3–4 symptoms]. Are any of these horribly painful [agonizing] or disabling? [continue to repeat as necessary]
Strengths	With standardized measures, such as the SIRS, it is highly effective. It also appears to be easily adapted to other structured measures of the *DSM-IV* symptoms.
Limitations	Unless embedded in the assessment process, potential malingerers may be able to recognize this detection strategy.

Symptom Selectivity

Definition	This strategy assesses whether the potential malingerer is indiscriminantly endorsing symptoms. Very few genuine patients endorse more than 2/3 of symptoms when presented with a broad array.
Example	Broad arrays of symptoms are provided by structured interviews and symptom checklists.

(*Continued*)

TABLE 2-2. (CONTINUED)

Strengths	This strategy is effective with several structured interviews (i.e., the SIRS and the SADS).
Limitations	Despite its potential, it has not been tested with symptom checklists.

[1]It is unusual for loss of appetite (typically a depressive symptom) to be paired with accelerated thinking (typically a manic symptom).

strategies used in standardized assessments of malingering. The purpose of this section is twofold. First, it provides forensic experts with a brief and updated review of detection strategies. These experts are likely to have in-depth knowledge of detection strategies and their applications via *Clinical Assessment of Malingering and Deception*. Second, it familiarizes criminal attorneys with detection strategies, giving them definitions, examples, and a nontechnical summary of their strengths and limitations.

The first three strategies (*rare symptoms, improbable symptoms,* and *erroneous stereotypes*) address variations of atypical symptoms. Of these, *rare symptoms* are the most extensively tested and have proven effective across a range of clinical and forensic settings. *Improbable symptoms* are far more extreme than *rare symptoms*. By definition, these preposterous symptoms are unlikely to be true except in the most rare circumstances. Their extremeness helps to rule out genuine patients that are attending to the clinical inquiries. This same extremeness means that many potential malingerers will correctly identify these symptoms as bogus thereby decreasing their effectiveness. *Erroneous stereotypes* are more subtle than are *rare symptoms*. Based on empirical validation, these problems and symptoms are commonly misperceived by nondisordered individuals as characteristic of genuine patients. They are erroneous stereotypes because their actual rate of endorsement by genuine patients is relatively low. The subtlety of this strategy is likely an advantage with sophisticated malingerers.

The next three strategies (*symptom combinations, unlikely patterns of psychopathology,* and *obvious vs. subtle symptoms*) address atypical symptom patterns. Based on extensive SIRS data, *symptom combinations* appear to be highly effective in their use of unusual symptom pairs. These symptom pairs must be developed with great care and should be empirically validated. *Unlikely patterns of psychopathology* are represented by the malingering index (see Morey, 1996) of the Personality Assessment Inventory (PAI; Morey, 1991). This strategy examines unexpected patterns between pairs of scales or subscales. *Obvious vs. subtle symptoms* strategy capitalizes on malingerers' desires to appear severely impaired. These three strategies are sophisticated and unlikely to be discerned by many malingerers.

The final two strategies (*symptom severity* and *symptom selectivity*) examine atypical endorsement patterns. Rather than focus of specific symptoms, symptom pairs, or scale differences, these strategies adopt the broadest perspective, namely the overall endorsement patterns. *Symptom severity* examines the overall proportion of severe (i.e., disabling or excruciating) symptoms. *Symptom selectivity* simply evaluates the overall proportion of endorsed symptoms. Given the marked variability among genuine patients, these final strategies are especially effective with extreme levels of endorsement.

DETECTION STRATEGIES FOR FEIGNED COGNITIVE IMPAIRMENT

As previously noted, standardized measures for the assessment of feigned cognitive impairment face formidable challenges since this type of dissimulation simply requires a poor performance accompanied by a display of apparently "genuine effort." Importantly, judgments about "effort" are inferential and unnecessarily complicate the assessment of feigned cognitive impairment. Despite the potentially misleading terminology used by some forensic clinicians (i.e., "suboptimal effort" and "incomplete effort"), the following observation is imperative: Standardized measures of feigning do *not* assess effort, they evaluate performance. Therefore, feigned cognitive impairment should be evaluated on the basis of performance without introducing subjective inferences about effort and its underlying motivation.

Rogers, Harrell, and Liff (1993) are credited with the first systematic examination of detection strategies for feigned cognitive impairment. As summarized in Table 2-3, these strategies have been augmented by several additional methods. These detection strategies are highly variable regarding their validation and demonstrable accuracy. Forensic experts are often challenged in deciding which detection strategies and standardized measures should be used in particular forensic cases.

Rogers and Bender (2003) categorized detection strategies in two domains: *excessive impairment* and *unexpected patterns*. For *excessive impairment*, malingerers are detectable by their gross deficits in performance. In contrast, strategies based on *unexpected patterns* systematically assess unlikely relationships among different items or response choices. In general, potential malingerers should need greater sophistication to foil successfully strategies based on *unexpected patterns* because they require an appreciation of the relationship among items and responses. Table 2-3 outlines the various strategies subsumed under each domain.

Three strategies (*floor effect, symptom validity testing,* and *forced-choice testing*) are based on *excessive impairment*. Of these, *floor effect* is a commonly

TABLE 2-3. DETECTION STRATEGIES FOR FEIGNED COGNITIVE IMPAIRMENT

Floor effect	
Definition	This strategy uses items that are so simple that most patients with genuine impairment are successful. Potential malingerers may not recognize the simplicity of the items. In addition, some instructions intend to mislead patients about the complexity of the test (i.e., Rey-15).
Example	"Who is older, you or your mother?"
Strengths	The strategy can be easily operationalized by sets of very simple items with high success rates (e.g., 90 or 95%). Some measures based on floor effect have proven to be moderately effective.
Limitations	Extensive validation is required to ensure that the results are not explainable by genuine disorders. Standardized measures must be tested to see if their results hold both singly and in combination for the following conditions: different brain injuries, learning disorders, mental retardation, and Axis I disorders.
Symptom validity testing (SVT)	
Definition	In a forced-choice format, this simple yet elegant strategy identifies malingerers based on their below-chance performance. Some potential malingerers may not calculate the proportion of errors found among persons with total incapacity.
Example	Given three choices, the error rate should never significantly exceed 67%.
Strengths	With sufficient trials, this measure can produce highly accurate results at classifying malingerers with substantially below-chance performances. These results are not confounded by mental retardation or comorbidity.
Limitations	At best, only about one-third of probable malingerers are identified by this strategy.
Forced choice testing (FCT)	
Definition	This strategy attempts to evaluate lower-than-expected performances on certain cognitive tests. As an analogue to floor effect, it expected that some malingerers will fail too badly and be identified.
Example	On a forced-choice format, short-term memory performance is very poor although above chance levels.
Strengths	Despite its popularity, this strategy does not have any specific strengths. Unlike floor effect, its items are not specifically selected for their discriminability.
Limitations	It has all the limitations of the floor-effect strategy without its advantage.
Magnitude of error	
Definition	This strategy is based on the finding that genuine patients often make predictable errors, especially in a forced-choice format. Potential malingerers may pay more attention about which items to fail rather than how to fail them.

(Continued)

TABLE 2-3. (CONTINUED)

Example	Consider the following sequence: 35, 28, 21, __. When responding incorrectly, patients with genuine impairment are still likely to understand the general direction (i.e., decreasing numbers) even if their calculations are inaccurate. In this example, genuine patients are more likely to answer "16" than "46."
Strengths	As items become more challenging, potential malingerers may find it difficult to foil this strategy. Initial results are very promising.
Limitations	Although likely less vulnerable than forced-choice testing,[1] this strategy needs to be tested with different populations.

Performance curve

Definition	As items increase in difficulty, a predictable pattern emerges with increased errors. This pattern of performance is typically a curve. Potential malingerers are unlikely to take into account item difficulty and produce a different pattern.
Example	In remembering numbers of different lengths, the proportion of accurate digits should decrease as the length increases until the person has reached his or her maximum abilities.
Strengths	Potential malingerers have problems foiling this detection strategy especially when the items are presented in a random order. With specific measures, this strategy has proven successful.
Limitations	Extensive validation is required to establish different levels of item difficulty; a performance curve cannot be discerned if items are too easy (i.e., all correct) or too difficult (i.e., chance-level performance).

Violation of learning principles

Definition	This strategy is a compilation of expected results based upon established learning principles. Marked violations of learning principles may detect potential malingerers.
Example	In learning a list of words, performance at recognition almost always exceeds recall.
Strengths	Learning principles are well-established rules based on extensive empirical data.
Limitations	Standardized methods with learning principles have not been extensively tested.

Consistency across comparable items

Definition	For genuine patients, performance within the same test on comparable items is likely to form predictable patterns, either consistent or attenuation (e.g., fatigue or frustration). Malingerers not attending to these patterns may evidence atypical variations in performance.
Example	Frederick's work on the Validity Indicator Profile (VIP; Frederick, 1997) represents a rigorous testing of item comparability.

(Continued)

TABLE 2-3. (CONTINUED)

Strengths	When rigorously tested, consistency across comparable items can be examined explicitly.
Limitations	Consistency across comparable items may not be as effective as other strategies. When not tested but simply assumed, comparisons cannot be systematically evaluated and should be considered as "atypical presentation" strategy.
Psychological sequelae	
Definition	As a result of brain injury, genuine patients may manifest additional symptoms (e.g., indifference to their loss of abilities). A potential strategy is to test whether these additional symptoms and problems (i.e., sequelae) differentiate between malingerers and genuine patients.
Example	Frequency of reported rage reactions for patients with concussions versus those feigning concussions.
Strengths	If carefully developed, systematic differences could be examined on items that are not intuitive.
Limitations	Current research on whether uninjured persons could recognize common sequelae has not proved successful. Further research on genuine and bogus sequelae is needed.
Atypical presentation	
Definition	This strategy simply refers to unexpected findings, such as marked variations on similar tests. Because certain organic disorders (e.g., dementias) sometimes result in variable abilities, this strategy should be used with great caution. In a minority of cases unusual patterns of neuropsychological functioning are reliably established. In most cases, this is a residual category.
Example	A discriminant analysis of the WAIS-R scales for simulators and genuine patients.
Strengths	When carefully established, this strategy is difficult to feign. As a residual category, no specific strengths are noted.
Limitations	Unlike other detection strategies, this approach lacks a firm conceptual basis. Predictably, empirical findings are often variable.

[1] Types of errors (e.g., magnitude of error) rather than overall performance (e.g., forced-choice testing) may reflect basic cognitive processes that occur irrespective of comorbidity.

used strategy that entails items which are "too simple to miss." This strategy is the most effective when items are embedded with other strategies to avoid the transparency of the *floor-effect* strategy. *Symptom validity testing* evaluates below-chance performance on equiprobable choices. The real strength of this strategy is that extreme failure rates are only explainable by feigning. Unfortunately, the majority of malingerers do not "fail" at below-chance rates. Because *symptom validity testing* does not identify many malingerers, researchers have attempted to replace it with *forced-choice testing* based on lower than expected performances. This strategy lacks the discriminability of *floor effect* and the minimization of false-positives found with *symptom validity testing*. Therefore, *forced-choice testing* is not recommended for forensic practice.

Three strategies (*magnitude of error, performance curve,* and *violation of learning principles*) represent the *unexpected performance* domain and have been tested across multiple measures. While not extensively researched, *magnitude of error* appears to be one of the most effective strategies (Bender & Rogers, 2004) in its examination of *how* feigners fail items. The *performance curve* is a robust strategy that examines success rates on items of increasing difficulty. Malingerers tend to show a flatter curve than genuine patients with less "success" on comparatively easier items. *Violation of learning principles* is a constellation of related strategies addressing memory and related functions. This strategy generally produces positive results, although the magnitude of these results is often modest.

The final three strategies (*consistency of comparable items, psychological sequelae,* and *atypical presentation*) also represent the *unexpected performance* domain but are more limited in their validation. While appearing straightforward, the establishment of *consistency of comparable items* requires carefully selected items and careful validation. At present, Frederick and Foster's (1997) work on the Validity Indicator Profile exemplifies the needed research. *Psychological sequelae* has considerable promise that has yet to be realized in establishing additional symptoms and associated features that may accompany brain injury. Lastly, *atypical presentation* is a residual category that produces mixed results. It is not recommended for forensic practice, unless empirical research is used to verify atypical patterns of test results.

The next step is the selection of detection strategies for use in forensic practice. This selection will depend on the availability of standardized methods, the defendant's presentation, and the relative effectiveness of individual strategies.

STANDARDIZED ASSESSMENT OF MALINGERING

The determination of malingering is a superordinate issue that "trumps" all other considerations in forensic cases. If a criminal defendant is classified as a malingerer, a defense claim relying on mental impairment is critically undermined. Any testimony about malingering, however weak and unsubstantiated, may override even strong evidence to the contrary. We have been involved in several cases where the "say-so" of one expert overrides all objective data that the criminal defendant is *not* malingering. As an example from South Carolina, one expert prevailed in his opinion on malingering, despite extensive data to the contrary and the fact he had not even evaluated the defendant.

Forensic psychologists and psychiatrists bear a heavy responsibility in assessing malingering. Experts want to minimize the likelihood that malingerers avoid detection and evade their responsibilities to the criminal justice system. However, the misclassification of a person with a mental disorder as a malingerer is a momentous error. Such inaccurate expert testimony may not only result in an erroneous decision on a specific mental health issue, but also discredit the defendant completely. In cases where the only defense is a mental health issue (e.g., insanity), such grave errors may be a chief determinant in the outcome of the case for which experts must accept personal responsibility.

This chapter cannot cover all the requisite data needed for empirically validated assessments of malingering. Experts need to be grounded in both the detection strategies and the clinical methods (see Rogers, 1997). Especially in complex cases, criminal attorneys will need their own experts in making sense out of a plethora of measures that often yield divergent findings. We begin with feigned mental disorders.

ASSESSMENT OF FEIGNED MENTAL DISORDERS

As a brief review, forensic experts must decide which standardized measures should be employed in order to assess comprehensively the potential malingering of mental disorders. Importantly screens, such as the Miller Forensic Assessment of Symptoms Test (M-FAST; Miller, 2001), have a useful function for identifying potential feigners (Jackson, Rogers, & Sewell, in press) but should not be used for the determination of malingering.

Appendix B is a reproducible overview of detection strategies and standardized methods. Some forensic experts may wish to reproduce this appendix as a visual display for educating the judge and jury about different detection strategies and their methods of assessment. Appendix B reviews clinical interviews and five standardized measures often used in the evaluation of feigned mental disorders. A nontechnical summary of measures is provided:

- *Structured Interview of Reported Symptoms (SIRS).* The SIRS (Rogers, Bagby, & Dickens, 1992) is a specialized measure for feigned mental disorders that uses 8 detection strategies (see Appendix B) and has been extensively validated with forensic populations. Importantly, the SIRS makes very few errors (false-positive rates of 2–3%) in classifying malingerers.

- *Minnesota Multiphasic Personality Inventory—2 (MMPI-2).* The MMPI-2 (Butcher, Dahlstrom, Graham, Tellegen, & Kaemmer, 1989) is a multiscale inventory that assesses patterns of psychopathology and response styles. Extensive research examines feigned mental disorders, although determinations are sometimes challenging given the range of validity scales and their respective cut scores.
- *Personality Assessment Inventory (PAI).* The PAI (Morey, 1991) is a new-generation multiscale inventory that has psychometric advantages over the MMPI-2. It uses two strategies (see Appendix B) and is moderately effective.
- *Millon Clinical Multiaxial Inventory-III (MCMI-III).* The MCMI-III (Millon, 1994; Millon, Davis, & Millon, 1997) is a multiscale inventory that attempts to assess both Axis I syndrome and Axis II disorders while using only 175 items. It does not rely on clearly specified detection strategies for feigned mental disorders and is not clinically effective (Schoenberg, Dorr, & Morgan, 2003).
- *Malingering Probability Scale (MPS).* The MPS (Silverton & Gruber, 1998) is a self-report inventory designed to assess feigned mental disorders. It has not been extensively validated with forensic populations and has limitations in its validation (Nicholson, 1999).

Clinical interviews are an integral component of forensic evaluations because of their versatility in addressing case-specific issues. By themselves, clinical interviews cannot evaluate systematically specific detection strategies. As summarized in Appendix B, the effectiveness of these empirically validated strategies simply cannot be demonstrated for clinical interviews. Therefore, interviews are described as "unknown" for two reasons:

1. *Subjectivity.* The evaluator's level of sophistication and threshold for making such decisions are likely to be highly variable.
2. *Lack of validation.* Without systematic data, the bases for such conclusions cannot be empirically tested or validated.

A coterie of forensic experts has a reputation for routinely concluding that a defendant is likely malingering either in (a) the absence of standardized data, or more alarmingly (b) despite standardized data to the contrary. For defense counsel in particular, this type of testimony is very problematic. Cross-examination is often not fruitful because these experts have developed a repertoire of responses to questions about standardized methods. These responses are often structured as "yes-but" responses or what Brodsky (1991) characterizes as "admit–deny" replies to cross-examination. As an example, the expert may respond, "Although many psychologists use the MMPI-2, I have found that a detailed clinical examination ... " After multiple attempts the attorney becomes stymied in his or her efforts to clarify the limitations of the expert's conclusions.

No single approach will be successful with a seasoned expert attempting to obfuscate the bases of his or her findings and their limitations. Because any testimony about malingering is likely to have a chilling effect on any criminal defense, attorneys must be especially well prepared to address this matter. Review of past testimony by the expert can be invaluable in preparing questions and possibly in impeaching the expert's credibility.

Experts substituting their own judgments about malingering for standardized assessment can be divided into two groups:

1. Experts knowledgeable about standardized methods.
2. Experts ignorant of standardized methods.

Attorneys will need to decide which type of expert is testifying in each case. Many experts qualify for the second option either because of a lack of training or because they have not stayed current with the burgeoning literature on malingering and deception. For these cases, illustrative cross-examination is presented in Box 2-4.

Box 2-4 provides illustrative cross-examination that attempts to disrupt the canned responses developed by glib experts who ignore or discount standardized methods for the assessment of feigning. The goal is for the attorney to establish his or her framework for the cross-examination rather than allowing the expert to dictate or obscure the direction. This example uses detection strategies as the framework. Please note that its focus is simply to document to the judge or jury, via testimony and visual displays, the number of holes in the expert's evaluation and findings. If there are more "holes than fabric," then the weight of the testimony is likely to be vitiated. This strategy is more likely to succeed than more direct efforts aimed at forcing a highly verbal expert to acknowledge his or her shortcomings.

The following standard for forensic practice is recommended: *When feasible, standardized methods for the assessment of malingering should always be used in forensic evaluations*. The proviso "when feasible" is included to address those infrequent cases where standardized measures lack sufficient validation. An example might be a defendant with moderate mental retardation attempted to feign a psychosis.

Box 2-4   ILLUSTRATIVE CROSS-EXAMINATION FOR CONCLUSIONS ABOUT
MALINGERING BASED ONLY ON CLINICAL JUDGMENT

1. *Is your court report dated ___ an accurate reflection of your evaluation? . . . Are there any significant findings were that accidentally or deliberately left out of this report? . . . Any significant conclusions that you left out of this report?*
2. *Doctor, are you qualified to render an expert opinion about malingering in this particular case?*
3. *Are you knowledgeable about the malingering literature? . . . What malingering books do you rely upon as references?*
4. [if reports *Clinical Assessment of Malingering and Deception* or "the Rogers book"] *In this reference that you use, what are the detection strategies for feigned mental disorders?*
5. [if not aware of *Clinical Assessment of Malingering and Deception*] *What are the detection strategies for feigned mental disorders?*
6. [if only 2 or 3] *Are you aware that you recalled only ___* [number] *strategies? . . . What are the other primary strategies used in this book that you rely on?*
7. *Please define "rare symptoms" for the court. . . Please define "symptom combinations" for the court . . . Please define "indiscriminant symptom endorsement."* [term used in 1997 book for "symptom selectivity"]
8. *Doctor, turning to your court report dated ___, please show me specifically where you listed the rare symptoms for my client.* [Use a visual display to keep track of the *absence* of examples as you go through the different detection strategies.]
9. [An option is to repeat this process using detection strategies for "feigned cognitive impairment."]
10. *You were being truthful when you testified earlier that your report included all your relevant findings and conclusions, isn't that correct?*
11. *Please answer honestly and directly "yes" or "no," is this display an accurate representation of your findings with respect to these detection strategies? . . .* [Cut off obfuscations] *Thank you, doctor, for those insights into your evaluation.*

Forensic experts should typically choose at least two standardized measures for evaluating feigned mental disorders. In reviewing Appendix B, this choice will likely entail measures that are validated for more than one detection strategy. In addition, many experts will adopt a multi-method model combining different clinical methods (i.e., a structured interview plus a multiscale inventory). As a result, more forensic evaluations of feigning will include the Structured Interview of Reported Symptoms (SIRS; Rogers, Bagby, & Dickens, 1992) and either the MMPI-2 (Butcher, Dahlstrom, Graham, Tellegen, & Kaemmer, 1989) or the PAI (Morey, 1991). A synopsis of these three methods is provided below.

MMPI-2. The MMPI-2 is the traditional, time-honored method for assessing malingering and other response styles. Its original authors,

Hathaway and McKinley, were among the first investigators to recognize the importance of assessing response styles and their effects on clinical profiles. In its early development, three validity scales were developed to assess malingering and defensiveness. Since that time, more than a dozen scales and indices have been formulated. Because of its complexity, many clinicians do not devote sufficient time to maintain their expertise in using the MMPI-2 for the assessment of malingering. Both forensic experts and criminal attorneys should be aware that some clinicians use outdated knowledge in drawing their conclusions.

Rogers, Sewell, Martin, and Vitacco (2003) conducted a comprehensive meta-analysis of the MMPI-2 and malingering with 65 feigning studies plus 11 diagnostic studies. They found large effect sizes that demonstrated marked group differences between feigning and genuine clinical samples. Listed below are four major findings:

1. The F(psychiatric) or Fp scale appears to be the most effective with a very large effect size ($d = 1.90$) that works well with different diagnostic groups with a fairly narrow range of cut scores. An Fp raw score of greater than 9 is recommended for likely feigning.
2. The traditional F scale, while having a very large effect size ($d = 2.21$), had two major concerns: (a) no consensus about the best cut score and (b) likely problems with certain diagnoses.
3. The Fb scale appeared less effective than F but suffered from similar problems; see (a) and (b).
4. The Ds scale produced a large effect size ($d = 1.62$) with a consistent cut score that works well across diagnostic groups. A Ds raw score of greater than 35 is recommended for likely feigning.

The MMPI-2 can be useful, especially when extreme elevations are achieved, at evaluating cases of likely feigning. The use of Fp supplemented by Ds and possibly F can provide useful data based on an impressive database, encompassing more than 60 studies and 4,000 participants (see Appendix D).

Despite these important achievements, the MMPI-2 should not be used with all forensic referrals because certain conditions have not been adequately tested. In the absence of research data, the MMPI-2 should *not* be used to assess feigning under these circumstances:

1. Patients requiring an audiotaped version of the MMPI-2,
2. Patients requiring a Spanish-language version of the MMPI-2,
3. Patients responding inconsistently,
4. Patients with mental retardation.

Attorneys should systematically screen *all* MMPI-2 reports that address feigning to ensure that *none* of these conditions are present. Although these criteria are straightforward and noncontroversial, experts occasionally ignore them. In an egregious example from a Federal Correctional Institute, an experienced forensic psychologist concluded that a defendant was malingering on the MMPI-2 despite the defendant's mental retardation, the inconsistent profile, and the audiotaped administration of the Spanish-language version. Regrettably, these significant lapses were only discovered after the trial was complete; attempts by the defense counsel for a retrial were unsuccessful.

One challenge that attorneys and opposing experts are likely to face is the occasional forensic clinician who is willing to conclude that high but not extreme elevations (65T to 90T) on the MMPI-2 F or Fb scales are evidence of feigning. Rogers et al. (2003) demonstrated convincingly the dangers of these conclusions. For courtroom use, Appendix D includes in a reproducible format several key findings from the Rogers et al. meta-analysis as they relate to Scales Fp, F, and Fb.

Consider, for example, the MMPI-2 results for a defendant with a well-documented history of schizophrenia. How can the attorney address an expert's unwarranted conclusions that the defendant is malingering because of marked elevations (*T* scores about 80) on scales F and Fb? One option is to use Appendix D as the basis of cross-examination. After asking the expert to review Appendix presented as a visual display, cross-examination might include the following:

1. *You agree, doctor, that the defendant was diagnosed with schizophrenia long before his current circumstances?*
2. *Please inspect the meta-analysis by Rogers and his colleagues presented on the visual display. Isn't it true, doctor, that genuine patients with schizophrenia have average scores on scales F and Fb in the 80T range?*
3. *And isn't it true, that the defendant scored in this same range?*
4. *Based on this meta-analysis, what is the approximate standard deviation of the F scale for persons with schizophrenia?*
5. *Given that standard deviation, isn't it likely that genuine patients may score one and possibly two standard deviations above average? ... So it very possible for a genuine patient with a history of schizophrenia to have an F score above 100T?*
6. [if quibbles] *Come on doctor, do the math. What is 80* (average) *plus 23* (standard deviation)? *... [optional] And what is 80 plus 46?*

In complicated cases involving the MMPI-2 and malingering, we recommend the use of consulting and rebuttal experts. Attorneys should remain cognizant of the numbing effects of numbers. Visual displays are vital, even in this comparatively simple example of cross-examination.

PAI. The PAI (Morey, 1991) is a new-generation multiscale inventory that is designed to assess both response styles and patterns of psychopathology. In general, the PAI offers a number of advantages over the MMPI-2 that include easier reading comprehension (grade 4), different levels of responses ("false," "slightly true," "mainly true," and "very true"), and superior internal consistency for its scales and subscales.

Response styles on the PAI has been subjected to more than a dozen investigations during the last decade. While outstripped by decades of MMPI-2 feigning research, many forensic experts are likely to opt for the PAI for two reasons. First, its research has been tested by both simulation design and known-groups comparisons. Second, PAI results focus on consistent cut scores rather than the range of cut scores found with the MMPI-2. The selection of a multiscale inventory should be made on a case-by-case basis weighing individual characteristics of each case.

Two investigations by Rogers and his colleagues (Rogers, Sewell, Cruise, Wang, & Ustad, 1998; Rogers, Sewell, Morey, & Ustad, 1996) provide the most extensive data on the PAI and feigning. The Rogers et al. (1996) study was a sophisticated analogue study with 176 simulators feigning one of three conditions (schizophrenia, major depression, and generalized anxiety disorder) being compared with 221 genuine patients with a diagnosis corresponding to one of these three disorders. The Rogers et al. (1998) study was a large known-groups comparison from two correctional-forensic settings with 57 probable malingerers and 58 genuine patients. Combining across these studies, the major findings are outlined:

1. *Rule-out.* Most probable malingerers from correctional-forensic settings (83.9%) had at least moderate elevations ($\geq 77T$)[4] on the Negative Impression (NIM) scale. Therefore, forensic referrals without clinical elevations can often be ruled out (i.e., not considered further for feigning) if there is no other evidence of potential malingering.
2. *Screen.* Malingering should be extensively evaluated in both forensic and nonforensic referrals having at least moderate elevations on the NIM scale ($\geq 77T$).
3. *Probable feigning.* Malingering is very likely to occur in both forensic and nonforensic settings with extreme elevations on either NIM ($\geq 110T$) or the Malingering Index (≥ 5).

---

[4]To decipher this shorthand, "$\geq$" means "greater than or equal to," and "T" refers to the standardized T score that is based on a mean of 50 and a standard deviation of 10.

The same caveats hold for the PAI as the MMPI-2 with respect to unresearched versions (audiotaped and Spanish versions) and mental retardation, and inconsistent responding. Therefore, attorneys to review systematically any PAI with conclusions about feigning for any of these four conditions.

In closing, attorneys are likely to find fewer egregious errors with PAI conclusions about feigning than the MMPI-2. These differences reflect on the training and preparation of experts, not on the measures themselves. Nonetheless, attorneys and opposing experts should be alert for over-interpretation that link weak PAI findings to malingering.

SIRS. The SIRS (Rogers et al., 1992) is a structured interview developed specifically to assess feigning and related response styles. It consists of eight primary scales that cover most of the established detection strategies for feigned mental disorders. Seven scales cover the detection strategies reported in Appendix B with *obvious vs. subtle* being divided into two scales. In addition, the eighth scale examines "reported versus observed symptoms," focusing on overt verbal and nonverbal behaviors. Recently, Rogers, Jackson, Sewell, and Salekin (in press) performed a confirmatory factor analysis (CFA) on the SIRS primary scales using the original validation data ($N = 403$) that was supplemented with three additional samples ($N = 255$). The CFA yielded two underlying dimensions: Spurious Presentation (highly atypical presentation of often bogus symptoms) and Plausible Presentation (marked overreporting of potentially legitimate symptoms).

The SIRS has been extensively validated with forensic populations. With trained interviewers, it yields highly reliable results for the primary scales. The major findings for the SIRS are summarized:

1. *Validation.* The SIRS has been extensively validated by its authors and independent investigators with highly positive results (for updated summary, see Rogers, 2001). Importantly, the research has included both simulation (analogue) design and known-groups comparisons.
2. *Discriminant validity.* Each primary scale clearly differentiates between feigning and genuine populations. Across clinical samples, the effect sizes are very large (mean Cohen's $d = 1.74$) for SIRS primary scales.
3. *Classification.* The scale development and resultant cut scores were developed to minimize the possibility of false-positives (i.e., misclassifying a genuine patient as a feigner). As a result, the SIRS has a very high positive predictive power (e.g., .97) to reduce false-postives.

In summary, the SIRS is a well-validated measure that has been tested in a range of forensic and correctional settings. Its results can be easily explained to the courts by addressing its detection strategies, validity, and resulting accuracy. Most forensic experts will consider the SIRS to be an essential component of their assessment repertoire.

Two significant problems have been observed with the SIRS in forensic practice, namely expert discounting and exposure to feigned results. These problems are examined individually:

1. *Expert discounting*. Rogers, the author of the SIRS, is approached periodically by forensic experts who are seeking to "explain away" SIRS results indicating a high likelihood of feigning. As a highly standardized, objective method, the SIRS results should not be discounted simply because they did not fit with preconceived notions. Occasionally, the SIRS is administered to patients who are incapable of responding relevantly to its inquiries. In these infrequent cases, however, the examiner should have terminated the interview immediately after observing the patient's inability to focus or respond meaningfully to the specific questions. The failure to do so indicates a lack of sufficient expertise in SIRS administration.

2. *Exposure to feigned results*. Occasionally, defendants with feigned SIRS results will be given access to their "failed" SIRS protocol. Not surprisingly, a subsequent SIRS administration does not yield the same results. In one egregious case, a male psychologist attempted to dismiss the feigned protocol and assert the accuracy his subsequent administration. Although the SIRS is resistant to general coaching, exposure to failed results at feigning is very likely to compromise subsequent administrations.

Prosecutors, in particular, should be aware of these efforts to discount or manipulate SIRS results in order to avoid classifying a defendant as feigning. Whether through discounting or exposure, these practices are incompatible with the SIRS administrative guidelines. The discounting practice is sometimes referred to as "cherry picking" whereby the expert attempts to manipulate the assessment process by selectively choosing "favorable" test interpretations and discarding the rest.

Assessment of Feigned Cognitive Impairment

Dozens of psychological measures have emerged during the last two decades ranging from commercially published tests to focused research applications. Many attorneys will initially feel overwhelmed by the plethora of measures, many with only modest validity. The purpose of this section is to provide those experts not specializing in neuropsychological assessments and criminal attorneys with a conceptual framework for understanding these measures and their detection strategies. Importantly, experts and attorneys should not conclude that a commercially published test is necessarily well validated. Reviews (see Rogers & Bender, 2002) demonstrate considerable variability in test validation for both published and unpublished measures.

The aphorism that a "little knowledge is a dangerous thing" is trite but true in describing the complex literature surrounding feigned cognitive impairment. What makes this literature so complex? Contributing factors include the following:

1. The complexity results from the sheer number of (a) published and unpublished measures and (b) specialized applications to strategies to intellectual and neuropsychological tests.
2. Among four research designs (see Rogers & Bender, 2002), one design is clearly inapplicable. In particular, the *differential prevalence design* has limited usefulness and should *not* be used in forensic practice. This design simply assumes that more forensic than non-forensic cases may feign. Not only does this design yield data of questionable value, it is overtly biased against forensic cases.
3. For many studies, the focus of the research (i.e., the experimental instructions and scenarios) has only marginal relevance to criminal forensic practice.

Given these complexities, attorneys and many experts will need their own consultants in navigating through the mishmash of research findings and methods. The only exception for attorneys will likely involve the most blatant cases of sciolism.

Application of detection strategies. The most sensible course of action is for attorneys to focus on the basic detection strategies underlying measures of feigned cognitive impairment. Toward this end, Appendix C provides a representative summary of measures and strategies. When questioned by attorneys, experts need to have a thorough understanding of each measure and their reasons for selecting or deselecting it. This understanding must include its two basic parameters: (a) the extensiveness of its validation and (b) usefulness of its detection strategies. Even without detailed preparation, cross-examination can sometimes expose sciolism, when the expert appears lost and confused with comparing detection strategies and explaining his or her choices of measures. Some experts will attempt to defend their choice by "experience" and "familiarity." While these reasons are understandable, they do not represent scientific evidence. Science is not based on insularity (*my* experience and familiarity) but a comparative analysis of tested methods. This matter is addressed in Chapter 3 with illustrative cross-examination.

The general effectiveness of detection strategies appears to be closely related to specific feigning measures. Unlike feigned mental disorders, general efficacy of particular detection strategies is more difficult to demonstrate. However, the following observations appear warranted:

1. *Below-chance performance on symptom validity testing is convincing evidence of feigning.* No other detection strategy provides such convincing evidence. Detection via symptom validity testing can stand on its own; however, we strongly recommend that experts seek additional corroborative data. Because less than one-third of the feigners are detected by this strategy, experts must also rely on other less accurate methods.

2. Three strategies (performance curve, floor effect, and magnitude of error) appear to have some strong empirical bases. Confidence in conclusions drawn from these detection strategies is enhanced if two conditions can be met: (a) feigning is determined by at least two of the three strategies, and (b) potential confounds (e.g., mental retardation and severe Axis I disorders) can be ruled out.

Synopsis of feigning measures. This subsection provides a brief summary of the feigning measures presented in Appendix C. The first eight measures are either commercially published (TOMM, VIP, WMT, VSVT, and CARB) or widely available (PDRT, Rey-15, and DCT). The remaining two measures (NSI and TOCA) have limited research and presently should not be used determinations of malingering, although they may yield ancillary data about detection strategies. In the following paragraphs, we provide nontechnical summaries of these measures. In referring to these measures, experts and attorneys are faced with two unappealing alternatives: refer either to measures by their initials which appears arcane, or by their full names which is often cumbersome. In this subsection, we use initials because this usage is common in the professional literature.

The Test of Malingered Memory (TOMM; Tombaugh, 1996) is a well-validated measure for evaluating feigned nonverbal memory deficits. Its strengths include the use of multiple detection strategies and extensive data, predominantly from VA samples. However, its use with defendants presenting with severe cognitive deficits is strongly questioned. Teichner and Wagner (2004) found that more than 70% of genuine patients with dementia failed the TOMM[5]. Equally concerning is the observation by Smith (1998). In the validation of the TOMM, some cognitively impaired patients were "helped out" (e.g., refocused on the task and given expanded instructions). Because this coaching is not allowed in the standard administration of the TOMM, an unknown percentage of genuine patients with severe impairment are likely to be wrongly classified. For forensic practice, we recommend that the TOMM only be used under the following conditions:

- *Persons with severe Axis I disorders have been excluded.* The TOMM does appear to be effective for persons with mild depression and anxiety (Ashendorf, Constantinou, & McCaffrey, 2004) but its usefulness with severe disorders requires more study.[5]
- *Defendants have no significant problems sustaining attention.*
- *Persons with moderate to severe dementia have been excluded.* The TOMM may misclassify the majority of individuals with dementia as feigning even though their impairment is genuine (Teichner & Wagner, 2004).

The TOMM may occasionally yield important data about feigning based on a violation of a learning principle. In one California case, the defendant's scores were low (i.e., floor effect) but possibly explainable by his severe depression. However, the defendant has scored substantially better on delayed (approximately a 30-min interval) than immediate memory. Given learning principle (i.e., memory decay over time), an *improvement* of more than 20% is highly unexpected. On the basis of this and other findings, we concurred with the expert's opinion that the defendant was likely feigning.

The Validity Indicator Profile (VIP; Frederick & Foster, 1997) is a sophisticated measure for assessing patients level of sustained effort on verbal and nonverbal cognitive tasks. Its strengths include extensive validation and considerable sophistication in developing a range of detection strategies. Although some of the promotional literature is potentially misleading, its test manual conscientiously describes its validation and clinical applications. As noted by Frederick and Foster (1997), many "invalid" profiles are *not* feigned but represent either (a) poor effort but motivated to do well (described as "careless") or (b) some intention to perform poorly but not a sustained effort (described as "irrelevant"). In addition, Rogers and Bender (2002) examined data presented in the test manual and concluded

---

[5]Weinborn, Orr, Woods, Conover, and Feix (2003) found inpatients with little motivation to malinger failed the TOMM at problematic rates: 16.7% for Trial 2 and 11.5% for Retention.

that the VIP missed more than 90% of feigning cases. In forensic cases, we recommend that the VIP only be used to assess overall effort but not for the determination of feigning or malingering. The VIP should only be used under the following conditions:

- *Persons with severe Axis I disorders have been excluded.*
- *Persons with mental retardation have been excluded.* As noted in the test manual, the VIP is mostly inaccurate (95.0%) with this population.
- *Persons with suspected or documented learning disorders have been excluded.* Persons with these learning disorders were systematically excluded from the VIP validation. This exclusion has important implications for criminal forensic evaluations; nearly two-thirds of state inmate populations have learning disorders (Bureau of Justice Statistics, 2003).
- *Persons with documented brain injury should be excluded.* More than one-third of this population produced "invalid" results on at least one of the two VIP subtests.

The Word Memory Test (WMT; Green, Astner, & Allen, 1996) presents 20 pairs of words and tests the memory abilities for recognition and recall at two intervals (immediately and after a 30-min delay). Substantial research has examined the clinical usefulness of detection strategies for feigned memory impairment. Unfortunately, the test manual (Green, Allen, & Astner, 1996) does not integrate these studies in establishing utility estimates; this complicates its forensic applications. In forensic practice, the WMT should only be used under the following conditions:

- *Persons with severe Axis I disorders have been excluded.*
- *Persons with mental retardation have been excluded.*
- *Persons lacking fluency in English oral and written comprehension have been excluded.*

The WMT has the potential for evaluating performance curve by examining learning tasks of varying difficulty. *Pair associates* (e.g., "cat–mouse") are a very simple form of recall. The examiner supplies the first word of the pair (e.g., "cat") and the patient responds with the second (e.g., "mouse"). In contrast, delayed free recall is demanding; it requires that patient to recall as many words as possible after a 30-min delay. Therefore, experts can evaluate the patient's performance curve by examining comparative success on subtests of varying difficulty.

The Victoria Symptom Validity Test (VSVT; Slick, Hopp, Strauss, & Thompson, 1997) is a 48-item computer-administered version of the

Hiscock Digit Memory Test that requires the recognition of five-digit numbers when offered two alternatives. Below-chance performance on symptom validity testing is highly effective, but found in only a minority of cases (Slick, Hopp, Strauss, Hunter, & Pinch, 1994). The VSVT has no exclusions in forensic practice as along as it relies solely on symptom validity testing.

The Portland Digit Recognition Test (PDRT; Binder & Willis, 1991) evaluates recognition memory for numerical sequences in a two-choice format. It provides a distraction task and longer intervals than some alternative methods (e.g., the SVST and CARB). Like these measures, its symptom validity testing works in only a minority of cases. Test validation tends to focus on the strategy of forced choice testing, which has very limited applicability in forensic cases. In forensic practice, the PDRT can be used if limited to symptom validity testing.

The Computerized Assessment of Response Bias (CARB; Allen, Conder, Green, & Cox, 1997) is a commercially published measure utilizing multiple detection strategies (forced choice testing, floor effect, and reaction time) to assess recognition memory. It is intended to assess "secondary gain, incomplete effort, feigning, symptom exaggeration, faking, and malingering" (p. 1). It has been primarily validated for brain-injured groups in compensation settings. Like the many other specialized measures, the following conditions should be observed:

- *Persons with severe Axis I disorders have been excluded.*
- *Persons with mental retardation have been excluded.*

Lezak (1995) is the primary source for two traditional screens for feigned cognitive impairment based on Rey's formulations. These include the Rey-15 involves the recall memory of 15 items (numbers, letters, and geometric shapes) that are organized so as facilitate memory. Used as a screen, it may identify cases requiring further evaluation. However, the Rey-15 lacks sufficient accuracy to be used in the determination of feigning with a wide range of classification rates (see Schretlen, Brandt, Krafft, & Van Gorp, 1991). The second screen, Dot Counting Test, utilizes performance curve under tasks of varying difficulty (i.e., grouped and ungrouped dots). Comparisons of relative time appear to be moderately useful at detecting likely feigners (Binks, Gouvier, & Waters, 1997).

The two remaining measures have limited research has should only be used for ancillary data about detection strategies for feigned cognitive impairment. The Neuropsychological Symptom Inventory (NSI; Rattan, Dean, & Rattan, 1989) was originally developed to survey reported symptoms associated with neurologic and mental disorders. Subsequently, the NSI has been used with simulators feigning mild closed head injuries

(Gelder, Titus, & Dean, 2002). The NSI primary detection strategy is psychological sequelae, although it also uses atypical presentation (i.e., overall symptom impairment and unusual items on the Lie scale). The Test of Cognitive Abilities (TOCA; Rogers, 1996) provides data about cognitive abilities and response styles. With respect to the latter, the TOCA systematically evaluates floor effect, magnitude of error, performance curve, symptom validity testing. These detection strategies are combined with reaction time. Bender and Rogers (2004) found that magnitude of error was very accurate at identifying both simulators (positive predictive power = .94) and genuine patients (negative predictive power = .93). Both floor effect and performance curve were effective while symptom validity testing was not.

CONCLUSIONS ABOUT FEIGNED COGNITIVE IMPAIRMENT

Despite great strides during the last decade, the assessment of feigned cognitive impairment represents a patch quilt (some might say a crazy quilt) of measures, detection strategies, and special scores/formulae. In addition, these measures are often limited in type of cognitive abilities being assessed. Most measures are focused narrowly on specific cognitive abilities. Experts and attorneys should consider whether the feigning measure matches the purported deficits:

- Measures addressing only *recognition memory* (i.e., recognize the correct response given two choices): TOMM, PDRT, VSVT, and CARB.
- Measure addressing only *recall memory*: Rey-15.
- Measure addressing a range of memory abilities (i.e., recognition, cued recall, and free recall): WMT.
- Measure addressing word knowledge and nonverbal reasoning: VIP.
- Measure addressing simple calculation: DCT.
- Measure addressing verbal and nonverbal reasoning, verbal comprehension, spatial abilities, and working memory: TOCA.

In general, these measures are potentially useful in cases whether the defendant is purporting major deficits in attention and concentration because these capacities form the basis for all cognitive abilities. Therefore, feigned deficits in basic concentration are likely to be detected by most specialized measures.

Experts should attempt to select measures that assess abilities related to a particular defendant's purported deficits but must sometimes compromise between well-validated measures and tests focused on purported deficits. Reports to the court should be forthright about the decision process so that it can be scrutinized by attorneys and other experts. In those cases where the expert appears to be using measures based on convenience rather than purported deficits, attorneys may wish to inquire about this decision:

1. *But doctor, what tests or measures did you administer that addressed __* [specific deficits in question]?
2. *Yes or no: would it be fair to say, that you have no data that directly addresses whether __* [specific deficits in question] *are genuine?*

SUMMARY

The assessment of response styles is a bedrock issue that underlies all forensic evaluations. This chapter focuses on critical issues related to malingering, which are organized into three levels: domains (mental disorders and cognitive impairment), detection strategies, and standardized measures. The complexity of this material underscores the science of forensic psychology and psychiatry and the need for a sophisticated understanding of the material. Of the other response styles, defensiveness will be addressed in several chapters (i.e., Chapters 7 and 11) with special attention to sex offenders and substance abusers.

3

The Nature of Experts
and Their Testimony

Forensic textbooks (e.g., Heilbrun, 2001; Melton et al., 1997; Rogers & Shuman, 2000a) often delay the subject of the selection and presentation of expert testimony to the final chapters to serve as a capstone for forensic practice. We have reversed the order to encourage experts and attorneys to consider the "final" product from the development of the case to its ultimate resolution. The chapter briefly explores the nature of experts before a transition to its major focus, their testimony.

THE NATURE OF EXPERTS

One way to think about the selection and presentation of mental health experts is by analogy to shopping in a consignment store. All experts seem slightly battered and chipped, their value is difficult to judge, and none come with reliable guarantees. Many attorneys are undiscriminating shoppers: they do not look closely for flaws. Some tend to overvalue their selections, and others miss great bargains. A few attorneys seek assurances that cannot be found and will lead to much frustration. Prudence cautions that attorneys:

- *Look for cracks.* Attorneys should routinely check with the relevant state licensing boards (Simon & Shuman, 1999) and require as part of their professional agreements the disclosure of any current or pending (a) legal actions against the expert or (b) ethical complaints (Rogers & Shuman, 2000a). Informal networking among colleagues is also invaluable for avoiding obvious mistakes.
- *Beware of promises.* Attorneys using the occasional expert whose testimony can seemingly be bought (i.e., the "hired gun") are betting on the obtuseness of the judge or the naivete of the jury deciding the case. If the fact-finer is discerning, the coziness of the attorney–expert relationship and the glibness of the expert will be quickly realized.

The consignment-shop metaphor, however, is incomplete in describing the expert's role in criminal proceedings. It is true that attorneys are responsible for their initial selection of retained forensic experts and even the occasional termination of experts from their cases. Yet, it is also true that seasoned experts select attorneys in deciding which cases to accept. Selection aside, the real focus is on their relationship. Which relationships will work well? Which relationships will work poorly?

Working Styles

Attorneys are invested in developing a good working relationship with their experts. How is this achievable? Self-reflection is an important aspect of establishing a workable attorney–expert relationship. Attorneys need to consider what made the difference between good and poor working relationships in past cases. Beyond the particular demands of a specific case, we postulate that the attorney's own personality and style of lawyering play a major role.

A key issue for criminal attorneys is to select competent experts with compatible working styles. A general understanding of differences in working style may help both attorneys and their experts to achieve this. As a first step, attorneys may wish to consider three general dimensions:

1. *Big picture vs. detailed picture.* Attorneys favoring the *big picture* perspective tend to favor experts who prefer narrative responses

and are skilled at "telling the story." The big-picture perspective becomes obvious even in the qualifications of an expert; for example, "Doctor, tell us about your professional background." In contrast, attorneys subscribing to the *detailed picture* want a more organized presentation with their own systematic input toward "building the story." In working together, attorneys will want experts that are compatible with their basic style.

2. *Emotional vs. logical.* Like experts, attorneys vary considerably in their approach to their use of emotions to influence the jury. Some attorneys paint emotional images for the jury that works best with experts that manifest controlled passion in their testimony. Other attorneys function more quietly using logic and arguments of persuasion. They focus on building evidence and a convincing fact pattern.

3. *Unidirectional vs. bidirectional.* Attorneys vary greatly in their types of interactions with forensic experts. Some attorneys seek to "keep their own counsel;" they alone are responsible for managing the criminal case. The relationship tends to be unidirectional; input is typically sought for very focused issues. In contrast, other attorneys seek greater participation from experts and openly discuss courtroom strategies as it relates to mental health issues (i.e., bidirectional relationship).

Common frustrations are experienced when working styles are polar-opposite. For instance, a "big-picture–unidirectional" attorney is likely to experience frustration with an expert that is detail-oriented (small picture) and accustomed to discussing many facets of the case (bidirectional). One option is to avoid experts with apparently incompatible working styles. An alternative, described in the next subsection, is to develop explicit expectations that take into account these differences in personality and working style. All professionals (attorneys and their experts) are influenced by their personalities that affect their workstyles.

Experts also bear considerable responsibility in acknowledging differences in working styles and attempting to resolve potential issues. Frank discussions can avert major conflicts. For example, an attorney may want an expert to appear fresh and unrehearsed. In changing prepared testimony, the attorney may not realize the consequences to the attorney–expert relationship. Beyond potential problems with the immediate response (e.g., surprise and possible consternation), this unidirectional perspective may damage the expert's trust in the attorney. An expert wary of the next "surprise" is unlikely to perform optimally.

CLARIFICATION OF EXPECTATIONS

Experts and attorneys are vulnerable to false expectations. In professional relationships, false expectations are rarely the result of active deception or subterfuge. Rather, they result from an unexpressed unwillingness to clarify the nature of the relationship and its professional boundaries.

An important issue in establishing professional boundaries is for experts and attorneys to be explicit about what conduct is expected. For many experts, these boundaries may include

- Do not ask me to cover up the "bad news," which is a part of every case.
- Do not manipulate the information; I respond badly when potentially damaging information is withheld.

For many attorneys, these boundaries may include

- Do not sweet talk me; I need to know every weakness in this case.
- Do not act so important; the case is not about you but about this defendant's life.

Many expectations between attorneys and experts address important, though mundane issues, such as the expert's availability and financial remuneration (Gutheil, 1998a). These expectations should be reduced to writing to minimize any misunderstandings for both conceptual and mundane issues.

PROBLEMATIC EXPERTS

Recent reviews of experts and their testimony focus predominantly on process, giving little attention to the *types* of experts that become involved in mental health issues (Ewing, 2003; Resnick, 2003). We address two types of forensic experts that are often problematic for opposing counsel and experts. These types consist of *technicians* and *self-absorbed experts*.

Technicians

A substantial minority of "experts" does not understand the *science* of forensic psychology and psychiatry, and are content to follow established procedures without a sophisticated understanding of their empirical strengths and limitations. They are also unlikely to have more than a superficial understanding of the relevant legal issues. We describe these experts as *technicians* because of their emphasis on methods and procedures. In this regard, we offer an informal distinction:

- *Professionals* are competent in both the science and practice of their specialities. Their practice is informed by research and empirically validated methods.
- *Technicians* are moderately competent in the practice of their specialties but do not understand its scientific underpinnings. Outside of the courtroom, technicians might even admit, "I do it this way because I was taught to do it this way."

Experts are unlikely to admit to being merely technicians. Nonetheless, this simple distinction may assist criminal attorneys in making decisions both in the selection of their own experts and the cross-examination of opposing experts.

The most effective cross-examination of technician-type experts is often highly individualized in its attempt to uncover inadequacies in training and knowledge. The most commonly observed example of technician-type evaluations involves the routinized use of computerized interpretations, or their predecessors, cookbook interpretations (see Box 3-1). Computerized interpretations are typically overly inclusive and do not discriminate a small number of well-validated data from a plethora of weakly supported statements or conjecture (Rogers, 2003b). From several pages of interpretation, the technician-type clinician handpicks based on preference rather

---

BOX 3-1 "TECHNICIANS" IN THE COURTROOM: ILLUSTRATIVE
CROSS-EXAMINATION

[This example is geared for mid-career expert who has been using the same measures for one or more decades.]

Expertise
1. *Doctor, when did you first learn to administer* __ [a test, such as the Rorschach or the MMPI-2]?... *Who taught you how administer it?... Did* [select: he or she] *do a good job?*
2. *About how many studies have been done of the* __ [test] *in the last decade?... Have you stayed current on the* __ [test]?... *How many of the* __ *studies have you carefully reviewed?... Were any worth remembering?... What are their names?*
3. [if applicable] *So you read less than 10% of the studies and can't remember even one title?*
4. *When you made this conclusion* (repeat a relevant sentence with a *noncontroversial* conclusion from the report), *how did you do it?...* [if quibbles]

(*Continued*)

Doctor, I am not asking for trade secrets, just tell me about the process. What was the first step?

5. [if relies on a computerized report for some or all of the interpretation] *Is this computerized report valid? . . . Is it your testimony that its interpretations and conclusions have sufficient validity as to be considered as valuable evidence in this case?*

Biased Interpretations

6. *Doctor, do you have of that computerized report with you?* [These computerized reports typically available to counsel.] *. . . How many pages of interpretations and conclusions are provided about the defendant?* [typically 2–3 pages] *. . . I noticed your report on __ [test] is less than a page long, isn't that correct?*

7. [key issue] *Please read to the court all the interpretations that you left out.* [if quibbles after a short while] *. . . Doctor, this court is interested in the whole truth. Please read all the interpretations and conclusions, not just the ones you hand picked.*

8. *Doctor, are you familiar with the term "cherry picking?" . . . What does it mean when applied to test interpretations? . . . So like cherries, you take the ones you like and leave the rest?*

9. *In all fairness, doctor, isn't that what you did—just takes the ones you liked?* [if disagrees] *What were the scientific reasons for leaving out __ [relevant interpretation]? What about __ [relevant interpretation], what were the scientific reasons for leaving it out?* [repeat as necessary]

Proprietary Interpretations

10. *Doctor, what is "proprietary information?" . . . Isn't it true that test firms don't tell you where they got their "proprietary information?"*

11. *How much proprietary information was used in the computerized interpretation of __ [test]? . . . [if "none"] How do you know that?*

12. *Which interpretations are based on proprietary information?* [cannot possibly know]

13. *Doctor, what are the ethical concerns in using interpretations or conclusions based on proprietary information?*

14. [for psychologists] *What is Ethical Standard 9?* [if doesn't know] *Doesn't it establish the standards for ethical practice as it relates to evaluations?*

15. *Doesn't Ethical Standard 9.09 require that you take professional responsibility for all your interpretations, including those which are computerized?* [Download the American Psychological Association's Ethical Standards from its website to use in cross-examination.]

16. *How can you possibly take responsibility for something that is proprietary when you don't even know its source or validation?* [if strongly disagrees] *Take __ [an interpretation that was included in the report], what was the source and validation of that finding?*

17. [if applicable] *First you testified the test may have proprietary interpretations, then you testified you don't know which interpretations are proprietary. Isn't it true that we can't put much faith in any of these interpretations?*

than science. If less than one-third of the possible interpretations/findings are used, the likelihood of cherry-picking looms large. *Cherry-picking* is the biased process of choosing desired interpretations and discarding the rest. "Cherry-picking constitutes an extreme form of confirmatory bias and should not be used in clinical or forensic practice." Rogers (2003b, p. 317).

Many testing services do not reveal the sources of their data or the underlying validation. Because all experts are responsible for their conclusions, such "proprietary information" is highly problematic. If an expert does not know the source or bases of a specific interpretation, the expert cannot know whether it is valid. The American Psychological Association (2002) code of ethics requires that psychologists know and take responsibility for their test interpretations, irrespective of whether an automated system is used. Psychologists risk engaging in unethical conduct if they cannot substantiate their conclusions (Bersoff & Hofer, 2003).

Box 3-1 attempts to tackle the more egregious issues found in technician-type testimony—absence of expertise, biased interpretations, and reliance on unverifiable proprietary information. Computerized and cookbook[1] interpretations involving multiscale inventories (e.g., the MMPI-2 and MCMI-III) and projective tests (e.g., the Rorschach) present problems. The illustrative cross-examination in Box 3-1 presupposes a technician-type expert who is willing to acknowledge at least some of his or her limitations. With especially recalcitrant experts, rebuttal testimony may be the best alternative.

Box 3-1 addresses three facets of technician-type experts that attorneys may wish to cover. Tackling both *biased interpretations* and *proprietary interpretations* may be overkill in some cases. The first set of questions (i.e., Expertise) is rather innocuous and only serves to point out the expert's lack of current training and up-to-date knowledge.

The questions on *biased communications* have the potential of unsettling some technician-type experts who are comfortably ensconced in their routinized use of automated test interpretations. Such questions can be especially effective when the expert's bias is obvious, for instance, including only those interpretations that cast the defendant in a sympathetic light. An example would be an MMPI-2 interpretation that emphasized depression and impaired functioning but somehow neglected to mention the antisocial features, potential feigning, and possible substance abuse. As noted above, "cherry-picking" in which the expert takes the best and disregards the rest is an egregious practice.

---

[1]Cookbook interpretations refer to texts with extensive lists of possible interpretations; some are valid and others speculative.

Attacking the expert's reliance on unverifiable proprietary information requires careful preparation that relies on the APA ethical standards. The danger is that the trier-of-fact will get "lost in the details" especially when presented in convoluted responses. Therefore, it is imperative that attorneys have a firm grasp on the underlying logic. Stripped to the bone, the logic is simple:

- Proprietary information is unverifiable.
- Conclusions based on unverifiable information are unethical and substandard.
- Because computerized reports do not differentiate proprietary from nonproprietary information, all computerized-based conclusions are suspect.

Self-Absorbed Experts

Narcissism exists in every profession including forensic psychology and psychiatry. A common variant of narcissism is presence of the *self-absorbed experts*. These experts are sometimes problematic to cross-examining attorneys because they exude confidence and superiority, which unchallenged, may sway the jury. As outlined in Table 3-1, the self-absorbed expert can be identified by three cardinal characteristics: superiority, totality of knowledge, and insularity. Totality of knowledge and insularity are closely related. The basic attitude is "I know all that is needed to be known." Other experts or sources of data are summarily dismissed as nonmeritorious. The expert's perspective must be insular in order to protect the aura of superiority. After all, superiority "dies at the stake" when other equally valid perspectives are recognized.

TABLE 3-1. THE SPECIAL CASE OF THE SELF-ABSORBED EXPERT SYNDROME

A common variant of narcissism is the *Self-Absorbed Expert* that is distinguished by the following characteristics:

3. *Superiority*: The self-absorbed expert expresses a superior attitude that is implicitly dismissive of attorneys and other experts. Alternative opinions are summarily discounted.
4. *Totality of knowledge*: The self-absorbed expert expresses a full command of the data relevant to the current case. As a corollary (see #3), information beyond the expert's command is simply deemed to be *not* relevant.
5. *Insularity*: The self-absorbed expert is unwilling to consider methods other than his or her own to address the forensic issue. In particular, the expert is often dismissive of standardized methods because they are likely to question his or her superiority (see #1).

Many criminal attorneys are ineffective with self-absorbed experts. An important aspect of an effective cross-examination of a self-absorbed expert is whether to focus on *content* or *process*. The crucial distinction follows:

- *Content focus.* The attorney attempts to wrestle admissions from the self-absorbed expert that his or her major points have weaknesses. The *content focus* is familiar ground for the self-absorbed expert and admissions are rarely forthcoming.
- *Process focus.* The attorney works on the credibility of the self-absorbed expert by highlighting his or her superiority and insularity. Rather than seeking admissions, the goal is the opposite. Namely, it illustrates why the expert "could not possibly be wrong." Such unbridled arrogance weakens credibility and may alienate the jury.

As illustrated in Box 3-2, two tactics with self-absorbed experts involve their overweening confidence and dismissiveness of other experts and their methods. A useful approach is to allow such experts to "inflate with their self-importance" and to facilitate this process by being friendly and even solicitous. The alternative is a more hostile approach, ranging from subtle irony to heavy-handed sarcasm. However, the goal is for the expert, not the cross-examining attorney, to alienate the jury. The goal is realized when the self-absorbed expert's excessive arrogance is revealed.

Box 3-2   Self-Absorbed Expert: Illustrative Cross-Examination

[These questions are to be asked in a friendly, possibly solicitous, manner to provide the jury with an ample opportunity to experience expert's superior and arrogant attitudes.]

Overweening Confidence
1. *Doctor, in your testimony today, you seemed very confident in your findings, is that correct?*
2. *Are very certain of all your findings or are there one or two that you have less confidence in?* [follow up any admissions of "uncertain findings"]
3. *Would it be fair to say that your report in this case was also very confident in its findings?*
4. *Please tell us, doctor, any doubts at all that you have about any of your findings in this case? . . .* [if none] *You sound very sure that you are right in this case, is that correct? . . . Positive of your conclusions?* [add other questions if necessary; remember your goal is to expose expert's arrogance]

Dismissive of Other Experts
5. *If you are positive about your findings, I guess that would make Dr. __'s conclusions wrong, wouldn't it? . . .* [likely to equivocate] *Well then, tell us the*

(Continued)

merits of Dr. __'s conclusions. . . . [if applicable] *Maybe I missed something; what are the <u>major strengths</u> of Dr. __'s conclusions?*

6. *How can you be confident that you are right when Dr. __ disagrees with you? . . . How confident are you, 80%, 90%, 100%?*

Dismissive of Other Methods #1: The Expert Relies Only on Clinical Interview

7. [if applicable] *I noticed you relied on your own clinical interview and did not use standardized measures in your evaluation, is that correct?*

8. *You didn't use* __ (e.g., a multiscale inventory) *in your evaluation, is that correct? . . . Is* __ *a well-validated measure?*

9. *You didn't use* __ (e.g., a structured interview) *in your evaluation, is that correct? . . . Is* __ *a well-validated measure?* [repeated as necessary, covering only the best-validated measures given by your own expert]

10. *Why didn't you need these standardized measures in your assessment of the defendant? . . . So basically your interview covered all the relevant findings in this case? . . . I take it you did <u>your</u> best job in this case?*

11. *Objectively, doctor, do you see anything wrong with you saying I can do better alone, with just my clinical interview, than all the validated measures in the world? . . .* [if negative] *I didn't think you would, doctor.*

Dismissive of Other Methods #2: The Expert Relies on Clinical Interview and Mental Status Examination

12. *In your report, you stated you conducted a mental status examination, is that correct?*

13. *Which mental status examination did you use?* [most common is the Mini-Mental State Examination or MMSE]

14. [if not MMSE] *Are you aware that the Mini-Mental State Examination is the best-validated mental status examination?*

15. [if MMSE, try to illustrate how it is not helpful with the common diagnostic issues] *How many items on the MMSE directly assess schizophrenia?* [none] *. . . Depression?* [none] *. . . Anxiety disorders?* [none] *. . . Mental retardation?* [none]

16. *You didn't use* __ (e.g., a multiscale inventory) *in your evaluation, is that correct? . . . Is* __ *a well-validated measure?*

17. *You didn't use* __ (e.g., a structured interview) *in your evaluation, is that correct? . . . Is* __ *a well-validated measure?* [repeated as necessary, covering only the best-validated measures given by your own expert]

18. *Why didn't you need these standardized measures in your assessment of the defendant? . . . So basically your interview covered all the relevant findings in this case? . . . I take it you did <u>your</u> best job in this case?*

19. *Objectively, doctor, do you see anything wrong with you saying I can do better just my clinical interview and a mental status exam, than all the validated measures in the world? . . .* [if negative] *I didn't think you would, doctor.*

Dismissive of Other Methods #3: Attacking The Expert's "Expertise"

[This approach is intended to supplement either #1 or #2. Unlike earlier components (friendly, even solicitous, approach), it becomes confrontational.]

(Continued)

20. *When you rejected* __ (e.g., a multiscale inventory), *was that based on knowledge or ignorance?* . . . [if you know the expert has no or very limited training in psychometrics or standardized assessments] *Please impress us with how many* __ (e.g., a multiscale inventory) *you have personally administered. . . . At least, tell us how many you have personally interpreted.* [if none] . . . *So if this is not based on ignorance, tell us which of the standard textbooks on* __ (e.g., a multiscale inventory) *you have closely read.*

21. *Are you even qualified to evaluate the merits of* __ (e.g., a multiscale inventory)? . . . [if "yes"] *Would that be based on knowledge or guesswork in this case?* . . . [if at least some knowledge] *Let's see how well you can do. Here is* __ [select a complex profile such as the MMPI-2 or PAI]. *What are the specific conclusions you can draw from this profile?* [You will need further preparation by your expert about specific scales and codetypes.]

Most experts are reticent to criticize their colleagues and self-absorbed experts are likely to be no exception. However, these experts can easily be put in a bind (i.e., "backing-down" or "putting-down") if their overweening confidence has been amply presented. Here is the bind:

- *Backing-down.* They acknowledge the comparable contributions of other experts and openly disavow their own superiority.
- *Putting-down.* They maintain their superiority at the expense of their credibility as they derogate their colleagues' expertise.

Many self-absorbed experts do not want to be bogged down by standardized measures that constrain their superiority and threaten their insularity. Some experts avoid all standardized measures while others may include a general screen, such as mental status examinations. Among the dozens of mental status examinations, most have little validity and survive on the basis of tradition rather than science (Rogers, 2001). Of mental status examinations, the Mini-Mental State Examination (MMSE; Folstein et al., 1975) is the most commonly used and does have circumscribed applicability in screening for cognitive impairment, such as found with moderate and severe dementias. It is not helpful in evaluating Axis I disorders (e.g., schizophrenia and major depression) or key symptoms (e.g., paranoid delusions or command hallucinations) that are often central to criminal forensic evaluations. Occasionally, experts will attempt to misrepresent the MMSE as a comprehensive measure. A useful approach is to bring a copy of the MMSE to the courtroom and demonstrate to the triers-of-fact the simplicity of its 11 items. Copies can be easily downloaded (e.g., http://www.healthsci.clayton.edu/nurs4220/mmsexam.htm) from the Internet.

Attorneys have two alternatives for self-absorbed experts depending on whether they use the MMSE or other mental status examinations. These questions underscore the self-absorbed experts' willingness to disregard decades of research and well-validated measures in deference to their own narcissistic self-importance.

The final set of illustrative questions takes an entirely different tack. If the self-absorbed expert continues to appear credible, he or she is often vulnerable to insularity. Self-absorbed experts rarely bother to examine closely the validity of methods that they do not personally use. This insularity often leads to *exclusion through ignorance*. In adopting a confrontational approach, the cross-examining attorney seeks to expose the expert's ignorance. If the expert's refuses to back-down, the last subset of questions (#21) illustrates the potential vulnerability of this intransigence.

EXPERT TESTIMONY

The second major section of this chapter focuses on the presentation of expert testimony. It is devoted to the general structure and principles underlying the examination of the expert by the party offering the expert that applies across the spectrum of criminal issues. Examination of the expert is divided into three phases: (1) qualification of the expert, (2) direct examination of the expert, and (3) redirect examination of the expert. Each phase is critical to building the credibility and persuasiveness of the expert. Cross-examination is addressed extensively in subsequent chapters.

Our assumption is that the attorneys and experts will work collaboratively on the development of each successive phase. In our experience, both attorneys and experts often focus on the direct examination itself, paying short shrift to either qualifications or redirect. Assuming the purpose of expert testimony is persuasion, each of the three phases plays an important and complementary role in persuading the fact-finder. We ask that attorneys rethink expert testimony as an interrelated process rather than three discrete steps.

EXPERT QUALIFICATIONS

Any person who has perceived relevant information may be compelled to testify about those perceptions as a lay witness in a trial. Expert witnesses, in contrast with lay witnesses, are permitted to draw inferences or offer opinions about facts that have been perceived by the expert or others, to assist the fact finder in deciding the case. In most jurisdictions, a ruling on the qualification of a witness as an expert only occurs if an opposing party objects to a witness's testimony on that grounds. Absent an objection, there may be no ruling from the court that a witness offering expert opinion is qualified as an expert.

When an objection is raised, the trial judge is called upon to determine whether the expert has scientific, technical, or specialized knowledge that will assist the fact-finder to understand the evidence or decide a question of fact. Two overarching principles guide this determination. First, expertise is contextual not generic. It is impossible to know whether a witness may qualify as an expert without knowing the specific issue on which the expertise is sought. Professional distinction standing alone does not guarantee qualification as an expert, rather what is required is a demonstration of relevant expertise (e.g., malingering in a case in which incompetence to stand trial is claimed to be feigned). Second, the trial court's determination of the expert's admissibility is regarded deferentially by the appellate courts and is unlikely to be overturned on appeal. Thus, this portion of the examination of the expert should anticipate all of the challenges that could be raised even if it is unlikely that they will be raised.

Once a court concludes that the issue on which the expert is offered is one on which the jury might benefit from expert assistance, the party offering the expert must address the *Daubert v. Merrell Dow Pharmaceutical, Inc.* (1993) and *Frye v. United States* (1923) issue—is the information claimed by this group of experts sufficiently reliable to permit it to be presented to the jury? The *Frye* test, articulated by the District of Columbia Court of Appeals, was applied in many federal courts prior to the enactment of the Federal Rules of Evidence. It is still applied in many state courts, when a challenge is made to the reliability of scientific evidence. With the *Frye* rule, the trial court is charged with gauging its "general acceptance" in the scientific community to which it belongs:

> Just when a scientific principle or discovery crosses the line between the experimental and demonstrable stages is difficult to define. Somewhere in this twilight zone the evidential force of the principle must be recognized, and while courts will go a long way in admitting expert testimony deduced from a well-recognized scientific principle or discovery, the thing from which the deduction is made *must be sufficiently established to have gained general acceptance in the particular field in which it belongs*. (Emphasis added; p. 1014)

When the Federal Rules of Evidence were adopted in 1975, they made no mention of *Frye* which had come under increasing criticism in the 1960s and 1970s because of the absence of clarity about what general acceptance meant, as well as why it was an appropriate standard for scientific validity or reliability. Not until 1993 in *Daubert v. Merrell Dow Pharmaceutical, Inc.*

did the Supreme Court clarify that *Frye* did not survive the adoption of the Federal Rules of Evidence. Rather, the Court concluded that the rules specified that trial judges were to admit expert testimony that is relevant and reliable, requiring them to determine "whether the reasoning or methodology underlying the testimony is scientifically valid and of whether that reasoning or methodology properly can be applied to the facts in issue" (pp. 592–593). In the context of judging the reliability of scientific experts the Court noted:

> The adjective "scientific" implies a grounding in the methods and procedures of science. Similarly, the word "knowledge" connotes more than subjective belief or unsupported speculation. The term "applies to any body of known facts or to any body of ideas inferred from such facts or accepted as truths on good grounds." ... Of course, it would be unreasonable to conclude that the subject of scientific testimony must be "known" to a certainty; arguably, there are no certainties in science ... But, in order to qualify as "scientific knowledge," an inference or assertion must be derived by the scientific method. (p. 590)

To make this preliminary determination when the admissibility of scientific evidence is challenged on reliability grounds, without limiting the trial court's discretion to consider other factors, the Court in *Daubert* offered four general considerations:

- Whether falsifiability of the scientific evidence can be evaluated. The court determined, "a key question to be answered in determining whether a theory or technique is scientific knowledge that will assist the trier of fact will be whether it can be (and has been) tested" (p. 593);
- Whether the theory or technique has been subjected to peer review and publication;
- Whether the known or potential rate of error of the technique and procedures can be established; and
- Whether the theory or technique has general acceptance in the relevant scientific community.

Daubert did not explain how these factors should be applied, noting instead that flexibility was a guiding consideration. "The inquiry envisioned by Rule 702 is, we emphasize, a flexible one. Its overarching subject is the scientific validity."(p. 594)

The next chapter in the Supreme Court's *Daubert* trilogy was *General Electric Co. v. Joiner* (1997). *Joiner* resolved that the abuse of discretion standard should apply when federal appellate courts review federal trial court decisions to admit or exclude expert testimony. Most states follow a similar rule. One important lesson of *Joiner* for experts is to understand that the trial judge is likely to have the final say on admissibility and therefore preparation for presenting or excluding expert testimony in the trial courts should include all relevant scientific information. Second, the abuse of discretion standard leads to the possibility of conflicting admissibility decisions in different trial courts on the same issue and same methodology. Thus, experts and attorneys must know each judge's approach to the admissibility of controverted expert evidence.

The third chapter in the Supreme Court's *Daubert* trilogy was *Kumho Tire Co., Ltd. v. Carmichael* (1999). *Kumho* answered the question left open by *Daubert*, whether it was restricted to offers of hard science expert testimony as addressed in *Daubert*. The Court in *Kumho* concluded that *Daubert issues* applied to all types of expert testimony but that trial courts enjoy broad discretion in apply these factors:

> We also conclude that a trial court may consider one or more of the more specific factors that Daubert mentioned when doing so will help determine that testimony's reliability. But, as the Court stated in Daubert, the test of reliability is "flexible," and Daubert's list of specific factors neither necessarily nor exclusively applies to all experts or in every case. Rather, the law grants a district court the same broad latitude when it decides how to determine reliability as it enjoys in respect to its ultimate reliability determination. See General Electric Co. v. Joiner, 522 U.S. 136, 143, 118 S.Ct. 512, 139 L.Ed.2d 508 (1997) (courts of appeals are to apply "abuse of discretion" standard when reviewing district court's reliability determination). (p. 141–142)

The trilogy does not offer specific standards regarding the four components. As noted by Krauss and Sales (2003), the courts provide no guidance about what level of error rate is deemed unacceptable. Some debate can also occur over the correct calculation of error rate. On this point, different utility estimates should vary with the conclusion:

- When the forensic clinician concludes that a specific condition is *present* (i.e., "positive"), then the proper estimate of error rate is *1-PPP*. Positive predictive power is the accuracy of the measure for a specific defendant for measuring the presence of a condition; *1-PPP* is the error rate for this specific defendant.
- When the forensic clinician concludes that a specific condition is absent (i.e., "negative"), then the proper estimate of error rate is *1-NPP*. Negative predictive power is the accuracy of the measure for a specific defendant for measuring the absence of a condition; *1-PPP* is the error rate for this specific defendant.

If the *Frye/Daubert* issue of evidentiary reliability is not raised or is decided favorably for the offering party that party must substantiate the expert's expertise. This substantiation includes the witness's qualifications as an expert with relevant and reliable knowledge. Specifically, does this witness have the education, training, or experience to know what well-informed experts in the field know about the specific issue? This decision is also addressed to the discretion of the trial court.

Beyond legal requirements, the qualifications phase serves several valuable functions. First and foremost, it provides a preparatory period for the expert. Most experts put substantial effort into preparation. However, the psychological preparation is never completed until a short time *after* the expert takes the stand. Even with assurances by the court ("The doctor will be the first witness tomorrow."), cases rarely occur when they are scheduled. Other matters before the court or a missing juror often does delay proceedings. Given these uncertainties, the expert is never fully prepared until his or her testimony begins.

Familiar questions at the beginning of qualifications are very helpful because they help to focus and/or calm the expert. Of equal importance, attorneys should be relaxed and unhurried in these first few minutes of expert qualifications. Once the expert becomes settled and focused, the attorney can gradually change the pace and momentum to fit his or her own style and considerations of the particular case.

An additional purpose of expert qualifications is establishing the credibility of the expert. Jurors seek to make expert credibility determinations based on rational criteria—the expert's qualifications, reasoning, factual familiarity, and impartiality (Shuman, Champagne, & Whitaker, 1996). Thus, these rational considerations ought to be the center piece of the presentation, beginning with establishing the expert's qualifications to address the issue(s) which will be the subject of his or her testimony. Besides reviewing the expert's formal training and experience, a secondary task is to provide the judge and jury with an opportunity to get to know the expert. Credibility embraces trustworthiness (Melton et al., 1997). Whether brief personal glimpses of the expert is helpful has not been empirically studied. Given that expert testimony is often technical in nature, it could be argued that such efforts may help to humanize expert's testimony.

Experts with substantial accomplishments face an additional predicament in establishing their credibility. On one hand, they wish to communicate about these accomplishments so that the fact-finder is properly informed. On the other hand, they do not wish to appear as self-serving braggarts, cocksure in their superiority. Even seasoned experts may need to practice *how* to relate their impressive accomplishments with the obvious goal of engaging, not alienating, the judge and jury.

The expert's frankness and openness play an important role in how jurors may perceive him or her. As dimension of openness, the expert may be experienced as approachable versus distant. Beginning with qualifications, the expert can begin to establish rapport with the jury and indicate nonverbally his or her respect for their important function. This comment on openness should not be confused with disguised attempts at ingratiation or manipulation. Rather, it is based on well-established literature on genuineness and its positive effects, at least on therapeutic interactions (Klein, Michels, & Kolden, 2001).

DIRECT EXAMINATION

Forensic psychological and psychiatric texts often focus on legal and procedural issues (Ewing, 2003) or style of presentation (Gutheil, 1998a, 1998b; Melton et al., 1997; Resnick, 2003) rather than direct examination of an expert. Similar observations (Becker, 1997; Matson, 1994) are noted for expert testimony outside of mental health issues. Given this limited focus, attorneys and experts are offered little guidance in how to structure and present psychological and psychiatric testimony on direct examination.

Experts and attorneys are likely to fall, by default, into familiar patterns in their preparation for direct examination. We suspect that some experts have consistently structured their direct examination in the same pattern across years of their forensic practice. The primary purpose of this section is to provide experts and attorneys with four basic structures for the presentation of direct examination. Before addressing these basic structures, we should review the specific components of psychological and psychiatric testimony used in constructing a direct examination.

COMPONENTS OF DIRECT EXAMINATION

The basic components of psychological and psychiatric testimony on direct examination about the evaluation of a litigant are composed of methods, data, conclusions, and opinions. Beyond methods, the testimony reflects three levels of inference from the basic data (e.g., direct observations or clinical findings) to conclusions (e.g., the "meaning" of the clinical findings such as a diagnosis), and opinions (e.g., combining conclusions to address components of the referral question). Each component is described in detail.

Methods

Judges and juries need to be educated about the methods: *what they are* and *why they were used*. Care must be taken to not to "talk down" (e.g., treat them as if they were stupid) or "talk over" (e.g., be abstruse and make them feel stupid) to the fact-finder. With methods, we expect jurors to learn a new language (i.e., names and acronyms), specialized knowledge (e.g., what their findings mean), and science (e.g., reliability and validity of measures).

How many experts would like to be coerced (jurors did not volunteer) into learning a foreign language plus specialized knowledge without any study guides? We are astonished by how many experts expect this of the jury. Verbal presentation of methods should be supplemented with easily read visual aids and handouts. These materials must be prepared and presented in coordination with the attorney who retained them (who may have an obligation to present all proposed exhibits prior to trial), marked and offered into evidence as exhibits based on agreement of the parties or a ruling of the trial judge. In either case they must accurately reflect the evidence on which they rely and utilize methods that are sufficiently reliable to permit their admission into evidence. In addition, where individual juror handouts are sought, each handout must be identical.

Experts are sometimes reluctant to accept feedback about their effectiveness in describing clinical methods to nonprofessionals. When possible, we recommend that a co-counsel listen to this segment of direct-testimony preparation. His or her limited understanding of the testimony may be very instructive.

Data

Experts need to address what they found, namely their observations, test data, and clinical findings. In establishing key data, a broader perspective may include its determination (How do you know it?) and sources (Where did it come from?). With literally hundreds of data, experts are necessarily selective in what they present. From this perspective, data are not entirely separate from either conclusions or opinions.

What data should be presented? The basic metrics are competence, relevance, perspective, balance, and candor (Shuman & Greenberg, 2003). Experts should only address issues for which they have the education, training, and experience to provide competent forensic services. Experts should attempt to present all data relevant to the opinions they have been asked to address and nothing that is not. Experts should consider and address opposing perspectives on the relevant data in a balanced manner. Avoiding the practice of cherry-picking, experts should present data candidly without selecting only data that supports the conclusion of the party who retained them. By acknowledging possible weaknesses on direct, the expert may increase his or her credibility and diminish the effects of cross-examination (see Williams, Bourgeois, & Croyle, 1993).

Conclusions

Data by themselves may have little meaning. Conclusions provide a framework for organizing and understanding the data. Diagnostic conclusions help us to understand how symptoms assist in establishing the diagnosis (i.e., inclusion criteria) and what conditions or syndromes should *not* be present (i.e., exclusion criteria). Conclusions easily extend beyond diagnoses to address specific abilities (e.g., abstract thinking) or impairment (e.g., capacity to perform daily activities).

Opinions

Opinions are typically integrated conclusions that address issues relevant to the court. For example, diagnosis *per se* has little direct relevance to most criminal forensic standards (Greenberg, Shuman, & Meyer, 2004). However, specific incapacities arising from several Axis I disorders may well be very relevant to a specific legal issue, such as competency to stand trial.

The early common law limited expert witnesses from testifying to opinions that embraced the ultimate issue in the case. The modernization of evidence law did away with the ultimate issue rule because it resulted in much confusion as courts had difficulty determining which issues were ultimate and because jurors are unlikely to fall prey to ultimate opinions that are not supported by sound reasoning (Fulero & Finkel, 1991; Rogers, Bagby, Crouch, & Cutler, 1990). Notwithstanding this change in legal rules permitting experts to testify to the ultimate opinion in the case, a small but vocal contingent of commentators has campaigned vigorously against the use of ultimate opinions in any criminal or civil matter (Melton, Petrila, Poythress, & Slobogin, 1987, 1997; Melton, 1999) arguing that mental health experts have no expertise on the legal or moral issues that are bound up with the ultimate issue.

While the desire to limit mental health experts to their sphere of expertise was sensible, the reason courts abandoned the ultimate issue rule is that they could not make sense of it. If lawyers and judges cannot easily distinguish ultimate from nonultimate issues, how can mental health professionals whose expertise is not law be expected to do so? Restricting mental health professionals to opinions within their expertise requires criteria in a mental health professional's sphere of expertise—do the data provide reliable support for the opinion (Rogers & Shuman, 2000a; Rogers & Ewing, 2003). Rather than trying to figure out legal rules for which they have no training, mental health experts should concentrate on their professional expertise—is there a scientifically sound basis for this opinion? Only in the federal courts and California, as a consequence of John Hinckley's successful insanity defense, are there external legal constraints on ultimate issue testimony beyond what the science might support when an expert is testifying to the mental state of a criminal defendant. And that is the only setting in which experts should categorically avoid testifying in terms that embrace the ultimate issue in the case. In all other cases, experts should consider whether there is good evidence to support their conclusions.

Attorneys may encounter forensic psychologists and psychiatrists who believe there are professional or ethical bans preventing them from rendering an ultimate opinion. As outlined in Rogers and Shuman (2000a), no such bans exist. The arguments against ultimate opinions are based on questionable assumptions or are not supported empirically. Forensic clinicians should critically reevaluate their positions on ultimate opinions. Critiques by Rogers and Ewing (1989, 2003) examine the major issues, which are also outlined in Appendix E.

AN OVERVIEW OF DIRECT EXAMINATION

We summarize in Table 3-2 two simple (Building-up and Unfolding) and two complex (Comparative Analysis and Critical Issues) models of direct examination. Attorneys and experts may wish to use these models in deciding on the best organization for a particular case. In the following subsections, each model is examined separately.

THE BUILDING-UP MODEL

The Building-up model is intuitively appealing. Early testimony with its clinically relevant details lays the foundation for subsequent conclusions and opinions (see Table 3-2). Jurors can easily understand how facts lead to conclusions which lead to opinions. Sometimes direct examination can create an aura of suspense. For example, an attorney may ask with understated curiosity, "So doctor, what does it mean that Mr. Smith heard voices and was fearful for his life?" The explanation about auditory hallucinations and paranoid ideation might then lead to questions about schizophrenia. In turn, questions about impairment arising from the schizophrenic disorder may lead to issues regarding Mr. Smith's rational understanding of his criminal proceedings.

Our major concern is that experts may automatically adopt the building-up model because their testimony has become routinized. Attorneys, pressed for time in trial preparation, may favor the building-up model because it takes less time to prepare. Formulaic questions (*What did*

TABLE 3-2. FOUR CONCEPTUAL MODELS FOR DIRECT EXAMINATION

Building-Up Model
Description: Testimony builds from simple to complex with observable data providing the bases for conclusions and opinions. Data (e.g., examples of persecutory delusions and command hallucinations) lead to conclusions (e.g., diagnosis of paranoid schizophrenia), which lead to opinions (e.g., "appreciate the criminality" prong of the ALI standard of insanity).
Advantages: First, the structure of the testimony is simple and easy to follow. Second, well-prepared testimony may actively engage triers-of-fact in the outcome as they consider the relevance of the data and conclusions to the final opinions.
Limitation: The testimony has a potential risk of becoming bogged down in details before the connections between data and conclusions are made.

Unfolding Model
Description: The testimony begins with the opinions and works backward to the opinions and data. It starts with the bottom-line issues and then offers substantiation. To be effective, such testimony the testimony should "unfold" so that the bases of conclusions are revealed in a manner that holds the interest of the triers-of-fact.
Advantages: First, this structure is also easy to follow. Second, the triers-of-fact know immediately the bottom-line issues and have little danger of becoming lost in the testimony.
Limitation: The triers-of-fact are not as engaged in "trying to figure it out"; one supposition is that triers-of-fact may be more persuaded by their increased involvement in determining bottom-line issues.

Comparative Analysis Model
Description: Testimony begins with 2 or 3 alternative explanations with data and conclusions being presented for each. Data and conclusions are marshaled for each alternative.
Advantage: The primary advantage is its potential to address directly the triers-of-fact's decisional process. Let us assume in the earlier example that the jury already heard expert testimony that the decapitating defendant was psychotic. Jury members are individually trying to decide between "mad"and "bad." By presenting the evidence side-by-side, this testimony may influence the jury's decisions.
Limitations: Unless presented clearly with visual aids, testimony runs the risk of confusing the triers-of-fact. In addition, this model only makes sense when the arguments for one alternative are compelling.

Critical Issues Model
Description. As a variation of the Build-Up Model, testimony may be organized into several individual components that are key to the case. Data, conclusions, and opinions are presented for each. For a competency-to-confess case, the expert may pose a series of questions:

⇒Was the defendant feigning his or her impairment?
⇒What is the defendant's current ability to waive his or her rights intelligently?
⇒What was the defendant's retrospective ability to waive these rights, given police custody and his or her intoxication?

Advantage: The basic advantage of this approach is to break down opinions into meaningful components. This model has merit when different clinical methods are used to address each component (e.g., feigning vs. Miranda rights).
Limitation: The approach may be needlessly complex for many criminal cases.

you do? ... What did you find? ... What are your conclusions?) require very little thinking and preparation time. We recommend the following:

- The Build-Up model should be actively chosen rather than accepted by default. This choice requires the active consideration of several alternatives.
- The Build-Up model should not be used for saving preparation time. On the contrary, this model may require more time to avoid routine questioning that may result in a lackluster performance from both the expert and the attorney.

THE UNFOLDING MODEL

The Unfolding model could be described simply as the "Build-Up model in reverse." After describing the nature of the evaluation and its methods, the attorney's questions jump to the bottom-line. The expert is asked his or her opinions in the case. Using the previous example of Mr. Smith, the expert may be queried about components of the competency-to-stand-trial standard and asked for opinions about each component. As part of this unfolding, the key question is simply, *"Doctor, how did you arrive at this opinion about __* (e.g., ability to consult with counsel)?" As part of that response, the expert is likely to refer to Mr. Smith's diagnosis of schizophrenia. The next level of inquiry may address the evidence for this disorder: *"What led you to the diagnosis of schizophrenia?"* Assuming delusions and hallucinations were part of the response, the next level of inquiry is about the symptoms themselves. For instance, *"what is the evidence that Mr. Smith has paranoid delusions?"*

The basic idea is for the case to unfold and gradually be disclosed to the fact-finder. With the proper flow and organization, its purpose is systematically to substantiate the opinions and conclusions. Rather than building up to opinions, the general thrust of testimony is to demonstrate convincingly why these opinions should be believed. As a simple analogue, advertising about the harmful effects of cigarette smoking often begins with the conclusions (e.g., "Cigarettes cause cancer.") and then works backwards to provide supporting evidence.

One option that attorneys and experts may wish to consider is the increasing certitude with the unfolding model. As the inquiries become closer the "data," confidence builds in the questions and responses. Concrete examples and specific observations can be stated directly without any reservations. Thus, direct examination ends on a strong note with clarity and certitude.

A risk of the unfolding model is that some jurors may become lost, especially if the diagnostic and legal issues are complex. Visual displays are almost always helpful in providing jurors with the progression of testimony. We recommend the use of visual displays to clarify this progression.

THE COMPARATIVE ANALYSIS MODEL

The Comparative Analysis Model provides the fact-finder with the logical options for explaining the defendant's functioning vis-a-vis the relevant legal standard (see Table 3-2). On the basis of an actual case, how do we explain the robbery and seemingly senseless decapitation of a compliant convenience-store clerk? Was the male defendant responding to command hallucinations? Was he simply malingering? Did his long-standing hatred of women from her ethnic background escalate a robbery into a bizarre murder? Logically, the jury in this case had to consider these options in reaching its verdict.

The Comparative Analysis model works best in cases where the judge or jury are confronted with several disparate explanations for the behavior in question. An example might be a wife-battering case where the verdict likely hinges on the issue of self-defense. Its goals are twofold: (1) convince the jury of the expert's thoughtfulness and objectivity, and (2) provide the jury with a well-reasoned argument for accepting the expert's conclusions.

We like the Comparative Analysis model for experts testifying after experts for other side. It provides a singular opportunity to criticize implicitly the limitations of earlier experts' conclusions. The expert does not even have to mention the opposing expert; he or she simply describes each model's strengths and limitations. As a concrete example, an expert tried to explain a male defendant's variable presentation as evidence of his psychotic disorder. A subsequent expert concluded this explanation was illogical and untenable. On the critical matter of delusions, she examined several alternatives for this variable presentation. She concluded that the variable presentation of beliefs could not possibly be delusions. Delusions, by definition, are fixed and firmly sustained.

The Comparative Analysis model is not effective in ambiguous cases where no compelling alternative emerges. Given its complexity, care must be taken to have a well-organized direct supplemented with visual displays.

THE CRITICAL ISSUES MODEL

The Critical Issues model is simply an elaborated version to the Build-Up model. Instead of one set of conclusions, the direct examination is organized by several critical issues. For example, the R-CRAS (Rogers, 1984) presents several key issues that may be addressed sequentially in insanity cases, such as malingering, diagnostic issues, and impairment. Each component could be addressed separately.

The Critical Issues model appears to be the most appropriate when each issue has its own standardized methods (see Table 3-2). For instance, the assessment of malingering requires the systematic use of detection strategies and typically relies on standardized measures. When considering key issues such as malingering separately, the fact-finder has a greater opportunity to understand the issue and its relevant methodology. This organization can also benefit the expert. By breaking the direct examination into meaningful components, the expert can address sequentially the relevant issues posed by a particular case.

REDIRECT EXAMINATION

The rules of evidence in state and federal courts grant trial judges broad control over the mode and order for the presentation of evidence. Commonly, this authority has been interpreted and applied to permit litigants to conduct a redirect examination (and then re-cross-examination) of a witness. The purpose of redirect is to address new matters that were raised on cross-examination, not matters that might have been forgotten on direct or that counsel wishes to reemphasize. There is no absolute right to conduct a redirect examination, thus its scope and content are subject to the discretion of the trial judge regarding the importance of the new matter being addressed.

As previously observed, preparation for redirect is often overlooked. This omission appears to be based on the premise that cross-examination is unpredictable. We question this premise on two grounds:

1. *All testimony has weaknesses.* Therefore, the expert and attorney can reasonably predict the likely points of cross-examination.
2. *Most attorneys develop a predictable style of cross-examination.* Therefore, the types of issues likely to be raised are also predictable.

Each attorney should look at each expert's planned testimony and its concomitant weaknesses. We have found that criminal attorneys are often reluctant to discuss these limitations. As an extreme example, a defense counsel in one high-profile case wanted to "bet the defendant's life" that the judge would limit cross-examination to the very specific issues raised on direct. If the defense counsel's objections were not consistently sustained, the expert would quickly become the prosecution's star witness. An honest appraisal of an expert's testimony, both its strengths and weaknesses, is absolutely essential.

Most weaknesses can be addressed on direct examination through such methods as "stealing thunder." They can also be considered on redirect. Attorneys are likely to be divided over the merits of saving some surprises for either cross-examination or redirect. On one hand, some relevant information may never be shared with the fact-finder. On the other hand, the need for such information is likely contingent on cross-examination. Without an attack, the reply is unnecessary.

Attorneys should follow closely the content of their expert's responses during cross-examination. They can identify those issues in which the expert did not have a full opportunity to elaborate on his or her responses. In a recent case, an expert was questioned about an opposing expert's conclusions based on a mental status examination. In responding, the expert raised doubts about the validity of this conclusion. The underlying issue (i.e., the opposing expert's misuse of clinical methods) was key to the case. On redirect, the attorney may ask the expert to expand on his or her doubts and their relevance to the differing conclusions in this particular case.

SUMMARY

Attorneys and experts must develop a good understanding of their important commonalities and differences. Working styles and expectations are critical to effective collaborations. This chapter provided insights into experts and their testimony. We encourage experts to broaden their models for direct examinations, taking into account the particular needs of the case and the preferences of the attorney. Subsequent chapters will address relevant issues of cross-examination as they relate to specific legal standards.

II

Specific Criminal Issues

4

Forensic Determinations of Diversion and Bail

The deinstitutionalization of the persons with chronic mental disorders was galvanized by the combination of increased legal protections for the mentally ill coupled with strong economic incentives to close inpatient facilities. Deinstutionalization has significantly reduced the number of inpatient psychiatric beds. Their availability has dropped approximately 1100% since 1955 (Lamb & Weinberger, 1998) and is likely to drop even further (Lamb & Bachrach, 2001). What happens to persons who are chronically disordered? In the absence of treatment, significant numbers become disruptive or engage in criminal behavior. Jails become a repository for thousands of persons with chronic mental disorders and have become "a poor man's mental health facility." (Teplin, 1984, p. 69).

The entry of mentally disordered offenders into the criminal justice system may trigger the consideration of two preliminary forensic issues—diversion and bail. For diversion, the goal is to substitute more appropriate mental health interventions for criminal sanctions. For bail, the goals are twofold in addressing both the likelihood of a nonappearance and potential dangerousness to the community. Diversion and bail will be addressed separately in the following paragraphs.

The most critical psychological and psychiatric involvement for most mentally disordered offenders concerns diversion. This determination addresses whether the defendant's behavior will be subjected to punitive sanctions by the criminal justice system or clinical interventions by the mental health system. Diversion to the mental health system can occur formally and informally at several stages in the processing of mentally disordered offenders. Steadman, Morris, and Dennis (1995) provided a valuable template for understanding the three possible stages of diversion:

1. *Prebooking*. Typically police officers or crisis counselors in conjunction with law enforcement intervene at the earliest point of contact and divert suspects to mental health services. This informal diversion commonly uses clinical services in the community.
2. *Prearraignment*. Jail staff, pretrial services, or specialized diversion programs identify jail detainees who may benefit from specialized forensic services.
3. *Postarraignment*. Jail staff, probation services, or mental health professionals provide for an evaluation regarding the appropriate disposition. In some cases, the criminal charges are put on hold, pending the defendant's completion of the designated treatment.

Forensic clinicians are most commonly appointed to evaluate defendants at the postarraignment phase, although some may serve as consultants to specialized diversion programs that operate during prearraignment. Therefore, this chapter emphasizes the role and responsibilities of forensic clinicians in postarraignment diversions.

Bail determinations, especially with mentally disordered offenders, should take into account psychological and psychiatric factors that may affect the likelihood of a nonappearance and issues of community safety. Unfortunately, forensic research has largely overlooked evaluative issues related to bail determinations. As a result, the empirical knowledge and specialized methods are substantially limited.

RELEVANT LEGAL STANDARDS

DIVERSION STANDARDS

Diversion decisions are framed by local law and policy and do not implicate constitutional guarantees limiting governmental power or recognizing an entitlement to beneficent government intervention. No Supreme Court decision recognizes a criminal defendant's constitutional right to be diverted and treated, rather than tried and punished. The existence and scope of diversion programs are shaped by pragmatic considerations rather than constitutional protections. In many jurisdictions, the courts have sought practical solutions to the criminalization of the mentally disordered. Diversion alternatives arise from agreements between judges, prosecutors, and defense attorneys that are often limited by the availability of financial resources (Belenko, 2001; Steadman, Corcozza, & Veysey, 1999).

A guiding legal principle buttressing the case for selected diversions is *therapeutic jurisprudence*. Therapeutic jurisprudence encourages an examination of the therapeutic and anti-therapeutic consequences of legal decision-making (Wexler & Winick, 1996). The diversion of mentally disordered offenders can be examined for its therapeutic outcomes. Does it provide a positive outcome for diverted offenders? Moreover, does it extend beyond the offenders in safeguarding the immediate community? Therapeutic jurisprudence recognizes the necessity to also consider the community and social contexts in weighing the benefits of its interventions (Daicoff & Wexler, 2003).

Statutory Provisions for Diversion

Individual states have enacted statutes that address diversion through a combination of criminal sanctions and treatment alternatives for impaired defendants. In many states, the potential for criminal sanctions is used as external motivation for specific groups of defendants. Statutes on diversion vary considerably from state to state. For example, Indiana (Ind. Code Ann. § 12-23-5-1) authorizes the "conditional deferment of judicial proceedings in a minor crime when mental illness is a 'contributing factor'" (Luskin, 2001, p. 219). California authorizes diversion of mentally retarded defendants charged with a misdemeanor (Cal. Pen. Code § 1001.20 [2004]). Kansas authorizes diversion "if it appears to the district attorney that diversion of the defendant would be in the interests of justice and of benefit to the defendant and the community" (Kan. Stat.Ann. § 22-2907 [2003]). In contrast, Utah law broadly authorizes that "[a]t any time after the filing of an information or indictment and prior to conviction, the prosecuting attorney may, by written agreement with the defendant, filed with the court, and upon approval of the court, divert a defendant to a non-criminal diversion program" (Utah Code Ann. § 77-2-5 [2004]).

STATUTORY PROVISIONS FOR SPECIAL COURTS

Some state legislatures have also created special courts to consider the needs of specific offenders and provide appropriate dispositions. The first drug court was created in Dade County, Florida, in the late 1980s under the leadership of then State Attorney Janet Reno, as an alternative response to the prosecution of drug-addicted defendants who had swamped the criminal justice system. Drug courts now exist in state courts across the country. Although they are highly individualized, their common characteristics include recognition of a need for immediate intervention, activist judicial involvement, and a collaborative rather than an adversarial approach (Thompson, 2002).

Drug courts have received widespread support for their effectiveness in reducing criminal offenses via treatment involvement (Brennan, 1998). The number of drug courts in the United States has more than doubled in the last several years (American University, 2000, 2003) and now exceeds 1,000. While the majority are devoted to adult offenders, specialized drug courts have also been established for both juveniles and families.

Mental health courts were developed more recently to address the needs of mentally disordered offenders, whose extensive contacts with the criminal justice system for minor offenses, are problematic. A number of factors contributed to their development including the concurring consequences deinstitutionalization and homelessness for overcrowded jails struggling to address the needs of persons with mental disorders whose had not been effectively served by community mental health treatment agencies (United States Department of Justice, 2000). The first mental health court was established locally in Broward County, Florida, in 1997. Common features of mental health courts include (see McGaha, Boothroyd, Poythress, Petrila, & Ort, 2002): (a) voluntary participation by defendants, (b) inclusion of disordered defendants for whom their mental disorders contributed to their criminal activities, and (c) active monitoring of treatment interventions by the court. Concern with public safety generally limits inclusion to low-level offenders without a history of violence. Some mental health courts are more willing to include more serious offenders than others. Mental health courts also differ in terms of the timing of their intervention. While some divert defendants prior to adjudication, others operate postconviction, generally following a guilty plea.

In 2000, the U.S. Congress passed and President Clinton signed into law American's Law Enforcement and Mental Health Project Act, Pub. L. No. 106–515 § 2 (codified as amended at 42 U.S.C. § 3796ii [2000]) which instructed the Attorney General to fund mental health court demonstration projects. The resulting grant program employs a flexible definition of mental health court that authorizes grants to not more than100 state and local government programs that provide an alternative to jail or prison for nonviolent offenders with serious mental disorders and train law enforcement personnel to identify and address the needs of disordered offenders.

BAIL DETERMINATIONS

For defendants who are not diverted prior to adjudication, psychologists and psychiatrists may play a critical role in bail determinations. Forensic clinicians may be asked to provide expert opinions related to (1) whether defendants should be detained or released pending adjudication and (2) what conditions of release should be considered. The section addresses the relevant legal standards for bail considerations.

Constitutional Right to Bail and Statutory Criteria

Historically, individuals charged with noncapital offenses were eligible for release on bail subject only to conditions intended to assure the defendant's attendance at trial. From the passage of the Judiciary Act of 1789, 1 Stat. 73, 91, to the present Federal Rules of Criminal Procedure, Rule 46 (a)(1), federal law has provided that a person arrested for a noncapital offense shall be admitted to bail. This traditional right to freedom before conviction permits the unhampered preparation of a defense and serves to prevent the infliction of punishment prior to conviction. "The statutes of the United States have been framed upon the theory that a person accused of crime shall not, until he has been finally adjudged guilty in the court of last resort, be absolutely compelled to undergo imprisonment or punishment, but may be admitted to bail, not only after arrest and before trial, but after conviction and pending a writ of error" (*Hudson v. Parker*, 1895, p. 285). "Unless this right to bail before trial is preserved, the presumption of innocence, secured only after centuries of struggle, would lose its meaning" (*Stack v. Boyle*, 1951, p. 4).

The prevalence of crimes committed by defendants released on bail prompted a retrenchment from this established position. The Federal Bail Reform Act of 1984 permits a federal court to deny a defendant bail prior to trial if the Government demonstrates by clear and convincing evidence that no conditions of release conditions "will reasonably assure . . . the safety of any other person and the community . . . considering the charges against the defendant, the evidence against the defendant, what is known about the defendant, and the risk posed by the defendant's release" (18 U. S. C. § 3142, 1982). The Federal Bail Reform Act specified the types of offenses for which community safety must be considered: (1) crimes of violence, (2) any offense with a maximum sentence of life imprisonment or death,

(3) any offense involving controlled substances carrying a 10-year sentence, and (4) a felony charge against a person who has been convicted of two or more of the preceding category of offenses (18 U.S.C. § 3142 (f) (1), 1982). However, any offense can result in a denial of bail when the defendant "presents a serious risk of flight or of obstruction or attempted obstruction of justice is subject to pretrial detention" (18 U.S.C. § 3142 (f) (2), 1982).

The Federal Bail Reform Act (18 USC § § 3142(c)(B), 1982) also delineated a lengthy list of release conditions that must be considered before the denial of bail. Those conditions of particular relevance to forensic clinicians include (1) medical, psychological, or psychiatric treatment (residential or outpatient), (2) restrictions on alcohol or narcotic use, (3) third-party custody, (4) restrictions on personal associations, (5) prohibitions on weapons, and (6) any other reasonable condition. Forensic consultations should address the potential usefulness of these release conditions.

In *United States v. Salerno* (1987) the Supreme Court upheld the constitutionality of the Federal Bail Reform Act concluding that protection of the community is a legitimate regulatory goal to justify pretrial detention. Salerno argued that the Bail Reform Act went beyond the limitations on governmental activities encompassed by the Due Process Clause of the Fifth Amendment and that it violated the Eighth Amendment's limits on excessive bail. The Court dismissed both arguments finding that the restriction on liberty in question is a permissible regulatory measure and does not constitute punishment. It concluded (p. 755), "We are unwilling to say that this congressional determination, based as it is upon that primary concern of every government—a concern for the safety and indeed the lives of its citizens—on its face violates either the Due Process Clause of the Fifth Amendment or the Excessive Bail Clause of the Eighth Amendment."

The Court has not decided other cases under the Bail Reform Act to identify the level of risk required to deny bail, instead permitting the lower federal courts to utilize the categories created by the Act. For example in *United States v Byrd* (1992), one Court of Appeals determined that the defendant's receipt by mail of a videotape depicting minors engaged in sexually explicit conduct did not alone constitute a crime of violence that posed a threat to the community to justify pretrial detention under the Act. In contrast, in *United States v Wen Ho Lee* (1999), another Court of Appeals upheld the denial of bail for a former employee of Los Alamos National Laboratory charged with espionage in downloading files of nuclear secrets, for which 7 of 10 files were still missing, based on the danger posed to the nation if the files were acquired by the wrong hands.

One federal circuit court in *United States v. Martin-Trigona* (1985) held that the Bail Reform Act does not authorize a judge to order the defendant to submit to a psychiatric examination on the issue of dangerousness as a condition of release on bail. It found no statutory authority under the Act to order a psychiatric examination on the issue of dangerousness. It ruled (p. 37), "Under the statute, judicial officers determining whether detention or conditions of release are appropriate must consider 'the available information concerning' the nature of the offense charged, the evidence against the defendant, personal history and characteristics of the defendant (including mental condition and litigation history), and the nature and seriousness of the danger presented by the defendant." No other reported decisions address the issue or the related issue of whether a different result is warranted when the government seeks an examination only after the defendant presents expert psychiatric or psychological testimony about dangerousness based on an examination of the defendant.

Some state statutes parallel the federal legislation in their denial of bail based on community safety. For example, Arizona denies bail to anyone charged with a capital offense, sexual assault, or sexual conduct or molestation of a minor under 15 where the proof is evident that person charged with one of these offenses is guilty (Arizona, 2003). Similarly, California permits bail to be denied in capital crimes and other felonies where the proof is great including:

(a) Felony offenses involving acts of violence on another person, or felony sexual assault offenses on another person, when the facts are evident or the presumption great and the court finds based upon clear and convincing evidence that there is a substantial likelihood the person's release would result in great bodily harm to others; or

(b) Felony offenses when the facts are evident or the presumption great and the court finds based on clear and convincing evidence that the person has threatened another with great bodily harm and that there is a substantial likelihood that the person would carry out the threat if released (Cal Const, Art I § 12 [2003]).

In summary, forensic clinicians will need to familiarize themselves with relevant statutory and case law requirements for bail and release determinations. A critical consideration is the level of risk necessary for these determinations. Given the relative infringements on personal freedom, denial of bail should require a much higher level of risk than the imposition of release restrictions. Risk assessments for bail determinations address a spectrum of issues from nonappearance to flight, obstruction of justice, and dangerousness. These issues are examined closely in the next section of clinical operationalization.

CLINICAL OPERATIONALIZATION OF DIVERSION AND BAIL DETERMINATIONS

Both diversion and bail determinations share common elements related to risk management. With both diversion and release decisions, forensic clinicians are concerned with the defendants' meaningful participation in the required programs and small likelihood of serious recidivism. However, these determinations are fundamentally dissimilar in their purposes and criteria. Therefore, separate subsections will address diversion and bail.

CLINICAL OPERATIONALIZATION OF DIVERSION

Diversion determinations typically do *not* involve legal criteria based on statutes or case law. Instead, diversion determinations are usually based on discretion involving either individualized or programmatic decisions. Therefore, this section focuses on two related issues: (1) the adoption and communication of professional standards for diversion consultations, and (2) pragmatism in the matching of the defendant's needs with available resources.

Professional Standards

Forensic clinicians must be aware of the potential for *therapeutic bias*. It is often manifested by practitioners, who appear vulnerable to unwarranted optimism even in cases of persistent treatment failures. Judges and prosecutors may become cynical about nondiscriminating experts who routinely recommend therapeutic interventions.

Forensic practice must establish its own professional standards. As articulated by American Academy of Psychiatry and Law (AAPL, 1995), forensic experts should strive for objectivity in their evaluations. Table 4-1 summarizes the fundamental issues that should be addressed and communicated to the court in all diversion consultations. In providing objectivity, a clearly presented and practicable diversion plan should be presented balanced in its presentation and plainly honest in its appraisal of strengths and weaknesses.

TABLE 4-1. A CHECKLIST FOR THE DIVERSION OF MENTALLY DISORDERED
OFFENDERS

Directions: Check the applicable level for each criterion.
1. Mental disorder: insight and motivation for change
   ☐ denial or lack of insight into the mental disorder
   ☐ nominal awareness of the mental disorder but no motivation to change
   ☐ awareness of the mental disorder and external motivation to change (e.g., please others)
   ☐ awareness of the mental disorder and internal motivation to change (e.g., personal distress)
2. Mental disorder and acceptance of treatment
   ☐ noncompliance with treatment
   ☐ partial compliance with treatment and "self-medication" (e.g., substance abuse complicates treatment)
   ☐ partial compliance with treatment and no "self-medication"
   ☐ full compliance with treatment
3. Mental disorder and treatment success
   ☐ noncompliance and no treatment success (e.g., based on several past attempts)
   ☐ compliance and no treatment success (e.g., based on several past attempts)
   ☐ compliance and modest treatment success (e.g., still markedly impaired)
   ☐ compliance and moderate treatment success (e.g., decompensation is a likely)
   ☐ compliance and substantial treatment success (e.g., capable of independent functioning)
4. Treatment availability
   ☐ Recommended treatment is not likely to be available (e.g., limited community resources)
   ☐ Recommended treatment is available but funding is uncertain (e.g., many community mental health programs ration services)
   ☐ Recommended treatment is available and funded
5. Mental disorder and criminal behavior
   ☐ criminal behavior is unrelated to the mental disorder (e.g., would have committed the offense if not disordered)
   ☐ criminal behavior is marginally related to the mental disorder (e.g., impulsivity increases its likelihood)
   ☐ criminal behavior is directly related to the mental disorder (e.g., committed the offense because of disorder)
6. Criminal behavior and treatment
   ☐ successful treatment does not target the criminal behavior (e.g., persecutory delusions do not improve with treatment)
   ☐ successful treatment does target the criminal behavior (e.g., persecutory delusions improve with treatment)

In the absence of professional standards, experts are vulnerable to their own biases. In this regard, Rogers and Bagby (1992) found marked variability in treatment alternatives provided by forensic psychiatrists. As the first step in standardizing diversion evaluations, we recommend that these consultations systematically address the relevant issues (see Table 4-1). The following professional standards are proposed for diversion consultations:

- Diversion reports should address the defendant's (1) mental disorders, (2) insight and motivation for change, and (3) acceptance and compliance with proposed treatment.
- Diversion reports should provide forensic conclusions regarding (1) likelihood of treatment success, (2) availability of the proposed treatment, (3) relationship of the alleged criminal conduct to the mental disorder, and (4) the likely effects of treatment on the alleged criminal behavior.

These professional standards acknowledge the court's responsibility to both the individual offender and the immediate community. Unsuccessful interventions serve neither the offender nor the community. Except in infrequent cases of civil commitment, the success of diversion cannot be achieved without the defendant's motivation for change and genuine acceptance of proposed treatment. Logically, treatment cannot be an effective alternative to criminal sanctions unless (1) success is expected, based on past or current interventions, and (2) the treatment is available and funded.

The professional standards recognize that diversion plans must take into account issues of community safety. With violent or otherwise serious offenses, the courts will be very interested in the relationship between the proposed treatment and reduced likelihood of recidivism (see Table 4-1). Unless the link from treatment to the reduction of criminal behavior can be demonstrated, the diversion plan does not meet professional standards for accountability. In contrast, community safety is less likely to be an issue for the courts when minor offenses arise from the defendant's impaired functioning (e.g., vagrancy). In these instances, the linkage is preferred but not required.

In summary, forensic clinicians are professionally accountable for articulating a clear and workable diversion plan to the courts. Based on these standards, the courts should be informed about nature of the problem (diagnoses, motivation, and criminal conduct), and the feasibility of the plan (treatment availability and likely success). In most cases, diversion plans are highly dependent on local programs. Therefore, the next section addresses the pragmatic issues of matching defendants to available diversion programs.

Pragmatism and Programs

Diversion programs vary significantly across jurisdictions on many parameters that include the legal mechanisms for diversion and ongoing court involvement. Legal mechanisms for diversion (see Steadman, Barbera, & Dennis, 1994; McGaha et al., 2002) include (1) dropping of the criminal charges, (2) keeping the charges open with subsequent status hearings, (3) treatment as a condition of bail, and (4) treatment as a condition of probation.[1] To enhance motivation, some diversion programs will expunge criminal records upon successful completion of treatment. In most cases, the court's continued involvement is likely to play an instrumental role in the likely success of the diversion plan.

Most of diversion programs utilize their own staff to screen candidates for admission. In many instances, case managers will be used with only modest (e.g., B.A.-level) training in assessment and treatment (Steadman et al., 1994). The role of forensic psychologists and psychiatrists may be circumscribed in jurisdictions relying heavily on agency-based assessments. Even so, experts in these jurisdictions can still conduct a thorough evaluation of the defendant including issues of treatment and community safety. However, issues of professional rivalry should be minimized. The overriding goal is informing the court with the best available information for making its determination. As a practical consideration, funding may become a critical issue with courts unwilling to pay for a "second opinion."

A potential weakness of agency-based diversion programs is that their decisions can become policy-driven rather than addressing the specific issues in a particular case. For example, many diversion programs systematically exclude violent offenses. Does that mean that no violent defendant should *ever* be diverted? Defense counsel may need to push for independent diversion evaluations in cases where agency-based programs categorically exclude certain types of defendants.

As part of the matching process, forensic clinicians must also familiarize themselves with specialized courts, including their objectives and procedures. For example, drug courts offer specific alternatives to criminal sanctions. They typically combine treatment, drug testing, and close supervision by criminal justice personnel. Eligibility for programs may include both pre-adjudication (diversion) and post-adjudication (sentencing).

Summary

The courts have not established specific criteria that must be satisfied in rendering diversion recommendations. As a result, forensic clinicians may have considerable flexibility in how they frame diversion issues and apply assessment methods. In the absence of legal criteria, we have

---

[1]Technically, this option involves sentencing rather than diversion. However, it can be used for diversion purposes when the defendant pleads guilty to a minor offense as part of a plea arrangement to ensure the court's continued oversight.

proposed basic professional standards for diversion consultations. These standards emphasize professional accountability in rendering opinions related to treatment amenability (e.g., likely success and availability of proposed interventions) and community safety. Table 4-1 provides a checklist for professional standards and their concomitant issues.

Diversion consultations are not abstract exercises. Quite to the contrary, they represent pragmatic and practical plans for increasing a particular defendant's adjustment while addressing concerns about community safety. Pragmatically, diversion plans must address the correspondence between the defendant's needs and available diversion programs.

CLINICAL OPERATIONALIZATION OF BAIL DETERMINATIONS

Bail determinations implicitly rely on clinical and social science data in predicting the defendant's functioning as it relates to future appearances and the absence of prohibited behaviors. Despite this centrality, forensic mental health professions are underutilized experts in bail determinations. A major contribution to this oversight is lack of professional literature on bail determinations. Indeed, standard textbooks in forensic psychology (e.g., Goldstein, 2003; Melton et al., 1997) and psychiatry (Rosner, 2003) virtually ignore clinical issues related to bail determinations.

Evaluations of bail extend beyond predictions of dangerousness to specific judgments regarding nonappearance, risk of flight, and obstruction of justice. Forensic clinicians are likely to have specialized knowledge that may assist the courts in a small number of cases involving nonappearance and dangerousness.

Nonappearances for grossly impaired defendants. A small minority of mentally disordered defendants lacks the basic capacity to organize and direct their behavior except for their most immediate needs. Historically, these persons would likely be hospitalized because of their limited capacity for self-care and goal-directed behavior. Forensic assessments focus on the defendant's overall functioning and level of purposeful behavior. An important consideration is family or community support, which may assist the defendant in making required appearances.

Flight risks for non-impaired defendants. Given ample opportunity to evaluate the defendant, the critical issue is whether the defendant has any substantive reasons *not* to flee. Logically, many defendants have some motivation to avoid prosecution and lengthy sentences. However, most defendants do not flee while on bail. The goal is to assess the defendant's motivation to stay for trial and face its potential consequences.

Flight risks for impaired defendants. Forensic clinicians must address the effects of the defendant's mental disorders on ability and willingness to participate in the trial. This issue raises the related matter of competency to stand trial. If the defendant has delusional fears, then his or her rational participation in the proceedings may be compromised. In rare cases, the defendant may have an Axis I episode that potentially contributes to flight risks. While not reported in the literature, diagnostic possibilities include severe manic episodes and fugue disorders.

Potential dangerousness on bail. Imminent threats of dangerousness are often more observations of violent behavior than actual predictions of dangerousness. Such instances can result in highly confident conclusions as they relate to bail. Long-term predictions are much more challenging. Balanced risk assessment must take into account both risk and protective factors. However, the only guidance that the Bail Reform Act and the decisions interpreting it provide is that for a defendant charged with the requisite class of offense, the government must demonstrate by clear and convincing evidence that no conditions of release will assure the appearance of the person or the safety of the community.

CLINICAL METHODS AND FORENSIC CONSIDERATIONS

Both diversion evaluations and bail determinations typically occur soon after arrest but serve very different objectives. Most diversion evaluations seek to avoid criminal prosecution through coercive but not punitive interventions. In contrast, most bail determinations are premised on criminal prosecution; they seek to balance the personal liberties of the defendant against the state's interest in ensuring the defendant's participation in further proceedings and protecting the community. Given their divergent goals, diversion evaluations and bail determinations will be examined separately.

DIVERSION EVALUATIONS

Diversion evaluations can be conceptualized in two categories, specifically prototypical cases and atypical cases. Prototypical cases are typified by their chronicity and nonviolence. Atypical cases are distinguished by their treatment amenability and infrequent but sometime severe offenses.

Prototypical Cases

Conceptualization. The primary goal for prototypical cases is the development of effective interventions for defendants charged with minor offenses whose functioning is typically impaired by a combination of mental disorders and substance abuse. Prototypical cases for diversion are characterized by the following: (1) chronic mental disorders, (2) variable compliance with treatment, (3) substance abuse, (4) unstable environment (e.g., marginal housing or homeless), and (5) frequent but minor offenses. Attorneys and forensic clinicians should be clear about the purpose of diversion in these prototypical cases: The goal of diversion is for the effective management of chronic but nonviolent cases.

The courts sometimes have unrealistic expectations about diversion. *The diversion of prototypical cases does not reduce future recidivism.* This point is demonstrated by a sampling of recent studies. For example, Cosden, Ellens, Schnell, Yamini-Diouf, and Wolfe (2003) found that nearly one-half (47%) of diverted offenders in an assertive community treatment program were rearrested in a 12-month follow-up. Using the same follow-up interval, Munetz, Grande, and Chambers (2001) found that 61.5% of diverted offenders were rearrested, although only 7.7% were for violent crimes. Likewise, Naples and Steadman (2003) found 44% of nonviolent offenders recidivated within one year of their diversions.

Using the *Checklist for the Diversion of Mentally Disordered Offenders* (see Table 4-1), prototypical cases are not likely to be "good candidates" for diversion based on their internal motivation and past treatment successes. A key issue is whether a diversion program can offer sufficient monitoring and external incentives to increase substantially treatment compliance. With prototypical cases, the potential for treatment success is not known because of offenders' noncompliance.

We recommend the use of *pattern analysis* to evaluate the track records of prototypical cases. These mentally disordered offenders often have years of documented failures. Within these records, forensic clinicians can sometimes find periods of relative adjustment with minimal involvement of the criminal justice system. Pattern analysis is simply a term to describe a longitudinal and systematic review of legal and clinical records with the goal of defining periods of adjustment and maladjustment while delineating the contributing factors.

Diversion plans for prototypical cases may require a fundamental rethinking of interventions for chronic mentally disordered offenders. Given the scarcity of resources, some diversion programs utilize a threshold model: What are minimal resources needed to maintain the offender in the community? A radical alternative is a saturation model: What combination of resources can be effectively used to build a sustained period of success and adjustment? Regarding the latter, daily urine samples may be necessary to minimize the relapse even though all samples are not necessarily tested.

Diversion recommendations for prototypical cases should only be offered when three critical conditions can be met:

1. *Adequate monitoring*. Without intensive monitoring, failure is almost guaranteed. Community-based housing is often a critical factor in monitoring the offender's adjustment.
2. *Adequate incentives*. The initial incentives are typically the avoidance of negative consequences (e.g., jail); however, the effectiveness of these incentives is generally short-lived. Without positive incentives (e.g., family contact or stable housing), eventual failure is almost guaranteed.
3. *Adequate interventions*. Many prototypical offenders "self-medicate" feelings of depression and despair; substance abuse may produce short-term relief and long-term failure. Active medication interventions may be more successful than passive medication management.[2]

Clinical Methods. Evaluations of prototypical cases cannot be accomplished in isolation. Instead, forensic clinicians must consider the "match" between a particular prototypical offender and the available diversion programs. In the absence of formal diversion programs, tailored interventions can be considered only if they meet the above conditions (monitoring, incentives, and interventions). All programs for prototypical cases require the involvement of a legal authority (e.g., judges) combined with mental health and community resources (Steadman et al., 1995).

Diversion assessment for prototypical cases requires an evaluation of Axis I disorders including substance abuse, and Axis II disorders. Many programs (e.g., Steadman et al., 1999) use standardized screens for substance abuse:

- Michigan Alcoholism Screening Test (MAST; Selzer, 1971) is a brief screen of that is only effective with admitting alcoholics.
- Drug Abuse Screening Test (DAST; Skinner, 1982) parallels the MAST as a screen for those admitting illicit substance abuse.

An alternative is the Substance Abuse Subtle Screening Inventory-III (SASSI-III; Lazowski, Miller, Boye, & Miller, 1998), which purports to screen for substance abuse regardless of persons' acknowledgment. One

---

[2]With the former, medical staff actively works to maximize adjustment. With the latter, medication is maintained until significant decompensation requires a reevaluation.

concern is that this measure may be capitalizing on antisocial attitudes thereby confounding its effectiveness in offender populations (Rogers & Shuman, 2000). Further research is needed to document its effectiveness for mentally disordered offenders denying their substance abuse.

We recommend that forensic clinicians consider the use of the Personality Assessment Inventory (PAI; Morey, 1991) that includes two scales for substance abuse: Alcoholism (ALC) and Drug Abuse (DRG). Written at a grade 4 level, the PAI addresses other critical issues, important to diversion evaluations:

- Axis I pathology (e.g., psychotic thinking and mood disorders);
- Response styles including the overreporting and underreporting of symptoms;
- Problematic behaviors (i.e., aggression and suicide);
- Problematic Axis II syndromes (i.e., antisocial and borderline);
- Treatment-related issues (e.g., treatment rejection and social support).

In addition to the PAI, forensic clinicians will likely want to document the prototypical offenders legal, diagnostic, and treatment history. Using a pattern analysis, they should attempt to evaluate which combination of factors promote adjustment and low criminality. The pattern analysis will combine clinical interviews with extensive documentation review.

Atypical Cases

Conceptualization.   Violent offenders pose an entirely different set of problems for diversion programs. Although their recidivism rates may be comparable to their nonviolent counterparts (Naples & Steadman, 2003), a key issue is community safety. Unlike the prototypical cases, we surmise that the courts are likely to be highly selective about the diversion of violent offenders. Setting a high standard, the term "atypical cases" is reserved for a minority of violent offenders for whom treatment may substantially reduce recidivism.

Domestic violence programs have demonstrated variable success with motivated offenders that successfully complete treatment. Effectiveness with these violent offenders appears to be linked to the type of program and its selection of spouse batterers. For example, Babcock and Steiner (1999) used certified treatment programs spanning 12 months with independent monitoring by probation. Treatment completers rarely engaged in spouse-battering (7.5%) as compared to noncompleters (22.5%) or those incacerated (61.8%). As a critical issue, the number of sessions attended was key to successful outcomes. The assessment of domestic violence via screens and scales had developed at an uneven pace with little attention to the prediction of treatment amenability (Dutton & Kropp, 2000). Any assessment for domestic violence should carefully evaluate violence toward children which also occurs with about 50% of male batterers (Saunders, 1994).

The *Checklist* in Table 4-1 is the template for evaluating atypical cases. Ideally, atypical offenders will be genuinely motivated for change. In each case, the proposed treatment should be available, accepted by the offender, and proven to be effective. Most importantly, the treatment effectively targets psychopathology associated with criminal behavior. These conditions (motivation, effective treatment, and reduced criminality) are likely to be met in only a small percentage (e.g., less than 5%) of violent cases.

Clinical methods. An extensive evaluation should be conducted to assess comprehensively Axis I and Axis II disorders that may have contributed to the criminal behavior. Structured interviews are important to the standardized evaluation of these disorders and their severity. Structured interviews may include

- Axis I disorders: the Schedule of Affective Disorders and Schizophrenia (SADS; Spitzer & Endicott, 1978a) or Structured Clinical Interview of *DSM-IV* Disorders (SCID; First, Spitzer, Williams, & Gibbon, 1997).
- Axis II disorders: the Structured Interview for *DSM-IV* Personality Disorders (SIDP-IV; Pfohl, Blum, & Zimmerman, 1995), International Personality Disorder Examination (IPDE; Loranger, 1999), or Structured Clinical Interview for *DSM-IV* Personality Disorders (SCID-II; First, Gibbon, Spitzer, Williams, & Benjamin, 1997).

The evaluation must also integrate relevant data from clinical and legal records with the diagnostic information. The forensic clinician is attempting to find clear linkages (see Table 4-1) between (1) the disorder and the criminal behavior, and (2) treatment and the amelioration of the criminal behavior. As a specific example, a young sex offender psychotically misconstrued certain behaviors (e.g., bending over) as explicit sexual invitations. Once treated with antipsychotic medications, his unwanted sexual advances desisted completely.

Atypical cases recommended for diversion should be based on demonstrable evidence that is specific to a particular offender. For instance, the forensic clinician should be prepared to establish that the criminal behavior occurred only during an Axis I episode, which responded to treatment.

In particular, specific symptoms related to the criminal behavior (e.g., manic-based spending) have substantially improved as a result of treatment. Attorneys should hold forensic clinicians to rigorous standards in atypical cases. Both the community and the offender suffer in cases of violent recidivism.

BAIL EVALUATIONS

Balanced risk assessments take into account both *protective* and *risk* factors in making clinical predictions (Rogers, 2000). Protective factors *reduce* the likelihood of the targeted behavior (e.g., nonappearance in court or dangerous conduct), while risk factors *increase* its likelihood. Protective and risk factors can be conceptualized as either *static* or *dynamic*. Static factors are not modifiable, often because they involve biological markers (e.g., male gender) or past events that cannot be changed. In contrast, *dynamic* factors are potentially amenable to change. Attorneys must determine whether risk assessments are balanced and address both static and dynamic protective and risk factors:

- *Static protective factors* may involve a physical disability, such as a drunken driver receiving permanent injuries that diminish his or her ability to ever drive again. They may also include demographic characteristics, such as gender or older age.[3]
- *Dynamic protective factors* typically involve interventions (e.g., medication), support (e.g., family assistance), or separation (e.g., removal from a high conflict marriage).
- *Static risk factors* commonly reflect the offender's past criminal activities, although sometimes gender and race are also included. See the opinion in *United States v. Webster* (1998, pp. 356–357), "Thus, although race per se is an irrelevant and inadmissible factor, the effects and experiences of race may be admissible. If a defendant can show that his life has been marked by discrimination or some other set of experiences, irrespective of whether the result, in part, of his race, then that properly might be admissible as relevant mitigating background or character evidence. But this is a far cry from using race in and of itself as a proxy for such a set of beliefs and experiences. Pigmentation does not define a person's character or background; the life that a person has led and the things that he has experienced do."

---

[3]Interestingly, older age (e.g., greater than 50) is a static predictor because it is not modifiable, while young age (e.g., less than 25) is a dynamic predictor.

TABLE 4-2. BAIL DETERMINATIONS: A BALANCED MODEL OF PROTECTIVE AND RISK FACTORS

Clinical Concerns	Protective Factors			Risk Factors		
	Inpatient	Outpatient	3rd party	Abuse	Associates	Weapons
Impaired behavior	+	+	+	+	?	+
Impulsivity	NA	+	?	+	+	+
Reactive aggression	NA	+	?	+	+	+
Instrumental aggression	NA	?	?	?	+	+

Note. 3rd party: third-party custody; abuse: substance abuse; associates: known persons likely involved in criminal activity.

- *Dynamic risk factors* frequently include interpersonal difficulties (e.g., anger problems) and personality dimensions (e.g., impulsivity and sensation-seeking).

In contrast, biased risk assessments rely heavily on static risk factors. The bias is twofold. By neglecting all protective factors, it unfairly characterizes most offenders as posing substantial risks. By neglecting dynamic risk factors, it unfairly characterizes most offenders as posing *permanent* risks.

Importantly, the risk-assessment model, as originally promulgated by Federal Probation Act, should be a balanced model. It requires that forensic clinicians consider both protective and risk factors in their bail determinations. Table 4-2 summarizes three potential protective factors (i.e., inpatient treatment, outpatient interventions, or third-party custody) and three potential risk factors (i.e., substance abuse, criminal associates, and the availability of weapons). Four clinical concerns are identified: impaired behavior, impulsivity, reactive aggression, and instrumental aggression.

Dynamic protective factors are likely to be the most successful with impaired offenders. For example, residential treatment may substantially reduce the likelihood of both nonappearances and criminal conduct. In some cases, a combination of outpatient treatment and third-party custody may increase significantly offenders' compliance with the conditions of probation. For instance, a young male offender with schizophrenia could be placed in the custody of his mother with mandated outpatient treatment. This combination is likely to be more successful than relying on a single protective factor.

Impulsivity is often linked with substance abuse (Moeller & Dougherty, 2000). Bail conditions that require outpatient treatment and actively monitor substance abuse may serve as effective protective factors in selected cases by reducing impulsivity and drug-seeking behaviors. A pattern analysis may be helpful in establishing which cases are likely to respond to these interventions. Clearly, repeated failures on random drug testing would question the feasibility of this intervention.

Aggression can be conceptualized as either reactive or instrumental. "Reactive" aggression occurs when the offender responds with strong emotions, such as anger and fear, when perceiving others as hostile and threatening. As noted by Sterling and Edelmann (1998), reactive aggression is experienced by some individuals irrespective of their antisocial backgrounds. Reactive aggression should be treatable by specific interventions focused on reducing hostile attributions toward others (see Dodge, Price, Bachorowski, & Newman, 1990) and the use of Stress Inoculation Training (Novaco, 1975). In contrast, "instrumental" aggression involves planned aggressive behavior toward achieving a criminal objective. Armed robbery would be an example of instrumental aggression. It is unlikely that any of the listed protective factors will play an appreciable role in reducing the risk of instrumental aggression.

Beyond aggression, most bail evaluations will likely include an assessment of psychopathy. The standard measure for its evaluation is the Psychopathy Checklist—Revised (PCL-R: Hare, 2003). While not a risk assessment measure per se, its four facets with interpersonal, affective, lifestyle, and antisocial dimensions are likely to offer valuable insights into the defendant's functioning.

Table 4-2 outlines potential risk factors that can be prohibited as conditions of bail. Prohibiting weapons and curtailing criminal associations should be evaluated in light of each offender's history. We recommend against *pro forma* prohibitions routinely applied to all cases. Forensic clinicians should also exercise care in recommending abstinence from alcohol or drugs as a condition of bail. These bail conditions only make sense when clinical interventions are available to offenders with diagnosed substance abuse disorders. Otherwise, these offenders are likely to fail the conditions of bail.

Bail evaluations must consider both Axis I and Axis II disorders. In most cases, structured interviews will be necessary to establish reliable diagnoses. The evaluations will also involve extensive assessment of substance abuse and its effects on the defendant's functioning. We strongly recommend pattern analysis of the clinical data to establish either (1) the necessary conditions for bail, or (2) the compelling reasons for denying bail. Table 4-2 provides a template for these pattern analysis. However, forensic clinicians must consider any other reasonable factor in making these determinations. This provision requires that forensic clinicians consider case-specific information. As a concrete example, a careful review of an offender's history may indicate that gainful employment provides sufficient stabilization to warrant bail.

Risk assessment measures are conspicuously absent from this discussion. The reasons for their absence are threefold:

1. Risk assessment measures were developed for "back-end" appraisals for the management and eventual release of sentenced offenders. Bail determinations are "front-end" assessments that include a much broader range of offenders, some of whom have not served substantial sentences.
2. Risk assessment measures do not adequately address protective factors.
3. Risk assessment measures typically are used to make long-term predictions (e.g., 1 to 5 years), whereas bail determinations often cover a much more limited time (e.g., less than 6 months).

POTENTIAL TRIAL ISSUES

Most diversion cases are resolved without an extended proceedings that include expert testimony. Occasionally, experts testify in diversion cases when issues of diversion are statutorily defined. In most other cases, diversion only occurs when the opposing counsel reach a mutual agreement. In rare instances, the court itself may request consideration of a mental-health alternative for minor but repetitive offenses.

PROTOTYPICAL DIVERSION CASES

Perlin (1994) introduces the concept of *pretextuality* to explain how criminal law often shapes legal principles and practices to reach its consequentialist goals. Prototypical cases of diversion are especially nettlesome for the criminal courts. The courts often look for some solution to problems that extend logically beyond their boundaries, such as the effective management of mentally disordered offenders. Understandably, both the courts and the jails do not want to become Teplin's (1984) "a poor man's mental health facility."

Most jurisdictions offer little statutory guidance for the diversion of prototypical offenders. In its absence, diversion programs are often influential in establishing policies for key decisions regarding diverted and nondiverted offenders. Criminal attorneys need to play an active role in ensuring the fairness and the accountability of the diversion decisions.

This section focuses primarily on direct examinations based on the premise that both prosecution and defense are attempting to find a practical and workable solution. Given this cooperation, we suggest that the focus in the courtroom should center on accountability for three reasons:

1. The Courts are more likely to use diversion for prototypical cases if they have some assurances that key issues are being addressed.
2. Individualized treatment plans have a greater likelihood of success than boilerplate models.
3. Requirements for accountability may provide sufficient justification of expanding funds to budget-strapped diversion programs.

We recommend that attorneys request expert evidence regarding an individualized treatment plan that (1) takes into account the defendant's needs and motivation, and (2) provides necessary monitoring and safeguards. Toward this objective, sample questions for direct examination are presented in Box 4-1. These sample questions could easily be adapted for cross-examination. However, the purpose shared by both defense and prosecution is establishing a workable solution.

Box 4-1   PROTOTYPICAL CASES OF DIVERSION: SAMPLE QUESTIONS
FOR DIRECT EXAMINATION

A. Treatment Needs
   1. *What treatment is necessary to reduce the likelihood* __ [the defendant] *does not appear in this court with similar charges?*
   2. *Is this treatment available?...How is it funded?*
B. Motivation
   3. *Would it be fair to say that* __ [the defendant] *is not highly motivated to seek out treatment on [his/her] own accord?...How do you intend to motivate* __ [the defendant] *to comply with treatment?*
   4. *What negative incentives are proposed for noncompliance?...Do you have any data that suggest that these incentives will be effective this time?*
   5. *What positive incentives are proposed for treatment involvement?...Do you have any data that suggest that these incentives will be effective this time?*
C. Monitoring and Safeguards
   6. *I understand that* __ [e.g., paranoid thoughts] *are problematic for* __ [the defendant]. *How will you monitor this?*
   7. *How will you monitor for substance abuse?* [likely urinanalysis]...*What frequency is needed to ensure maximum compliance?*
   8. *What intervention will be used if* __ [the defendant] *misses one appointment?*
   9. *What intervention will be used if* __ [the defendant] *misses several appointments in a row?*

Direct examination, as exemplified by Box 4-1, recognizes that most prototypical cases of diversion have long histories in both mental health and criminal justice systems. As previously noted, diversion has not demonstrated its effectiveness in reducing recidivism. Reasons for this failure likely include the complexity of diagnostic issues, lack of mental health resources, lack of an individualized plan, and lack of sufficient incentives. The focus on direct examination is threefold: (1) an individualized treatment plan, (2) negative and positive incentives, and (3) active monitoring. The court's continued involvement in negative sanctions (e.g., admonishments, stricter treatment conditions, and even jail) appear a key component of these programs (Griffin, Steadman, & Petrila, 2002).

Diversion Issues

Atypical Diversion Cases

The defense occasionally raises the issue of diversion for a particular offender charged with a very violent offense.[4] Unlike the cooperation found with prototypical cases, the nature of the offense is likely to produce adversarialness in the proceedings. Therefore, this section will focus of sample cross-examination issues to address the effectiveness of the diversion program and community safety.

A viable option is to reproduce Table 4-1, *A Checklist for the Diversion of Mentally Disordered Offenders*, and use it as the basis for cross-examination. As a demonstrative exhibit, the expert can be questioned about the defendant's treatment compliance and treatment effectiveness. Any pattern of past failures deserves rigorous cross-examination. The most challenging issue for experts is the linkage between effective treatment and community safety. In addition to case-specific questions, they must also grapple with general questions such as the following:

- *Doctor, would you be willing to stake your professional reputation on the conclusion that __ [the defendant] will not seriously injure another innocent person?*
- *What about your professional livelihood? . . . If your mistake seriously injures an innocent person, would you give up your practice as a forensic [select: psychologist or psychiatrist]? . . . [likely to decline] So you are willing to bet someone else's life but not even your own profession?*

---

[4]In contrast to common assault with superficial injuries, these offenses typically involve weapons and major injuries.

Bail Determinations

Forensic psychologists and psychiatrists are often unfamiliar with the legal standards and guidelines for bail evaluations. Attorneys must ensure that experts are both versed in the relevant legal standards and knowledgeable of the assessment methods required to address these standards. Cross-examination can elicit any limits in legal and clinical knowledge.

Cross-Examination for Testimony on the Denial of Bail

At least theoretically, bail plans can be constructed to address adequately issues of flight risk and community safety for most pre-bail defendants. Even in difficult cases, some combination of residential care, electronic monitoring, and treatment would likely be effective. When experts testify against bail, a key consideration is whether they carefully considered different alternatives in trying to construct an effective bail plan. Box 4-2 provides same questions for uncovering less-than-comprehensive consultations.

Forensic psychologists and psychiatrists have little knowledge and expertise about bail flight risks. Assuming the defendant did not disclose the intent to flee, these experts often have no way of knowing anything specific about flight risks. One real danger is that the forensic clinician will engage in a highly inferential process and extrapolate from what he or she might do under similar circumstances. A second danger is that the expert will simply rely on demographic data (e.g., homeless) in making these determinations. Instability in living quarters cannot be facilely equated with flight risks. Sample cross-examination is presented in Box 4-2.

Aggressive behavior can be conceptualized as either reactive or instrumental. In the former case, an offender's feelings of rage and impotence can sometimes be successfully treated with cognitive behavioral therapy (i.e., CBT) and other interventions. Sample inquiries (Box 4-2) illustrate how the expert may be put on the defensive, if these interventions were not adequately considered. Cross-examination can also address the treatment expertise customary for each discipline. Many forensic psychologists do not have a sophisticated understanding how pharmacological interventions might assist with aggression, while many forensic psychiatrists do not have a sophisticated knowledge of specific CBT techniques.

Cross-Examination of Testimony Recommending of Bail

The basic principles of cross-examination apply to bail recommendations. A prime issue is to underscore the uncertainties of complex

---

Box 4-2   SAMPLE CROSS-EXAMINATION FOR TESTIMONY ON THE
DENIAL OF BAIL

A. Bail Plans
1. *In the course of your testimony today, I did not hear you describe any effective plans to give* __ [the defendant] *bail, is that correct?*
2. *Let's make a list of the "bail" plans you considered. Please describe them one at a time and I will list them on this display board for you.* [likely will have only 1 or 2 poorly described ideas] ... *Is that all?*
3. *For the sake of argument, let's assume money is not an issue. What would be an effective bail plan for* __ [the defendant]? ... [if none] *What about house arrest with electronic monitoring?* ... [if still negative] *What about house arrest in the custody of* __ [e.g., a parent with no arrests] *and electronic monitoring?* ... [if still negative] *What about medication, house arrest, third-party custody, and electronic monitoring?* [continue to add conditions until the expert's extremeness and rigidity are patently obvious]

B. Flight Risk
4. *Has* __ [the defendant] *tried to escape?* ... *Did* [he/she] *tell you* [he/she] *was going to try to escape?* ... [in applicable] *So you have evidence that* __ [the defendant] *has tried to avoid prosecution?*
5. *Would you have any reason to call* __ [the defendant] *a liar?* ... *Isn't it true* [he/she] *promised to show up in court?* [if, negative response] ... *Well did you even ask* __ [the defendant] *about this?* ... [if, "no"] *Sounds like you had your mind all made up, doesn't it?*
6. [defendant's status; if relevant] *Are you biased against my client?* ... *Do you treat all poor persons fairly?* ... [optional] *How many poor persons have you had over to your house who weren't hired help?* ... *Just because* __ [the defendant] *is* __ [e.g., homeless], *you wouldn't hold that against* [him/her], *would you?* ... [if brings up the issue of stability] *Then you would be satisfied if the judge ordered* __ [the defendant] *to stay at* __ *shelter is that correct?*

C. Reactive Aggression
7. *According to the police,* __ [the defendant] *"blew-up" and struck* __ [the victim], *is that correct?*
8. *Do you have any first-hand knowledge of what actually occurred?* ... *Is it possible that there were extenuating circumstances that might make almost anyone blow-up?*
9. *Doctor, tell us how many anger management groups you have conducted.*
10. [if none] *How many have you participated in?* ... [probably none] *Or supervised directly?* ... [probably none] *With all due respect—isn't it true, doctor, that you are completely inexperienced at treatment that could help* __ [the defendant] *control outbursts and receive bail?* [likely to cite reading articles] ... *I didn't ask about book learning, I asked about real experience. Let me repeat the question.*
11. [if "yes"] *Were you an effective therapist?* ... *Were you able to create positive change in half of your clients?* ... *More than half?* ... *Why would you deny an effective treatment to my client?*

Box 4-3   SAMPLE CROSS-EXAMINATION FOR TESTIMONY ON THE
              RECOMMENDING OF BAIL

A. General Risk Factors
   1. *What factors would likely contribute to* __'s [the defendant's] *engaging
      in criminal activity?*
   2. *Are alcohol and drug use frequently associated with criminal activ-
      ity?... Do you have any specific knowledge of their role in this case?*
      [probably not]
   3. *Which of* __'s [the defendant's] *friends have criminal histories?* [dif-
      ficult to know]... *Which of* [his/her] *friends have participated with*
      [him/her] *in criminal activities?*
   4. *Beside asking* [him/her], *how did you rule-out* __'s [the defendant's]
      involvement in gangs?
B. Psychopathy as a Specific Risk Factor
   5. *What risk assessment measures did you use?... How were they vali-
      dated?*
   6. [if applicable] *What are the different methods available for evaluating
      of psychopathy?... What methods did you use?... Why?*
   7. *What is the* __'s [the defendant's] *level of psychopathy?... How was
      this evaluated?*

---

predictions, such as flight risk and risk assessments. Forensic clinicians are often unaware of critical predictors in a particular bail evaluation, including the role of substance and the involvement of criminal associates. As outlined in Box 4-3, these crucial issues compound the uncertainties of bail predictions.

A minority of forensic clinicians appears unaware of methodology applied to risk assessments. A small subset of questions seeks to examine the clinician's knowledge of these measures and their applicability. Although these measures have limited usefulness in bail determinations, these questions may be useful in testing the expert's knowledgability. In addition, psychopathy should be considered in many bail evaluations. Experts should be able to describe different methods for its assessment. In addition, they should be able to elucidate how the separate dimensions of psychopathy affect their conclusions about bail issues.

SUMMARY

Traditionally, forensic clinicians are underutilized during the initial processing of offenders on matters such as diversion and bail. This chapter provides cautious optimism for a slightly expanded role. Importantly, diversion evaluations are best conceptualized as two subtypes: prototypical (chronic minor cases for whom recidivism is likely) and atypical (a small minority of serious cases with demonstrable links between treatment and community safety). A balanced risk assessment model provides a conceptual underpinning for bail evaluations with its consideration of both risk and protective factors.

5

Miranda and Beyond: Competencies Related to Police Investigations

The United States Constitution recognizes a variety of individual rights that pertain directly to the criminal justice system. These include the right of the people "to be secure in their persons, houses, papers, and effects, against unreasonable searches and seizures" (U.S. Constitution, Amendment IV); not to be "compelled in any criminal case to be a witness against himself" (U.S. Constitution, Amendment V). Additional constitutional rights include "[in all criminal prosecutions, the accused shall enjoy the right to a speedy and public trial, by an impartial jury of the state and district wherein the crime shall have been committed, which district shall have been previously ascertained by law, and to be informed of the nature and cause of the accusation; to be confronted with the witnesses against him; to have compulsory process for obtaining witnesses in his favor, and to have the assistance of counsel for his defense]" (U.S. Constitution, Amendment VI). This chapter addresses 4th, 5th, and 6th amendment rights as they relate to police investigations.

The critical mental health issue with regard to these constitutional protections is the competence of suspects to waive their rights. With a valid waiver, a suspect may consent to be searched or confess to a criminal wrongdoing. Although courts presume that suspects are competent to waive their rights in the absence of evidence to the contrary, when the issue is raised, courts have sought to assure the presence of a threshold level of competence. This chapter addresses that threshold level of competence and its assessment.

Clinically, forensic experts must often evaluate retrospectively a defendant's decisions at these crucial points in time. Such retrospective evaluations address both the general comprehension and decisional capacities of a criminal defendant during critical stages of the investigation and subsequent arrest. Typically, suspects' decisions to consent to a search or to confess are made without the benefit of counsel (Gudjonsson, 2003); many defendants make rapid decisions without full knowledge and consideration of their alternatives. Months or even years later, defense attorneys may attempt to determine whether the waiver of rights met the legal litmus test, namely were these waivers *voluntary, knowing,* and *intelligent.*

"Confessions to crimes are valuable commodities, which once introduced to a judge or jury, are exceedingly difficult for defense lawyers to overcome. Unchallenged, inculpatory statements are devastating, typically taken as a clear sign of the defendant's guilt" (Goldstein, 2003b, p. 14). While less dramatic, other waivers, such as consent to search, may also have devastating consequences for the defendant.

The competence of criminal defendants to waive their legal rights during police investigations is often a pivotal issue in the case. The admission of either a confession or incriminating evidence from a "warrantless search" (i.e., a search without a search warrant) is understandably likely to weigh heavily with the fact finder. However, the admission of such evidence is contingent on the defendant's competence to make a voluntary, knowing, and intelligent decision to waive the relevant constitutional protections. Regrettably, forensic research has virtually ignored the competency-to-waive decisions, despite their prevalence and importance. *The frequency of Miranda waivers by impaired defendants' likely exceeds all other mental health issues at the pretrial phase.*

The defendant's appreciation of these constitutional rights and the consequences of a waiver of these rights can be impaired by either cognitive limitations (e.g., mental retardation) or interference by a mental disorder (e.g., schizophrenia). Focusing only on cognitive deficits, Grisso (1981, p. 98, Table 13) found that 8.9% of adult offenders were markedly impaired in their ability to understand the relevant *Miranda* warning. Two other estimates were used in calculating the prevalence of impaired *Miranda* understanding: (a) the annual arrest rate of approximately 13.7 million for adult offenders (Federal Bureau of Investigation, 2002) and percentage of confessions (40–50%) playing a pivotal role in subsequent convictions (Gudjonsson, 2003; Wrightsman & Kassin, 1993). The prevalence of defendants's *Miranda* waivers based on cognitive deficits alone is estimated at more than 400,000 per year (i.e., 8.9% impaired × 13.7 million suspects × 40% pivotal role [lower bound estimate] = 487,720).

The chapter begins with a preeminent issue, the legal bases for competence-to-waive decisions. The chapter then focuses on specific waiver decisions that include *Miranda* rights and warrantless searches. General (i.e., competency-to-waive decisions) and specific (e.g., *Miranda*) issues will be addressed together in discussing forensic conclusions and possible testimony.

RELEVANT LEGAL STANDARDS

COMPETENCE-TO-WAIVE STANDARD

Background

The general legal standard for waiving individual rights recognized by the U.S. Constitution was articulated by the U.S. Supreme Court in *Johnson v. Zerbst* (1938). *Johnson* involved a challenge to a conviction for passing counterfeit money by a defendant who had not been represented by counsel at trial, to which he was entitled under the Sixth Amendment. In the process of assessing whether the defendant had waived his right to counsel the Court articulated language, without flourish or fanfare, that would serve as a lens for a panoply of waiver decisions across the constitution:

> It has been pointed out that "courts indulge every reasonable presumption against waiver" of fundamental constitutional rights and that we "do not presume acquiescence in the loss of fundamental rights." A waiver is ordinarily an intentional relinquishment or abandonment of a known right or privilege. The determination of whether there has been an intelligent waiver of the right to counsel must depend, in each case, upon the particular facts and circumstances surrounding that case, including the background, experience, and conduct of the accused. (p. 463)

The remainder of the decision revealed little more about the meaning of this language. Because the lower court had not engaged in any findings regarding waiver, the Supreme Court remanded the issue and never applied the rule it articulated to this defendant. Nonetheless, *Johnson v. Zerbst*'s presumption against waiver of constitutional rights and intentional relinquishment of a known right standard have become the foundation for assessing waiver of a defendant's constitutional rights. Over time, the Court has conceptualized the elements of this standard as requiring that a waiver of constitutional rights be knowing, intelligent, and voluntary.

Substantive Criteria

The following paragraphs operationalize these three prongs of the waiver standard drawn from *Johnson v. Zerbst* (1938). While the Court has made clear that all three requirements must be satisfied to conclude that a challenged waiver is valid (*Edwards v. Arizona*, 1981), the Court has been less than clear in distinguishing these requirements from each other.

The *knowing* prong of the waiver standard has been explained by the Supreme Court in *Godinez v. Moran* (1993, p. 401) using the following language:

> The purpose of the . . . knowing . . . inquiry . . . is to determine whether the defendant actually does understand the significance and consequences of a particular decision . . . See Faretta v. California, supra, at 835 (defendant waiving counsel must be "made aware of the dangers and disadvantages of self-representation, so that the record will establish that 'he knows what he is doing and his choice is made with eyes open'") (quoting Adams v. United States ex rel. McCann, 317 U.S. 269, 279, 87 L. Ed. 268, 63 S. Ct. 236 (1942)); Boykin v. Alabama, 395 U.S. at 244 (defendant pleading guilty must have "a full understanding of what the plea connotes and of its consequence").

The "knowing" prong addresses the defendant's knowledge or appreciation of the implications of the waiver. In the context of a waiver of the right to counsel, the Court (*Patterson v. Illinois*, 1988, pp. 292–293) explained: "[T]he accused must 'kno[w] what he is doing' so that 'his choice is made with eyes open.' . . . [T]he key inquiry in a case such as this one must be: Was the accused, who waived his Sixth Amendment rights during postindictment questioning, made sufficiently aware of his right to have counsel present during the questioning, and of the possible consequences of a decision to forgo the aid of counsel?" Thus, this prong necessarily seeks to ascertain the defendant's basic grasp of legal rules and procedures governing the investigation and prosecution of a crime and how the defendant's waiver will affect the conduct of that prosecution.

The Supreme Court and lower federal courts have imposed no special requirements or thresholds for waiver of constitutional rights in the case of a mentally disordered defendant, noting only that it is a relevant consideration entitled to great weight in determining whether the defendant understood the consequences of his or her decision (*Edwards v. Arizona*, 1981;

Shafer v. Bowersox, 2003). Assessing whether a defendant with a history of mental illness had voluntarily waived his or her *Miranda* rights before confessing, the Eleventh Circuit Court of Appeals captured the role that courts have allocated to mental disability in this inquiry:

> There is little doubt that mental illness can interfere with a defendant's ability to make a knowing and intelligent waiver of his Miranda rights. Competency to make such a waiver is, of course, to be determined according to the totality of the circumstances. Johnson v. Zerbst, 304 U.S. at 464, 58 S. Ct. at 1023. This is not a field for inflexible rules. See North Carolina v. Butler, 441 U.S. at 375, 99 S. Ct. at 1758. Nonetheless, mental illness is certainly a factor that a trial court should consider when deciding on the validity of a waiver. If a defendant cannot understand the nature of his rights, he cannot waive them intelligently. Thus the Supreme Court has recognized that a juvenile defendant may be too young and inexperienced to make an intelligent waiver. See Fare v. Michael C., 442 U.S. 707, 725, 99 S. Ct. 2560, 2572, 61 L. Ed. 2d 197 (1979). The former Fifth Circuit held that mental retardation can render a defendant incapable of intelligently waiving the Miranda rights. Cooper v. Griffin, 455 F.2d 1142, 1145 (5th Cir.1972). n. 14 The Fourth Circuit has held that youthfulness and schizophrenia can combine to invalidate a waiver of rights, Moore v. Ballone, 658 F.2d 218, 229 (4th Cir.1981), and the Sixth Circuit has held that language difficulties can render a defendant's waiver of Miranda rights invalid. See United States v. Short, 790 F.2d 464, 469 (6th Cir.1986). (*Miller v. Dugger*, 1988, p. 1539)

Thus, while the presence of mental disorder may heighten the necessity for an inquiry into the defendant's competence to waive certain constitutional rights, it does not change the standard for that inquiry.

The Court explained the *intelligent* prong of the standard for waiver of constitutional rights in the very recent decision of *Iowa v. Tovar* (2004, p. 1387), noting:

> We described a waiver of counsel as intelligent when the defendant "knows what he is doing and his choice is made with eyes open." Adams, 317 U.S., at 279, 87 L. Ed. 268, 63 S. Ct. 236. We have not, however, prescribed any formula or script to be read to a defendant who states that he elects to proceed without counsel. The information a defendant must possess in order to make an intelligent election, our decisions indicate, will depend on a range of case-specific factors, including the defendant's education or sophistication, the complex or easily grasped nature of the charge, and the stage of the proceeding. See Johnson, 304 U.S., at 464, 82 L. Ed. 1461, 58 S. Ct. 1019.

The "intelligent" prong addresses the defendant's ability to manipulate knowledge about the legal rules and procedures for prosecution and how they will be affected by the waiver decision. Thus, the "intelligent" prong overlaps and is interrelated with the "knowing" prong. Indeed, the Court often describes them concurrently without separately distinguishing their meaning (*Iowa v. Tovar*, 2004, p. 1389): "'[T]he law ordinarily considers a waiver knowing, intelligent, and sufficiently aware if the defendant fully understands the nature of the right and how it would likely apply in general in the circumstances—even though the defendant may not know the specific detailed consequences of invoking it.' *United States v. Ruiz*, 536 U.S. 622, 629, 153 L. Ed. 2d 586, 122 S. Ct. 2450 (2002)."

The *voluntary* prong addresses the capacity of the suspect to choose freely without coercion whether to waive his or her rights. The Court has explained:

> The purpose of the "...voluntary" inquiry ...is to determine whether ...the decision is uncoerced. (*Godinez v. Moran*, 1993, p. 401)

A defendant's mental disorder standing alone will not render a confession involuntary under this criteria. Rather, courts have required the presence of coercive police activity related to that mental disorder to conclude that the waiver was not voluntary (*Colorado v. Connelly*, 1986). Yet, mental disorder, while not alone dispositive, is clearly relevant to the inquiry.

COMPETENCY TO CONFESS STANDARD

Background

The U.S. Supreme Court decision in *Miranda v. Arizona* (1966) was set against the background of its earlier decision *Escobedo v. Illinois* (1964) in which the Court found constitutionally inadmissable a confession obtained while the defendant was interrogated in police custody, handcuffed and standing, for four hours and denied his request to speak with his attorney. The *Escobedo* Court concluded that the interrogation had occurred at a critical stage of the proceedings triggering the constitutional right to counsel (*Escobedo v. Illinois*, 1964, pp. 490–491):

> We hold, therefore, that where, as here, the investigation is no longer a general inquiry into an unsolved crime but has begun to focus on a particular suspect, the suspect has been taken into police custody, the police carry out a process of interrogations that lends itself to eliciting incriminating statements, the suspect has requested and been denied an opportunity to consult with his lawyer, and the police have not effectively warned him of his absolute constitutional right to remain silent, the accused has been denied "the Assistance of Counsel" in violation of the Sixth Amendment to the Constitution as "made obligatory upon the States by the Fourteenth Amendment," Gideon v. Wainwright, 372 U.S., at 342, and that no statement elicited by the police during the interrogation may be used against him at a criminal trial.

Escobedo generated divergent lower court opinions and much confusion about what it required of law enforcement. The Court accepted review of the lower court decision in *Miranda* and several similar cases. Its purpose

(*Miranda v. Arizona*, 1966, pp. 441–442) was "to give concrete constitutional guidelines for law enforcement agencies and courts to follow."

Substantive Criteria

Chief Justice Earl Warren, writing the majority opinion in *Miranda*, delineated the rights of persons subjected to custodial interrogation.[1] First and foremost, the *Miranda* decision established the defendant's right to remain silent. The Court held that this fundamental right stands on the Fifth Amendment privilege against self-incrimination (p. 467) and expressed strong concerns that defendants might feel compelled to cooperate under the belief that "silence in the face of accusation is itself damning" (p. 467). Critical to this point, the Court reasoned that the right to silence must be protected against negative consequences at trial:

> In accord with our decision today, it is impermissible to penalize an individual for exercising his Fifth Amendment privilege when he is under police custodial interrogation. The prosecution may not, therefore, use at trial the fact that he stood mute or claimed privilege in the face of accusation. (p. 468)

A core element of the right to silence is the defendant's understanding that he or she will not be incriminated, or anyway penalized, by exercising this fundamental right. Without that understanding, the right to silence becomes an empty formality in the form of an illusory choice (i.e., "damned it you do, damned if you don't"). As addressed later in this chapter, forensic experts sometimes neglect to examine this core element that is essential to the right to silence.

The Court also held that defendants subjected to custodial interrogations have the right to counsel, which is "indispensable to the protection of the Fifth Amendment privilege" (p. 469). Beyond Fifth Amendment privilege, the Court determined that the right to counsel served other valuable purposes regarding coercion and misrepresentation. On the matter of coercion, the Court noted, "With a lawyer present the likelihood of coercion is reduced, and if coercion is nevertheless exercised, the lawyer can testify to it in court" (p. 470). Regarding misrepresentation, the Court observed that the presence of defense counsel can help to guarantee that the defendant's "statement is rightly reported by the prosecution at trial" (p. 470). In summary, the *Miranda* decision articulates three important safeguards afforded by the right to counsel: (a) protection against self-incrimination,

---

[1]Custodial interrogation is defined as "questioning initiated by law enforcement officers after a person has been taken into custody or otherwise deprived of his freedom of action in any significant way" (p. 444).

(b) protection against police coercion, and (c) protection against biased reporting of the defendant's statements.

The Court mandated that these constitutionally enshrined rights (i.e., silence and counsel) be communicated to the defendant in the form of a warning. It described (p. 479) the five basic components to be included in each warning:

1. "He must be warned, prior to any questioning, that he has a right to remain silent,"
2. "that anything he says can be used as evidence against him in a court of law,"
3. "that he has the right to the presence of an attorney,"
4. "that if he cannot afford an attorney one will be appointed for him prior to any questioning, if he so desires."
5. "Opportunity to exercise these rights must be afforded him throughout the interrogation."

The Court did not, however, articulate the specific language that should be used in the *Miranda* warnings. As a result, each jurisdiction is free to develop its own language (Helms, 2003) examined the sentence and reading complexity of federal and state standards and found reading differences that would suggest at least 31 distinct versions of *Miranda* warnings at the state level. Furthermore, a bewildering array of *Miranda* warnings likely occurs at the county level. For instance, Greenfield, Dougherty, Jackson, Podboy, and Zimmermann (2001) found 16 different *Miranda* versions being used throughout New Jersey counties.

Chief Justice Warren, writing the majority opinion, was cognizant of the coercive aspects of custodial interrogation. Even in the "absence of physical coercion and patent psychological ploys" (p. 457), he concluded that "It is obvious that such an interrogation environment is created for no other purpose that to subjugate the individual to the will of his examiner. This atmosphere carries its own badge of intimidation" (p. 457). Moreover, "The entire thrust of police interrogation there, as in all the cases today, was to put the defendant in such an emotional state as to impair his capacity for rational judgment" (*Miranda*, p. 465). Mental health professionals are, accordingly, obliged to evaluate the defendant's capacities in light of his or her circumstances at the time of the *Miranda* warning and waiver and in light of law enforcement methods.

Post-Miranda Modifications

Subsequent Supreme Court decisions have focused on procedural issues but left the substantiative criteria intact. In *Moran v. Brubine* (1986), the Court reaffirmed the rights recognized in *Miranda*, while explicating the procedural standard that governs their waiver under *Johnson v. Zerbst* (1938):

Echoing the standard first articulated in *Johnson v. Zerbst*, 304 U.S. 458, 464 (1938), Miranda holds that "[the] defendant may waive effectuation" of the rights conveyed in the warnings "provided the waiver is made voluntarily, knowingly and intelligently." 384 U.S., at 444, 475. The inquiry has two distinct dimensions ... First, the relinquishment of the right must have been voluntary in the sense that it was the product of a free and deliberate choice rather than intimidation, coercion, or deception. Second, the waiver must have been made with a full awareness of both the nature of the right being abandoned and the consequences of the decision to abandon it. Only if the "totality of the circumstances surrounding the interrogation" reveals both an uncoerced choice and the requisite level of comprehension may a court properly conclude that the *Miranda* rights have been waived. (p. 421)

Moran explained that the waiver of *Miranda* rights requires "full awareness of both the nature of the right being abandoned and the consequences of the decision to abandon it." For example, if the defendant believes (or is led to believe) that "cooperation" with the interrogation will have positive rewards (e.g., leniency), then his or her comprehension of the consequences of abandoning the right to remain silent may be compromised. Although the Court has cautioned that full awareness of the right may be found to be present "even though the defendant may not know the specific detailed consequences of invoking it" (*Iowa v. Tovar*, 2004, p. 1389), *Moran* clarifies that "the relinquishment of the right must have been voluntary in the sense that it was the product of a free and deliberate choice rather than intimidation, coercion, or deception."

The Supreme Court narrowed the reach of claims of mentally disordered defendant's regarding the voluntariness of their *Miranda* waivers in *Colorado v. Connelly* (1986). In *Connelly*, the defendant had returned to Colorado and confessed to a murder at the behest of his command hallucinations. The Court disallowed psychotically based internal coercion as the basis for a claim of coercion rendering the waiver of *Miranda* involuntary, arguing that its acceptance would force the courts to "divine a defendant's motivation for speaking and acting" (*Connelly*, p. 165). In an opinion that generated much controversy, the Court held (*Connelly*, p. 167) that a defendant's mental state alone does not render a statement involuntary: "[C]oercive police activity is a necessary predicate to the finding that a confession is not "voluntary." Miller (2003, p. 193) took strong issue with this decision as "reversing two hundred years of jurisprudence" in striking down "free will" as a precondition to voluntariness. Based on *Connelly*, a forensic expert may only address external coercion, such as police intimidation or trickery, as it applies to the voluntariness prong. In a more recent decision (*Watson v. DeTella*, 1997, p. 453), the Court clarified voluntariness, "A confession is voluntary if the totality of the circumstances demonstrates that it was the product of rational intellect and not the result of physical abuse, psychological intimidation, or deceptive interrogation tactics calculated to overcome the defendant's free will." However, it is unclear whether internal coercion can be completely exempted from voluntariness in such instances where external coercion interacts with internal coercion. In considering the totality of circumstances, we argue that a suspect's delusions of guilt cannot be ignored in evaluating the effects of police coercion. The cases simply note that:

> To determine whether a defendant's confession was voluntary, a court must consider the totality of the circumstances Withrow v. Williams, 507 U.S. 680, 693, 123 L. Ed. 2d 407, 113 S. Ct. 1745 (1993). These circumstances may include, among other things, the degree of police coercion, the length of the interrogation, its location, its continuity, and the defendant's maturity, education, physical condition, and mental condition. (*Smith v Bowersox*, 2002, p. 922).

COMPETENCY FOR WARRANTLESS SEARCHES

Background

The Fourth Amendment protects the right of the people "to be secure in their persons, houses, papers, and effects, against unreasonable searches and seizures" (U.S. Constitution, Amendment IV). In *Mapp v. Ohio* (1961), the Court held that an appropriate remedy for state searches that violated the Fourth Amendment's prescriptions was exclusion of the fruits of that search in any resulting prosecution. This ruling extended the exclusionary rule from federal to state prosecutions. Searches conducted without a warrant based on probable cause are "per se" unreasonable, subject to a limited number of exceptions. One important exception is consent.

Schneckloth v. Bustamonte (1973) concerned the definition of consent for purposes of the admissibility of warrantless searches. The defendant was a passenger in a car stopped at 2:40 A.M. with a headlight and license plate light that were burned out. At the officer's request, the six occupants of the vehicle stepped out of the car and the officer, now joined by two other officers, asked the driver if he could search the car to which the drive responded affirmatively. During the search the officers found checks that had been stolen from a car wash which formed the basis for the defendant's conviction for possessing a check with intent to defraud.

Substantiative Criteria

Justice Stewart, writing the majority opinion in *Schneckloth v. Busta-monte* (1973), observed that warrantless searches are generally unreasonable. An exception occurs when the suspect freely and voluntarily consents to the search. The Court openly acknowledged the challenges of establishing *voluntariness* as the criterion in reviewing past cases, "Those cases yield no talismanic definition of 'voluntariness,' mechanically applicable to the host of situations where the question has arisen" (p. 224).

The *Bustamante* decision carefully weighed several different conceptualizations of voluntariness. It rejected extreme formulations. On one hand, using the suspects' mere knowledge of their consent is inappropriate because it does not consider the possibility of coercion. On the other hand, insisting that the consent be "spontaneous" (i.e., irrespective of the police's request) would eliminate virtually all warrantless searches. Instead, the Court cited with approval *Culombe v. Connecticut* (1961):

> The ultimate test remains that which has been the only clearly established test in Anglo-American courts for 200 years: the test of voluntariness. Is the confession the product of an essentially free and unconstrained choice by its maker? If it is, if he has willed to confess, it may be used against him. If it is not, if his will has been overborne and his capacity for self-determination critically impaired, the use of his confession offends due process. (pp. 225–226)

In evaluating the totality of the circumstances, mental health professionals must consider (1) free and unconstrained choice, and (2) the closely related issue of critical impairment in self-determination. In making determinations of voluntariness, clinicians must take into account "subtly coercive police questions, as well as the possibly vulnerable subjective state of the person who consents" (p. 229). Importantly, given the facts of the case, the decision is limited to *noncustodial* suspects (p. 248).

The decision in *Schneckloth v. Bustamonte* (1973) provides an important parameter on the *right to refusal* as it relates to voluntariness. It held that prosecution did not have to prove the defendant's knowledge of his or her right to refuse cooperation. However, it affirmed that "the state of the accused's mind, and the failure of the police to advise the accused of his rights, were certainly factors to be evaluated in assessing the 'voluntariness' of an accused's responses" (p. 227). Therefore, the defendant's knowledge of the "right to refuse consent is one factor to be taken into account," but it is not "the *sine qua non* of an effective consent" (p. 227).

The Court was careful to distinguish the competency necessary to waive the constitutional protections against warrantless searches based on Fourth Amendment protections from those rights which "the Constitution guarantees to a criminal defendant in order to preserve a fair trial"

(p. 237). Fourth Amendment protections do not involve "the fair ascertainment of truth at a criminal trial" (p. 242); rather, they address improper intrusions by law enforcement. In light of this distinction, the Court held that the "requirement of a knowing and intelligent waiver" did *not* apply to competency for warrantless searches. Suspects do not have to consider all the implications of their choices (i.e., "knowing" waiver) or manifest a reasoned decision (i.e., "intelligent" waiver). Instead, the Court ruled that "consent was in fact voluntarily given, and not the result of duress or coercion, express or implied" (p. 248). Clinically, the *Bustamonte* decision involves two prongs: (1) capacity to choose and (2) freedom from coercion.

Regarding consent to a warrantless search given by a suspect in police custody, the context has affected the application of these rules but has not changed them. "It is generally recognized that coercion is more easily found if the person consenting to the search has been placed under arrest, but the fact that an individual is under arrest at the time he gives his consent is not, of itself, sufficient to establish that his consent was involuntary" (*United States v. Hall*, 1978, p. 928).

Subsequent case law has addressed the critical role of mental capacity in ascertaining the voluntariness of a consent. For example, relying on the Supreme Court decision in *United States v. Watson* (1976), the Fifth Circuit Court of Appeals noted in *United States v. Elrod* (1971, p. 365):

> No matter how genuine the belief of the officers is that the consenter is apparently of sound mind and deliberately acting, the search depending on his consent fails if it is judicially determined that he lacked mental capacity. It is not that the actions of the officers were imprudent or unfounded. It is that the key to validity—consent—is lacking for want of mental capacity, no matter how much concealed.

Whether *Elrod*'s focus on the mental capacity of the defendant independent of the behavior of the police survives *Connelly*'s requirement that coercion result from the behavior of the police to render the waiver involuntary has not been specifically addressed by the courts. However, *Elrod* is still cited with authority in *United States v. Rambo* (1986, p. 1297): We recognize that Rambo was possibly under the influence of a narcotic at the time of his arrest, Magistrate's Report at 5, and was highly disturbed. However, the mere fact that one has taken drugs, or is intoxicated, or mentally agitated, does not render consent involuntary. See United States v. Gay, 774 F.2d 368, 377 (10th Cir. 1985); United States v. Elrod, 441 F.2d 353, 355 (5th Cir. 1971). In each case, "the question is one of mental awareness so that the act of consent was the consensual act of one who knew what he was doing and had a reasonable appreciation of the nature and significance of his actions." Elrod, 441 F.2d at 355. The cases are fact-specific and offer little concrete guidance beyond their recognition that mental capacity is an integral part of the inquiry.

CLINICAL OPERATIONALIZATION OF WAIVER DECISIONS

Competency evaluations related to police investigations vary substantially based on the specific issue. For *Miranda* evaluations, the waivers must be knowing, intelligent, and voluntary. However, voluntariness is limited to external coercion and duress. In contrast, competency to consent to warrantless searches center directly on voluntariness and encompasses both (1) the capacity to choose and (2) implicit or explicit coercion.

Knowing Waivers

The litmus test of *knowing* waivers is that suspects understand the basic elements of waiver as it relates to their circumstances, the warning, and their rights. Sometimes overlooked by mental health professionals, defendants must have a basic appreciation of their circumstances, specifically that they are being questioned by law enforcement officers who are likely seeking evidence against them. Without an awareness of their circumstances, defendants cannot make a knowing waiver of their rights. For example, a female defendant may mistakenly believe that the police are eliciting her help regarding a roommate's drug offenses with no awareness that she is also the object of investigation. Without this key information, the knowing aspect of the waiver is compromised.

Knowing waivers also require an adequate comprehension of the legally mandated warning. In the case of *Miranda* warnings, the suspect should be able to understand both the vocabulary and the meaning of the *Miranda* statements. As a specific example, Grisso (1981) found that a significant minority of suspects had a poor understanding of the word "right" as it applies to *Miranda* warnings. In this context, "right" refers to the suspect's privilege or prerogative. If suspects are unclear about its meaning, then their understanding of their *Miranda* rights are seriously vitiated. Some suspects are able to understand the vocabulary of *Miranda* warnings but do not understand their meaning. The ability to paraphrase these warnings is the chief method of establishing a basic understanding of their content. For basic comprehension, we recommend the following for forensic clinicians:

1. "Tell me in your own words what it says." Suspects often resort to identical words as used in the warnings. Forensic clinicians will need to probe further, especially for words with legal meanings.
2. "What does that mean to *you* (or *your case*)?" The core issue is whether the suspect can apply the specific statements to him- or

herself. For example, good understanding of "used as evidence against him" from the *Miranda* warning might be "They will try nail me if I keep talking." In contrast, suspects cannot apply this component to themselves unless they recognize both (a) the adversarial relationship and (b) the grave risk of providing evidence against themselves.

A knowing waiver requires more than a transitory capacity. Many forensic clinicians make the erroneous assumption that comprehension at the very moment of the waiver was effectuated is sufficient for the waiver to be valid. With respect to *Miranda* warnings, the Court held that "Opportunity to exercise these rights must be afforded him throughout the interrogation" (p. 479). The "opportunity to exercise these rights" is premised on an awareness that these rights exist. For instance, a defendant with moderate dementia may be able to understand his or her *Miranda* rights, but be unable to retain this information for more than a minute or two. If this impairment is clearly demonstrable, then the suspect lacks a core element of *Miranda* understanding. When the suspect is subjected to a lengthy interrogation, then his or her recall should be tested after an extended interval (e.g., 1 hour or 2 hours). To emphasize this point, attorneys should be alert for incomplete evaluations: *Miranda evaluations should address the suspect's ability to recall their rights at intervals approximating the interrogation length.*

INTELLIGENT WAIVERS

Intelligent waivers, when reduced to essential abilities, require that suspects are able to accomplish three closely related cognitive tasks: (a) identify their alternatives, (b) understand the consequences of these alternatives, and (c) apply reasoning to their decision. Bonnie (1992) developed a framework for *decisional competence* in the context of competency-to-stand-trial determinations (see Chapter 6). This framework is also helpful in understanding *intelligent waivers*, in its accurate appraisal of relevant information and application of cost–benefit analysis. The first step is whether the suspect recognized his or her three basic choices that we have characterized as Confess, Outfox, and *Miranda*. We outline the advantages and disadvantages of each choice:

Confess. With this alternative, the suspect provides an inculpatory statement without the benefit of counsel.

1. Advantages:
   a. Immediate (that day) advantages: "approval of investigators," stop the stress of the interrogations, and end the uncertainty

b. Long-term (outcome of the case) advantage: none
2. Disadvantages:
a. Immediate disadvantages: "approval" ceases after the confession; new uncertainties arise about the case
b. Long-term disadvantage: high probability of a conviction with limited opportunity for plea bargaining

Outfox. With this alternative, the suspect attempts to outmaneuver the investigators by pretending to cooperate while denying criminal involvement in the alleged offense.

1. Advantages:
a. Immediate (that day) advantages: "feels" in control; hopes to deflect prosecution
b. Long-term (outcome of the case) advantage: very low probability of deflecting prosecution
2. Disadvantages:
a. Immediate disadvantage: interrogation is a confidence game with the suspect as the gull
b. Long-term disadvantage: high probability of either incriminating evidence or a confession

Miranda. In asserting his or her rights, the suspect remains silent and immediately requests counsel.

1. Advantages:
a. Immediate (that day) advantage: does no damage to the case
b. Long-term (legal outcome) advantage: maintains options including plea bargaining
2. Disadvantages:
a. Immediate disadvantage: must endure inferences about guilt (something to hide)
b. Long-term disadvantage: none

Legal and mental health professionals likely will contribute additional advantages and disadvantages to this outline. In many cases, confessing suspects trade immediate advantages for long-term and often devastating disadvantages (i.e., a conviction with limited opportunity for plea bargaining). Forensic clinicians are likely to be divided on whether this lack of reasoning is sufficient to question a suspect's *intelligent waiver*. We recommend that experts provide further evidence of the suspects' diminished abilities for verbal reasoning and decision making.

Suspects, who attempt to outfox investigators, often have a poor appraisal of the interrogation process. As described by Gudjonnson (2003), the interrogation process can be characterized as a "confidence game." However, it is the suspect, and *not* the investigators, who is typically conned. Using a variety of sophisticated psychological tactics (Inbau, Reid, Buckley, & Jayne, 2001), investigators attempt to manipulate suspects to confess, often through outright deception. Despite their poor appraisal of the interrogation process, many "outfoxing" suspects have sufficient rational abilities.

Intelligent waivers require that suspects are free from psychotic interference that markedly impair the decisional process. The most common impairment among psychotic symptoms is from delusions, especially paranoid delusions. Suspects with moderate to severe paranoid delusions may grossly misinterpret the nature of interrogation and misperceive interactions. For instance, paranoid suspects may misconstrue forceful questioning with imminent threats of physical violence. Persons with paranoid delusions may disengage from the interactions, respond with anger, or capitulate because of fear. Disengagement from the interrogation is unlikely to affect *Miranda* decisions. However, affective reactions to delusionally based perceptions may vitiate suspects' ability to waive intelligently their *Miranda* rights. Two possible delusional responses are

1. *Delusionally based capitulations.* Suspects with paranoid delusions may grossly misperceive their interrogators as physical threats endangering their lives or as supernatural forces that cannot be denied. Especially in the first instance, an aggressive interrogation style (e.g., intrusions on personal space and implicit threats) may contribute to persecutory ideations in suspects with psychotic disorders. Faced with formidable threats, some delusional suspects may capitulate to the inevitable outcome. Affectively, these capitulations are based on fear, arising from gross misperceptions.

2. *Delusionally based counterattacks.* Suspects with paranoid or grandiose delusions may also respond with anger because of perceived threats to their safety and/or personal importance. In "striking back," rational processes are likely to be absent. The suspect is preoccupied with generating threats and challenges to the interrogators. With grandiose delusions, the suspect's goal may be to protect his or her importance rather than considering the consequences of participating in the interrogation. Affectively, these counterattacks are based on anger, arising from gross misperceptions.

VOLUNTARY WAIVERS

Voluntariness under Miranda

The *Connelly* case severely curtailed the use of the defendant's mental state in the determination of voluntariness. For *Miranda* waivers, it equated voluntariness with a lack of *external* coercion, based explicitly on its skepticism of divining a suspect's motivation (see *Connelly*, p. 165). Therefore, command hallucinations and delusions of control cannot be regarded, standing alone, as dispositive of the voluntariness of a confession.

As affirmed in *United States v. Newton* (2004), there is little question that *Miranda*'s goal "to give concrete constitutional guidelines for law enforcement agencies and courts to follow" (*Miranda v. Arizona*, 1966, pp. 441–442) requires that police coercion or intimidation be judged by an objective standard. The question under an *objective* standard is whether a reasonable person under similar circumstances find the interrogators' conduct as coercive. For example, in *United State v. Barone* (1992), the Court of Appeals found a confession inadmissible when law enforcement did not scrupulously respect the defendant's right to cut off questioning. Although the court found that the statement was given voluntarily, it nonetheless rejected its admission. Its language (p. 1383) says much about judicial assessment of *Miranda* standards and the assessment of voluntariness:

> Thus, in determining the admissibility of a confession made in response to initial police questioning, Miranda directs courts to look at whether the law enforcement officers have followed specified procedures; if not, the suspect's confession is inadmissible, without inquiry into voluntariness. The presumption, of course, is that most confessions obtained without adherence to those procedures would be involuntary.

Voluntariness under Bustamonte

Although *Bustamonte* and *Connelly* appear at odds in their consideration of voluntariness, the Court sees the standards very differently. It held in *United States v. Rojas-Martinez* (1992, p. 418):

> Voluntariness depends upon the totality of the circumstances and must be evaluated on a case-by-case basis. Schneckloth v. Bustamonte, 412 U.S. 218, 226, 36 L. Ed. 2d 854, 93 S. Ct. 2041 (1973). Under Connelly, a confession is voluntary in the absence of official overreaching, in the form either of direct coercion or subtle forms of psychological persuasion.

The cases have been read to impose two separate, nonconflicting aspects of voluntariness. First, the totality of the circumstances must be considered. Second, then only if police coercion played a role in the totality of circumstances might the waiver be regarded as involuntary.

Like most psychological constructs, voluntariness is an ordinal construct that is expressed on a continuum. At the extreme, both the courts and clinicians are likely to concur that a person in a coma cannot consent to any decision. Less extreme and more common conditions occur with the diagnoses of substance-induced delirium. This disorder (see American Psychiatric Association, 2000a, p. 145) requires (1) disturbance of consciousness with a reduced ability to "focus, sustain or shift attention" and (2) substantial changes in cognition (e.g., disorientation, or deficits in language or memory) or perceptions. While arising from intoxication, DSM-IV-TR cautions that the diagnosis should only be made when cognitive symptoms exceed those found simply with intoxication and warrant "independent clinical attention" (p. 145). Specific diagnostic subtypes include the following substances: alcohol, amphetamine, cannabis, cocaine, hallucinogens, inhalants, opioids, phencyclidine, sedatives, hypnotics, and anxiolytics.

The first challenge for forensic clinicians is the establishment of the suspect's awareness of his or her environment. As a common example, a severely intoxicated suspect may still have a general awareness of the environment if he or she was oriented and able to communicate with communicate with the police officer. Deficits in memory may be difficult to assess retrospectively, given that blackouts may impair recollections.

Voluntariness for warrantless searches may also be affected by psychotic and mood disorders. For instance, command hallucinations or delusions of control may require the suspect's compliance against his or her will. Concomitant with severe depression and self-reproach, self-destructive impulses may override any rational choice.

CLINICAL METHODS AND FORENSIC CONSIDERATIONS

Forensic assessments of suspects' capacities are especially challenging in light of their retrospective nature, variability in legal standards, and limited availability of specialized measures. In particular, the retrospective nature places an onerous responsibility on forensic clinicians who must attempt to evaluate the defendant's abilities at the time of decision-making (confession or search). Any facile equation of current abilities with past competencies represents substandard practice.

Forensic clinicians will need to integrate case-specific methods with standardized measures in their evaluations of competencies related to *Miranda* and warrantless searches. Despite their limited validation, some forensic clinicians may wish to augment these evaluations with specialized forensic measures. This section of the chapter is organized by the specific legal competency, because of the fundamental differences between *Miranda* and warrantless searches standards.

MIRANDA

A primary issue in *Miranda* evaluations is whether the defendant had the cognitive capacity to make a knowing and intelligent waiver. The strongest evidence of incapacity is found in cases where the defendants have pervasive intellectual impairments, namely mental retardation. In particular, the chronicity of mental retardation as well as its potentially profound effects can be convincingly demonstrated. However, legitimate issues can also be raised whether the defendant's capacity can also be impaired by severe psychopathology. Viljoen, Roesch, and Zapf (2002) found that many defendants with schizophrenia evidenced marked impairment in their competence to understand their rights.[2] Therefore, *Miranda* evaluations should focus on both domains, namely cognitive and psychological impairments.

Standardized Measures

Cognitive impairment for *Miranda* issues can be either general or specific. In cases where the defendant appears to be unimpaired, forensic clinicians may wish to use the Wechsler Abbreviated Scale of Intelligence (WASI; Weschler, 1999) to estimate verbal and overall intelligence. In cases where the defendant appears to be impaired cognitively, a comprehensive assessment is recommended that addresses both general and specific deficits. This assessment would likely include

- Weschler Adult Intelligence Scale—Third Edition (WAIS-III; Weschler, 1997) is the best-validated individual intelligence test for adult populations. Importantly, the WAIS-III provides forensic clinicians with valuable data regarding verbal abilities including Verbal IQ and the Verbal Comprehension Index.
- Wechsler Individual Achievement Test 2nd Edition (WIAT-II; Psychological Corporation, 2002) yields grade-equivalent scores for word reading, reading comprehension, listening comprehension,

---

[2]Data on defendants with schizophrenia were collected primarily from an inpatient forensic hospital and therefore are not directly generalizable to pretrial defendants as a whole. Within this segment of disordered offenders, they had poor understanding of their rights; out of a total of 30 points, they averaged only 12.83 ($SD = 6.34$).

and oral expression. Specific deficits in reading and oral comprehension are particularly relevant to the understanding of *Miranda*
warnings.

Clinical research (Everington & Fulero, 1999; Fulero & Everington,
1995; Grisso, 1998) has been content to evaluate overall intelligence in relationship to *Miranda* comprehension rather than focus on specific verbal
abilities. Forensic clinicians must avoid such nonspecific and potentially
misleading analyses of overall intelligence (i.e., Full Scale IQ). In many defendants, comparatively strong nonverbal abilities (i.e., Performance IQ)
may obscure critical deficits in verbal abilities (i.e., Verbal IQ). Beyond Verbal IQ, careful consideration should be given to the Verbal Comprehension
Index that assesses acquired verbal knowledge and verbal reasoning.

The Vocabulary subtest offers useful data regarding the defendant's
knowledge of words and their meanings. Entirely separate from the *Miranda* vocabulary, it provides an independent and standardized measure
of the defendant's word mastery. This subtest can assist *Miranda* evaluations in corroborating that marked deficits in word meanings are broadly
based.[3]

The *Miranda* decision does not require that the warnings be read by
the suspect or that their waiver of rights be written. In general practice,
custodial suspects typically are presented their *Miranda* warnings in both
oral and written formats. Therefore, it is imperative that forensic clinicians
test the defendant's abilities consistent with the procedures used in his or
her warning. Considering the "totality of the circumstances" (*Colorado v.
Spring*, 1987, p. 573), either oral or written comprehension may be sufficient
to meet the *Miranda* requirements. An advantage of the WIAT-II is its standardization of oral and written comprehension. These data are presented
with grade-level equivalents that are easily understandable by persons
without mental health training. While the WIAT-II is recommended, other
achievement tests may be used if they (a) offer sufficient coverage for oral
and written comprehension and (b) have been normed for adult populations.

Forensic clinicians occasionally encounter well-educated defendants
with above-average verbal abilities. Given the grave consequences of
Miranda evaluations, forensic clinicians should administer the relevant
subtests of the WIAT-II so as not to short-change the consultation. *Criminal attorneys should be aware that commonly used screens for reading "ability" do not test for reading "comprehension."* Inapplicable screens include the

---

[3]Selective deficits, targeting only *Miranda* issues, would raise concerns about whether the
defendant was attempting to feign incompetency.

Wide Range Achievement Test (3rd ed., WRAT-3; Wilkinson, 1993) and the Slosson Oral Reading Test, Revised (SORT-R3; Slosson & Nicholson, 2002).

Assessment of psychological impairment must take into account the retrospective nature of the evaluation and the severity of Axis I symptomatology. As a standard reference, Rogers (2001) comprehensively reviews structured interviews for Axis I and Axis II disorders. For retrospective evaluations, the Schedule of Affective Disorders and Schizophrenia (SADS; Spitzer & Endicott, 1978) is the premier Axis I interview. The SADS has been validated for the evaluation of prior episodes. Unlike most Axis I interviews, the SADS provides accurate ratings of symptom severity. As criminal attorneys can readily attest, the simple presence of symptoms (e.g., auditory hallucinations) does not address the critical issue. For establishing *Miranda*-related abilities, the paramount issue is the *effects* of symptoms on the defendant's functioning. An abbreviated version of the SADS (SADS-Change Version or SADS-C; Spitzer & Endicott, 1978b) could be used with *Miranda* cases in which the defendant appears to be well adjusted.

Specialized Miranda Measures

Clinical researchers have attempted to develop specialized *Miranda* measures for assessing relevant vocabulary, recall, and verbal reasoning. Beyond isolated efforts at developing measures (Greenfield, Dougherty, Jackson, Podboy, & Zimmermann, 2001; Oberlander, Goldstein, & Goldstein, 2003), the bulk of research has addressed the Grisso's *Miranda* Instruments (GMI; Grisso, 1998). The GMI is a collection of four *Miranda* scales that were developed to evaluate the outdated St. Louis County *Miranda* warning.[4] Attorneys will likely need to be familiar with the GMI:

- Comprehension of *Miranda* Rights (CMR; 4 items) involves the paraphrasing of four statements from the outdated St. Louis County *Miranda* warning.
- Comprehension of *Miranda* Rights—Recognition (CMR-R; 12 items) involves recognizing relevant ideas based on four statements from the outdated St. Louis County *Miranda* warning.
- Comprehension of *Miranda* Vocabulary (CMV; 6 items) involves the definitions of difficult words found in the outdated St Louis County *Miranda* warning.

---

[4] According to Dr. Bruce Frumkin, an expert on *Miranda*, the tested GMI version is no longer used in St. Louis County (personal communication, March 6, 2004).

- Function of Rights in Interrogation (FRI; 15 items) is composed of four hypothetical situations that are read to the defendant (4–5 sentences in length); a series of questions are asked on the basis of these situations purported to assess three subscales: Nature of Interrogation (NI), Right to Counsel (RC), and Right to Silence (RS).

The American Psychological Association in conjunction with other professional organizations issued the authoritative *Standards for educational and psychological testing* (AERA/APA/NCME, 1999) that provides the requirements for all psychological measures whether they are referred to as tests, scales or instruments.[5] Rogers, Jordan, and Harrison (2004) provided a technical critique of the GMI and how its scales fail to satisfy even the basic requirements for test reliability and validity as set forth in the official *Standards*. As applied to adult offenders, the three most obvious failures are as follows: (1) reliability data are virtually nonexistent; (2) normative data used the wrong reference group; and (3) criterion-related validity is nonexistent.

Many forensic clinicians are likely to be misled by overly optimistic reviews (Frumkin, 2000; Grisso, 2003; Oberlander & Goldstein, 2001; Oberlander et al., 2003) of the GMI that overlook its fundamental weaknesses. Such reviews do a disservice to criminal attorneys and their experts by glossing over the GMI's failures to meet basic test requirements. As a result, attorneys will likely need to educate forensic clinicians regarding the limitations of the GMI. These limitations obviously have implications regarding the admissibility of the GMI in light of the *Daubert* criteria. Two *Daubert* criteria are not met:

- *Known or potential error rate.* The GMI fails to report any *standard errors of measurement*. This simple statistic tells us how much confidence, if any, can be placed in the accuracy of scale scores. Given its absence and the lack of external validation, error rates are completely unknown.
- *General acceptance by the scientific community.* Despite several "favorable" reviews, the GMI fails to meet the necessary scientific requirements established by its discipline.

One alternative for forensic clinicians is to use the GMI as a "behavioral sample" rather than a psychological measure. In this instance, the forensic

---

[5]To avoid circumvention of test requirements, the *Standards* (p. 3) affirm the following, "The applicability of the Standards to an evaluation device or method is not altered by the label applied to it (e.g., test, assessment, scale, inventory)."

clinician simply records his or her observations about the defendant's vocabulary, understanding of statements, and responses to scenarios. As a "behavioral sample," two restrictions must be observed:

1. The GMI must be described explicitly as a behavioral sample that is used exclusively for observations.
2. No scoring, norms, or interpretations can be presented either in writing or testimony.

Criminal attorneys will likely encounter forensic clinicians that misuse the GMI as a psychological measure. Sample cross-examination questions, presented in Box 5-1, exemplify several themes. First and foremost, any measure is useless if it lacks demonstrable reliability. We cannot put any faith in results if we cannot demonstrate (a) whether the scores are accurate (i.e., standard error of measurement), (b) whether different clinicians would get vastly different results (i.e., interrater reliability), and (c) whether the defendant's results will vary from day to day (i.e., test–retest reliability). Of equal importance, we must be able to demonstrate the GMI's validity. The GMI has little or no usefulness, unless we can demonstrate (a) its congruence with the *Miranda* warning be used in a particular jurisdiction (i.e., content validity) and (b) its relationship to a real-world standard, such as court findings in *Miranda* cases (i.e., criterion-related validity).

Box 5-1   MODEL CROSS-EXAMINATION ON GRISSO'S *MIRANDA* MEASURES
WITH ADULT OFFENDERS

Inadequate Validation

1. *Are the Miranda measures developed by Dr. Grisso sufficiently validated as to offer the court any useful information?*
2. *Were they adequately normed on adult suspects?* [likely affirmative]...*This is an important issue, doctor. You are testifying under oath that it was adequately normed on adult suspects, is that correct?*
3. *Then can you tell us why Dr. Grisso describes the adult offenders serving time in halfway houses?* [likely equivocates]...*Assume for the moment my description is accurate, these offenders were not suspects as far as we know, correct?*
4. *Would you agree with this statement, "Psychological measures must be reliable and valid before they used?"*
5. *Doctor, when were you going to tell the Court that there are no reliability data whatsoever on the Grisso's measures with adult populations?* [if attempts to use adolescent data]...*Even if it were applicable to adults, isn't it true there are no reliability data on three of the four Grisso measures for <u>adolescents</u>?*

(Continued)

6. [if applicable] *According to Dr. Grisso's test manual, how many subjects in the validation sample were diagnosed with a mental disorder?* [none] . . . *With mental retardation?* [none] . . . *With depression?* [none]

7. *Be honest, doctor, Grisso's measures were not validated on the critical populations, were they?* [if quibbles] . . . *Not on suspects?* . . . *Not on mentally retarded?* . . . *Not on mentally disordered?*

8. *By the way, did Dr. Grisso even to bother to test his results against some independent criterion, like the courts' rulings in Miranda cases?* [no]

Inadequate Validation #2: Introduction of an Exhibit

9. *Doctor, I would like to give you a summary pertaining to Grisso's Measures* [provide a visual display for the Court; sample is provided in Appendix F]. *Let's look the column entitled CMR; please tell the jury what CMR stands for* ["Comprehension of Miranda Rights"]

10. [Display of Appendix F] *Let's go down the first column. What do we know about its "standard error of measurement?"* . . . *What is "internal consistency?"* . . . *What is "interrater reliability?"* [continue as necessary; the point is to demonstrate the expert's lack of sophistication with these terms]

11. *Staying with CMR, what is its standard error of measurement?* . . . *Isn't it true that it has <u>never even been tested</u>?*

12. *Staying with the CMR, is its content validity directly relevant to this jurisdiction?* . . . [if applicable] *What Miranda warning is used in the Grisso measure?* [simple four statements] . . . [if current jurisdiction is much more complex] . . . *Which Miranda warning is used in <u>this</u> jurisdiction?*

13. *Isn't it true, doctor, that criterion-related validity tries to tell us how well a measure works in the real world?* [yes] . . . *Isn't it also true, that the Grisso measure did even attempt to look at its real world applications?* [yes]

14. *None of us like to admit that we are wrong. In fairness to the Court, wouldn't the truth be that you erred in administering ___* [defendant] *the Comprehension of Miranda Rights?*

15. *Let's be honest, doctor, the other subtests have just as many problems don't they?* . . . *Do we need to go through each one of them, or are you willing to admit that they are markedly deficient?*

16. [if necessary, go through #11–13 for each Grisso subtest]

One option is to begin with general questions about the GMI's total lack of reliability and markedly inadequate validity. If the expert engages in prevarications, a rebuttal expert may be necessary to expose these deceptions. If the expert appropriately concedes the unreliability and invalidity of the GMI, the attorney may wish to concretize these concessions through the use of an exhibit (see Appendix F). The second set of cross-examination questions provides an example of how this exhibit could be used with an expert that has the integrity to acknowledge the GMI's blatant shortcomings.

Miranda research has also investigated whether suggestibility plays a role in false confessions. Oberlander et al. (2003) recommended that the Gudjonsson Suggestibility Scale (GSS; Gudjonsson, 1984, 1992) may be useful in evaluating "interrogative suggestibility." By using a fictitious crime, the forensic clinician evaluates the defendant's ability to recall accurately up to 40 details. After being subjected to leading questions and negative feedback, changes in the defendant's account are tabulated. Many prosecutors are likely to be skeptical about whether the GSS has ecological validity. In plain English, can we assume the defendant's suggestibility similarly from the fictitious to the actual offense? In the fictitious case, the defendant is briefly exposed to many details that are irrelevant to his or her predicament. In the actual case, the defendant is relating to his or her personal memory of events that are highly consequential.

Experimental evidence (e.g., Kassin & Kiechel, 1996) indicates that false confessions can be induced in presumably well-adjusted persons (i.e., college students) when confronted by persons in authority and presented with false evidence of their guilt. Issues of the believability and credibility of the defendant go far beyond the legal competencies required for Miranda and warrantless searches. Mental health professionals are likely to be divided on whether their expertise can directly address the believability of defendants' confessions and their subsequent retractions. In our opinion, this matter does not rely for forensic expertise and is beyond the scope of both this chapter and this book.

Case-Specific Methods

Forensic clinicians are hampered in their evaluations by the retrospective nature of most competency-to-waive Miranda evaluations and the invalidity of specialized Miranda measures. As a result, they are likely to rely heavily on the above-described standardized measures and case-specific methods. Case-specific methods are individualized in their focus on a specific defendant and his or her particular circumstances. These methods can be used to assess cognitive and psychological impairments.

Cognitive abilities. The challenge is to assess accurately the defendant's cognitive appreciation of Miranda at the time of the confession. The criminal justice system tends to educate defendants, both informally (e.g., conversations with other inmates) or formally (e.g., inquiries by defense counsel). As a result, the defendant may have learned about his or her Miranda abilities. However, it is very unlikely that the defendant "unlearned" Miranda rights. Therefore, forensic clinicians may have greater confidence for defendant who remain cognitively impaired than their unimpaired counterparts.

TABLE 5-1. CASE-SPECIFIC METHODS OF ASSESSING COGNITIVE IMPAIRMENT

Retrospective recall

- Goal: Ascertain memory of the interrogation and the original warning
- Methods: Questions address the identification of interrogators (e.g., names and physical characteristics) and recall of their statements; embedded in the inquiry are questions about the *Miranda* warning and the memory of its specific content.

Current understanding

- Goal: Discriminate current understanding from past memory
- Methods: Direct inquiries address the defendant's current understanding with follow-up probes where this information was learned.

Prompted understanding

- Goal: Test the defendant's immediate recall when presented with the *Miranda* warning
- Methods: The relevant *Miranda* warning is presented in the same mode (oral, written, or both) as used at the time of interrogation; the defendant paraphrases the warning.

Prompted understanding with delay

- Goal: Test the delayed recall of the *Miranda* warning in cases where the defendant did not immediately confess
- Methods: Delayed recall should parallel the time between the warning and the confession. After the appropriate interval with no intervening discussion of *Miranda*, the defendant's recall is retested.

Miranda rights

- Goal: Ascertain defendant's understanding of right to silence and right to an attorney
- Methods: Questions should address the defendant's understanding of the consequences of exercising his or her rights. Examples include (1) "What would have been the downside of *not* speaking to the police?" and (2) "Could this be used against in court?"

Miranda vocabulary

- Goal: Evaluate the defendant's comprehension of *Miranda* terms and phrases
- Methods: Difficult words or terms with legal meanings are formed into a vocabulary list and asked systematically of the defendant.

Table 5-1 outlines the key cognitive domains of *Miranda* rights with goals and suggested methods. The retrospective recall of the interrogation is likely to be the single most relevant facet of the evaluation. An unhurried and open-ended account beginning before defendant's entry into custody can provide a useful basis for evaluating other abilities. Leading (or misleading) questions should be avoided, such as "Did they give you time to think before asking you to sign the *Miranda* warning?" This information should emerge from the open-ended account.

The defendant's current understanding of the *Miranda* warning is often useful. This information is different from *prompted* understanding that is assessed by presenting the relevant *Miranda* warning to the defendant and asking for immediate recall. Because *Miranda* rights extend throughout the interrogation, it will be important to assess the interval of time between the *Miranda* warning and the confession. If an appreciable amount of time transpired (e.g., 15 minutes or more), then the defendant's recall must be tested to approximate the defendant's ability to recall this information at the appropriate interval. Other domains include *Miranda* rights and the defendant's reasoning (e.g., "What was given up?" and "What was accomplished?") and simple knowledge of *Miranda* vocabulary.

Psychological impairment. An unstructured interview can be used to assess diagnostic issues and other clinical considerations that may have affected the defendant's intelligent waiver of his or her rights. These issues are well covered under the section on *Clinical Operationalization.*

Forensic Considerations

Conclusions regarding *Miranda* rights must be based on the "totality of the circumstances." Specific deficits cannot be equated with an invalid waiver. Instead, the defendant's overall abilities must be considered. The first step is the completion of a thorough evaluation that adequately covers the relevant clinical issues. To assist criminal attorneys, Table 5-2 presents a convenient checklist to ensure the adequacy of *Miranda* evaluations.

TABLE 5-2. ATTORNEY'S CHECKLIST ON THE ADEQUACY OF MIRANDA EVALUATIONS

Clinical issue	Standardized assessment	Case-specific methods
Intelligence	Individualized IQ test	N.A.
Verbal intelligence	Verbal IQ from testing	Clinical observations of verbal abilities
Vocabulary	IQ Vocabulary subtest	Verbatim report of *Miranda*-related words
Reading comprehension	Subtest of individualized achievement	Verbatim paraphrasing after reading the *Miranda* warning
Oral comprehension	Subtest of individualized achievement	Verbatim paraphrasing after oral presentation of *Miranda*
Verbal reasoning	IQ Comprehension subtest	Verbatim list of pros and cons for waiving *Miranda* rights
Psychopathology	Structured interview with severity ratings	Results of clinical interview covering Axis I diagnoses
Genuineness: Cognitive	Validated scales assessing effort	Clinical observations of defendant's effort
Genuineness: Psychological	Validated screens and SIRS	Clinical observations for possible malingering

As with most forensic evaluations, we recommend a "bottom-up" approach whereby forensic clinicians systematically each component of *Miranda* and subsequently integrate these results in drawing their conclusions. This approach systematizes the clinical data and minimizes halo effects and other biasing effects.

The decisional process involves the integration of standardized measures with case-specific methods. This integration combines the strengths of the respective approaches. Standardized measures provide reliable and quantifiable information about the defendant's abilities and functioning. Case-specific methods provide invaluable information about an individual defendant's capacity to understand a specific standard under particular circumstances. Ideally, a defendant's lack of oral understanding of the *Miranda* warning can be partially corroborated by his or her impaired oral comprehension. This multimethod approach offers the court the best-available information for reaching its determination.

Forensic clinicians are sometimes faced with disparate findings that require further investigation. For instance, a defendant with a superior vocabulary may exhibit difficulties understanding most of the *Miranda* words. Clearly, issues of effort and possible malingering must be examined. In contrast, some defendants may have a good understanding of *Miranda* vocabulary but relative poor vocabulary on IQ tests. One possibility would be an overlearning of *Miranda* words from frequent exposure via television and other media outlets. In keeping with the "totality" perspective, disparities must be evaluated in light of the defendant's overall appreciation of *Miranda*.

WARRANTLESS SEARCHES

Forensic clinicians should rely on the *clinical operationalization* of voluntariness in their determinations of a defendant's capacity to waive his or her rights. The first step in conducting these evaluations is a thorough assessment of the defendant's diagnosis and overall impairment in functioning. While not exhaustive, three clinical conditions that are may lead to involuntary agreement are enumerated:

1. *Substance-induced delirium*. In severe cases, the defendant has markedly reduced awareness of his or her surroundings and a diminished capacity to choose rationally. Some defendants may have little comprehension of either the risks (e.g., stashed drugs) or their choices.

2. *Severe psychotic disorders.* Some defendants with severe psychotic symptoms may be grossly impaired in their ability to choose. For some defendants, their entire focus involves psychotic symptomatology (e.g., imminent threats arising from paranoid delusions) that markedly impairs their choicefulness. In a few instances, the psychotic symptoms may override the capacity to choose. Examples include (1) command hallucinations that demand compliance with police's request to search, and (2) delusions of control that involve persons in authority taking charge of the patient's autonomy.

3. *Severe acquiescence associated with marked cognitive impairment.* Acquiescence, the willingness to agree irrespective of content, is sometimes observed among defendants with mental retardation (Gudjonnson, 1990). For defendants with limited intellectual abilities, acquiescence is comparatively easy to evaluate because it is typically a pervasive response style when faced with high-status interviewers (Heal & Sigelman, 1995).

In the absence of prevalence data, we surmise the substance-induced delirium has the most common occurrence but is rarely referred for a forensic consultation. For example, a severely impaired male driver with substance-induced delirium "consents" to a warrantless search of his vehicle. The defense counsel can only question his client's capacity to waive by presenting strong evidence *against* him on impaired driving charges. Of course, one possibility is that the defense counsel could raise the issue of an invalid waiver as part of a plea-bargaining strategy.

No specialized measures are available to assess directly the defendant's voluntariness. Therefore, the subsequent sections will address briefly standardized assessments and case-specific methods.

Standardized Assessments

Forensic clinicians should be able to screen a defendant effectively in deciding which areas of inquiry should be pursued. Such screening should address substance-induced delirium, severe psychotic disorders, and acquiescence associated with mental retardation. In some instance, additional diagnostic inquiry will be needed to address cognitive disorders, such as dementias, or to evaluate other severe mental disorders, such a major depression with delusions of guilt or dissociative disorders. This screening should combine the defendant's clinical presentation with collateral data (i.e., witnesses statements, arrest reports, and mental health records).

Substance abuse.   Substance abuse is difficult to assess because clients are often (1) deceptive about their drug use, (2) poor historians because of intoxication or delirium, and (3) simply unaware of the actual drugs and their potency (see Rogers & Kelly, 1997). One option is the administration of the Structured Clinical Interview of *DSM-IV* Disorders (SCID; First et al., 1997) which includes most Axis I disorders and has extensive coverage of alcohol and substance abuse disorders. This section of the SCID is divided into 8 major categories of substance abuse with a systematic review of as many as 15 clinical characteristics for each category. We strongly recommend that forensic clinicians obtain written permission from the defendant prior to the SCID administration for a collateral SCID, collecting data from a significant other about the defendant's substance abuse. Data suggest that simply the knowledge that corroboration is being sought may improve a substance abuser's forthrightness.

A second rarely used option is hair analysis as a laboratory-based method of assessing retrospective drug use. Because scalp hair grows approximately half inch every 30 days, analysis of longer hair can provide corroborative information about general drug use at discrete times in the past (Rogers & Shuman, 2000). Naturally, hair analysis cannot offer precise information about substance abuse at the time of the search.

Severe psychotic disorders.   As described before, the SADS provides an unmatched ability to assess some discrete period (e.g., time of the warrantless search), the severity of Axis I symptoms. While less detailed for psychotic symptoms, the SADS still provides comprehensive coverage of psychotic symptoms, including those rarely observed in clinical populations. This coverage has two advantages. First, it allows forensic clinicians to focus on both overall impairment (i.e., global functioning) and specific symptoms (e.g., delusions of control and thought insertion). Second, indices are available to assess whether malingering is likely to be a salient issue (Rogers, 1997).

Mental retardation.   As previously addressed, the WAIS-III is the best-standardized test of intellectual abilities. Other individually administered intelligence tests (e.g., the WASI) could be considered but are not recommended when mental retardation is suspected.

Acquiescence.   Winkler, Kanouse, and Ware (1982) developed the Acquiescence Response Set (ARS), a scale composed of 12 items that are logically opposite. The ARS is available in the Winkler et al. (1982) article.[6] In a large community sample, very few opposite responses were strongly endorsed with a mean of 1.48 ($SD = 1.55$). Its advantage is mainly

---

[6]These items should be randomly sorted before used clinically; they are rated on a 5-point scale from *strongly agree* to *strongly disagree*.

standardization, as well as relevant though limited research with defendants (Gudjonnson, 1990).

Case-Specific Methods

In most search-waiver cases, the critical threshold issue is a severe clinical condition or diagnosis. A recommended approach is to investigate diagnosis and impairment first, followed by a more detailed analysis of competency-related abilities.

Substance-induced delirium. The assessment of substance-induced delirium will be highly dependent on witnesses' accounts of the defendant at the time of the search. If the diagnosis is applicable, the defendant's account is likely to be poor and unreliable. As a complicating issue, defendant's efforts to remember what did occur is often distorted by others, such as witnesses' accounts or questions (e.g., "Do you remember laying down in the street?). Defendants with a detailed and accurate account are *not* likely to warrant the diagnosis of substance-induced delirium.

The usefulness of police reports varies substantially with their level of detail. They are likely to describe impaired behavior as initial justification for their intervention (e.g., erratic driving and slurred speech). However, the description of the consent is often cursory without any comments of the suspect's capacity. The ideal corroborative sources are persons observing the interactions who are both unimpaired and not the subject of police investigation. Unfortunately, most consent-to-searches are not witnessed by disinterested persons.

The strongest evidence of an invalid waiver is grossly disorganized, possibly disorientated, person whose capacity for purposeful behavior is very limited. A clear example would be an incapacitated person found on the sidewalk, unable to stand, whose responses to questions are mumbled sentences that are difficult to comprehend. Most cases are less clear and require inferences about choices and perceived options that are highly dependent on the accurate recall of witnesses.

Severe psychotic symptoms. The recommended format for retrospective assessments of Axis I symptoms is an unstructured account followed by standardized assessments and case-specific probes. As discussed more extensively with insanity evaluations (see Chapter 7), the defendant is encouraged to relate in as much detail as possible the events leading up to the interaction with police. Questions are asked about the defendant's actions, thoughts, and emotions. This unstructured account provides the framework for more detailed probes. In many cases, the account reveals no impairment by psychotic symptoms. In a few instances, the effects of severe psychotic symptoms on the waiver decision will require close examination. Issues related to voluntariness include the following:

- Did the defendant understand what was being asked? Did he or she have an appreciation of the potential consequences?
- Was the defendant overwhelmed by his or her psychotic symptoms to the extent that choice was not actively considered?
- Was the defendant directed by delusions of control, thought insertion, or command hallucinations to comply against his or her will?

Acquiescence in a cognitively impaired defendant.   The first step is the establishment of the substantial cognitive impairment, which is often mental retardation although cognitive disorders such as dementias must be ruled out. The main focus is to assess whether the defendant indiscriminantly assents to questions asked by persons of high status or authority. Finlay and Lyons (2001) have outlined three methods for directly assessing acquiescence in persons with mental retardation:

1. *Asking pairs of questions with an opposite meaning* (also referred to as "item-reversal techniques"). An example would be (a) "Do you like to spend most of your time with friends?" and (b) "Do you like to spend most of your time alone?"
2. *Asking pairs of questions with a similar meaning.* An example would be (a) "Do you enjoy your friends most of the time?" and (b) "Are you almost always happy when you are with your friends?"
3. *Asking nonsense questions.* An example would be, "Does the sun shine into your house at night time?"

Opposite-item pairs (#1) provide the clearest evidence of acquiescence (Gudjonnson, 2003). The strength of this approach is that it is adapted to different contents in demonstrating the persistence and pervasiveness of the acquiescence. For waivers (searches and *Miranda*), we recommend that forensic clinicians also use opposite-item pairs with leading questions. This variation likely parallels the methods used in police investigations. An example would be (a) "You're lying to us, aren't you?" and (b) "You wouldn't lie to us, would you?" These types of questions are likely to intensify the acquiescence because of their leading nature and increased complexity.

In addition to a general evaluation of acquiescence, we also recommend a specific assessment related to the police investigation. When the defendant has given a statement, one option is to turn the sentences in that statement into a series of leading questions. As a forensic example, a highly acquiescent male defendant with mild mental retardation was evaluated for his *Miranda* abilities. Using the statement as an outline, a series of questions, paralleling the defendant's own sentences, were asked that implicated the defendant. Examples include (a) "You were there that night, weren't you? (b) "You threw her to the ground didn't you?" and (c) "You raped her, didn't you? Later, a parallel set of leading questions were asked with opposite content. Examples include (a) "You weren't there that night, were you?" (b) "You have never pushed her to the ground, have you?" and (c) "You have never raped her, have you?" If additional data are needed, opposite pairs of leading questions can be asked about a fictitious crime (e.g., assaulting the city mayor).

Forensic Considerations

Criminal attorneys are provided with a checklist in Table 5-2 to evaluate the adequacy of the consent-to-search evaluations. They should realize that these consultations represent uncharted territory for most forensic clinicians. As a result, the methodology is less developed than most areas of forensic psychology and psychiatry.

The procedural rule that governs who must raise and who must prove what and what assumptions the courts make was stated succinctly by the Second Circuit Court of Appeals in *United States v. Downs-Moses* (2003, p. 267):

> A defendant may make a valid waiver of his rights under Miranda if he does so voluntarily, knowingly and intelligently. Miranda, 384 U.S. at 444; United States v. Palmer, 203 F.3d 55, 60 (1st Cir. 2000). The district court must begin with the presumption that the defendant did not waive his rights. Palmer, 203 F.3d at 60. The government bears the burden of proving a valid waiver by a preponderance of the evidence. See id.; United States v. Rosario-Diaz, 202 F.3d 54, 69 (1st Cir. 2000).

A common perception among law enforcement (Rogers, 2004) is that all or nearly all criminal defendants understand their *Miranda* warnings. This common misperception is reinforced by innumerable television dramatizations in which *Miranda* warnings are provided. Defense attorneys should be cognizant of this concern. Their goal is to overcome the frank skepticism, especially in cases involving substance-induced delirium and cognitively impaired acquiescence. In stark contrast, prosecutors will want to build on this skepticism by arguing that perpetrators are responsible for their decisions and should not be able to "take back" their choices. From a prosecutorial standpoint, it could be argued, "They chose to become intoxicated and now they want to be exempted from any responsibility."

Defense attorneys may wish to raise issues regarding the validity of warrantless searches for reasons beyond a favorable ruling. In bench trials, testimony about the defendant's capacity may have an ameliorative effect on the subsequent sentencing. In addition, some attorneys may view complicating factors such as consent-to-search as incentives for reaching a satisfactory agreement in plea-bargaining.

GENERAL CROSS-EXAMINATION ISSUES

In keeping with the *legal-empirical-forensic* model, attorneys should vigorously question experts who lack sufficient knowledge and understanding of the legal issue. Many forensic clinicians have not developed expertise for *Miranda* and competency to consent to search consultations. Attorneys must ensure that experts have an adequate knowledge base on their determinations. For example, does a particular forensic clinician have a firm understanding of *Miranda*? Model cross-examination questions for attorneys are presented in Box 5-2. The primary purpose of these questions is to test the expert's knowledge of the *Miranda* warning and rights. In particular, many defendants and possibly a few experts are unaware that their exercise of the right to silence cannot be used against them in subsequent proceedings. A secondary purpose is to influence and possibly persuade the court that a *Miranda* waiver is a legitimate issue, which deserves serious consideration. As noted, the commonsensical notion is that *everybody*, except possibly persons with mental retardation, must understand *Miranda*. These sample questions attempt to counteract this pervasive notion. As a possible gambit, some experts may not realize that the right to silence is protected; the objective of #5 would be to use the expert's mistaken understanding to impeach his or her credibility.

Box 5-2   General Cross-Examination Questions for *Miranda* Waivers

Knowledge of Miranda Warnings and Waivers
1. *What is your understanding of the Miranda warning in __ [county or jurisdiction]? . . . Can you tell it to us in your own words?*
2. [if states it verbatim] *Please tell us in your own words what it means to you.* [If the expert has trouble with this, it may signify that he or she has not thought carefully about its meaning and import.]
3. *Do all experts agree on this meaning for this particular Miranda warning?* [only valid answer is likely "don't know"] . . . *In your opinion, doctor, what would be some areas the other experts might disagree?* [if, "not sure"] . . . *Doctor, please take a minute to seriously consider this important issue. . . . Were you able to think of any areas of possible disagreement?*

(Continued)

---

4. *In the Miranda warning, it uses the word "exercise"* [substitute other language as appropriate]. *Could you define the word "exercise"? . . . What about the word "afforded"* [substitute other language as appropriate]; *could you define the word "afforded" for the jury?* [The judge may begin to pay close attention to these definitions; look signs of skepticism; if present, press for certainty] *. . . Doctor, are you winging these definitions or is this your firm understanding of these words? . . . So you are definite that others, such as the judge, would not disagree with you?*

5. [optional] *Doctor, what is meant to the "right to silence"? . . . Isn't it true that the courts will find out __ [the defendant] had something to hide? . . . So, is it your understanding that the prosecutor can bring this out at trial as evidence of guilt? . . . By the way, how did you assess the defendant's understanding about this? . . . How could __ [the defendant] make an intelligent waiver, if [he/she] believed they would be nailed whether they talked or not?*

Voluntary waivers

6. *Is it true, doctor, that waivers of Miranda rights must be voluntary? . . . [any equivocation] Isn't it true, doctor that the Supreme Court in the Miranda case requires that all Miranda waivers are voluntary?*

7. *What does the word "voluntary" in this setting?*

8. *Isn't it true that our participation in the courtroom is sometimes not voluntary? . . . For example, could you just leave the courtroom right now if you felt like it?*

9. *Even members of the jury are required to be here, aren't they? . . . Would it be fair to say that you don't have to be mentally ill to have your actions be involuntary?*

10. *Now the police station is different from the courtroom, wouldn't you agree?*

11. *Do most suspects wander into the police station on their own? . . . How do police officers "motivate" suspects to come into the police station? . . . Do some suspects come in handcuffed?*

12. *When they are being interrogated in an interrogation room, is that the thing they most want to be doing in the whole world? . . . Maybe the least thing? . . . Why don't they just leave?*

13. *Do you have any expertise whatsoever about why defendants confess? . . . What are some tactics used by the police to "motivate" persons to make statements against their own self-interest? . . . Is it legal for police to lie to persons being interrogated? . . . Is it done often? . . . Did it occur with this defendant?* [anything except a denial] *Based on your expertise, what would be likely things for the police to lie about?*

14. [denial] *You seem awfully confident in your opinion? . . . And you weren't there were you? . . . No videotape spanning custody to confession? . . . Any chance that your assertion is just wishful thinking?*

As with all forensic evaluations, attorneys bear a heavy responsibility to ensure that experts utilize well-validated methods in conducting their consultations. Tables 5-2 and 5-3 outline the important clinical issues and the methods (standardized and case-specific) for their assessments. Given that assessment of the capacity to waive both Fourth amendment and

TABLE 5-3. ATTORNEY'S CHECKLIST ON THE ADEQUACY OF CONSENT-TO-SEARCH EVALUATIONS

Clinical issue	Standardized assessment	Case-specific methods
Substance abuse disorder	SCID Substance Abuse module	Clinical and collateral interviews
Intoxication vs. delirium	N.A.	Witness interviews and police reports
Severe psychotic symptoms	SADS	Interviews focused on the effects of psychotic symptoms
Mental retardation	Individualized IQ test	Evidence of adaptive functioning
Dementia	MMSE and screens for dementia	Evaluate memory disturbances, especially capacity to assimilate new information, and decisional abilities
Acquiescence	ARS (optional)	Tailored interview systematically applying opposite-item pairs for general and crime-specific items

Note. N.A. = Not applicable.

Miranda rights are retrospective, multiple methods and multiple sources are essential. The strongest case for the adequacy of the assessment methods can be made when standardized methods and corroborative sources are convergent with case-specific information. The weakest case for the adequacy of the assessment methods occurs when the expert relies heavily on defendant's retrospective account. In its worst form, the expert engages in exorbitantly priced parroting of the defendant's words. The sample cross-examination, presented in Box 5-3, addresses an expert's overreliance on the defendant's account.

BOX 5-3   SAMPLE CROSS-EXAMINATION FOR UNSUBSTANTIATED OPINIONS REGARDING *MIRANDA* RIGHTS

Unsubstantiated Conclusions about an *Invalid* Waiver

1. *Doctor, who told you that* [he/she] *couldn't understand the Miranda warning?*
2. *Please tell the jury what is meant by a "self-serving" statement? . . .* [very optional] *If I told you that* [he/she] <u>*did*</u> *understand the Miranda warning, would you believe* <u>*me*</u>*? . . . Can you think of a reason why you would believe* [him/her] *over me, besides the fact his attorney is paying you and I am not?*
3. *When you interviewed the police officer interrogating __* [the defendant], *what was* [his/her] *conclusions? . . . Didn't bother to interview the police officer?*

(Continued)

4. *When you administered standardized tests to evaluate his intelligence, what did you find? ... Didn't bother with IQ testing either?*
5. *When you used structured interviews to evaluate his level of psychological impairment, what did you find? ... Didn't bother with structured interviews either?*
6. [very optional] *Doctor, would you prefer the term "slipshod" or "grossly deficient" to describe your evaluation?*

Unsubstantiated Conclusions about a *Valid* Waiver

7. *I believe it was your testimony on direct that __ [the defendant] gave a valid waiver of [his/her] right, is that correct? ... And you based this on your __ hour interview of the defendant and a written copy of his statement to police?*
8. *When did you complete your interview? ... When was the interrogation? ... So __ months transpired between the two, correct? ... Would you concede that a lot can happen in __ months?*
9. *Are you aware that __ [the defendant] told me [he/she] was __ [e.g., "very upset" or "hearing hallucinations"] at the time the statement? [should be "no"] ... Doctor, is that because you didn't even bother to contact me?*
10. *Are you aware of [his/her] psychiatric records? ... Did you bother to ask me about them? ... Isn't it true that might change your opinion in this case? ... [if quibbles] Aren't we all after the truth? ... [very optional] Even if it goes against who pays your check?*
11. [as needed, augment with Questions 3–6]

SUMMARY

Legal competencies related to police investigations are often overlooked in criminal trials. The adequacy of *Miranda* waivers dwarfs other psycholegal issues in terms of their widespread prevalence and potentially pivotal role with the subsequent verdict. This chapter outlines the key issues, legal and forensic, related to *Miranda* and warrantless searches. It provides a template for conducting waiver evaluations and cautions against the use of unvalidated measures, such as the GMI.

6

Competency to Stand Trial

Competency-to-stand-trial (CST) cases predominate forensic referrals in the criminal domain. Annually, estimates of competency referrals range from 50,000 (Skeem, Golding, Cohn, & Berge, 1998) to 60,000 (Bonnie & Grisso, 2000) with mental health issues arising in as many as 10–15% of criminal cases (Melton, Petrila, Poythress, & Slobogin, 1997). CST consultations enjoy two benefits often not present in other criminal consultations— the clarity of the legal standard and the existence of standardized assessment methods. The legal standard for competency to stand trial was articulated in the Supreme Court's decision in *Dusky v. United States* (1960; hereinafter *Dusky*) and the Court has not vacillated in its approach to CST since that time. In addition, the assessment methods for CST evaluations have been standardized and refined for more than four decades. Accordingly, CST consultations have benefited greatly from the consistency and uniformity of the relevant legal standard and the empirical research on its standardized assessment.

RELEVANT LEGAL STANDARD

THE FEDERAL STANDARD

Substantive Standards

Competency to stand trial (CST) is a central focus of forensic practice in the criminal justice system. Although CST does not directly address the defendant's culpability, it addresses constitutionally guaranteed rights that are essential to a fair and accurate assessment of culpability. As the Supreme Court articulated in *Riggins v. Nevada* (1992, pp. 139–140), "Competence to stand trial is rudimentary, for upon it depends the main part of those rights deemed essential to a fair trial, including the right to effective assistance of counsel, the rights to summon, to confront, and to cross-examine witnesses, and the right to testify on one's own behalf or to remain silent without penalty for doing so." The failure to raise or address CST is a common ground for appealing the conviction of an incompetent defendant; it is a violation of due process that can be raised at any stage of the proceedings (*Pate v. Robinson*, 1966). Although CST and the insanity defense both raise issues of the defendant's mental state, they differ in temporal frameworks and legal standards. Indeed, the "entry of a plea of not guilty by reason of insanity . . . presupposes that the defendant is competent to stand trial and to enter a plea" (*Medina v. California*, 1992, p. 449).

The denial of the constitutional rights implicated by the trial of an incompetent defendant arises from portions of the Federal Constitution that applies in federal and state court trials. Therefore, the legal focus of this chapter centers on federal court decisions interpreting and applying these constitutional rights. However, the states are permitted within the parameters of federal decisions to augment their state laws with additional criteria. Therefore, we also address several state variations with added CST requirements.

The primary source of the constitutional requirements for CST is a 1960 United States Supreme Court decision, *Dusky v. United States*. In a one-page opinion with no elaboration or explanation, the Court stated that the test for CST is whether the defendant "has sufficient present ability to consult with his lawyer with a reasonable degree of rational understanding—and whether he has a rational as well as factual understanding of the pro-ceedings against him" (p. 402). This test imposes several requirements that must be satisfied before finding a defendant competent to stand trial. Correlatively, failure to meet any requirement should result in finding the defendant not competent to stand trial.

Consult-with-counsel prong. The first prong, "whether he has suffi-cient present ability to consult with his lawyer with a reasonable degree of rational understanding," focuses on the defendant's present abilities to assist his or her lawyer. As explained in *Cooper v. Oklahoma* (1996) and *Godinez v. Moran* (1993), this prong requires that the defendant possess the situational awareness, capacity, and ability to assist in trial preparation, consideration of settlement options, acceptance or rejection of settlement options, and the trial itself. These cases arguably elaborate upon the definition of the accused's awareness of procedural rights found in *Dusky* and *Drope v. Missouri* (420 U.S. 163 [1974]). They address competency as involving the accused's ability to either participate in case settlement (i.e., a guilty plea) or trial with basic knowledge and understanding of trial procedures, procedural rights, and the substantive issues in the case at hand. For preparation, these capacities include (a) identifying sources of tangible evidence and witnesses, (b) identifying issues for the confrontation of adverse witnesses, and (c) providing information relevant to defenses (e.g., alibi or self-defense). In addition, at the time of trial, the capacity for decision-making requires that, in consultation with counsel, the defendant address such issues as whether to have the defendant testify (see *Riggins v. Nevada*, 1992).

The defendant's capacity to consult "with a reasonable degree of rational understanding" does not require an idealized intellectual capacity. The *Dusky* standard requires only a *reasonable* degree of rational understanding. The term, *reasonable*, is contextual in the law and requires that the circumstances be considered (*Yarborough v. Alvarado*, 2004). As described by Rogers and Mitchell (1991), the requisite level of rational understanding is generally greater for a complex crime (e.g., securities fraud) than a less complex crime (e.g., assault). For example, in *Morris v. Slappy* (1983), the Supreme Court rejected an argument that the Sixth Amendment guarantees a meaningful attorney client relationship, as it would fail to take into account the complete context of the case including the interests of the victim in undergoing another trial. The term, *reasonable*, is a relative, not an absolute judgment. The "defendant is entitled to a fair trial, but not necessarily to a perfect trial" (*State v. McClendon*, 1968, p. 425).

The temporal framework for *Dusky*'s consult with counsel is "sufficient present ability." Unlike criminal responsibility, which addresses *past* mental capacity, the test for CST addresses *present* mental capacity. A novice error in CST evaluations occurs when forensic clinicians broaden to temporal framework beyond the defendant's current abilities.

The consult-with-counsel prong of *Dusky* distinguishes *choice* to consult from *capacity* to consult in its focus on the defendant's "ability to consult with his lawyer." Only incapacity is germane to CST determinations with uncooperative defendants. Otherwise, defendants could delay indefinitely their trials by refusing to cooperate. For this reason, the courts are loathed to conclude that disruptive courtroom behavior is, by itself, proof of incompetency to stand trial (*United States v. Holmes*, 1987).

Factual and rational understanding prongs. The *Dusky* requirement, "whether he has a rational as well as factual understanding of the proceedings against him," has been construed as either two separate prongs (factual understanding and rational understanding) or a single prong combining both levels of understanding. Commentators are divided on the best conceptualization with those favoring two separate prongs (Grisso, 2003; Otto et al., 1998) and those relying on one encompassing prong (Melton et al., 1997; Shuman, 1996). The *Dusky* decision offers no further guidance on this point. As described under *Clinical Operationalization*, recent research by Rogers et al. (2003a) provides strong empirical support for the utility of conceptualizing *Dusky* as three prongs (i.e., factual understanding of the proceedings, rational understanding of the proceedings, and rational ability to consult with counsel). However, these data speak to the clinical practicalities and not to legal precedent.

The factual understanding prong is the easiest to articulate. Factual understanding addresses the defendant's basic knowledge of the courts and the proceedings. At its simplest level, does the defendant know about the role of judge, jury, prosecutor, and defense lawyer? Is he or she aware of the consequences of conviction? This level of knowledge is not envisioned as sophisticated understanding. Rather, it seeks to assess, whether the defendant, with assistance of counsel, can grasp his or her circumstances. "Not every manifestation of mental illness demonstrates incompetence to stand trial; rather, the evidence must indicate a present inability to assist counsel or understand the charges ... Likewise, neither low intelligence, mental deficiency, nor bizarre, volatile, and irrational behavior can be equated with mental incompetence to stand trial." *Burket v. Angelone* (2000, p. 192).

The rational understanding prong addresses the defendant's ability to have reality-based perceptions, thoughts and decisions regarding the legal process. In both *Cooper* and *Godinez*, the Court requires part of the reality-base to involve a basic, understanding of the procedures and a rational understanding of the current case. As a clear example, a criminal law professor was evaluated by one of the authors. While having outstanding factual knowledge plainly surpassing that of his evaluators, his rational understanding was compromised by delusional thinking centered on the judge and a larger conspiracy of attorneys. As with factual understanding, the requisite level of rational understanding is typically rudimentary. Many defendants make poor, emotionally based decisions that do not accurately capture the potential risks and benefits (Rogers, Tillbrook,

& Sewell, 2004). However, their basic abilities are not compromised by mental disorders. The lack of rational understanding in *Dusky* requires a major impairment of cognitive abilities arising from a mental disorder and defect.

Requisite mental condition. The *Dusky* test does not mention mental disorder in conjunction with its standard, let alone specify any type or severity of mental disorders as necessary in meeting the standard, although it is commonly assumed that a mental disorder will be the source of the problem. A defendant with substantial psychopathology but not warranting any particular diagnosis could be deemed incompetent. Conversely, no diagnoses can be equated with incompetency. Despite early misconceptions by testifying experts (Robey, 1965), the mere presence of a psychotic disorder cannot be accepted as presumptive evidence that the defendant is incompetent (*Burket v. Angelone*, 2000). Rather, the *Dusky* standard is based on functional abilities. It is concerned with the impairment and its specific effects on the defendant's competency-related capacities.

One form of mental impairment that has arisen frequently in CST cases is amnesia, especially amnesia for the time of the alleged offense. The courts (e.g., *United States v Villegas*, 1990) have resisted recognizing a *per se* rule that defendants suffering from amnesia are automatically incompetent. Instead, the effects of amnesia on the defendant's ability to consult with counsel is simply a factor to be taken into account in each case. As articulated in *United States v. Villegas* (1990, p. 1341), "Factors to be considered include whether the defendant has any ability to participate in his defense, whether the amnesia is temporary or permanent, whether the crime and the defendant's whereabouts at the time of the crime can be reconstructed without his testimony, whether the government's files will be of assistance in preparing the defense, and whether the government's case is strong or weak."

Procedural Standards

The case law has mandated a number of procedural rules governing CST determinations. Importantly, there is no requirement that all defendants be examined and found competent prior to trial. In the absence of evidence to the contrary, defendants are presumed competent to stand trial (*Medina v. California*, 1992). The state may require a defendant to bear the burden of proving incompetence to stand trial, but not by a higher standard of proof greater than the preponderance of the evidence (*Cooper v. Oklahoma*, 1996). Because the conviction of an incompetent defendant violates due process, the judge must conduct a hearing on the issue whenever the evidence raises a "bona fide doubt" about the defendant's competence, even if the issue is not raised by the defense lawyer or the prosecutor (*Pate v. Robinson*, 1966).

The consequences of being found incompetent to stand trial vary from jurisdiction to jurisdiction. A defendant in a federal criminal trial, found incompetent to stand trial, is subjected to commitment for up to 4 months. The statutory requirements (18 U.S.C.A. § 4241, 2003) are clearly set forth: "whether there is a substantial probability that in the foreseeable future he will attain the capacity to permit the trial to proceed" and thereafter "for an additional reasonable period of time until—(A) his mental condition is so improved that trial may proceed, if the court finds that there is a substantial probability that within such additional period of time he will attain the capacity to permit the trial to proceed; or (B) the pending charges against him are disposed of according to law; whichever is earlier." Although due process requires the suspension of criminal proceedings against an incompetent defendant until he or she regains competence, constraints are placed on both the types of treatment that may be imposed, and the length of time a defendant may be confined as incompetent.

In *Sell v. United States* (2003), the Supreme Court relied on its prior decisions in *Riggins v. Nevada* (1992) and *Washington v. Harper* (1990) and concluded that it is constitutionally permissible for the government to administer antipsychotic drugs to defendants against their will under certain conditions. Determinations must be made regarding whether (1) serious criminal charges are involved and that the proposed treatment (2) is medically appropriate, (3) is unlikely to have side effects that will threaten the fairness of the trial, (4) took into account less intrusive alternatives, and (5) is likely to advance government interests related to the trial. The court must first find that important governmental interests are at stake given the serious crime for which the defendant stands accused. Second, the court must find that involuntary administration of the medication will significantly further the government's interests by rendering the defendant competent to stand trial while at the same time unlikely to have side effects that will interfere with the defendant's ability to assist counsel. Third, the court must conclude that the administration of the drugs is in the defendant's best medical interest (i.e., medically appropriate).

In *Jackson v. Indiana* (1972), the United States Supreme Court addressed the length of time a defendant may be confined as incompetent to stand trial. It concluded that indefinite commitment of an incompetent defendant, under less restrictive standards than those applicable to civil commitment, was a violation of due process and equal protection of the laws under the Fourteenth Amendment. The Court held:

that a person charged by a State with a criminal offense who is committed solely on account of his incapacity to proceed to trial cannot be held more than the reasonable period of time necessary to determine whether there is a substantial probability that he will attain that capacity in the foreseeable future. If it is determined that this is not the case, then the State must either institute the customary civil commitment proceeding that would be required to commit indefinitely any other citizen, or release the defendant. (*Jackson v. Indiana*, 1972, p. 738)

The question of what constitutes a "reasonable period of time" for competency restoration has not yielded easy answers. As articulated in *United States v. Sahhar* (1995), the federal courts have rejected the argument that the maximum period of penalty, if convicted, constituted a "reasonable period of time." The Court of Appeals reasoned that this defendant may not be punished because he has not been convicted. Instead, the grounds for his continued confinement rests on his mental disorder and concomitant dangerousness.

State Law Augmentation

Substantive Standards

Because the United States Supreme Court established only a few constitutionally mandated requirements for the competency process, states through statutes and appellate opinions also have addressed substantive and procedural issues. Unlike *Dusky*, for example, the majority of state statutes have an explicit requirement that incompetence must result from a mental disorder or disability (Brakel et al., 1985). Beyond that general requirement, these statutes provide little assistance in identifying the requisite diagnosis or defect. They neither define nor delimit the type of mental disorder or defect that may be considered on the question of competence to stand trial. When the defendant is found not competent to stand trial and unlikely to be able to be restored to competence within a reasonable time, some states (e.g., Oklahoma, 2004) ask the fact finder to address whether the defendant meets the jurisdiction's criteria for civil commitment.

Other states have statutorily augmented the capacity required to be competent to stand trial. For example, Wyoming statutory law (2002) articulates that to be tried, sentenced, or punished, the defendant must possess the capacity to

1. comprehend his position;
2. understand the nature and object of the proceedings against him;

3. conduct his defense in a rational manner; and
4. cooperate with his counsel to the end that any available defense may be interposed.

These criteria do not add much to *Dusky's* requirements as they concretize them. For example, the statutory requirements that the defendant "comprehend his position" and "understand the proceedings against him" is simply a concrete way of asking the *Dusky* question "whether he has a rational as well as factual understanding of the proceedings against him." Similarly, asking about cooperating with counsel to interpose any available defense concretely addresses the *Dusky* prong for consult with counsel. It may have specific relevance in those infrequent cases where the defendant will not even consider a mental health defense because of his or her impaired insight. The third point (conduct his defense in a rational manner) captures the essence of the inquiry underlying competence to stand trial. "The rule in relation to trial for crime has been well stated in Corpus Juris Secundum, with the collection in the notes of many pertinent comments and authorities: 'The test of insanity of an accused precluding his being put on trial for a criminal offense is usually stated to be his capacity to understand the nature and object of the proceedings against him and to conduct his defense in a rational manner; and, if he passes this test, he may be tried, although on some other subjects his mind may be deranged or unsound.' 44 C.J.S. Insane Persons § 127, p. 284" (*Lee v. Wiman*, 1960, p.165).

Florida statutory law identifies the *Dusky* criteria as its standard for competence to stand trial and then identifies six components of the defendant's capacity that the examiner should consider and include in their report. The statute (Fla. Stat. Ann. § 916.12 [2004]) enumerates the following capacities:

1. Appreciate the charges or allegations against the defendant;
2. Appreciate the range and nature of possible penalties, if applicable, that may be imposed in the proceedings against the defendant;
3. Understand the adversarial nature of the legal process;
4. Disclose to counsel facts pertinent to the proceedings at issue;
5. Manifest appropriate courtroom behavior; and
6. Testify relevantly.

Many states have made no attempt to alter *Dusky's* substantive requirements in their legislative response to the decision (e.g., Cal. Pen. Code § 1367 [2004]; 50 Pa. Stat. Ann. § 7402 [2004]; Tex. Code Crim. Proc. art. 46B.003 [2004]). These statutes simply restate *Dusky's* language without explanation or commentary. In other states, case law provides some specification on how the *Dusky* criteria should be applied. In one of the most detailed list, a concurring opinion of a Nebraska Supreme Court Justice in *State v. Guatney* (1980, p. 545) suggested that the following factors be considered:

1. That the defendant has sufficient mental capacity to appreciate his presence in relation to time, place, and things;
2. That his elementary mental processes are such that he understands that he is in a court of law charged with a criminal offense;
3. That he realizes there is a judge on the bench;
4. That he understands that there is a prosecutor present who will try to convict him of a criminal charge;
5. That he has a lawyer who will undertake to defend him against the charge;
6. That he knows that he will be expected to tell his lawyer all he knows or remembers about the events involved in the alleged crime;
7. That he understands that there will be a jury present to pass upon evidence in determining his guilt or innocence;
8. That he has sufficient memory to relate answers to questions posed to him;
9. That he has established rapport with his lawyer;
10. That he can follow the testimony reasonably well;
11. That he has the ability to meet stresses without his rationality or judgment breaking down;
12. That he has at least minimal contact with reality;
13. That he has the minimum intelligence necessary to grasp the events taking place;
14. That he can confer coherently with some appreciation of proceedings;
15. That he can both give and receive advice from his attorneys;
16. That he can divulge facts without paranoid distress;
17. That he can decide upon a plea;
18. That he can testify, if necessary;
19. That he can make simple decisions; and
20. That he has a desire for justice rather than undeserved punishment.

Although cited with approval by other state courts, this list of suggestive factors was never formally adopted by the Nebraska Supreme Court.

The merits of an exhaustive listing of CST abilities could easily be debated, both because of its level of details and possible omissions. Nevertheless, the specific criteria articulated by either statute or case law should have a salutary effect in standardizing CST assessments and subsequent reports.

Procedural Standards

Two temporal benchmarks set important parameters for decision making concerning competency to stand trial—the length of time defendants may be committed to determine whether their competency is likely to be restored and, if so, the length of time they may be committed to restore their competency. The constitutional boundaries set by the Supreme Court in *Jackson v. Indiana* (1972, p. 738) articulated that a defendant could only be confined because of incompetence to stand trial for a "'reasonable period of time' necessary to determine whether there is a substantial chance of his attaining the capacity to stand trial in the foreseeable future" before civilly committing or releasing the defendant. This limitation, while binding on the states has been amplified by statutes in many states (Brakel et al., 1985). Some states limit the period of time that a defendant may be committed to restore competency to the maximum period the defendant could have been sentenced for the crime (Colo. Rev. Stat. 16-8-114.5 [2003]; 725 Ill. Comp. Stat.5/104-25 [2004]). Other states have chosen some arbitrary time such as 6 months (Ind. Code Ann. § 35-36-3-3 [2004]; Iowa Code § 812.5 [2003]).

Many states, like the previously cited federal statute, also limit the time period for the defendant's commitment to determine whether competency is likely to be restored. For example, Arizona limits this commitment to 30 days with the possibility of a 15-day extension for extraordinary circumstances (Ariz. Rev. Stat. § 13-4507 [2004]). Other states have longer commitments, such as 90 days in Indiana (Ind. Code Ann. § 35-36-3-3 [2004]) and 120 days in Texas (Tex. Code Crim. Proc. art. 46B.073 [2004]).

A fundamental question that has plagued the courts for many years is whether the standards of competence to waive constitutional rights standard differs depending on the particular constitutional right. For example, a waiver of the right to counsel leaves a criminal defendant without legal guidance. Therefore, should more intelligence or capacity be required to waive this right than is necessary to stand trial with the benefit of counsel? In *Godinez v. Moran* (1993), the U.S. Supreme Court addressed whether the standard for competence to enter a guilty plea or waive counsel is higher than the standard for competence to stand trial. The Court rejected the argument that competence to plead guilty or waive counsel should be measured by a higher or different standard than the standard for competence to stand trial. After making this determination, the Court proceeded to examine whether there should be any differences in this assessment and noted that there are differences:

> A finding that a defendant is competent to stand trial, however, is not all that is necessary before he may be permitted to plead guilty or waive his right to counsel. In addition to determining that a defendant who seeks to plead guilty

> or waive counsel is competent, a trial court must satisfy itself that the waiver
> of his constitutional rights is knowing and voluntary ... In this sense there is a
> "heightened" standard for pleading guilty and for waiving the right to counsel,
> but it is not a heightened standard of competence. (*Godinez v. Moran*, 1993, p. 401)

This ruling by the Supreme Court requires that the trial court engage in an additional set of inquires for assessing waiver of the right to counsel beyond those inquiries required to assess competency to stand trial. In particular, the trial court must address whether the waiver of counsel is an uncoerced decision based on accurate information. The Supreme Court in *Godinez* (1993, p. 401) observed that: "The purpose of the 'knowing and voluntary' inquiry, by contrast, is to determine whether the defendant actually does understand the significance and consequences of a particular decision and whether the decision is uncoerced." Where these competencies are at issue, the trial court must consider not only the defendant's intelligence but also the defendant's grasp of the implications of the specific right sought to be waived (e.g., How will a guilty plea change the process and affect the likelihood and length of confinement?) and the existence of coercion affecting his or her decision.

CLINICAL OPERATIONALIZATION
OF THE COMPETENCY STANDARD

Rogers, Jackson, Sewell, Tillbrook, and Martin (2003) differentiated between models that extend beyond legal requirements of *Dusky* and its progeny (i.e., *extrapolated* models) from those that focused specifically on the legal criteria (i.e., *explicit* models). *Extrapolated* models provide theoretically interesting hypotheses regarding extralegal modifications of the CST criteria. For example, Bonnie (1992, 1993) provides his own conceptualization of competency that encompasses elaborate hypotheses about decisional capacities extending well beyond the *Dusky* standard. Other commentators have focused on broadly construed volitional abilities (Miller, 2003) and general capacity to communicate effectively (Abrams, 2002). Because extrapolated models extend beyond the legally relevant criteria, they will not be examined here further.

Rogers (2001; Rogers, Tillbrook, & Sewell, 2004) described three *explicit* models for operationalizing the *Dusky* Standard. These models (Discrete Abilities, Competency Domains, and Cognitive Complexity) are outlined below.

The *Discrete-Abilities* model divides the *Dusky* standard into three separate though related prongs: (a) factual understanding of the proceedings, (b) rational understanding of the proceedings, and (c) rational ability to consult with counsel. Early efforts (e.g., Grisso, 1986; Roesch & Golding, 1988) simply enumerated specific abilities without attempting to address particular *Dusky* prongs. More recently, clinical investigators (e.g., Grisso, 2003; Otto et al., 1998; Rogers, Grandjean, Tillbrook, Vitacco, & Sewell, 2001) have utilized the three prongs of *Dusky* as separate components in their research and development of forensic measures. A major advantage of the *Discrete-Abilities* model is that forensic clinicians do not lose specificity in their evaluation of a defendant's particular capacities and incapacities.

The *Competency-Domains* model has been favored by prominent legal commentators including Melton et al. (1997) and Shuman (1996). Syntactically, the *Dusky* standard uses hyphenation to divide the ability to consult with counsel from factual and rational understanding of the proceedings. Conceptually, the ability to relate meaningfully to a defense counsel appears to be a different domain than the defendant's understanding of the proceedings. The "ability to consult" is clearly an interpersonal and interactive capacity. In contrast, factual and rational understanding has much more of an individual focus on the particular trial and its options.

The *Cognitive-Complexity* model capitalizes on the level of reasoning and rational ability required by each prong. Two prongs (i.e., rational understanding of the proceedings and rational ability to consult with counsel) require complex cognitive abilities entailing perceptions, judgments, and decisions. In direct contrast, factual understanding typically involves the simple recall of overlearned material (i.e., semantic memory), such at the role of the judge. Rogers et al. (2001) found some initial support for the cognitive complexity model.

Rogers et al. (2003) systematically tested the three competing models via confirmatory factor analysis. For this purpose, they used the Evaluation of Competency to Stand Trial—Revised (ECST-R; Rogers, Tillbrook, & Sewell, 1998, 2004) because of its sophisticated scale development. Specifically, the ECST-R items were developed specifically to assess the *Dusky* prongs; their representativeness of individual prongs was formally tested via prototypical analysis using recognized experts.

In operationalizing the *Dusky* standard, what model should forensic clinicians use? The key findings from Rogers et al. (2003) are outlined:

- The *Discrete-Abilities* model with three separate but related prongs was the strongest model. Its robust comparative fit index of .90 met the benchmark for relative fit indices (Dunn, Everitt, & Pickles, 1993) with evidence of good fit on the Standardized Root Means Square Residual (SRMR = .06).
- The *Competency-Domains* model evidenced the poorest fit (e.g., RCFI = .79) that was substantially worse ($\chi^2_{change}[1] = 105.50$, $p < .01$)

than the *Cognitive-Complexity* model (e.g., RCFI = .86). However, neither model demonstrated an adequate fit even when multivariate recommendations were followed.

CLINICAL ISSUES

The current data are clear: *Forensic clinicians should consider each prong of Dusky separately.* The next issue is ensuring adequate clinical coverage of each prong in the forensic assessment. Based on the prototypical analysis by Rogers, Tillbrook, and Sewell (2004), Table 6-1 summarizes the most prototypical criteria for each prong. The next subsections focus on each *Dusky* prong separately.

TABLE 6-1. WHAT FORENSIC CLINICIANS NEED TO ADDRESS: A PROTOTYPICAL ANALYSIS OF THE DUSKY PRONGS

Rating	Prototypical items	A sampling of clinical considerations
Consult with Counsel		
6.60	Inability to communicate one's thoughts coherently	Formal thought disorder, disturbances of speech, incoherence
6.60	Inability to participate in one's defense	Lack of autonomous thoughts (e.g., thought insertion or withdrawal) and self-destructive motivation (e.g., delusions of guilt)
6.00	Incapacity to make decisions	Cannot describe or recognize alternatives and severely impaired decisions (e.g., psychotic interference)
5.40	Expectations about the case and defense counsel	Psychotically based expectations
Factual Understanding of the Proceedings		
6.60	Lack of understanding of the defense counsel's role	Unaware of counsel's efforts to help the defendant and minimize punishment
6.00	Lack of understanding of judge's role	Unaware of judge's role in running the court, verdicts, and sentencing
5.60	Lack of understanding of his or her criminal charges	Unaware of the seriousness of the charges and possible penalties

(Continued)

TABLE 6-1. CONTINUED

Rating	Prototypical items	A sampling of clinical considerations
5.40	Lack of understanding of the prosecutor's role	Unaware of prosecutor's role in bringing charges, guilty verdicts, or maximizing punishment
5.40	Lack of understanding of the jury's role	Unaware of jury's role regarding verdict and possible sentencing
5.20	Lack of understanding of the courtroom process	Unaware of trial process (e.g., opening statements, evidence, and jury deliberation)
Rational Understanding of the Proceedings		
7.00	Inability to rationally participate in defense	Unaware of possible defense strategies; participation influenced by psychotic symptoms or motivated by self-harm
6.80	Lack of awareness of his or her involvement as the defendant	Denial of being a defendant; denial of the possibility of being found guilty and sentenced
6.40	Lack of understanding of the adversarial process	Inability to understand conflicting roles between prosecution and defense
6.00	Lack of investment in the trial's outcome	Uninterested in the verdict; cannot grasp its potential consequences
5.60	Self-defeating motivation	Potentially interested in sabotaging case

Consult Prong

The ability to consult with counsel can be conceptualized as three prototypic items that are summarized succinctly as brief inquiries. First, can the defendant communicate understandably and rationally? Second, does the defendant operate as an autonomous person motivated by self-interest? Third, does the defendant have a reality-based working relationship with his or her attorney?

The most prototypic item for the consult prong addresses the defendant's basic capacity to communicate coherently. This essential ability constitutes the necessary prerequisite to all rational communications. Based on structured or unstructured interviews, forensic clinicians can ascertain the defendant's ability to communicate his or her thoughts clearly. Clinicians may wish to evaluate two facets of these communications:

- *Is the defendant generally coherent, i.e., able to make meaningful statements that are related to the interviewer's questions and comments?*
- *Does the defendant have selective intrusions on this coherence, such as ideas of reference or neologisms, that impair communication?*

The second most prototypic item considers whether the defendant can rationally participate in his or her defense. One clinical issue overrides all others in establishing this rational participation: *Is the defendant an autonomous individual acting out of self-interest?* As the product of psychotic symptoms, the defendant's thoughts may be experienced as alien and external. Salient examples include "thought insertion" and "thought extraction," whereby the defendant experiences his or her thoughts as being fundamentally altered by some external force. More commonly, defendants may experience delusions or command hallucinations that compromise rational participation. Affectively, severe depression occasionally leads to self-destructive motivation, thereby altering the defendant's capacity to act in his or her self-interest.

The third prototypical item addresses the interpersonal dimensions of the consult-with-counsel prong. What is the defendant's understanding and expectations about his or her attorney? What does the defendant believe the attorney expects of him or her? The capacity to develop mutually agreed-upon goals is essential to a working attorney–client relationship. Examples of clinical issues include the following:

- *Does the defendant have a marked distrust of the attorney to the extent that it impairs their working relationship?*
- *Does the defendant idealize his or her attorney to the extent that the defendant is unconcerned about trial, believing its positive outcome is virtually assured?*
- *Does the defendant grossly misperceive the defense counsel as derogating the defendant to the point that trying to participate in his or her defense appears to be a futile exercise?*

A crucial determination is whether the working relationship between the attorney and the defendant has been substantially compromised by any of the following prototypic items: (a) grossly impaired communication, (b) the defendant's lack of autonomy and self-interest, or (c) markedly distorted expectations of the attorney. One litmus test of a working relationship is the capacity for consensus through discussion. Simply put, *Can the defendant reach a shared understanding with his or her attorney about important aspects of the case?* A critical distinction must be made between consensus and capitulation. Consensus building recognizes areas of agreement and disagreement, and attempts to establish an optimal course of action toward a common goal. With capitulation, the defendant simply accedes to the attorney's ideas.

Factual-Understanding Prong

The *factual understanding of the proceedings* requires a simple recall or recognition of basic courtroom roles. With the exception of criminal charges, most facets of factual understanding require general information that is not specific to the defendant's case. The most prototypic item addressed the defendant's ability to understanding the purpose and duties of the defense counsel. Without this rudimentary understanding, the defendant's capacity to participate in the proceedings is negated. The key issue is summarized: *Is the defendant aware that the defense counsel is trying to help him or her?*

Other prototypical items address the roles and responsibilities of other positions in courtroom proceedings and trials, such as the judge, prosecutor, and jury. Informing these roles is the defendant's appreciation of the adversarial system. Naive defendants often make erroneous assumptions about the potential helpfulness of the prosecutor and the judge. They do not realize that the prosecutor's role is typically opposite the defendants' own self-interests and that judges aspire to impartiality (i.e., disinterest) in the cases before them. In contrast, jaundiced defendants may develop a markedly cynical view toward all participants in the legal system. For the purposes of factual understanding, the key issue is whether the defendant understands the expected roles (e.g., What is the judge *supposed* to do?). The discrete abilities can be summarized as follows, *"Does the defendant understand the roles and responsibilities of key persons (i.e., prosecutor, judge, and jury) in the courtroom?"*

The criminal charges and to a lesser extent the courtroom processes relate to the defendant's particular case. Obviously, the defendant must have a basic understanding about his or her charges. In some instances, the defendant faces many charges and may understandably be aware of only the more serious offenses (e.g., murder) with little interest in relatively minor crimes (e.g., marijuana possession). Simply put, *"Does the defendant understand the major charges against him or her?* The courtroom process is often shaped by the type of criminal charges and the defense strategy. Forensic clinicians must be careful about possible intrusions on privileged communications with the client and his or her defense counsel.

Rational-Understanding Prong

A rational understanding of the legal proceedings extends beyond factual understanding to a consideration of alternatives and reasoned choices. Such choices include an awareness of his or her basic procedural rights (e.g., trial, plead guilty, call witnesses, and testify). The most prototypical item is the defendant's basic capacity to decide. Basic alternatives, common to most trials, include method of resolution (trial vs. plea bargaining) and type of trial (bench vs. jury). The key issues are

- *Is the defendant aware of his or her basic choices?*
- *Can the defendant articulate some reasons for how he or she may decide?*

Most important decisions, including those by defendants, are not subjected to a formal cost–benefit analysis. Consequently, forensic clinicians do not weigh closely the quality of the defendant's reasoning. Rather, they consider whether important decisions are grossly irrational and thereby impaired.

Several prototypical items involve the defendant's recognition of his or her personal role in the proceedings and their potential consequences. Simply put, *Does the defendant know he or she is on trial?* Also, the defendant's investment in the outcome of the trial must also be considered, including the possibility of sabotaging his or her defense. Several important considerations are outlined:

- *Does the defendant understand the gravity of the case and the potential consequences of a conviction?*
- *Is the defendant motivated to be found guilty?*

A final prototypical issue for rational understanding is a clear appreciation of adversarial process. In making decisions, is the defendant clear about the adversarial process. If the defendant views the prosecutor on his or her side, then the decisional process may be compromised. In other words, *"Does the defendant appreciate his or her need to work with the defense counsel against the efforts of the prosecutor?"*

Summary

As summarized in Table 6-1, forensic clinicians must consider individually the clinical issues associated with each *Dusky* prong. Importantly, this prototypical analysis covers the key issues but is, by no means, exhaustive. In evaluating competency to stand trial, the next section addresses traditional interviews and standardized (i.e., measure-based) evaluations.

FORENSIC ASSESSMENT METHODS

Traditional interviews should be a component of every competency evaluation because of their versatility in assessing unique aspects of the individual defendant in the context of his or her particular circumstances. Such case-specific information cannot be achieved by standardized evaluations. In most cases, standardized evaluations provide a systematic appraisal of the defendant's functioning on competency-relevant issues. These methods complement each other with their respective strengths, i.e., the versatility of traditional interviews and validation of standardized methods. *As a general guideline, forensic clinicians should consider the integration of both clinical interviews and standardized assessment as the recommended standard of practice.*

Traditional Interviews

The format for traditional interviews is likely to move from general impairment to specific competency-related abilities. Following the initial notification of the defendant regarding the competency evaluation, many forensic clinicians prefer to gather very brief background data about the defendant's past, especially his or her history of mental disorders and interventions. As a caution, psychosocial history is, at best, only peripheral to the current, cross-sectional assessment of competency to stand trial. Importantly, past information may be irrelevant to the referral issue and represent an ethical violation in its unnecessary invasion of privacy (Ethical Standard 4.04, Minimizing Intrusions on Privacy; American Psychological Association, 2002, downloaded via http://www.apa.org/ethics/). Moreover, this past information potentially has a prejudicial rather than probative effect on the triers of fact.

The first major goal of traditional interviews is the assessment of the defendant's diagnosis and impairment. The purpose of diagnosis is to provide structure and organization to the clinical assessment. Specifically, it assures that the major components of psychotic, mood, and others disorders are not overlooked. Our preference is that *DSM-IV* multiaxial diagnoses are established first to ensure adequate coverage, followed by an assessment of impairment. Impairment takes into account the debilitating effects of symptoms, syndromes, and disorders. The Global Assessment Functioning (GAF; American Psychiatric Association, 2000) provides an initial estimation of the defendant's functioning. In competency cases, the forensic clinician will want to examine the defendant's psychological functioning in more detail regarding his or her ability to communicate, make decisions, and establish relationships.

The second major goal is the assessment of the defendant's response style. While a primary interest is whether the defendant is feigning his or her disorders/impairment, forensic clinicians must also consider that some defendants may wish to limit their contact with mental health professionals. In doing so, they may attempt to minimize the severity of their disorders and even deny current episodes. Therefore, traditional interviews should consider both malingering and defensiveness as possible response styles. As noted in Chapter 2, malingering must be established by validated methods and never be simply inferred by oddities in the defendant's clinical presentation.

The third major goal is systematically evaluating the defendant's competency-related abilities for each *Dusky* prong. The particular challenge for traditional interviews is found with the marginal cases, especially those cases where the defendants have severe mental disorders but their effects on competency-related abilities are either mixed or unclear. Forensic clinicians must be able to consider the various clinical issues associated with each prong and evaluate them comprehensively. Box 6-1 summarizes the critical considerations from the previous section, Clinical Issues. For clinicians relying predominantly on traditional interviews, Grisso's (1988) monograph provides some useful guidelines.

BOX 6-1   CRITICAL CLINICAL ISSUES IN EVALUATING THE DUSKY PRONGS
FOR COMPETENCY TO STAND TRIAL

These issues, presented in the text, are summarized here for forensic clinicians and attorneys. Forensic clinicians can use them to guide their CST evaluations. Attorneys can use them to systematically evaluate the comprehensiveness of the competency evaluation. In questioning the adequacy of the evaluation, an attorney can simply ask, *"Where in your report did you address ..."*

Consult with Counsel Prong
1. Is the defendant generally coherent, i.e., able to make meaningful statements that are related to the interviewer's questions and comments?
2. Does the defendant have selective intrusions on this coherence, such as ideas of reference or neologisms, that impair communication?
3. Is the defendant an autonomous individual acting out of self-interest?
4. Does the defendant have a marked distrust of the attorney to the extent that it impairs their working relationship?
5. Does the defendant idealize his or her attorney to the extent that the defendant is unconcerned about trial, believing its positive outcome is virtually assured?

(Continued)

6. Does the defendant grossly misperceive the defense counsel as derogating the defendant to the point that trying to participate in his or her defense appears to be a futile exercise?
7. Can the defendant reach a shared understanding with his or her attorney about important aspects of the case?

Factual Understanding Prong

8. Is the defendant aware that the defense counsel is trying to help him or her?
9. Does the defendant understand the roles and responsibilities of key persons (i.e., prosecutor, judge, and jury) in the courtroom?
10. Does the defendant understand the major charges against him or her?

Rational Understanding Prong

11. Is the defendant aware of his or her basic choices?
12. Can the defendant articulate some reasons for how he or she may decide?
13. Does the defendant know he or she is on trial?
14. Does the defendant understand the gravity of the case and the potential consequences of a conviction?
15. Is the defendant motivated to be found guilty?
16. Does the defendant appreciate his or her need to work with the defense counsel against the efforts of the prosecutor?

The assessment of consult-with-counsel prong of *Dusky* is particularly challenging. Many forensic clinicians formulate their opinions on the basis of the typical attorney. This approach has merit when the defendant is clearly competent or incompetent. In marginal cases, consideration should be given to inviting the defense counsel to participate in part of the competency evaluation. Such participation provides the expert with first-hand knowledge of the attorney–client relationship and capacity for reality-based communications.

Our major concern, especially in marginal cases, is that some forensic clinicians have a tendency to "hit the highlights" and not investigate thoroughly different elements of rational abilities. Please note that the critical issues in Box 6-1 are comprehensive but not exhaustive. On a case-by-case basis, other competency issues may be especially salient. The careful coverage of rational abilities is essential, as related specifically to the defense counsel and more generally to a reality-based appreciation of the proceedings.

In summary, all competency evaluations use traditional interviews as a critical component of their assessment. Traditional interviews provide versatility in evaluating case-specific information about a particular defendant, and his or her current situation. We recommend that traditional interviews be used in conjunction with (a) structured interviews (see Rogers, 2001) for reliable diagnostic information plus (b) forensic measures for standardized assessment of competency-related abilities. The next section examines forensic measures designed specifically for CST referrals.

Specialized Methods

Grisso (2003) provides comprehensive coverage of the major CST measures with the exception of Evaluation of Competency to Stand Trial—Revised (ECST-R; Rogers et al., 2004), which was published too recently to be included. In this section, we provide a distilled review of the main CST measures as an easy-to-use reference for forensic clinicians and criminal attorneys. Table 6-2 provides a useful overview of CST measures with general information about their formats and coverages. Nearly all CST measures favor an interview-based rather than written format. Interview-based approaches have two main advantages. First, they minimize problems with reading comprehension and potential confusion in the defendant's recording of his or her responses. Second, they allow forensic clinicians to ask follow-up inquiries to clarify the defendant's responses. Because of these advantages, we recommend the use of interview-based CST measures.

The coverage across CST measures varies dramatically. As noted in Table 6-2, CST measures differ remarkably in whether they explicitly address individual *Dusky* prongs and in the extent of that coverage. Even when CST items are designated for evaluating a particular prong, their content warrants close scrutiny. For example, the Georgia Court Competency Test (GCCT; Johnson & Mullett, 1987) has three items for addressing Consult with Counsel, yet two of these items are too rudimentary (i.e., the attorney's name and contact information) to be useful. By the same token, the MacArthur Competence Assessment Tool—Criminal Adjudication (MacCAT-CA; Poythress et al., 1999) has eight items designated for the consult-with-counsel prong, but coverage of the attorney–client relationship and the defendant's capacity to communicate is marginal at best. Specifically, these items are not relevant to the defendant's own attorney. They do not address (1) the nature of their attorney–client relationship, or (2) the defendant's perceptions or possible delusions about his or attorney or (3) the defendant's ability to communicate ideas to this attorney about pending case. Problems with CST coverage are especially concerning when counsel is having problems relating to the defendant but a particular CST measure does not reveal any appreciable impairment.

The next critical step in selecting CST measures is deciding on their purpose (screening vs. evaluation) and investigating their validation. For screening purposes, two measures should be considered: the Lipsett's

TABLE 6-2. DESCRIPTIVE CHARACTERISTICS OF COMPETENCY MEASURES

Measure	Items	Format	Ratings	Coverage			Description
				Con	Fac	Rat	
L-CST	22	Written	0–2	6a	13a	2a	Incomplete sentences that were intended as a screen
CAI	13	Interview[a]	1–5	3a	4a	6a	Individual ratings of specific competency-related abilities
GCCT	21[b]	Interview	Vary	3	16a	1a	Rapid interview of key competency issues
CAST-MR	50	Interview[c]	0–1	4h	25	15	Interview for mentally challenged defendants with definitions, hypotheticals, and current case
FIT-R	16[d]	Interview	0–2	7	6	3	Interview, derived from the CAI, is focused on the Canadian standard
Mac-CAT-CA	22	Interview	0–2	8h	8h	6	Interview based primarily on a hypothetical assault in a pool hall
ECST-R	21[e]	Interview	0–4	6	6	9	Interview based on the *Dusky* prongs and augmented with feigning items

Note: Con = consult with counsel; Fac = factual understanding of the proceedings; Rat = rational understanding of the proceedings. For measures, L-CST = Lipsett et al. Competency Screening Test; CAI = Competency Assessment Instrument; GCCT = Georgia Court Competency Test; CAST-MR = Competence Assessment for Standing Trial for Defendants with Mental Retardation; FIT-R = Fitness Interview Test—Revised; Mac-CAT-CA = MacArthur Competence Assessment Tool—Criminal Adjudication; ECST-R = Evaluation of Competency to Stand Trial—Revised. For ratings, a = assumed; h = hypothetical unrelated to the defendant's case.
[a]Sample interview questions are provided but not required for the CAI.
[b]An 8-item screen for feigning was subsequently added.
[c]Questions and multiple-choice alternatives are also presented in written form.
[d]Seventy-four questions are used to derive ratings on the 16 items.
[e]For competency alone; additional items as used as a screen for feigning.

Competency Screening Test (L-CST[1]; Lipsett, Lelos, & McGarry, 1971) and the Georgia Court Competency Test (GCCT; Johnson & Mullett, 1987). The L-CST is historically important as the first standardized approach to CST.

[1]Because we used CST for "Competency to Stand Trial," we modified the original acronym (CST) by adding its senior author, Lipsett (i.e., L-CST).

As noted by Grisso (2003), the L-CST does not attempt to assess case-specific information, limiting its usefulness in forensic practice. The GCCT provides brief coverage of competency-related issues and includes a simple screen for possible feigning (Gothard, Rogers, & Sewell, 1995). Regarding its construct validity, research has failed to establish stable factors that are congruent with the *Dusky* standard. In choosing between the L-CST and the GCCT, the latter has substantially more research, provides case-specific information, and screens for possible feigning. Therefore, we recommend the GCCT as a screening measure that can be used in high-volume settings to identify CST cases requiring full evaluations.

Three CST measures are commonly used in American jurisdictions: (1) the Competency to Stand Trial Assessment Instrument (CAI; McGarry & Curran, 1973); (2) MacArthur Competence Assessment Tool—Criminal Adjudication (Mac-CAT-CA; Poythress et al., 1999); and (3) Evaluation of Competency to Stand Trial—Revised (ECST-R; Rogers et al., 2004). A fourth measure is sometimes used with mentally retarded defendants: Competence Assessment for Standing Trial for Defendants with Mental Retardation (CAST-MR; Everington & Luckasson, 1992). The psychometric properties of these measures will be evaluated.

CAI. The CAI was built on a model that varies slightly from *Dusky* standard. Its three basic components include cooperation with counsel, understanding the nature and quality of the proceedings, and understanding the consequences of the proceedings. The CAI de-emphasizes *Dusky*'s requirement of active participation (i.e., "cooperate" vs. "assist") and rational understanding (i.e., "nature and quality" being only one element). The CAI is composed of 13 rationally derived functions that are intended to assess three basic components. In Grisso's (2003) review, he notes that the CAI offers a "conceptual tool" (p. 128) but does not have the status of an instrument.

The CAI continues to be used by a surprising number of forensic clinicians. We have seen a "revised version," referred to as the "CAI-R," used occasionally in forensic practice. Importantly, this so-called revision has not been validated and is not recognized in recent scholarly reviews (Grisso, 2003; Stafford, 2003). Attorneys should observe that the CAI was not intended as a formal psychological measure and that its research has largely been limited to early studies. Consistent with its original purpose, we recommend its use as a general outline of relevant issues. If the CAI (or CAI-R) is misrepresented as a formal measure, then forensic clinicians are vulnerable to vigorous cross-examination on both *Daubert* and ethical grounds.

Mac-CAT-CA. The Mac-CAT-CA was originally part of a large research program that was intended to operationalize Bonnie's (1992, 1993; Bonnie et al., 1997) theory of legal competence. Bonnie's elaborate theory is substantively different from the *Dusky* standard. Therefore, subsequent efforts to retrofit the MacArthur data to the *Dusky* standard faced formidable challenges. As a concrete example, *Dusky* requires the defendant's incapacities as they relate to his or her *own* case; the Mac-CAT-CA relies heavily on hypothetical data that is immaterial to the defendant's case.

Rogers (2001) critically reviewed the MacCAT-CA and its usefulness in CST evaluations. Its primary strength lies in its ability to assess the rational-understanding prong. While not eliciting case-specific information, it poses useful questions to evaluate the whether the defendant's reasoning is reality-based. However, this review also underscored three fundamental limitations:

- The consult-with-counsel prong is poorly represented on the Reasoning Scale, which has no items addressing the attorney–client relationship or their ability to communicate with each other. Without considering their own attorney–client relationship or their own circumstances, defendants are asked to complete two cognitive tasks based entirely on a hypothetical case: (a) differentiate relevant from irrelevant information (five items), and (b) make decisions about plea bargaining (three items).
- The factual-understanding prong does not address the defendant's case, trier of fact, criminal charges, type of trial (bench or jury), or likely sentences. Rather than questions about the defendant's own pending charges, he or she is asked about an alleged assault. It is of considerable significance that the *defendant is discouraged from describing his or her own personal case* (see Poythress et al., 1999, p. 11, under "personalization/editorializing").
- The complexity of the hypothetical data militates against an accurate appraisal of the defendant's competency-related abilities. For example, Item 14 assumes the defendant has rapidly assimilated hypothetical data; it presents the defendant verbally with a 30-word dilemma, two lengthy alternatives of 57 and 66 words respectively, and a 39-word summary/question.

In conclusion, the MacCAT-CA is a reliable measure and extensive normative data. As noted, its practical usefulness for assessing CST cases is limited by its lack of congruence with the *Dusky* standard, its hypothetical extrapolations, and its unnecessary complexity. However, the MacCAT-CA does provide useful information in cases where questions arise about the rational-understanding prong.

ECST-R.   The ECST-R (Rogers et al., 2004) was designed to address key elements of the *Dusky* standard. The ECST-R items were carefully constructed based on a prototypical analysis of the *Dusky* prongs. To maximize comprehension with impaired defendants, competency items worded simply and average 7.67 words per question. The simple wording is understandable by many defendants with limited cognitive functioning (Tillbrook, 1997). Its three competency scales correspond to the *Dusky* with strong empirical support via a confirmatory factor analysis (Rogers et al., 2003). In addition to its construct validation, criterion-related validity has been demonstrated with independent experts, the MacCAT-CA, and clinical impairment on the SADS-C (see Rogers et al., 2004).

The ECST-R is distinguished from other competency measures by its addition of multiple scales that screen for feigned incompetency. These scales employ multiple detection strategies and yield effective utility estimates (see Rogers, Jackson, Sewell, & Harrison, 2004). In addition to screening, the ECST-R can provide ancillary data in competency cases where unequivocal evidence of feigning is found. In particular, the ECST-R Atypical scales can help to determine the *type* of feigning, specifically whether a high probability exists that a particular defendant is attempting to feign incompetency to stand trial. These data on feigned incompetency are not available with other standardized measures.

CAST-MR. The CAST-MR (Everington & Luckasson, 1992) used an informal method of generating items that were deemed relevant to the *Dusky* standard. Ten experts from law and mental health rated "understanding of the proceedings" highly with respect to content validity. Unfortunately, these experts were sharply divided on the "assist-defense" dimension of *Dusky*. Based on Table 2 (Everington & Luckasson, 1992, p. 31), no expert perceived "assist-defense" items as average. Instead, they were split with about 28% of the experts rated the items as "poor to below average" and 53% as "above average to excellent."[2]

The authors claim that the CAST-MR items are written simply and subsequently refined with input from 55 graduate students on the "appropriateness of the vocabulary, syntax, and content for people with mental retardation" (Everington & Luckasson, 1992, p. 21). However, the items of the "assist-defense" scale appear unduly complex. The item stems average 29.46 words in length, ranging from 17 to 61 words.

Criminal attorneys should be alert to unsubstantiated assertions presented in the test manual. According to the manual, "The CAST-MR is designed for use with individuals who function in the range of mild to moderate mental retardation—that is, individuals who have Weschler Adult Intelligence Scale IQ scores of approximately 35 to 75" (Everington & Luckasson, 1992, p. 9) and meet other guidelines. However, the average IQ scores for Studies 2 and 3 range from 56 to 67, which are solidly in the mild mental retardation range. Although the manual neglected to report ranges

---

[2]Ten experts (see p. 21) were used, but data in Table 2 appears to be missing two experts.

and standard deviations, it is extremely unlikely that there is adequate representation for the moderate range of mental retardation.[3] Furthermore, test standards (AERA/APA/NCME, 1999) require that developers demonstrate the applicability of their validation to specific populations.

In conclusion, the current version of the CAST-MR was validated with Studies 2 and 3 that relied on modest samples of mentally retarded defendants (combined total = 68). Its interrater reliability appears adequate but is only expressed in percentages. Grisso (2003) expresses appropriate concern about its validation. At best, the CAST-MR should be used to provide ancillary data for defendants with mild mental retardation. Low scores, especially on "assist-defense," should simply be used to denote the need for a more comprehensive evaluation.

GENERAL CROSS-EXAMINATION ISSUES

Attorneys must be competent in confronting an array of forensic clinicians on CST issues. Clinicians range remarkably in the depth of their forensic training and the breadth of their clinical experience. This section includes general strategies and sample cross-examination that are potentially effective on forensic clinicians with either superficial knowledge or wrong-headed thinking.

We begin on a cautionary note. In our experience, the majority of CST referrals are "cut and dry" cases. Irrespective of the forensic clinician's expertise, the outcome of the CST proceedings is virtually assured. Examples include (1) grossly impaired defendants who are incoherent, and more commonly (2) unimpaired defendants with no mental health histories. In both instances, an extensive evaluation may be either infeasible or unnecessary. This section focuses on the marginal cases for whom comprehensive evaluations are required.

UNTUTORED EXPERTS

We are continually surprised at the number of forensic clinicians in CST cases who lack the requisite knowledge of the legal framework, forensic issues, and specialized methods. Relatively few are stumbling novices that venture beyond their expertise. More common are mid-career forensic clinicians who have become routinized in their clinical methods and ostensibly unaffected by the exponential growth in specialized knowledge on CST.

---

[3]Given that mental retardation has an upper range of approximately 70, most scores would need to cluster in the 50–70 range.

The sample cross-examination presented in Box 6-2 challenges the expert to defend his or her expertise on CST issues and methods. The sample questions are direct and specific; they explicitly contest the expert's expertise. The underlying rationale is simple: insular experts (see Chapter 2) are skilled at deflecting general nonconfrontational questions.

The focus of Box 6-2 centers on forensic assessment instruments (FAIs; see Chapter 1). The reasoning is twofold: (1) after more than four decades of research, FAIs provide specialized knowledge on CST issues, and (2) FAIs are directly relevant to admissibility of expert evidence under *Daubert*.

BOX 6-2 SAMPLE CROSS-EXAMINATION OF COMPETENCY EVALUATIONS
WITHOUT SPECIALIZED MEASURES

1. *Doctor, would you consider yourself an expert as assessing competency to stand trial?*
2. *As part of that expertise, have you remained current with major developments in the assessment of competency to stand trial? ... Are you aware that experts sometimes "get lazy" and don't stay current? ... Has this happened to you, doctor?*
3. *As a major advance in the field, can you tell the court what competency-to-stand-trial measure was published in 1999 after years of research on the more than 700 criminal defendants? ...* [if doesn't know] *Would it be the MacArthur Competence Assessment Tool—Criminal Adjudication? ... Is that commonly called the MacCAT-CA?*
4. *In all honesty, doctor, was your decision not to use of MacCAT-CA based on expert knowledge or simple ignorance?*
5. [likely to equivocate] *Well Doctor, how many times have you administered the MacCAT-CA measure? ... Have you even reviewed its test manual? ...* [if "yes"] *Can you describe for the court something as simple as its three scales?* [answer: Understanding, Appreciation, and Reasoning] *... Which of its scales assess the defendant's ability to consult with counsel?* [answer: Reasoning]
6. *You didn't administer the Evaluation of Competency to Stand Trial—Revised did you? ... Is it typically called the ECST-R?* [phonetically "X-ster"]
7. *Is your explanation for not using the ECST-R, based on expert knowledge or simple ignorance? ...* [if knowledge] *How does ECST-R address the Daubert's standard issue of error rates?* [answer: "standard errors of measurement" and "interprets the level of certitude"]
8. [very optional; only if arrogantly asserting expertise] *You didn't administer the MultiState Competency Exam did you?* [answer: it doesn't exist] *... Was* this *decision based on knowledge or ignorance?* [if claims knowledge]
9. *Do you have or could you develop sufficient expertise to administer the MultiState Competency Exam?*
10. *Would you be surprised to know that the MultiState Competency Exam doesn't exist? ... Can we give your testimony any credence when you pretend to know a nonexistent measure?* [move to have testimony stricken]

With reference to the former, only the most arrogant expert would attempt to summarily dismiss the importance of FAIs. With respect to the latter, many trial courts are sensitized to the differences between scientifically based and self-professed expertise.

Untutored experts simply do not make the commitment to stay current on developments in forensic psychology and psychiatry. As observed by Phillipsborn (2004), simplistic, intuitive consultations uninformed by empirical advances have no place in competency hearings. As outlined in Box 6-2, untutored experts are challenged as unprepared (lazy) and unknowledgeable (ignorant). In defending their reputations, attorneys may motivate such experts to speak plainly and possibly admit their shortcomings.

Ploys are rarely successful in the cross-examination of forensic clinicians. However, arrogant experts may become highly offended at questions that unmask their lack of expertise. Attorneys must decide for themselves whether a particular expert's arrogance supercedes his or her integrity. In rare cases, challenging such an expert's ignorance may reveal deceptive testimony (see 8–10, Box 6-2).

Conceptual Issues

Attorneys must closely review CST consultations to ensure that forensic clinicians address thoroughly *Dusky's* prongs. A natural temptation is to address the simplest aspects of CST referrals, namely factual understanding. Most defendants, including those found incompetent, have a rudimentary understanding of such overlearned concepts as judge, jury, verdict, and defendants. Much more relevant are the rational prongs as they relate to the proceedings and ability to consult with counsel.

Box 6-3 presents sample cross-examination questions that are organized by abilities and by measures. Many forensic clinicians engage in an inferential process in their evaluation of rational abilities. Because the defendant responds rationally to the interview questions, they may simply assume that reasoning abilities will be comparable for trial-related issues. Such extrapolations are unnecessary shortcuts. Certain delusions are only uncovered when the topics are thoroughly investigated. The sample of cross-examination questions illustrates the importance of evaluating rational understanding as it applies to both the courtroom proceedings and the attorney–client relationship.

The ability to consult with counsel is the most challenging prong of *Dusky* to evaluate. In most cases, forensic clinicians do not have an opportunity to observe attorney–client interactions. They must resort to separate accounts by defendant and his or her counsel. Several measures included "consult-with-counsel" scales that address hypothetical issues rather than

---

BOX 6-3   SAMPLE CROSS-EXAMINATION ON DUSKY-BASED
RATIONAL ABILITIES

A. Rational Understanding of the Proceedings
   1. [if relevant] *Doctor, you submitted a competency report on* ___ [the
      defendant] *did you not?* ... *Does this report accurately reflect your
      findings?* ... *Please take a moment to consider. Did you leave out any
      important findings about the defendant?* ... *Any findings that address*
      [his/her] *ability to stand trial?*
   2. *The Dusky standard* [or relevant statute] *includes the phrase "rational
      understanding of the proceedings." What is your understanding of this
      phrase?* ... *What does the word "rational" mean to you?*
   3. *What issues in this case require a rational understanding?* ... *Would a
      decision whether to testify require a "rational understanding?"* ... *Would
      a decision whether to accept a plea require a rational understand-
      ing?* ... *What about a decision whether to have a bench or jury trial,
      wouldn't that also require a rational understanding?* ... [add case spe-
      cific examples]
   4. [if relevant] *Doctor, please turn to your report. Where did you address*
      [his/her] *rational understanding of testifying?* ... *Where did you ad-
      dress* [his/her] *rational understanding of accepting a plea?* ... *Where
      did you address* [his/her] *rational understanding for different types of
      trials?* [add case-specific examples] ... *In all fairness, doctor, didn't
      you neglect critical elements of rational understanding?*
B. Consult with Counsel: General
   5. *The Dusky standard* [or relevant statute] *includes the phrase "consult
      with his lawyer with a reasonable degree of rational understanding."
      Doctor, what is your understanding of this phrase?*
   6. *What are the major issues that should be considered in addressing the
      rational ability to consult with counsel?*
   7. *What decisions has* ___ [the defendant] *and* [his/her] *counsel already
      made in this case?* ... *What was the defendant's reasoning?* ... *Did they
      consider a change in venue?* ... *Whether to accept a plea?* [add case-
      specific examples]
   8. [if relevant] *Please refer back to your report. Where are these important
      issues, regarding rational ability to consult with counsel, summarized?*
C. Consult with Counsel: MacCAT-CA
   9. *You testified that* the defendant [choose: possesses/lacks] *ability
      to consult with counsel, based in part on the MacCAT-CA, isn't that
      correct?*
   10. *Isn't it true that there are* no questions *on the MacCAT-CA that relate
       to* ___*'s* [the defendant's] *ability to consult with counsel?*
   11. *Isn't it true that there are* no observational items *on the MacCAT-CA
       that relate to* ___*'s* [the defendant's] *ability to consult with counsel?*
   12. *Isn't is also true, that the MacCAT-CA relies on some fictional case in-
       volving Fred and Reggie's altercation in a pool hall?* ... *Anything about
       that remotely similar to the current case?* ... [if appropriate] *Is it rele-
       vant to the current case whether Fred has a girlfriend?* ... *Or went to a
       baseball game?*

(Continued)

13. *Isn't it true, doctor, that these questions are irrelevant to __* [the defendant]?

D. Consult with Counsel: CAST-MR

14. *You did use Scale II "Skills to Assist Defense" to evaluate the defendant's ability to consult with counsel, isn't that correct?*

15. *Isn't it true that all 15 items on this scale begin with "Let's pretend" or "What if?" ... So these items are hypothetical, isn't that correct? ... So none of them deal with __'s* [the defendant's] *case and* [his/her] *attorney?*

16. *Doesn't one question start with "Let's pretend you got arrested?"* [answer: Question 27] ... *Isn't that a dumb question? ... Wasn't* [he/she] *arrested? ... How can you pretend something, if it really happened?*

17. [if defendant's IQ is below 50] *What is __'s* [the defendant's] *IQ? ... Isn't it true that the CAST-MR included only a few* [choose: competent/incompetent] *defendants with IQs this low?* [answer: yes]

18. *Does this IQ mean* [he/she] *has limited verbal abilities? ... When you interviewed* [him/her] *did you ask complicated questions? ...* [if 'no"] Why not?

19. *Would you be surprised to learn that each item on the CAST-MR "Skills to Assist Defense" scale averages about 30 words in length?* [average = 29.47 words] ... *And that doesn't even include the multiple-choice answers?*

20. *Isn't it true, that the CAST-MR does not evaluate the Dusky prong's consult with counsel?*

case-specific information. Box 6-3 includes sample cross-examination to underscore the limitations of the Mc-CAT-CA and the CAST-MR for assessing the consult-with-counsel prong of *Dusky*.

SUMMARY

CST evaluations predominate clinical-forensic issues raised at trial. In the last decade, sophisticated research has increased our conceptual understanding of *Dusky* and substantially improved our specialized methods. Many forensic psychologists and psychiatrists have benefited from this advancing knowledge and specialized measures. Regrettably, many others are entrenched in traditional approaches and obsolete information. Criminal attorneys must discern each expert's level of sophistication and be prepared to tackle major shortcomings.

7

The Insanity Defense

Legal and mental health professionals are not immune to the pervasive misperceptions concerning the operation of the insanity defense. Approaching mythic proportions, widespread erroneous beliefs are firmly held regarding the frequency and success of this defense. Contrary to these beliefs, insanity defense is raised in less than 1% of cases and is successful only about one-fourth of the time (Silver, Cirincione, & Steadman, 1994). Despite polarized views in high-profile cases, nearly one-half of successful insanity cases are resolved by a consensus between the prosecution and defense (Cirincione, 1996). Notwithstanding a few highly publicized exceptions, most NGRI (i.e., "not guilty by reason of insanity") patients are institutionalized for extended periods of time.

Why dwell on misbeliefs and mythology? The "insanity defense" itself is on trial in every insanity case. A jury cannot consider an insanity acquittal without grappling, at least implicitly, with its validity and imagined consequences. Likewise, the insanity defense is on trial whenever jurors have adopted the "principled" rejection of the insanity defense, dismissing it as a "common loophole for criminals," a "ploy of the wealthy," or a "contrivance of malingerers." Defendants are seriously disadvantaged by these misperceptions of the insanity defense, and defense attorneys must seek ways to educate juries and neutralize entrenched biases. Prosecutors are likely to be divided in their opinions on whether to capitalize on jurors' misbeliefs.

This chapter outlines the legal framework for insanity defenses and operationalizes the specific components of the different insanity standards. It distills the specialized knowledge of insanity evaluations, focusing on clinical methods and provides a useful introduction for criminal attorneys and forensic clinicians. For a more comprehensive treatment, we recommend Rogers and Shuman (2000a), *Conducting Insanity Evaluations*. The chapter concludes with an examination of trial issues with an emphasis on cross-examination.

RELEVANT LEGAL STANDARDS

A conviction for most serious criminal offenses in the United States requires proof of both a proscribed mental state (mens rea) and physical act (actus reus). Only minor offenses (e.g., parking violations) impose liability for the commission of the proscribed act without the requirement of an accompanying mental state. For other offenses, the mental state required for conviction can be negated by mental health evidence that either invalidates the specific intent requirement for the offense, or raises an affirmative defense that has come to be known as the insanity defense.

The insanity defense has been controversial for most of its history. Recently, the insanity defense had come under attack following John Hinckley's insanity acquittal for his attempted assassination of President Reagan. Faced with public outcry, several states repealed their insanity defenses. As an alternative, these states only permit exculpatory evidence that the defendant lacks the mental state required as an element of the offense charged (mens rea). Negation of mens rea is generally regarded as imposing a more demanding standard than proof of an insanity defense (Nusbaum, 2002). However, negation of mens rea, unlike a successful insanity defense, results in an unconditional release from confinement. Other states have either modified their insanity standards or added an alternative verdict of Guilty But Mentally Ill (GBMI). An implicit goal of the GBMI verdicts is to decrease the number of insanity acquittals.

The United States Supreme Court has never directly addressed whether an insanity defense is mandated by the U.S. Constitution. However, a number of its decisions cast doubt on the likelihood that the Court would find an insanity defense constitutionally compelled. For example, in *Leland v Oregon* (1952) the Court rejected an argument that the constitution mandated the use of a particular insanity defense or prohibited a state from requiring a defendant prove the defense by proof beyond a reasonable doubt. In *Patterson v. New York* (1977) the Court concluded that New York's decision to shift the burden to the defendant of proving extreme emotional disturbance to reduce the crime from murder to manslaughter did not offend due process. When asked to address the constitutionality of insanity defense repeal in light of these decisions, state supreme courts have found no federal constitutional impediment (*State v. Herrera*, 1995; *State v. Korell*, 1984; *State v. Searcy*, 1990). Thus, federal constitutional law has not defined the substance of state insanity defense laws.

After wading though the substantial jurisprudence, attorneys and forensic clinicians are left to ponder what are the actual effects of different standards governing the insanity defense. Available evidence (e.g., Steadman, McGreevy, Morrissey, Callahan, Robbins, & Cirincione, 1993; Wettstein, Mulvey, & Rogers, 1991) indicates that the legal nuances in different insanity tests have a small but appreciable effect.[1] Research by Finkel and his colleagues (Finkel, Shaw, Bercaw, & Koch, 1985; Finkel & Slobogin, 1995) suggests that jurors' commonsensical analysis of insanity may overshadow the effects of semantic differences. Nonetheless, the insanity defense looms large in the criminal justice system and defines the parameters of psychological and psychiatric input on issues of criminal responsibility.

SUBSTANTIVE STANDARDS

The M'Naghten Test

The *M'Naghten* test arose from a judicial commission empaneled following Daniel M'Naghten's controversial insanity acquittal. M'Naghten attempted to assassinate the British Prime Minister but mistakenly killed his secretary instead. For the *M'Naghten* test, the panel framed the issue as an affirmative defense requiring the defendant to plead and prove that he or she was "labouring under such a defect of reason, from disease of mind as not to know the nature and quality of the act he was doing; or if he did know it, that he did not know he was doing what was wrong" (*M'Naghten*, 1843). Absent a defendant's assertion of the defense, the defendant is presumed to be sane. Organized into its major components, the *M'Naghten* test established two general conditions, specifically a "defect of reason" caused by a "disease of the mind." The core of the test is composed of two cognitive prongs: the "nature and quality of the act," and its wrongfulness.

The *M'Naghten* standard almost exclusively focuses on cognitive impairment. Its first requirement is that the defendant experience a "defect of

---

[1]Care must be taken not to overstate these results; the effects are profound for the small number of cases where the standard is pivotal to the acquittal.

reason," which limits his or her capacity to engage in rational thinking. The case law has not focused independently on the meaning of this language, but has rather considered it in relationship to other components of the test (Fingarrette & Hasse, 1979).

Disease of the mind. The test requires that the defect of reason arise from a "disease of the mind." This phrase has been understood to refer to serious mental disorders and mental defects, such as mental retardation (Goldstein, 1967). While the meaning of this phrase was not addressed in *M'Naghten*, subsequent decisions have addressed its parameters. The judicial construction of the term has been both broad and functional; it is not limited to a particular diagnosis or category of mental disorders. For example, the District of Columbia Court of Appeals in *McDonald v. United States* (1962, p. 851) reasoned:

> What psychiatrists may consider a 'mental disease or defect' for clinical purposes, where their concern is treatment, may or may not be the same as mental disease or defect for the jury's purpose in determining criminal responsibility. Consequently, for that purpose the jury should be told that a mental disease or defect includes any abnormal condition of the mind which substantially affects mental or emotional processes and substantially impairs behavior controls. Thus the jury would consider testimony concerning the development, adaptation and functioning of these processes and controls.

Therefore, this component should be viewed as broadly encompassing a spectrum of disorders with its emphasis on legally relevant impairment rather than specific diagnoses. One major exception is voluntary intoxication. The case law has consistently excluded conditions that result from the "voluntary" use of drugs or alcohol (e.g., see *Griggs v. Commonwealth*, 1979).

Knowing. The two prongs of the *M'Naghten* standard rest on the defendant's ability to *know* his or her actions and their wrongfulness. Courts have generally failed to distinguish knowing the "nature and quality of the act" from knowing its wrongfulness (*State v. Esser*, 1962). The term "know" with the *M'Naghten* standard is generally limited to instances in which the impact of the "mental disease or defect" is on the defendant's cognitive rather than volitional capacity (Goldstein, 1967). However, some courts have broadened this construct to include emotional or behavioral deficits by interpreting "know" as knowledge fused with affect (*People v. Wolff*, 1964).

Nature and quality. The defendant must be aware of his or her physical actions and their immediate consequences. For this standard, "nature" is simply defined as an awareness one's actions and circumstances (Davidson, 1965). The term "quality" involves an appreciation of the degree of harmfulness associated with this conduct. As described by Rogers and

Shuman (2000a), quality requires an understanding of the potential or actual consequences for the victim. This first prong, nature and quality, requires only the most basic cognitive abilities. As a result, relatively few defendants qualify as insane under this prong.

Wrongfulness. The second prong, wrongfulness, is a pivotal component of the *M'Naghten* standard. All jurisdictions accept *legal* wrongfulness as meeting the *M'Naghten* standard. What about *moral* wrongfulness? Cases occur where the defendant fully recognizes that his or her actions are contrary to the criminal statutes but believe they are required by a divine authority. Interestingly, the *Bellingham* case, which preceded the *M'Naghten* standard, did encompass *moral* wrongfulness. Wrongfulness was construed as the ability to "distinguish good from bad, right from wrong" and must know that his conduct is "not only against the laws of God but against the laws of his country" (cited in Robitscher, 1966, p. 56). Following M'Naghten's acquittal, the House of Lords (1843) propounded a new standard[2] limited to legal wrongfulness that was "contrary to the law of the land."

Many jurisdictions have reintroduced moral wrongfulness as an element of the *M'Naghten* standard. In the oft cited opinion of the New Yolk Court of Appeals, *People v. Schmidt* (1915, p. 957), Judge Cardozo reasoned that *M'Naghten* is intended to encompass knowledge of both moral and legal wrongdoing:

> The judges expressly held that a defendant who knew nothing of the law would none the less be responsible if he knew that the act was wrong, by which, therefore, they must have meant, if he knew that it was morally wrong. Whether he would also be responsible if he knew that it was against the law, but did not know it to be morally wrong, is a question that was not considered. In most cases, of course, knowledge that an act is illegal will justify the inference of knowledge that it is wrong. But none the less it is the knowledge of wrong, conceived of as moral wrong, that seems to have been established by that decision as the controlling test.

Moral wrongfulness can be construed (see Brooks, 1974) with reference to public (e.g., a recognized religion) or private (e.g., individual values) perspective. The courts have limited moral wrongfulness to marked impairment of generally held, public beliefs, often involving a divine authority. Privately held beliefs would create insolvable conundrums for the criminal justice system because each insanity case would rely on the defendant's own perspective of moral wrongfulness. The Supreme Court of Arizona spoke to the heart of this matter in *State v. Corely* (1972, p. 473):

---

[2]Jury instructions in the M'Naghten trial included moral wrongfulness that addressed a "wrong or wicked act" ... "violating the laws both of God and man."

The interpretation of the word "wrong" as used in M'Naghten has been an enigma since the standard was almost uniformly adopted. A few courts have adhered to the view that the word should be restricted to a legal sense, i.e., if the defendant was suffering from a mental disease and did not know he was violating the laws of the state when he committed his act he will be declared insane... This view has been criticized, however, because it makes ignorance of the law a defense... Most courts have adopted the position that wrong should be expanded to include both legal and moral wrong, i.e., that defendant will be declared insane if he was suffering from a mental disease and not aware at the time he committed his act that it was in violation of community standards of morality... We find no authority upholding the defendant's position that one suffering from a mental disease could be declared legally insane if he knew that the act was morally and legally wrong but he personally believed that act right. We believe that this would not be a sound rule, because it approaches the position of exonerating a defendant for his personal beliefs and does not take account of society's determination of defendant's capacity to conform his conduct to the law.

In a recent survey Gee (2003) found that 24 states currently use some form of the *M'Naghten* standard. Gee reported that six states have augmented *M'Naghten* with some version of an irresistible impulse standard: Colorado, Georgia, Iowa, Kentucky, New Mexico, Oklahoma, and Virginia. For example, in Georgia, the insanity defense is augmented to include conduct explained by a delusional compulsion:

A person shall not be found guilty of a crime when, at the time of the act, omission, or negligence constituting the crime, the person, because of mental disease, injury, or congenital deficiency, acted as he did because of a delusional compulsion as to such act which overmastered his will to resist committing the crime. (Ga. Code Ann. § 16-3-3 (2002)

States use different language to describe the irresistible-impulse prong. For example, Oklahoma supplements its nonresponsibility defense to include "Persons who committed the act, or make the omission charged, while under involuntary subjection to the power of superiors" 21 Okl. Stat. § 152 (2004). Likewise, Virginia, provides that "The irresistible impulse defense is available when the accused's mind has become so impaired by disease that he is totally deprived of the mental power to control or restrain his act." (*Bennett v. Commonwealth*, 1999, p. 447).

AMERICAN LAW INSTITUTE STANDARD

As part of the Model Penal Code, the American Law Institute (ALI) standard was carefully crafted from 1952 to 1962 by a distinguished group of judges, law professors, and behavioral scientists. While most insanity defense standards (e.g., *M'Naghten*) have been reactions to public outcry and dismay, the ALI standard was a proactive endeavor to formulate a workable and fair insanity test. The ALI standard (American Law Institute, 1962) exculpates under the following circumstances:

> A person is not responsible for criminal conduct if at the time of such conduct as a result of mental disease or defect he lacks substantial capacity to either appreciate the criminality (wrongfulness) of his conduct or to conform his conduct to the requirements of law. As used in this article, the terms "mental disease or defect" do not include an abnormality manifested only by repeated criminal or otherwise antisocial conduct.

The ALI standard is composed of two general conditions and two specific prongs. The two general conditions are composed of "mental disease or defect" and "lacks substantial capacity." When these conditions are met, the principal consideration involves the two prongs: "appreciate the criminality [wrongfulness]" and "conform his conduct."

Mental disease or defect.   Relying on a 1962 DC Court of Appeals opinion in *McDonald v. United States*, "mental disease or defect" has generally been interpreted broadly to refer to nearly any diagnosis that impairs functioning. In another amplifying opinion, the Supreme Court of Missouri explained in *State v. Garrett* (1965, p. 240) that this term includes "any mental disease or defect regardless of its medical label or source, whether it was present at birth or developed later as a result of injury or physical or mental disease, or whether it is capable of improving or deteriorating."

The ALI standard sought to exclude any clinical condition that is "manifested only by repeated criminal or otherwise antisocial conduct." While commonly interpreted as eliminating Antisocial Personality Disorder (APD), this diagnosis is not necessarily excluded by this language because many defendants with APD evidence a developmental pattern of maladjustment. As a practical matter, however, a defendant with a primary diagnosis of APD is unlikely to prevail on an insanity defense.

Substantial impairment.   The ALI sought to avoid extremes (i.e., the necessity for total impairment) in its formulation of insanity. *Substantial* impairment was changed to address defendants with markedly diminished abilities. It was based on the following reasoning (American Law Institute, 1962):

> To identify the degree of impairment with precision, is, of course, impossible both verbally and logically. The recommended formulation is content to rest upon the term 'substantial' to support the weight of judgment; if capacity is greatly impaired, that presumably should be sufficient. An expert witness, called upon to assess a defendant's capacity at a prior time (which, of course, the witness probably did not observe), can hardly be asked for a more definitive statement—even in the case of extreme conditions.

Appreciate criminality. The ALI substituted the word "appreciate" for *M'Naghten's* use of the word "know." "Appreciate" goes beyond simple cognitive awareness to include emotional understanding, namely the importance of magnitude of the actions. It contemplates that the defendant was mentally capable of both understanding what he or she was doing and that it was wrong (*United States v. Dysart*, 1983). The original wording, criminality, refers to conduct that violates criminal statutes. The alternative term, wrongfulness, is slightly more inclusive and may embrace conduct involving moral wrongfulness.

Conform conduct. The second specific prong of the ALI standard addresses the defendant's capacity to control his or her criminal actions. Similar to irresistible impulse, *conform conduct* is construed more broadly. It addresses severe impairment in the defendant's capacity to choose and exert behavioral control (Rogers & Shuman, 2000).

The ALI standard is currently operative in 22 states (Gee, 2003). These states are composed of the following: Alabama, Alaska, Connecticut, Hawaii, Illinois, Indiana, Kansas, Kentucky, Maine, Maryland, Massachusetts, Michigan, Missouri, New York, North Dakota, Oregon, Rhode Island, Tennessee, Vermont, West Virginia, Wisconsin, and Wyoming.

Federal Insanity Defense Reform Act of 1984

John Hinckley Jr.'s insanity acquittal for his attempted assassination of President Reagan caused a public furor and rush to reform the insanity defense. The Hinckley case provides a contemporary parallel to the *M'Naghten* aftermath. Like *M'Naghten*, the Federal Insanity Defense Reform Act (IDRA, 1984) sought to assuage the public and assure that future "Hinckleys" would not be acquitted. Unlike *M'Naghten*, the IDRA has had a circumscribed sphere of influence as most insanity defense claims are raised in state courts. The IDRA is a throwback to the original *M'Naghten* standard, even adopting some of its language:

> It is an affirmative defense to a prosecution under any Federal statute that, at the time of the commission of the acts constituting the offense, the defendant, as a result of a severe mental disease or defect, was unable to appreciate the nature and quality or the wrongfulness of his acts. Mental disease or defect does not otherwise constitute a defense.

Substantively, the fundamental change enacted by the IDRA was the removal of the volitional prong. Ironically, the volitional prong was not central to Hinckley's acquittal (Low, Jeffries, & Bonnie, 1986). With its passage, the IDRA reverted insanity in federal cases to a cognitively-only model that incorporates *M'Naghten's* "nature and quality" with already existing "wrongfulness."

The IDRA sought to further restrict insanity acquittals by adding several descriptors. It applies the term "severe" to the required "mental disease or defect." While mental disorders such as schizophrenia (*United States v. Knott*, 1990) may meet this requirement, the IDRA's use of "severe mental disease or defect" is intended to impose a limitation on past practices. "[T]he legislative history of [the IDRA] . . . states: The concept of severity was added to emphasize that non-psychotic behavior disorders or neuroses such as an 'inadequate personality,' 'immature personality,' or a pattern of 'antisocial tendencies' do not constitute the defense" (*United States v. Salava*, 1992, p. 323). Interestingly, this choice of terminology is not consistent with the current nosology. Last appearing in *DSM-II* (American Psychiatric Association, 1968), the architects of the IDRA appeared to be battling nonexistent diagnoses.

In the passage of IDRA, Congress specifically intended to exclude from mental disease or defect conditions resulting from the voluntary use of alcohol or drugs (*United States v. Garcia*, 1996). While not limiting the defense to particular diagnoses, the IDRA is also intended to restrict the scope of disorders. This effort has had limited success. In *United States v. Rezaq* (1996, p. 467), a federal district court observed:

> A court's 'severity' analysis . . . consists of more than locating the magical word 'severe' in the diagnosis. Rather, it contemplates a more thoroughgoing approach, in which a court reviews the diagnosis for overall indications of the severity of defendant's mental disease or defect. The mere presence of the word 'severe' in a diagnosis that suggests a mild condition will not constitute a defense under [the IDRA]. Similarly, the absence of the word 'severe' will not necessarily mean that the condition diagnosed does not meet the standards of [the IDRA]." In essence, the court is relying on level of impairment rather than diagnostic categories. This functional analysis parallels practices prior to the IDRA.

The IDRA sought to limit issues of criminal responsibility to the insanity defense. This limitation is found in the sentence: "Mental disease or defect does not otherwise constitute a defense." Defenses such as diminished responsibility or diminished capacity which most circuits had previously upheld, were repealed as separate defenses by the IDRA (see *United States v. Westcott*, 1996). The question that has often arisen is whether this IDRA restriction also negates use of a mental disease or defect to negate the mens rea or specific intent requirement of the offense charged. Although not all circuits agree, most hold that the IDRA does not prohibit the defendant from introducing evidence of a mental disorder to negate mens rea or specific intent (*United States v. Cameron*, 1990; *United States v. Bartlett*, 1988; *United States v. White*, 1985). However, not all evidence of mental disease or defect claimed to be related to mens rea or specific intent is admissible. In *United States v. Westcott* (1996, p. 1358), the 11th Circuit of the US Court of Appeals held that while such evidence is admissible under the IDRA for purposes other than an insanity defense, it is necessary to limit such evidence to the legally acceptable theory of mens rea. Otherwise, it would allow defenses akin to justification. Accordingly, the court determined that:

> Psychiatric evidence is admissible to negate *mens rea* when the evidence focuses on the defendant's specific state of mind at the time the offense was committed...Evidence that a defendant lacks the capacity to form *mens rea* is to be distinguished from evidence that the defendant actually lacked mens rea...While the two may be logically related, only the latter is admissible to negate the *mens rea* element of an offense.

In jurisdictions that retain an insanity defense, the substantive standard has increasingly approached the test established following Daniel M'Naghten's acquittal on insanity grounds in the wake of his attempt to assassinate a popular political figure. Spurred by John Hinckley's acquittal on insanity grounds, progressive efforts to redefine the insanity defense have been curtailed. Efforts at curtailment include the guilty-but-mentally-ill (GBMI) verdict.

Guilty but Mentally Ill Verdict

The adoption of GBMI does not by itself change the insanity defense standard applicable in a particular jurisdiction. Rather, its adoption offers the jury another option in addition to guilty, not guilty, and not guilty by reason of insanity.[3] GBMI's ostensible goal is to convict the defendant but indicate concern that the defendant receives treatment during confinement. However, all inmates are entitled to rudimentary treatment. The GBMI verdict does not appear to offer inmates any tangible difference in treatment or programming. States with GBMI alternatives include the following: Alaska, Delaware, Georgia, Illinois, Indiana, Kentucky, Michigan, New Mexico, Pennsylvania, South Dakota, and Vermont. To reach this verdict under the GBMI model adopted in these states the jury must conclude that the defendant committed the act charged; suffers from a mental disorder; but, does not meet the test for acquittal by reason of insanity. Defendants found GBMI are sentenced to serve the sentence otherwise imposed with the additional direction that they are provided necessary treatment. The termination of treatment has no bearing on release from the sentence imposed. The substantive legal issues for the GBMI verdict are examined in Chapter 8.

---

[3]Montana's decision to repeal its insanity defense and adopt GBMI leaves jurors with only three options: guilty, not guilty, and GBMI.

Mens Rea Alternatives

Idaho (2003), Kansas (2003), Montana (2002), and Utah (2003) do not recognize the use of an insanity defense to a criminal prosecution. Instead, evidence of a mental disorder or disability is admissible to prove that the defendant lacked the mental state required for the offense (mens rea). Thus, the criteria for admission of evidence of the defendant's mental disorder in these states will be defined by the mental state requirement for the offense charged. For example, Idaho defines murder and the requisite malice as follows:

- "The unlawful killing of a human being . . . with malice aforethought or the intentional application of torture to a human being, which results in the death of a human being." (Idaho, 2003, § 18-4001)
- "Such malice may be express or implied. It is expressed when there is manifested a deliberate intention unlawfully to take away the life of a fellow creature. It is implied when no considerable provocation appears, or when the circumstances attending the killing show an abandoned and malignant heart." (Idaho, 2003, § 18-4002)

Absent an insanity defense, evidence that the defendant did not manifest "a deliberate intention unlawfully to take away the life of a fellow creature," *as the result of a mental disorder*, would be relevant. Beyond mens rea, evidence of the defendant's mental disorder may also be admissible as mitigation evidence in sentencing, specifically in capital sentencing (*Atkins v. Virginia*, 2002; *Lockett v. Ohio*, 1978; *Penry v. Johnson*, 2001).

PROCEDURAL ISSUES

Privilege and Discovery

Constitutional protection against self-incrimination does not typically apply to a defendant's participation in a court-ordered insanity examination. Most courts (e.g., *State v. Herrera*, 1995) have held that raising the insanity defense waives the privilege in as far as evidence of mental state is concerned. Thus, a defendant who refuses to participate in a court ordered examination may be denied the right to present expert testimony in support of an insanity defense. However, this waiver does not permit evidence from such an examination to be used to prove the defendant's commission of the act charged (*Walters v. Hubbard*, 1984).

A forensic assessment of a criminal defendant by a psychologist or psychiatrist retained by the defendant is protected by an attorney–client or work-product privilege, not a therapist–patient privilege. If the defendant chooses not to raise an insanity defense, the privilege remains, and the communications between the forensic examiner and defense counsel are not discoverable. If the defendant chooses to raise an insanity defense, the privilege is waived for any expert called to testify. Jurisdictions disagree about whether privilege applies to uncalled defense experts once the insanity defense is raised. Many jurisdictions (e.g., *People v. Lines*, 1975; *Smith v. McCormick*, 1990) hold that raising the insanity defense does not waive the privilege as to experts retained but not called by the defendant. However, an increasing number of jurisdictions hold that raising the insanity defense waives the privilege as to all defense experts (*People v. Edney*, 1976; *State v. Hamlet*, 1997).

The Ultimate Issue Rule

Modern evidence law (Fed. R. Evid. 704, 1975) has eliminated the ultimate opinion rule, which prohibited expert opinions that embraced the ultimate issue in the case. The reason for its elimination was both practical and conceptual; the ultimate opinion rule was considered difficult to apply and unnecessarily restrictive (Fed. R. Evid. 704, 1975). One reaction to John Hinckley's insanity acquittal was a circumscribed revival of the ultimate opinion rule focused on federal criminal prosecutions on the issue of the defendant's mental state:

> No expert witness testifying with respect to the mental state or condition of a defendant in a criminal case may state an opinion or inference as to whether the defendant did or did not have the mental state or condition constituting an element of the crime charged or of a defense thereto. Such ultimate issues are matters for the trier of fact alone. (Fed. R. 704(b))

Thus, an expert testifying in a federal criminal trial may offer an opinion about the defendant's diagnoses and impairment at the time of the offense. However, the expert is prohibited from stating an opinion about sanity that embraces the issue of whether the defendant had the mental state or condition constituting an element of the crime or a defense there to such as "appreciate the nature and quality or the wrongfulness of his acts." Unfortunately, this ban is nothing more than a semantic exercise (Rogers & Ewing, 1989) with no appreciable effects on juries.

California has enacted a similar rule on ultimate opinions. It stated

> In the guilt phase of a criminal action, any expert testifying about a defendant's mental illness, mental disorder, or mental defect shall not testify as to whether the defendant had or did not have the required mental states, which include, but are not limited to, purpose, intent, knowledge, or malice aforethought, for the crimes charged. The question as to whether the defendant had or did not have the required mental states shall be decided by the trier of fact. (California, 2003)

Daubert Issues

Expert testimony typically plays an instrumental though not decisive role in insanity evaluations: "The issue of insanity is not strictly medical, and expert witnesses, although capable of giving testimony that may aid the jury in its determination of the ultimate issue, are not capable of dictating determination of that issue" (*Schuessler v. State*, 1986, p. 329). Although an insanity defense verdict may rest entirely on lay testimony, it is common for defendants to offer expert testimony in support of an insanity defense. The procedural requirements for the admission of expert testimony have undergone a transformation in the federal courts and many state courts in the past decade. Spurred by a series of United States Supreme Court decisions (*Daubert v. Merrill Dow Pharmaceuticals*, 1993; *General Electric Co. v. Joiner*, 1997; *Kumho Tire v. Carmichael*, 1999), trial courts have increasingly been asked to play a gatekeeper role in the admissibility of expert testimony to ascertain whether proffered expert testimony meets a threshold of evidentiary reliability and relevance to the task at hand. Federal trial courts, and the state courts that have adopted this approach, have employed a set of pragmatic criteria that examines (1) whether the underlying theory or technique can be and has been tested, (2) whether the theory or technique has been subjected to peer review and publication, (3) what is the theory or technique's error rate and methods for controlling, and (4) acceptance of the theory or technique in the relevant scientific community.

Daubert and its progeny (see Chapter 3) hold the potential to raise the standards for forensic assessment by demanding the use only of methods and procedures that have been validated. When unvalidated tests and clinical methods are applied to insanity evaluations, they invited a *Daubert* challenge or a vigorous cross-examination. But the application of *Daubert* and its progeny are most often used in categorical challenges to the use of particular syndromes or disorders to support an insanity defense. Examples include Premenstrual Syndrome, Vietnam/Gulf War veterans' post-traumatic stress disorder, battered woman syndrome, and postpartum psychosis.

CLINICAL OPERATIONALIZATION
OF THE INSANITY STANDARDS

The retrospective nature of insanity evaluations poses a formidable challenge for forensic psychologists and psychiatrists. In conducting insanity evaluations, forensic clinicians must distinguish between ongoing and prior episodes (see Rogers, 2002). With *ongoing* episodes, they have a general opportunity to observe Axis I symptoms and concomitant impairment that are often similar to those experienced at the time of the offense. With *prior* episodes, the defendant's diagnoses and impairment must be entirely reconstructed from his or her accounts, witnesses' observations, and physical evidence.

This section addresses the major components of insanity evaluations with an emphasis on general domains. Forensic clinicians are responsible for consulting with attorneys regarding the specific statutes and case law governing the particular interpretation of insanity in their jurisdictions. Beyond consultations, experts should review and familiarize themselves with the substantive issues of specific insanity standards.

This portion of Chapter 7 is organized into three main sections directly relevant to insanity standards (1) retrospective diagnoses and impairment, (2) cognitive impairment, and (3) volitional impairment. The brief summary of standardized and specialized methods will be integrated into these three sections; for more expanded treatment, please see Rogers and Shuman (2000a).

RETROSPECTIVE DIAGNOSES AND IMPAIRMENT

Structured Interviews

Diagnoses, as described earlier, provide a useful method of organizing symptoms, syndromes and disorders and appraising their overall impairment. However, the method of achieving diagnoses is critical to its scientific underpinnings (see Chapter 12 for a fuller discussion). Traditional interviews are often imprecise, leading to missed diagnoses and misdiagnoses (Rogers, 2003a). As a result, forensic clinicians are strongly encouraged to use structured interviews that standardize both the diagnostic questions and the symptom ratings. Rogers (2001), *Handbook of Diagnostic and Structured Interviewing*, is standard reference for clinical and forensic practitioners.

In selecting an Axis I interview, the SADS offers significant advantages over the SCID when conducting insanity evaluations. The applicability of the SADS to insanity evaluations has been specifically examined (see Rogers & Shuman, 2000a). Other advantages include research on past diagnoses and reliable measurement of Axis I symptoms. SADS research has examined its usefulness with (1) worst period of the current episode and (2) prior episodes. While the SCID focuses primarily on diagnostic reliability, the SADS is distinguished from other Axis I interviews by its extensive data on the reliability of Axis I symptoms. To reemphasize a critical point: *For insanity evaluations, establishing retrospective diagnoses is not sufficient.* While Axis I diagnoses are helpful, forensic clinicians must be able to establish the presence and severity of specific Axis I symptoms. In this regard, the SADS produces excellent data for both interrater and test–retest reliabilities (Rogers, 2001).

Many forensic clinicians will also use the SIRS (Rogers et al., 1992) for assessing the possibility of feigned mental disorders (see Chapter 2). Although preliminary data are promising on its retrospective applications (Goodness & Rogers, 1999), the SIRS is only validated for current and ongoing episodes. If the defendants are feigning their *current* impairment, then their credibility for *prior* impairment is brought into question. However, attorneys and forensic clinicians should avoid the simplistic logic: Once a malingerer, always a malingerer. On the contrary, malingering appears much more a response to situational contingencies than a stable personality trait.

In general, insanity evaluations should begin with general, unstructured interview and move to more standardized methods, such as structured interviews. We recommend that forensic clinicians elicit a detailed account from the defendant of his or her actions, emotions, and thoughts for the time period leading to the alleged criminal behavior. Following these general accounts, structured interviews offer standardized questions and reliable ratings.

Multiscale Inventories

Most forensic clinicians will supplement traditional and structured interviews with formal tests, such as multiscale inventories. For assessing patterns of psychopathology, two multiscale inventories should be seriously considered: the Minnesota Multiphasic Personality Inventory—second edition (MMPI-2; Butcher, Dahlstrom, Graham, Tellegen, & Kaemmer, 1989) and the Personality Assessment Inventory (PAI; Morey, 1991). Two caveats must be borne in mind. First, these inventories assess the defendant's current functioning, not their functioning at the time of the crime. Second, they are *not* diagnostic measures; rather, they provide useful data about clinical characteristics. Between the MMPI-2 and PAI, which multiscale inventory is preferable in insanity evaluations?

The MMPI-2 has a proud tradition spanning six decades. Originally developed by empirical keying, a radical movement is underway to restructure the clinical scales completely and revamp their validation (Tellegen et al., 2003). Its greatest strength is the extensive research on feigned mental disorders (Rogers et al., 2003; see Chapter 2). In addition, MMPI research has investigated its usefulness in insanity evaluations (see Rogers & Shuman, 2000a). Importantly, forensic research has consistently failed to find clinical elevations or code types that differentiate sane and insane defendants. Shortcomings of the MMPI-2 include its comparatively high reading level (grade 8), considerable length (567 items), psychometric problems with subscales (variable alphas), and cookbook interpretations that conflate empirical data with traditional formulations.

The PAI is a much more recent addition to multiscale inventories. As a result, the PAI benefited from psychometric advances. Its nonoverlapping scales and subscales have superb internal consistencies. These features improve its clinical interpretability and discriminant validity. Its low reading level (4th grade) is especially useful in forensic populations. Its interpretations are based on empirical data with little influence from traditional formulations. Unlike the MMPI-2, the PAI lacks the extensive research on feigned mental disorders and other response styles.

Many forensic clinicians will notice that the Millon Clinical Multiaxial Inventory—3rd Edition (MCMI-III; Millon, 1994; Millon, Davis, & Millon, 1997) is missing from this discussion. Indeed, McCann and Dyer (1996; also Dyer & McCann, 2000) have strongly promoted the use of the MCMI-III in a variety of forensic settings. However, a critical review and meta-analysis by Rogers, Salekin, and Sewell (1999) concluded that the MCMI-III presented troubling *Daubert* issues in light of its validation and error rates. Even more disturbing, Rogers, Salekin, and Sewell (2000) found criterion contamination[4] in MCMI-III validation. Therefore, we cannot recommend the MCMI-III for insanity or other forensic cases.

Projective Methods

Controversy surrounds the use of projective methods in insanity evaluations (Rogers & Shuman, 2000a). Debate can even be found on whether projective measures are truly projective. As summarized by Erdberg (1990), the stimulus-to-fantasy approach hypothesizes that projective responses are symbolic of important internal dynamics, while the perceptual-cognitive approach sees responses to ambiguous material as more of a decisional than projective process. The most popular projective method is the Rorschach. Others methods include other inkblot methods, human figure drawings, the Thematic Apperception Test (TAT), and incomplete sentences. This section focuses on the Rorschach.

Approximately two-thirds of forensic clinicians *never* use the Rorschach in conducting insanity evaluations (Borum & Grisso, 1995). The

---

[4]This fatal flaw in research occurs when results are not entirely independent but influenced by "insider information." In this case, some "independent" clinicians were exposed to the MCMI-III results.

percentages were surprisingly consistent between forensic psychologists (68%) and psychiatrists (70%). Significantly, attorneys must realize that the Rorschach is not a single measure. Although the inkblots remain identical, psychologists may (1) use one of several administration/scoring systems, or (2) their own idiosyncratic approach. For the last several decades, the Exner system has predominated the administration/scoring systems. Recently, this system has become embroiled in controversy regarding its reliability and validity.

Attorneys should be even more concerned about idiosyncratic uses of the Rorschach in insanity evaluations. Characterized by Weiner (1995) as "subjective" interpretations, many psychologists do not use standardized scoring and interpretation, but rely on their own idiosyncratic hypotheses. Psychiatrists sometimes rely on these reports, incognizant of their subjectivity and unreliability. Through questioning or copies of the Rorschach scoring, attorneys can ascertain whether subjective interpretations were used. By their very nature, subjective interpretations lack falsifiability, error rates, peer-reviewed research, and general acceptance. Using *Daubert*, attorneys may argue to exclude subjective Rorschach interpretations based on their lack of evidentiary reliability. Alternatively, testimony based on idiosyncratic methods is very vulnerable to attack.

The Rorschach is not a diagnostic measure and does not yield *DSM-IV* disorders (see Chapter 12). Regarding its forensic applications, the Rorschach has not been extensively studied in criminal forensic populations. An early study of insanity cases (Boehnert, 1985) yielded modest results (overall classification of 51.6%). Studies of malingering indicate that the Rorschach is vulnerable to response styles (see Schretlen, 1997). Although participants may have difficulty feigning a specific disorder, such as schizophrenia, they can still produce Rorschach protocols that appear substantially impaired.

In conclusion, routine use of the Rorschach and other projective methods in insanity evaluations would appear to invite criticism and forceful cross-examination. In problematic cases, forensic clinicians struggle to address clinical issues relevant to the courts and may consider the potential contributions of projective measures. The consideration on a case-by-case basis is whether the potential value of projective methods to an insanity case outweighs the problems associated with these methods.

COGNITIVE ISSUES AND INSANITY

With the exception of the now-defunct *Durham* test, all insanity standards require that forensic clinicians address explicitly cognitive issues

TABLE 7-1. OUTLINE OF COGNITIVE ISSUES FOUND WITH INSANITY EVALUATIONS

Nature and Quality

1. Is the defendant's account generally consistent with the physical evidence?
2. Can the defendant describe his or her actions chronologically?
3. Did the defendant appear to understand the immediate consequences of his or her noncriminal (e.g., food preparation for breakfast) actions?
4. Did the defendant appear to understand the immediate consequences of his or her criminal (e.g., firing a weapon) actions?
5. In general, was the defendant engaged in purposeful behavior prior to the criminal actions?
6. Was did the defendant hope to achieve by his or her the criminal actions?

Wrongfulness

7. Were the criminal actions motivated by a grossly misperceived need for self-defense?
8. Were the criminal actions motivated by a grossly misperceived need to carry out official duties of an authorized government agent?
9. Were the criminal actions in direct response to grossly misperceived commands from a governmental authority?
10. Were the criminal actions an attempt to minimize or prevent what was grossly misperceived as a much greater harm?
11. [if jurisdictions where it is warranted] Were the criminal actions in direct response to grossly misperceived commands from a divine authority?

---

with reference to insanity. Cognitive issues can involve the "nature and quality" of the criminal conduct (*M'Naghten* and IDRA) and its wrongfulness (*M'Naghten*, IDRA, and ALI). Knowledge of wrongfulness is predicated on an awareness of the nature and quality. While it might be argued that "nature and quality" component is superfluous, forensic clinicians need to address each component of the standard. Where relevant, incapacity on both cognitive components may be persuasive to the triers of fact.

Table 7-1 outlines the key cognitive issues as a series of inquiries for "nature and quality" and wrongfulness. These cognitive prongs are addressed separately.

Nature and Quality

The defendant's free-flowing account of his or her actions at the time of the alleged offense is the most relevant information regarding "nature and quality." With minimal prompting, many defendants can provide an accurate account with a correct sequencing of actions and events. Often this accounting is consistent with witnesses' reports and the defendant's own statement at the time of his or her apprehension. In such cases, it is very likely that the defendant understands the "nature" of his or her criminal conduct.

A potential complication occurs with postarrest memory changes. A defendant may be inadvertently "educated" about events of the offense through police investigations or attorney interviews. Moreover, subsequent treatment may make the defendant's account appear more rational than what he or she was experiencing at the time of the offense. Unfortunately, no simple remedy is available to postarrest memory changes. Occasionally, collateral sources, such as the victim, will have had extensive contact with the defendant at the time of the offense and be able to produce a convincing account of events.

A frequent issue is the lack of memory registration as a result of alcoholic blackouts (see discussion of substance abuse in Chapter 5). As previously noted, voluntary intoxication does not qualify as a mental disease for the purposes of the insanity defense. This exclusion does not necessarily apply to alcohol-induced disorders, such as Alcohol-Induced Persisting Amnestic Disorder. A novice misjudgment is any equation of the defendant's lack of memory at the present time with a lack of awareness at the time of the offense. On the contrary, blackouts are commonly observed in persons who had engaged in purposeful, goal-directed behavior at the time of intoxication (see Rogers & Shuman, 2000a).

The pivotal issue in establishing the "quality" of the criminal act is an ascertainment of its meaning to the defendant. For example, one psychotic mother was completely convinced that Satan had assumed the likeness of her 4-year-old son. While clearly understanding her physical actions, she was unaware of the "quality" of her criminal conduct when her attempt to vanquish Satan resulted in the death of her child. Of the potential issues outlined in Table 7-1, the key consideration involves a knowledge of immediate consequences. Many insane defendants know the consequences of their behaviors that are not delusionally based. For example, a male defendant may realize that his 911 call will result in emergency services and possible police investigation. At the same time, he may have been unaware that frantic baptism of his baby in response to divine wishes would cause its asphyxiation.

The defendant's goals are often relevant to establishing the quality of his or her criminal conduct. Related inquiries may address (1) what the defendant achieved and (2) what the defendant hoped to achieve. Occasionally, an inquiry about their goals uncovers an elaborate delusional plan. More often, inquiries help to confirm rational goals with their intended consequences.

Wrongfulness

Within the cognitive domain, the most crucial determination is the defendant's knowledge or appreciation of wrongfulness. As observed in the commentary on the *M'Naghten* standard, the clearest evidence of impaired wrongfulness occurs when the defendant's conduct would be justified if his or her beliefs were true. What beliefs would justify the defendant's criminal conduct? Common explanations (see also Table 6-1) include

- *Self-defense or defense of others.* Through markedly distorted perceptions or beliefs, the defendant misinterprets his or her life or another's as being threatened by a third party. The defendant's motivation is either self-preservation or the protection of others.
- *Officially sanctioned duties.* Through markedly distorted perceptions or beliefs, the defendant misinterprets his or her criminal conduct as officially authorized by the government.
- *Misconstrued exigencies.* The law recognizes a defense of justification when the actor believes his action is necessary to avoid a greater harm to himself or others (e.g., breaking into a burning home to save an unconscious occupant).
- *Divine authority.* Through markedly distorted perceptions or beliefs, the defendant misinterprets his or her criminal conduct as officially commanded or sanctioned by a divine authority.

Impaired knowledge of wrongfulness is most commonly observed with instances of misperceived necessity for self-defense. We use "self-defense" as a descriptive term to represent the defendant's general motivation and not as strictly defined affirmative defense. A person with a chronic psychotic disorder may attempt to kill those imminently "threatening" his or her life. However, the immediacy of the threat varies from case to case. In one case, the defendant may believe he had already been poisoned by his wife. In a second case, the defendant may believe his coworker was attempting to poison him but had not yet succeeded. Conclusions about impaired knowledge of wrongfulness must take into account the degree of threat (e.g., death vs. slanderous letters) and its immediacy.

Occasionally, defendants are evaluated who believed their actions were sanctioned officially by a government agency, such as the CIA. If these delusional beliefs were true, then their actions might be legally justified. The challenge for forensic clinicians is establishing that the beliefs were fixed and held against incontrovertible evidence to the contrary. The challenge is often compounded by the defendant's "secret" or "covert" governmental role.

Appreciation of wrongfulness can also be impaired by misconstrued exigencies. While recognizing the illegality of the act, the defendant believes his or her actions are justified by the prevention of greater harm. In one instance, a female defendant "knew" that her neighbors had long engaged in hostile acts against her and her son. That morning, she firmly believed they were attempting to gain access to her house to torture slowly and eventually kill both of them. Faced with inevitable death, she sought to obviate the suffering by killing herself and her son as painlessly as possible.

Insanity cases occasionally occur where the defendant has psychotic and nonpsychotic motivations. As a further illustration of misconstrued exigencies, a male defendant attempted to save the world from a looming natural disaster that threatened to flood all the continents and drown their inhabitants. His delusions were well documented with hundreds of floridly psychotic letters to scientists and governmental agencies. As a desperate attempt to capture the government's attention, he mailed body parts with his theory. It could be argued that his awareness of wrongfulness was severely compromised by misconstrued exigencies. However, the decedent was his wife's extramarital lover, likely killed in a jealous rage. Therefore, the primary motivation for the killing itself appeared to be nonpsychotic.

Compliance with divine authority can also result in impaired knowledge of wrongfulness. In such cases, the defendant must fully accept the divinity and believe that it is his or her role to obey divine wishes or commands. Prototypically, obedience should be automatic and unquestioning. In contrast, selective obedience after substantial intervals suggests that the defendant is taking an active role in deciding when and what to obey. In these instances, nonpsychotic motivations should be actively considered.

VOLITIONAL ISSUES AND INSANITY

Post-Hinckley campaigns by the American Bar Association (1983) and American Psychiatric Association (1983) tried to convince both legal and mental health professionals that volitional abilities were impossible to assess accurately. In referring to nonexistent research, they attempted to persuade lawmakers of an artificial dualism that extolled the cognitive prong and denounced the volitional prong of the ALI insanity standard. These large-scale efforts have left a lasting impression on many forensic clinicians, who question their abilities to assess volitional abilities.

Rogers (1987; see also Rogers & Shuman, 2000a) found that forensic clinicians had comparable abilities in assessing cognitive and volitional abilities. Using a structured approach, the Rogers Criminal Responsibility

Assessment Scales (R-CRAS; Rogers, 1984), reliabilities were almost identical for cognitive (kappa = .75) and volitional (kappa = .80) prongs. In addition, experienced forensic psychiatrists appear more confident in their conclusions about the volitional than the cognitive prongs (Wettstein, Rogers, & Mulvey, 1986).

In summary, the empirical research does *not* support the challenges concerning the evaluation of the volitional prong. While not conclusive, the available research finds the experienced forensic psychologists and psychiatrists are generally comparable in their clinical abilities for assessing cognitive and volitional prongs. *Efforts to discredit the volitional prong of insanity standards are politically motivated and empirically unsubstantiated.*

Volitional impairment is conceptualized as two closely related constructs: "irresistible-impulse" for the augmented *M'Naghten* standard and "conformity of conduct" for the ALI standard. Table 6-2 summarizes the relevant issues that are presented as a series of inquiries. Despite their substantial overlap, these constructs are addressed individually.

Irresistible-Impulse

The irresistible-impulse prong of the augmented *M'Naghten* standard requires that the defendant is markedly impaired in his or her abilities to *delay* and to *choose*. If the defendant is able to delay the criminal actions for any extended period of time, then these impulses were resisted. However, the typical process for impaired defendants is an intensification of impulses. This intensification can be either gradual or abrupt. Therefore, the capacity to delay must be considered for the most intense period.

The power to choose is the pivotal issue in evaluating the irresistible-impulse prong (see Rogers & Shuman, 2000a). To operationalize this prong, "What issues were taken into consideration before acting on the impulse?" Forensic clinicians must take care to evaluate the defendant in the context of his or her circumstances. For instance, waiting until witnesses have left likely involves a rational choice by the defendant. In contrast, the manifest disregard of circumstances may suggest but not prove an impaired choicefulness. One stringent example is the policeman-at-the-elbow rule. Simply put, would the defendant have committed the act in the presence of law enforcement?

Evidence of choicefulness is often discovered in the details of the offense. Examples may include efforts to avoid the (1) detection of the crime, (2) identity of the defendant, or (3) apprehension of the defendant. Often in the commission of the crime, decisions are made about the victims, potential evidence, and eventual departure (e.g., when and how) from the crime scene. We recommend simple open-ended questions as the forensic clinician collects a moment-by-moment, highly detailed account. These differences need to be highlighted with salient examples:

- *Simple open-ended questions*: "What happened next?" What thoughts do you remember?"
- *Open-ended questions with a biasing assumption*: "In making that decision, what was your thoughts?" "Given your strong beliefs about the victim, what were you thinking?"
- *Close-ended questions*. "Were you thinking about vengeance when you shot the victim?" "How did the prospect of being arrested affect your planning?"

The chief concern is that the forensic clinicians may impose their own assumptions of rationality and choice on defendants, features that were not present at the time of the offense. If the defendants accept these assumptions, they will likely appear much more rational and capable of choosing. This point is crucial to insanity evaluations: *Forensic clinicians should avoid encumbering their clinical inquiries with implicit motivations.*

To be considered under the *M'Naghten* standard, impaired impulses must arise directly from a severe mental disorder or defect. The clearest example is observed occasionally with severe manic episodes. No cognitive mediation occurs as the individual acts on a driving impulse. When arising from a mental disorder, the forensic clinician expects to see multiple examples of impaired impulses that involve both criminal and noncriminal matters. In contrast, an isolated example that conveniently excuses the criminal conduct raises the index of suspicion regarding its genuineness.

Traditional psychodynamic formulations are rarely invoked in insanity evaluations as explanations for criminal conduct. One formulation would be to consider most criminal behavior as id drives that were only allowed expression because of deficits in the superego (technically called superego lacunae). Therefore, impulses for criminal behavior could not be resisted. Problems with the formulation are manifold, especially in light of the *Daubert* standard. Importantly, the formulation itself posits a structure of intrapsychic mechanisms that cannot be disproved (i.e., the falsifiability criterion of *Daubert*). In addition, its error rate is unknown and likely unknowable. Its general acceptance in forensic psychology and psychiatry is very much at question. In summary, such formulations are sweepingly broad, empirically untested, and unlikely to meet the *Daubert* criteria for the admissibility of expert testimony.

In summary, determinations of irresistible impulses often rely on an exhaustive review of the alleged offense with moment-by-moment accounts. If available, witnesses are interviewed with the same attention to detail. Issues of delay and choice are closely examined. When marked deficits are found, the forensic clinician evaluates the basis of these deficits and whether they arise from a severe mental disorder or defect.

CONFORMITY OF CONDUCT

The ALI prong, "conformity of conduct to the requirements of law," generally parallels irresistible impulse. It is slightly broader in its interpretation because ALI has a less-stringent rule, specifically that the loss of volitional abilities must meet the "lacks substantial capacity" criterion. Like the augmented *M'Naghten* standard, the crux of the determination is the defendant's capacity to choose. Evidence of this capacity can be observed at different phases of the alleged crime including (1) planning, (2) preparation, (3) execution, and (4) post-event actions. Each phase should be painstakingly evaluated.

Table 7-2 summarizes the salient clinical issues that should be addressed in relation to the conformity-of-conduct prong. As noted (see #1 and #2), the criminal conduct must be experienced as compelled; the rational exercise of choice about the commission of the alleged offense is

---

TABLE 7-2. OUTLINE OF VOLITIONAL ISSUES FOUND WITH INSANITY EVALUATIONS

Irresistible Impulse

1. What was the defendant's capacity to withhold or discontinue the criminal behavior? Was he or she capable of delaying the criminal behavior?
2. Was the need to perform the criminal conduct overpowering? Was it a sudden, uncontainable impetus that directly arose from a mental disorder?
3. Would it satisfy "policeman-at-the-elbow rule"?[1]

Conformity of Conduct

4. What did the defendant perceive to be his/her options at the time of the criminal behavior?
5. Was the defendant compelled to commit the criminal behavior? What efforts did the defendant attempt to resist the criminal behavior?
6. Did the defendant choose to be in circumstances, where this loss of control could be foreseen?
7. If the capacity to conform became gradually more impaired, why did the loss of control occur at this time?
8. How was this loss of volitional capacity evidenced in other parts of the defendant's life?

---

[1]Simply put, this criterion examines whether the criminal act was committed with total disregard for criminal apprehension (e.g., in the presence of law enforcement).

confirmation that this prong was not substantially impaired. Being compelled, the forensic clinician should look for data about the defendant's *disregard for apprehension*. Systematic efforts to minimize identification and apprehension suggest rational choices and a capacity to conform conduct.

Rogers (1987) emphasized the importance of evaluating the defendant's volitional abilities in light of forseeability and avoidability. If a delusional defendant chooses to put him- or herself at risk, this choice has bearing on the conformity-of-conduct prong. For instance, a male defendant with an amphetamine-induced delusional disorder may recognize from past experiences the dangers of carrying a concealed weapon when interacting with his former lover. The decision to place himself at an extreme risk is highly relevant to the subsequent loss of volitional abilities.

Based on a mental disorder or defect, the impairment of the conformity-of-conduct prong is a process not a momentary event. Forensic clinicians should evaluate the *pattern* of impaired volitional abilities. In some cases, the defendant evidenced a gradual decline followed by a seemingly minor precipitator. In other instances, the defendant's volitional abilities are marked by a fluctuating course with periods of control and dyscontrol.

In conclusion, the evaluation of the ALI conformity-of-conduct prong should consider volitional abilities, taking into account issues of questions and content raised in the "Irresistible-Impulse" subsection. Determinations of choice must consider both detail of the offense and patterns of volitional impairment arising from the mental disorder or defect. One hallmark for impaired volitional abilities is the defendant's disregard for apprehension.

SPECIALIZED METHODS FOR ASSESSING INSANITY

Efforts to develop well-validated specialized measures of insanity standards remain sparse, despite the complexity and importance of these evaluations. At present, two specialized measures are available: Mental State at the Time of the Offense Screening Evaluation (MSE-Offense; Slobogin, Melton, & Showalter, 1984) and the Rogers Criminal Responsibility Assessment Scales (R-CRAS; Rogers, 1984). These measures vary dramatically in their development, validation, and forensic applications. As a result, they will be examined separately.

MSE-Offense

The MSE-Offense is ambitious in its goals but modest in its validation. It was intended to assess three legal doctrines associated with criminal responsibility: the insanity defense, diminished capacity defense, and the unconsciousness defense (Slobogin et al., 1984, p. 307). However, its validation is limited to one modest study that pertains only to insanity. Although originally intended as a screen, Melton, Petrila, Poythress, and Slobogin (1997) recently advocated its use as a full measure, "MSE may be able to detect the obviously insane individual for whom a more comprehensive evaluation is unnecessary" (p. 235).

Rogers and Shuman (2000b) expressed strong reservations about construction of the MSE-Offense. It relies heavily on unstandardized questions and narrative information. It incorrectly uses DSM diagnoses and terms. As an alarming example, the screening for mood disorders does not even consider depressed or manic episodes. In addition, Borum (2003) was sharply critical of the MSE-Offense and its psychometric validation. He observed that the MSE-Offense neglects entirely any form of reliability or standardization. These prominent omissions violate official test standards (AERA/APA/NCME, 1999) for any evaluative device or procedure.[5]

The validation of the MSE-Offense is fundamentally flawed. It relies exclusively on ultimate opinions (i.e., potential legal defense: yes or no) in its validation with an inadequate sample (36 cases) and experts that are likely biased by demand characteristics. As noted by Rogers and Shuman (2000a), its results are very modest and statistically nonsignificant (kappa = .26; $p = .17$).

Poythress, Melton, Petrila, and Slobogin (2000) attempted to defend the MSE-Offense. Most telling was their concession regarding its psychometric inadequacies; they acknowledged "minimal disagreement" (p. 30) with the Rogers and Shuman (2000b) critique. They quarreled with the characterization of "obviously insane individual" as being an ultimate opinion; they asserted it is only a "preliminary report to the attorney" (p. 31) with the unstated inference that experts could discount their opinions on the ultimate issue, if asked at trial.

R-CRAS

The R-CRAS was developed as a method to "quantify essential psychological and situational variables at the time of the crime and to implement criterion-based decision models for criminal responsibility" (Rogers, 1984, p. 1). In constructing the R-CRAS, a study group of forensic

---

[5]Poythress et al. (2000, p. 31) try to escape criticism by claiming the MSE-Offense is not a "test" but only a "protocol." However, the official standards (AERA/APA/NCME, 1999, p. 3) prevent any evasions via semantic distinctions with their inclusive definition: "A test is an evaluative device or procedure in which a sample of an examinee's behavior in a specified domain is obtained and subsequently evaluated and scored using a standardized process."

psychologists and psychiatrists operationalized the ALI standard and standardized ratings for assessing ALI components. Additional criteria were subsequently developed to address the M'Naghten and Michigan-based GBMI standards.

Validation data were composed of 260 insanity cases collected from six forensic centers. For individual items, the test–retest reliability after a 2.7-week interval was generally moderate ($Mr = .58$), although modest for several items with very limited range. This paradigm is very rigorous in relying on retrospective accounts (i.e., time of the offense) and type of reliability (test–retest reliability). Reliability for components of the insanity standard was generally high (M kappa $= .81$) with almost perfect agreement about the final decision (kappa $= .94$).

Validation research focused primarily on construct validity. Hypothesized patterns for sane and insane defendants were consistently observed in three separate studies (Rogers, 1984). More recently, Rogers and Sewell (1999) combined the original data with newer samples ($N = 413$ insanity cases) and applied discriminant models to each component of the ALI standard. Each component produced highly discriminating patterns with an average hit rate of 94.3%. Of equal importance, the pattern variables related to the discriminant function was conceptually sound. Beyond construct validation, external criteria have produced robust results. In particular, comparisons to legal outcome have produced an excellent concordance rate of 88.3% with a phi coefficient of .723.

The R-CRAS provides a useful template for organizing insanity evaluations. Forensic clinicians wanting to use the R-CRAS should be informed regarding its development and validation (see Rogers, 1984; Rogers & Sewell, 1999). Several recent reviews (Borum, 2003; Shapiro, 1999) provide a balanced treatment. The primary criticisms (Melton et al., 1997; Ogloff, Roberts, & Roesch, 1993) involve its use of ultimate opinions. Importantly, forensic clinicians who feel uncomfortable with ultimate opinions are not compelled by the R-CRAS to address them. In addressing both sides of this debate, Borum (2003) noted that a national survey of forensic psychologists and psychiatrists found that fewer than 20% believed that rendering ultimate opinions were inappropriate.

GENERAL CROSS-EXAMINATION ISSUES

Contested insanity trials, perhaps more than other criminal issues, may lead to a polarization of forensic clinicians as they play a pivotal role. In some instances, the verdict itself appears to rest on the strength and substance of each expert's testimony. Attorneys may attempt to capitalize on the competitiveness and even rivalry between experts. Experts, susceptible to this polarization, are vulnerable on cross-examination because competitiveness and partisanship weaken their credibility.

This section of cross-examination issues is necessarily selective in its coverage. It begins with intrapsychic models, which may pose a major challenge to cross-examination. Next, the cross-examination on standardized measures is considered with antipodal issues of unwarranted overconfidence and summary dismissal. The section concludes with a discussion of prosecutorial and defense biases.

Intrapsychic Models

Experts, adopting intrapsychic models of criminal motivation, may insulate themselves from careful scrutiny by their use of language and theory. Experts sensitive to criticism may misread this statement as a wholesale indictment of intrapsychic theory and practice. This is simply not the case. It focuses only on criminal motivation. It addresses only the potential for obscuration; nothing in intrapsychic models prevents a lucid and easily comprehensible presentation of findings.

Intrapsychic models are often equated with psychodynamic thinking. Attorneys should be aware that this conceptualization is too circumscribed; other prominent examples include Jungian and Adlerian theories. Moreover, psychodynamic thinking is not monolithic. Instead, major variations of psychoanalytic theory and ego psychology continue to thrive. Given this complexity, attorneys may need their own consulting expert to clarify seemingly abstruse material.

This subsection presents general ideas that can be used to cross-examine experts espousing intrapsychic models. We focus on *intrapsychic conflicts* because of their relevance to criminal behavior.

The initial goal of cross-examination is a clarification of the expert's intrapsychic model, including its name, leading proponents, and any authoritative sources. This clarification will assist in cross-examination and hopefully minimize any "theoretical drift" into eclecticism. Once the model is established, an examination of its assumptions may prove useful. As an example, *"According to your understanding, Doctor, what are the causes of crime?* Or more specifically, *"Was the crime in this case caused or affected by intrapsychic conflicts?"*

One option for cross-examination is pleasantly but persistently to pursue scientific evidence regarding the validity and universality of intrapsychic conflicts. Box 7.1 includes illustrative cross-examination. Jurors may be skeptical about intrapsychic conflicts as an "excuse" for criminal conduct, especially if everyone has such conflicts but very few apparently

---

Box 7-1   ILLUSTRATIVE CROSS-EXAMINATION: INTRAPSYCHIC
CONFLICTS AND INSANITY

A. Intrapsychic Conflict: Universal and Valid?
   1. *Can we ever solve this intrapsychic conflict so that it goes completely away?*
   2. *Does everyone have it? . . . Both women and men? . . . Is it universal?*
   3. *Not to put you on the defensive, doctor, but what is the evidence that intrapsychic conflict is universal?*
B. Divergent Theories about Intrapsychic Conflict
   4. *There are two-sides to every coin; what is evidence that intrapsychic conflicts are not universal?*
   5. *Would it be fair to say that many* [select: psychologists/psychiatrists] *embrace theories that do not include intrapsychic conflicts?*
   6. [for psychologists] *Isn't the most common theory among psychologists "cognitive-behavioral therapy" or CBT? . . . And that theory does not embrace intrapsychic conflicts, does it? . . . Doctor, are you telling the Court that the majority of psychologists are wrong and that you are right?*
   7. [for psychiatrists] *Would it be fair to say that many psychiatrists embrace biological theories that do not include intrapsychic conflicts? . . . Are you really disputing the knowledge and expertise of these psychiatrists and neuroscientists who have made great strides in treating the mentally ill? . . . Are you telling the Court that these renowned psychiatrists are wrong and that you are right?*
C. Applying Intrapsychic Conflicts to the Trial
   8. *What about my neighbor who seems so quiet, peaceful, and self-accepting—Is she harboring these intrapsychic conflicts? . . . And my* [pastor/rabbi], *is* [he/she] *plagued with them as well?*
   9. *Aren't you telling us that all the members of the jury are beset with intrapsychic conflicts?*
   10. *Aren't your ideas about intrapsychic conflict based only on hindsight analysis? . . .* [if "no" or "uncertain"] *Before it happens, do you have any idea whose intrapsychic conflicts could get them into trouble? . . .* [optional; a sarcastic inquiry] *Given your expertise, who on the jury should we watch out for?*
   11. *Your ideas about intrapsychic conflict would apply to most criminals, wouldn't they? . . . Do you have any personal or professional reservations about making excuses for criminals? . . .* [likely to object] *Come on doctor, aren't you saying its not their fault?*
   12. [optional] *Doctor, you are not immune to intrapsychic conflicts, are you? . . . How are your intrapsychic conflicts affecting your testimony today? . . .* [may equivocate] *Isn't the truthful answer, doctor, that you don't really know how they are affecting you at this moment?*

---

engage in serious criminal acts. This skepticism is likely to be heightened by the knowledge that the majority of psychologists and psychiatrists do not espouse intrapsychic conflicts as a primary explanation for deviant or antisocial behavior.

Attorneys may wish to underscore that fact that no one in the courtroom is exempt from intrapsychic models. Sample questions in Box 7-1 illustrate (1) the implicit judgments about jury members (e.g., they are "sicker" than they realized) and (2) carte blanche excuses for many criminals (e.g., their "unconscious" was responsible). The general thrust of these illustrative questions is to marginalize the expert testimony because of its negative implications about juries and positive inferences about criminal defendants: Do they see everyone "at war with themselves?" What credence do they give to a theory that could be used to "explain away" most criminal behavior?

Occasionally, experts espousing intrapsychic theory will attempt to obscure issues by offering abstruse terms or unexplained interpretations. Sometimes attorneys attempt to compete with these experts by showing off their own knowledge and erudition. This strategy does not make sense. Instead, we advise attorneys to take the perspective of a juror and ask simple direct questions. Convoluted responses can be summarized on a visual display so that each component can be carefully queried. Recalcitrant experts can be exhorted to speak plain English.

Test Results and Diagnostic Data

Criminal attorneys are likely to encounter forensic clinicians with faulty knowledge and limited expertise at the use of standardized data. Tests and other standardized measures offer valuable information that can augment insanity evaluations. Their strengths lie in systematic methods of addressing diagnostic issues, impairment, and response styles (e.g., malingering). Their limitations lie in their circumscribed relevance to retrospective functioning and to the assessment of legally defined cognitive and volitional abilities. Significant problems are observed from two types of unbalanced perspectives:

1. Overly confident experts extol the strengths and discount the limitations of standardized measures.
2. Summarily dismissive experts discount the strengths and magnify the limitations of standardized measures.

1. Overly Confident Experts

The greatest danger with overly confident experts is that they will draw improper conclusions from standardized data about components on a particular insanity standard. This danger is escalated when substantial time has passed since the alleged offense and changes have occurred in the defendant's functioning (i.e., a prior episode). With limited exceptions (e.g., the SADS), inventories and diagnostic measures are not validated for prior episodes.

The MMPI-2 is commonly used by forensic psychologists and psychiatrists in conducting insanity evaluations. As previously noted, it may provide valuable data about the defendant's current functioning and response styles. What possible strategies should be used by attorneys if experts overstep the boundaries of MMPI-2 validation?

As described in Chapter 3, many forensic clinicians will rely on computerized MMPI-2 interpretations. Their resulting testimony is highly vulnerable on cross-examination (see Box 3-1). In addition to the issues raised in Box 3-1, none of the interpretations/conclusions provided by the MMPI-2 computerized reports will address (1) discrete episodes in the past or (2) components of the insanity defense. Examples of potential cross-examination are provided:

- *Isn't is true, doctor, that the MMPI-2 was administered __ months after the crime in question? And that many events have occurred including __* [e.g., incarceration, hospitalization, or treatment]? *In all honesty, you don't know what* [his/her] *MMPI-2 profile would have looked like on the day of the offense, do you?*
- *You were aware that the MMPI-2 was not validated for assessing past diagnoses, weren't you? . . .* [optional] *When you took an oath to tell the "whole truth" did you have your fingers crossed? . . . Then why didn't you fully disclose the limitations of your findings?*

Some forensic clinicians will maintain that the MMPI-2 was useful in establishing their conclusions about the defendant's sanity. These inferences are simply unsupported by the clinical and empirical literature. For example, Rogers and McKee (1995) conducted a descriptive analysis of the MMPI-2 and insanity evaluations and did not find conceptually based differences. As summarized in Appendix G, sane defendants with Axis I diagnoses tended to have *higher* elevations than those who met either M'Naghten or ALI criteria. Cross-examination may take into account the Rogers and McKee study by making copies of Appendix G:

- *Are you aware of the study by Rogers and McKee that found the MMPI-2 could not differentiate between sane and insane defendants?*
- *Are you aware that <u>sane</u> defendants scored higher on clinical scales than those evaluated as <u>insane</u>? . . .* [if negative, ask the expert to review the findings in Appendix G and read to the court the key results and conclusion]

2. Dismissive Experts

Arguments can be made on a case-by-case basis for why standardized measures would have little bearing on a particular insanity case. However, these arguments should be based on sound knowledge and compelling logic. As noted in Chapter 3, insularity and ignorance are not adequate reasons. Moreover, experts bear the ongoing responsibility of remaining current on specialized knowledge and training. Therefore, professional indolence cannot be used as an excuse.

One option is to approach standardized measures via the expert's current training. Sample cross-examination questions are provided:

- *What is your formal training in conducting insanity evaluations?* . . . [if responds with supervised experiences] *Doctor, that was not the question. The question was, "What is your <u>formal training</u> in conducting insanity evaluations?"*
- *What is your formal training with the Rogers Criminal Responsibility Assessment Scales? In keeping current on forensic [psychology/psychiatry], have you carefully reviewed its test manual?* . . . [if "no"] *Would it be fair to say that your decision whether to use the Rogers Criminal Responsibility Assessment Scales was based on inadequate training and ignorance?* . . . [if quibbles] *Doctor, you already admitted that you weren't trained in it and had not reviewed its test manual. Let's face it, you don't know the Rogers Criminal Responsibility Assessment Scales, do you?* . . . *Then your decision not to use it was based on ignorance, wasn't it?*

Prosecutorial and Defense Biases

Expert track records on insanity cases can reveal systematic biases for the prosecution or the defense. Some experts have developed reputations, whether deserved or not, that they always appear on a particular side. Cross-examination can address both their track records and their conceptualization of the relevant insanity standard. Regarding track records, cross-examination questions might include the following:

1. *How many times in your career have you testified in insanity cases?* . . . *How many times was there an expert on the other side disagreeing with you?* . . . *Did some of the cases have more than one expert disagreeing with you?* . . . *Please give us an honest estimate of how many* [select: dozens/hundreds]*of experts disagree with you?*
2. *Do you have a reputation of being friendly to the* [select: prosecution/defense]? . . . [likely to deny "friendliness"] *Who calls*

you to testify the majority of the time? ...More than 60% of the time? ...More than 70%?

3. *Do you deny "being in the pocket" of the* [select: prosecution/defense]?
4. *Were the experts who disagreed with you well trained? ... What percentage of the time were they right and you were wrong?*
5. [if highly disproportionate] *So you are telling us that you are better than __% of well-trained experts, isn't that correct? ... Doctor, are you conceited? ...* [if "no"] *Then, what's your proof that you are so much better?*
6. [if about equal] *Then we shouldn't take your word over that of Dr. __* [an opposing expert in this case], *should we?*

A second option is to examine the expert's conceptualization of the particular insanity standard. Systematic differences may reflect prosecutorial (i.e., narrowly defined) or defense (i.e., broadly defined) biases in applying components of the insanity standard. Please consider the following examples:

1. *You disagreed with Dr. __ about whether the defendant* [select: knew/appreciated] *wrongfulness, didn't you?*
2. *With reference to __ insanity standard, what is your definition of wrongfulness?*
3. *I would like to understand your concept of wrongfulness. If the person thought* [he/she]*was acting in self-defense, would that likely qualify? ... What about if [he/she] was carrying out official duties, like the CIA, would that likely qualify? ... Or responding to a divine authority, would that likely qualify? ... Or protecting society from a terrible catastrophe would that likely qualify?*

The point of this cross-examination is twofold. First, it tests the expert's knowledge of the insanity standard and the wrongfulness prong. Hesitations or equivocations should be addressed in detail. For example, *"I noticed you that hesitated. Would you share with the court your reservations?"* Second, it provides a framework for questioning the expert about the current case. One option includes the following:

4. *How does your understanding of wrongfulness differ from Dr. __* [an opposing expert] *in this particular case?*
5. *What changes in your understanding of wrongfulness would allow you to agree with Dr __?*

SUMMARY

Contested insanity cases often provide high drama in their polarization of forensic experts. Experts conducting insanity evaluations have ethical and professional responsibilities of maintaining sophisticated knowledge about relevant insanity standards and specialized training in assessment methods. Attorneys must hold experts to high standards of practice and be prepared to cross-examine them on any deficiencies in their use of sources, specialized methods, and conclusory opinions.

8

Beyond Insanity: Other Issues of Criminal Responsibility

Considerations of criminal liability extend beyond insanity to mens rea and automatism (Goldstein, Morse, & Shapiro, 2003). The legal foundations for these standards of criminal responsibility are subjected to considerable debate with formulations including justifications, excuses, and partial excuses (Buchanan, 2000; Goldstein et al., 2003; Reznek, 1997). Rather than enter this debate, we introduce affirmative defenses and mental health issues involving the failure to prove the requisite elements of the prima facie case.

Affirmative defenses exculpate the defendant even when the prosecution proves all of the elements of its prima facie case. To invoke an affirmative defense successfully, the defense must be raised and proved by the defendant. As discussed in Chapter 7, the insanity defense is an affirmative defense for which marked impairment of legally specified abilities renders the defendant nonresponsible. Affirmative defenses may involve variants of self-defense in which the defendant responds to misperceived threats. Originally described as "psychological self-defense"(Ewing, 1987), we examine these types of self-defense with the framework of *psychological context evidence*. A common example is a female defendant, who claims that her experiences as a battered spouse psychologically altered her perceptions of the necessity to use deadly force in self-defense.

The prosecution must prove the requisite elements (i.e., mens rea and actus reus) of the case. Failure to prove these elements may result in either an acquittal or a reduction in the degree of the offense to which the defendant is found guilty. A common example is a failure to prove the required intent for an offense, such as first-degree murder, in the case of a severely impaired defendant.

RELEVANT LEGAL STANDARDS

The conviction of a crime requires proof of a voluntary act proscribed by the law (i.e., actus reus) as well as proof of a guilty state of mind (i.e., mens rea). Evidence of a mental disorder that negates either of these requirements disproves an essential element of the state's prima facie case required for conviction. Indeed, in those jurisdictions that have repealed the insanity defense (Idaho, Montana, and Utah), demonstrating the absence of mens rea may be the only context in which exculpatory evidence (in contrast with mitigation evidence at sentencing) of the defendant's mental disorder is legally relevant and admissible. In these jurisdictions, the form and content of permissible exculpatory evidence of mental disorder to negate mens rea will turn on the distinctions between the mens rea requirement for the offense and the insanity defense. The differences between these standards may appear nuanced or subtle in examining the effects of a mental disorder on (1) the intention to commit a criminal act (mens rea) or (2) the comprehension of its wrongfulness (insanity defense). However, the differences in outcome under these standards are profound. Defendants found not guilty by reason of insanity are generally subject to automatic commitment. Defendants found not guilty because the state did not prove an element of the prima facie case are not subject to any punishment, if lesser-included offenses do not apply.

A specific context in which exculpatory evidence of the defendant's mental state may present an issue for mens rea, actus reus, and the insanity defense involves evidence of automatism. Automatism refers to involuntary behavior that occurs in an unconscious state. The courts are divided on how to address automatism: some courts address it under the insanity defense, others under mens rea, and still others under actus reus (see Automatism section below). Its categorization affects both the conditions of admissibility as well as the consequences of its successful use.

Evidence of a mental or emotional disorder may also be relevant, not specifically to address mens rea, actus reus, or an insanity defense, but to provide a context in which the fact finder is being asked to apply a well-recognized affirmative defense, such as self-defense. Where admissible, evidence that the defendant suffered from battered woman syndrome may be relevant to help the fact finder to comprehend the reasonableness of the defendant's claim of self-defense when she faced no imminent threat of serious bodily harm that would necessitate the use of deadly force. When evidence of battered woman syndrome is successful in persuading the fact finder to accept the affirmative defense of self-defense, the defendant's use of deadly force is permitted and the defendant is entitled to be released from confinement.

Evidence of a defendant's mental disorder may also bear on the guilty-but-mentally-ill verdict. In contrast with the previous standards, which negate an element of the state's case in chief or support an affirmative defense, this use of the defendant's mental disorder results from a finding that the defendant suffers from a mental disorder whose impact or severity does not rise to the level necessary to find the defendant not guilty by reason of insanity. The finding of guilt results in the defendant's confinement for the period of time associated with punishment for the offense but the place or conditions of confinement may be altered to address issues of treatment.

Mens Rea

The impact of a defendant's mental disorder on criminal responsibility may overlap the insanity defense and mens rea. However, a fundamental difference exists between them. As described by Morse (1984, p. 6):

> [A] defendant claiming no mens rea because of mental disorder is not asserting some lesser form of legal insanity, that is, he is not claiming that he is partially or less responsible for the crime charged. Rather, the defendant is straightforwardly denying the prosecution's prima facie case by attempting to cast doubt on the prosecution's claim that a requisite mental element was present at the time of the offense. He is claiming that he is not guilty of that crime at all, although he may be guilty of a lesser crime if all the elements of the latter are proven.

Many jurisdictions permit a defendant to choose whether to introduce exculpatory evidence of a mental disorder to support an insanity defense or to negate mens rea. However, a few jurisdictions limit exculpatory evidence of a mental disorder to mens rea, while others limit such evidence to an insanity defense.

Mens rea is said to comprise the subjective aspect of criminal culpability and actus reus is said to comprise the objective aspect of criminal culpability (Dan-Cohen, 2000). This characterization is intended to imply that the criminal law considers actus reus largely based on external or observable considerations (i.e., what *did* the defendant do?). In contrast, mens rea is largely based on internal considerations (i.e., what did the defendant *intend* to do?). These rough categorizations are best understood in context and against the background of the common law approach to distinguishing the general and specific intent requirement for mens rea. As the Supreme Court has noted in *United States v. Bailey* (1980, pp. 403–404):

> Few areas of criminal law pose more difficulty than the proper definition of the mens rea required for any particular crime . . . At common law, crimes generally were classified as requiring either "general intent" or "specific intent." This venerable distinction, however, has been the source of a good deal of confusion. As one treatise explained: "Sometimes 'general intent' is used in the same way as 'criminal intent' to mean the general notion of mens rea, while 'specific intent' is taken to mean the mental state required for a particular crime. Or, 'general intent' may be used to encompass all forms of the mental state requirement, while 'specific intent' is limited to the one mental state of intent. Another possibility is that 'general intent' will be used to characterize an intent to do something on an undetermined occasion, and 'specific intent' to denote an intent to do that thing at a particular time and place." . . . This ambiguity has led to a movement away from the traditional dichotomy of intent and toward an alternative analysis of mens rea . . . This new approach, exemplified in the American Law Institute's Model Penal Code [in which] the ambiguous and elastic term "intent" is replaced with a hierarchy of culpable states of mind. The different levels in this hierarchy are commonly identified, in descending order of culpability, as purpose, knowledge, recklessness, and negligence . . .

Conviction of a criminal offense requires a finding that the defendant performed a proscribed act along with an accompanying guilty state of mind. The guilty state of mind required to convict is not generic for all crimes, but is offense specific. These requirements are best understood in the context of a particular system and how it defines the corresponding offenses it criminalizes. The Model Penal Code of the American Law Institute (ALI) has been a major influence on substantive criminal law in the United States since its completion in 1962. The Model Penal Code has, to varying degrees, influenced the penal codes of 34 states—Alabama, Alaska, Arizona, Arkansas, Colorado, Connecticut, Delaware, Florida, Georgia, Hawaii, Illinois, Indiana, Iowa, Kansas, Kentucky, Nebraska, New Hampshire, New Jersey, New Mexico, New York, North Dakota, Maine, Missouri, Minnesota, Montana, Ohio, Oregon, Pennsylvania, South Dakota, Texas, Utah, Virginia, Washington, and Wyoming (see the Model Penal Code, Forward; ALI, 1962). The Texas Penal Code § 6.03 (2004), reflecting the categorical definitions described in the Model Penal Code (ALI, 1962), distinguishes the range of culpable mental states as follows: (a) A person acts intentionally, or with intent, with respect to the nature of his conduct or to a result of his conduct when it is his conscious objective or desire to engage in the conduct or cause the result. (b) A person acts knowingly, or with knowledge, with respect to the nature of his conduct or to circumstances surrounding his conduct when he is aware of the nature of his conduct or that the circumstances exist. A person acts knowingly, or with knowledge, with respect to a result of his conduct when he is aware that his conduct is reasonably certain to cause the result. (c) A person acts recklessly, or is reckless, with respect to circumstances surrounding his conduct or the result of his conduct when he is aware of but consciously disregards a substantial and unjustifiable risk that the circumstances exist or the result will occur. The risk must be of such a nature and degree that its disregard constitutes a gross deviation from the standard of care that an ordinary person would exercise under all the circumstances as viewed from the actor's standpoint. (d) A person acts with criminal negligence, or is criminally negligent, with respect to circumstances surrounding his conduct or the result of his conduct when he ought to be aware of a substantial and unjustifiable risk that the circumstances exist or the result will occur. The risk must be of such a nature and degree that the failure to perceive it constitutes a gross deviation from the standard of care that an ordinary person would exercise under all the circumstances as viewed from the actor's standpoint.

The Complexity of Mens Rea Exemplified by Texas Law

We use extended examples from Texas statutes and case law to underscore the complexity of mens rea issues. Other states vary their definitions and applications of intent. Because that extended treatment is not possible in this chapter, attorneys must educate themselves and their experts by assembling the relevant case law for their jurisdictions.

The case law provides examples of their meaning in context. The Texas Penal Code specifies that to act intentionally or with intent requires that the defendant consciously desires engaging in proscribed conduct or producing a proscribed result. Direct evidence of intent is not necessary but may be inferred from the surrounding circumstances (*Schexnider v. State*, 1997). The intent to do what the law forbids provides sufficient proof of intent. By way of illustration, the Texas courts found that there was sufficient evidence to conclude that a defendant's aggravated assault of a police officer was *intentional* where the evidence showed that the defendant lunged at the officer with two knives and failed to heed the officer's orders to drop them (*Meza v. State*, 2002). However, unless the defendant adopts and ratifies the intent of another, the defendant is to be judged by his or her own intent (*Steen v. State*, 1934).

The Texas Penal Code specifies that a defendant acts knowingly or with knowledge when the defendant is aware that his or her conduct is reasonably certain to cause the proscribed result. How does this differ from intentionality?

> [T]he distinction between knowing and intentional is narrow, and is preserved only because of the criminal law's traditional creation of specific intent offenses such as burglary, arson, and theft. We say "only" because there is little difference, in terms of blameworthiness, between one who wills a particular result and one who is willing for it to occur—between, for example, one ... who shoots into a moving car, intending to kill the driver, and one who shoots into a moving car he knows is occupied. The formulated distinction between intentional and knowing, as to results, is thus between desiring the result and being reasonably certain that it will occur ... Proof of knowing conduct requires more than a showing that the defendant was aware of but consciously disregarded a substantial and unjustifiable risk that the result would occur (*Dusek v. State*, 1998, p. 134).

By way of illustration, a defendant's conviction for *knowing* possession of a controlled substances was upheld on the basis of evidence that the arresting officer observed the defendant's speech was slurred, eyes were bloodshot, and found a glass crack pipe on the floor between the defendant's legs (*Palmer v. State*, 1993).

The Texas Penal Code specifies that a person acts recklessly or is reckless when he or she consciously disregards a substantial risk that and that disregard amounts to a gross deviation from what would be expected of an ordinary person as viewed from the actor's standpoint. In contrast with criminal negligence, which involves inattentive risk creation, recklessness involves conscious risk creation (*Lewis v. State*, 1975). By way of illustration, a conviction for *reckless* injury to a child was upheld where the evidence supported a finding that the defendant placed a young child in a tub of hot water (*Mills v. State*, 1987).

The Texas Penal Code specifies that a person acts with criminal negligence or is criminally negligent when the defendant ought to be aware of a substantial risk and that failure is a gross deviation from the care that an ordinary person would exercise under the circumstances. By way of illustration, evidence that the defendant drove at an excessive speed in a residential neighborhood near a bus stop at a time when children could be expected to be on their way to school was sufficient to support a conviction for *criminally negligent* homicide (*Thompson v. State*, 1984).

Applying this range of culpable mental states to the crime of murder, the Texas Penal Code (Texas, 2004, at § 19.02) states that a person commits the offense of murder only if he or she (1) intentionally or knowingly causes the death of an individual; (2) intends to cause serious bodily injury and commits an act clearly dangerous to human life that causes the death of an individual; or (3) commits or attempts to commit a felony, other than manslaughter, and in the course of and in furtherance of the commission or attempt, or in immediate flight from the commission or attempt, he commits or attempts to commit an act clearly dangerous to human life that causes the death of an individual.

The *intentional or knowing* mental state to convict parents for murder of their child was supported by evidence that child was emaciated, that the grandparents had urged the parents to seek medical help, and that the parents had denied the child food and medical care (*Kohler v. State*, 1986). A defendant's conviction for murder based on an *intent to cause serious bodily injury* was affirmed notwithstanding the defendant's statement that he did not intend to kill him when he cut his throat (*Martinez v. State*, 2000). And, the defendant's conduct resulting in the death of the victim during an *attempt to commit a felony* (i.e., robbery) supplied the mental state necessary for the crime of murder (*Foster v. State*, 2000).

By way of contrast, reckless conduct (conscious disregard of a substantial and unjustifiable risk) which results in the death of another constitutes manslaughter (Texas, 2002, § 19.02) and criminally negligent conduct (disregard of a substantial and unjustifiable risk of which the defendant ought to be aware) which results in the death of another constitutes criminally negligent homicide (Texas, 2004, § 19.02).

Absent an insanity defense, the admissibility of evidence of a mental disorder to negate mens rea turns on the intent requirement for the crime. Notwithstanding efforts to escape the confusion engendered by the common law's general and specific intent dichotomy, Texas courts and the courts in most states that follow *M'Naghten* standard continue to make this distinction. Except when the defendant raises an insanity defense, the Texas Court of Criminal Appeals has held (*Cowles v. State*, 1974, pp. 609–610) that evidence of the defendant's mental disorder is admissible to disprove mens rea only where the crime demands proof of specific intent:

> In States following [*M'Naghten*] it is settled that proof to the effect that the accused was the victim of mental weakness or emotional disturbances falling short of the inability to distinguish between right and wrong does not raise the issue of insanity ... An exception to this rule is where specific intent is an element of the offense for which the accused is being tried, as in the different degrees of murder and the "with intent" crimes ... The reasoning behind the exclusion of this type of evidence is that if the accused can distinguish between right and wrong and understands the nature and consequences of his acts, and is therefore legally sane, the fact that he suffers from a weak mind or from emotional problems does not excuse his act, and is consequently immaterial on the question of guilt and would only confuse the jury if admitted into evidence.

Thus, proof that a defendant whose actions resulted in the death of another was, as the result of a mental disorder, unable to formulate a "conscious objective or desire to engage in the conduct or cause the result" would be relevant to negate the require specific intent mental state required for murder in Texas. If persuaded that a reasonable doubt exists as to the presence of that culpable mental state, the fact finder should return a verdict of not guilty of murder, unless intent is supplied by the felony-murder provision of § 19.03(3). Alternatively, the mens rea required for criminal negligence demands proof of general intent (i.e., defendant ought to be aware of substantial and unjustifiable risk) but not specific intent. Thus, in the case of a charge of criminally negligent homicide, absent an insanity defense, evidence of the defendant's mental disorder is not admissible to disprove mens rea.

Mens Rea in Federal Jurisdictions

In the federal courts, a defendant seeking to introduce exculpatory evidence of a mental disorder is permitted to decide whether that evidence is relevant and tactically most beneficial to support an insanity defense or to negate mens rea. If the defendant does not raise an insanity defense, the admissibility of evidence of a mental disorder to disprove mens rea is limited to crimes involving a specific intent requirement (*United States v. Cameron*, 1990; *United States v. Yockel*, 2003). Federal case law provides its own formulation of specific intent.

The concept of specific intent in the federal courts has been tied to whether the intent requirement for the crime turns on an objective or subjective standard. Crimes that require proof of the defendant's *subjective* intent are regarded as specific intent crimes for which evidence of mental disorder may be relevant to negate mens rea. Conversely, crimes requiring only proof of *objective* intent are regarded as general intent crimes for which evidence of a mental disorder is not relevant to negate mens rea. The following opinion of the District of Columbia Court of Appeals in *United States v. Brawner* (1972, p. 999) is frequently cited by the federal courts to illustrate this distinction: "An offense like deliberated and premeditated murder requires a specific intent that cannot be satisfied merely by showing that defendant failed to conform to an objective standard." For those offenses whose mens rea requirement is satisfied by an objective standard, exculpatory evidence of a mental disorder in federal court is only admissible in support of an insanity defense. Thus, in *United States v. Yockel* (2003), the Eighth Circuit Court of Appeals concluded that bank robbery is a general intent crime and that the intimidation requirement for the crime is to be judged by an objective standard (i.e., whether the defendant engaged in conduct reasonably calculated to put another in fear). In the absence of a specific intent requirement, it was irrelevant whether the defendant intended to intimidate the teller. Thus, the Court of Appeals concluded that in the absence of an insanity defense, the trial court correctly excluded evidence of the defendant's history of mental illness to negate mens rea.

The Mens Rea Alternative to Insanity

States, which repealed the insanity defense, place heightened importance on evidence of a mental disorder to negate mens rea. As an example, Montana (2003) law explicitly provides that: "Evidence that the defendant suffered from a mental disease or defect or developmental disability is admissible to prove that the defendant did or did not have a state of mind that is an element of the offense." (Montana, 2003). To the same effect, Utah's (2003) articulated the following: "(1) (a) It is a defense to a prosecution under any statute or ordinance that the defendant, as a result of mental illness, lacked the mental state required as an element of the offense charged."

The mental state required in states with only mens rea defenses also varies by the type of offense. In Utah, for example, assault does not have a specific mental state required as an element of that offense, which it defines as "an act committed with unlawful force or violence that causes harm to another" (Utah, 2003a). However, the more serious offense of aggravated assault requires proof of the elements of assault as well as "intentionally causing serious bodily injury to another" (Utah, 2003b).

Prohibiting Mens Rea Testimony

Several states that have retained an insanity defense, such as Arizona (*State v. Mott*, 1997) and Michigan (*People v. Carpenter*, 2001), do not allow psychological or psychiatric evidence to negate specific intent, but only to support an insanity defense. Fearing the consequences of an unconditional acquittal for a mentally disordered defendant, these states have limited exculpatory evidence of mental disorder to instances in which the defendant will likely be confined in prison or a maximum security mental hospital. This reasoning is expressed in a Michigan Supreme Court ruling:

> We agree with the Supreme Court of Wisconsin that where . . . the statutes provide that a person found not guilty by reason of insanity is to be committed to a mental treatment facility until recovered and until his return to society presents no danger to the public, the introduction of evidence of mental condition on the question of impaired capacity to form intent during the guilt phase of the trial could well be required to acquit the defendant, sane or insane, without ever inquiring into the issue of sanity and without regard to the provisions of the statute requiring treatment of those pleading and establishing insanity (*People v. Carpenter*, 2001, p. 283).

AUTOMATISM

Criminal culpability, as noted above, requires that the defendant be found to have engaged in an unlawful act (actus reus) contemporaneously accompanied by a guilty state of mind (mens rea). The requirement of actus reus has been understood to necessitate a finding that the defendant has voluntarily committed a proscribed act. If the defendant's movement is controlled or precipitated by a force other than the defendant, it does not satisfy the requirement of actus reus. Accordingly, the majority of jurisdictions address claims of automatism as a negation of actus reus (*Sellers v. State*, 1991; *State v. Caddell*, 1975; *Fulcher v. State*, 1981). This focuses the case on the question whether the defendant engaged in a voluntary act, as reflected in the Supreme Court's interpretation of a bank robbery statute in *Carter v. United States* (2000, p. 269):

> [A] general intent requirement suffices to separate wrongful from "otherwise innocent" conduct. Section 2113(a) [punishing the use of force or violence to take something from a bank] certainly should not be interpreted to apply to the hypothetical person who engages in forceful taking of money while sleepwalking (innocent, if aberrant activity), but this result is accomplished simply by requiring ... general intent—i.e., proof of knowledge with respect to the actus reus of the crime.

This approach is also reflected in Section 2.01 of the Model Penal Code (ALI, 1962):

> A person is not guilty of an offense unless his liability is based on conduct that includes a voluntary act or omission to perform an act of which he is physically able ... The following are not voluntary acts within the meaning of this section ... a bodily movement during unconsciousness or sleep.

Typical cases decided under this standard involve a spouse, usually a husband, who claims that he was sleepwalking when he killed his sleeping wife. In the context of a violent death, this defendant presents expert testimony which asks the fact finder to conclude that "somnambulism or sleepwalking is a dissociative state wherein an individual performs motor acts without waking consciousness [and] that a sleepwalker could perform intricate maneuvers while asleep and could commit acts of violence" and that the defendant did so in this instance (*Sallee v. State*; 1975, pp. 905–906). Other courts (e.g., *State v. Jones*, 2000, p. 706) regard acts committed in a somnambulistic state as negating both actus reus and mens rea: "Unconsciousness is a complete defense to a criminal charge because it precludes both a specific mental state and a voluntary act."

These approaches generally extend beyond the parameters of the insanity defense. The reason that most courts do not consider unconsciousness under an insanity defense is that the conduct sought to be excused is not ordinarily explained by a mental disorder, which affected the defendant's cognitive capacity to distinguish right from wrong as contemplated by the insanity defense (*Fulcher v. State*, 1981). Nonetheless, when behavior in an unconscious state is sought to be explained by a mental disorder, courts have generally been receptive to consider it under an insanity defense. Consider the reasoning in *McClain v. State* (1997, p. 108):

> While automatistic behavior could be caused by insanity, "unconsciousness at the time of the alleged criminal act need not be the result of a disease or defect of the mind"...Consistent with this view, we hold that McClain's evidence of automatism as pleaded does not need to be presented under the insanity defense. We understand McClain's defense to consist of automatism manifested in a person of sound mind. To the extent involuntary behavior is contended to result from a mental disease or defect, the insanity statute would apply.

In general, the case law does not distinguish the cause of the unconsciousness. It has included instances of somnambulism, cerebral concussion, delirium from fever or drugs, diabetic shock, and epileptic blackouts when addressing the sufficiency of evidence of unconsciousness on a case-by-case basis (*State v. Caddell*, 1975).

Knowledge of predisposition to unconsciousness may negate the automatism defense. For example, a person drives with knowledge of his or her history of blackouts may not qualify (*Gov't of Virgin Islands v. Smith*, 1960). Also, the defense is not available where it is induced by the defendant's voluntary use of alcohol or illegal drugs (*Lewis v. State*, 1943; *State v. Williams*, 1979).

Although every jurisdiction recognizes that voluntary intoxication does not exculpate criminal responsibility, it may bear on whether the defendant formed the necessary intent to commit the crime charged. As articulated by the Supreme Court of Kansas:

> It necessarily follows that drunkenness so extreme as to prevent the forming of a purpose to kill might under our statute reduce what would have been murder at the common law to manslaughter, and in a proper case instructions to that effect should be given...It is to be borne in mind, however, that 'the fact of intoxication,' no matter how complete and overpowering, is not conclusive evidence of the absence of an intent to take life...for a person to be too drunk to entertain an intent to kill it would seem that he would have to be too drunk to entertain an intent to shoot (*State v. Harden*, 1971, pp. 60–61).

Psychological Context Evidence

Psychological research has been used as framework evidence to provide a background for deciding a variety of factual questions at trial from assisting in understanding eyewitness identification to the prediction of dangerousness (Walker & Monahan, 1987). We refer to this as *psychological context evidence*. Not generally intended to recognize a new defense, it uses expert testimony to expand the scope of a recognized defense through a richer understanding of the defendant and his or her unique circumstances. Examples include battered spouses (*Ibn-Tamas v. United States*, 1979) or special circumstances faced by African Americans (*People v. Ferguson*, 1998). The admissibility of this psychological context evidence turns on its satisfaction of the jurisdiction's threshold scrutiny for expert evidence (i.e., *Daubert* or *Frye*), as well as the jurisdiction's application of its rules governing the defense it is intended to support (e.g., its willingness to consider a defendant's subjective perspective in support of a claim of self-defense).

Deadly force, which would otherwise be criminal, is permitted (privileged) to prevent the imminent use of unprivileged deadly force. The Connecticut statute (2003) typifies most states in articulating of the circumstances under which the use of deadly force is privileged for self-defense:

> [A] person is justified in using reasonable physical force upon another person to defend himself or a third person from what he reasonably believes to be the use or imminent use of physical force, and he may use such degree of force which he reasonably believes to be necessary for such purpose; except that deadly physical force may not be used unless the actor reasonably believes that such other person is (1) using or about to use deadly physical force, or (2) inflicting or about to inflict great bodily harm.

The use of deadly force which may kill or cause serious injury is permitted when there is a reasonable belief on the part of the person who seeks to use force in self-defense that an attack involving deadly force or great bodily harm is imminent and no time exists to pursue other options to avoid harm.

The majority of jurisdictions apply an *objective* standard to assess the reasonableness of the defendant's beliefs. The question under the objective standard is what a reasonable person, not necessarily the defendant, would have believed under these circumstances. Take the example of spousal abuse. To justify the use of force in self-defense to respond to an imminent threat of severe battering, the objective standard applies. When domestic violence objectively appears inevitable although not imminent, the objective standard does not sanction the use of force in self-defense, assuming that sufficient time existed to seek police assistance or to flee to safety. In this setting, the use of psychological context evidence on battered woman syndrome is intended to assist in applying the self-defense doctrine to the unique circumstances of battered women by explaining the reasonableness of their beliefs about the imminence of the battering.

The battered woman syndrome was first described in Lenore Walker's book, *The Battered Woman* (1979). It hypothesized that battered women commonly experience Posttraumatic Stress Disorder and experience a cycle of violence from tension building to battering to then appeasement. Battered woman syndrome is intended to explain why battered women (1) often remain in abusive relationships while aware of the predictable escalation of violence, and (2) may defend themselves before the violence escalates and they are unable to do so (Burke, 2002). In addition, proponents claim that battered woman syndrome is explained by Seligman's theory of "learned helplessness" postulating that women who are victims of repeated domestic violence have "learned" that they are powerless to change their circumstances.

A vigorous debate continues on the admissibility of such testimony with argument both for (e.g., Monacella, 1997) and against (e.g., Faigman & Wright, 1997). Criticisms of Walker's research methods as unscientific and theoretically inconsistent will be addressed under Clinical Operationalization. This debate is mirrored in court decisions. Several states find the syndrome is not sufficiently reliable to meet their test for admissibility of expert evidence (*Buhrle v. State*, 1981; *State v. Thomas*, 1981), but most states have chosen to admit relevant evidence of battered woman syndrome, either by case law (e.g., *Bechtel v. State*, 1992; *State v. Hodges*, 1986) or statute (e.g., California, 2004; Maryland, 2003; Missouri, 2004; Ohio, 2004).

The admissibility of battered woman's syndrome extends beyond the *objective* standard and permits at least some elements of the *subjective* standard. Evidence typically addresses whether a female defendant *perceived herself* to be in imminent danger (*Ibn-Tamas v. United States*, 1979; *State v. Kelly*, 1984; *State v. Kelly*, 1984). This extension beyond the objective standard is well articulated in *State v. Koss* (1990, p. 974): "Thus, admission of expert testimony regarding the battered woman syndrome does not establish a new defense or justification. Rather, it is to assist the trier of fact determine whether the defendant acted out of an honest belief that she was in imminent danger of death or great bodily harm and that the use of such force was her only means of escape."

Other psychological context evidence to inform existing defenses has not fared as well as battered woman syndrome. The construct of "black rage" garnered public attention when raised in the Colin Ferguson trial. However, it has not seen much success in persuading judges or juries that the use of deadly force was justified by the defendants' rage over his or her experience of racial injustice (e.g., *People v. Ferguson*, 1998; *State v. Lamar*, 1984). Defenses based on urban psychosis or television intoxication have experienced a similar fate (Falk, 1996).

The Guilty but Mentally Ill (GBMI) Standard

The GBMI verdict, first enacted in Michigan in 1975, is an alternative verdict intended to reduce the number of insanity acquittals (LeBlanc-Allman, 1990). It supplements but does not supplant the insanity defense and purports to address the defendant's need for treatment while incarcerated. Statutes embodying this approach have been adopted in Alaska (2003), Delaware (2003), Georgia (2002), Illinois (2004), Indiana

(2004), Kentucky (2003), Michigan (2003), New Mexico (2003), Pennsylvania (2004), South Carolina (2003), and South Dakota (2003).

The Michigan statute is the prototype for state statutes that have adopted the GBMI supplemental verdict option. It applies only when the defendant asserts an insanity defense. Beyond the traditional verdicts (i.e., guilty, not guilty, or not guilty by reason of insanity), the Michigan statute (MCLS § 768.36 [2003]) requires the GBMI verdict to be considered with the following criteria:

(a) The defendant is guilty beyond a reasonable doubt of an offense.
(b) The defendant has proven by a preponderance of the evidence that he or she was mentally ill at the time of the commission of that offense.
(c) The defendant has not established by a preponderance of the evidence that he or she lacked the substantial capacity either to appreciate the nature and quality or the wrongfulness of his or her conduct or to conform his or her conduct to the requirements of the law.

Thus, this GBMI verdict requires a finding that the defendant has committed the act(s) charged, while mentally disordered. Under the Michigan statute, the impairment arising from the mental disorder is clearly delineated; it must cause a substantial impairment in thought or mood (see Rogers & Shuman, 2000a). However, this disorder and concomitant impairment does not warrant the successful application of the insanity defense in that jurisdiction. Juries in some states that have adopted GBMI are informed of the consequences of the verdict, while those in other states are not.

Utah has repealed its insanity defense but retains a GBMI plea which operates as a plea of guilty. If the court finds the defendant is currently mentally ill, it is authorized to impose any sentence that could be imposed upon a nonmentally ill defendant convicted of the offense as well as commit the defendant with consideration of his or her need for treatment, care, custody, and security.

Several GBMI states, which use the *M'Naghten* insanity defense standard, have adopted the language of the ALI standard for the GBMI verdict. These states include New Mexico (N.M. Stat. Ann. § § 31-9-3 [1978], South Carolina, (S.C. Code Ann. § 17-24-20 [1976]. But see *State v. Grimes*, 355 S.E.2d 538 (S.C. 1987) reasoning that it was unlikely that the legislature intended to change the definition of *M'Naghten* insanity standard adopted by case law to an ALI standard for the GBMI verdict), and Pennsylvania (Pa. Cons. Stat. 18 § § 314 [1998]).

CLINICAL OPERATIONALIZATION OF CRIMINAL CULPABILITY STANDARDS

Portions of this chapter section might be aptly described as the *terra incognita* of forensic psychology and psychiatry. Unlike most criminal-forensic issues, the role of mental disorder in assessing criminal culpability beyond insanity (hereinafter referred to as simply "criminal culpability") is poorly understood and largely unexplored. As amply documented in *Relevant Legal Standards*, statutes and case law are often far from precise in delimiting the elements of mens rea and demarcating their appropriate applications to crimes of varying intent and complexity.

Issues of Admissibility

Mens rea is a required element of all but the most minor criminal offenses (i.e., parking violations). Nonetheless, the willingness of courts to admit expert evidence on mental abnormality to negate mens rea varies substantially. As noted above, several jurisdictions limit exculpatory evidence of a mental disorder to an insanity defense, and prohibit its introduction to negate means rea except for specific intent crimes. Other jurisdictions which have abrogated the insanity defense permit exculpatory evidence to be raised only to negate mens rea.

Several studies attempt to describe systemic patterns of admissibility. Goldstein, Morse, and Shapiro (2003) provided without citations the most conservative estimate: they reported that only about one-half of the states expressly allow *any* evidence of mental abnormality to address the requisite mens rea, while the remaining states markedly restrict its admissibility. As Goldstein et al. (2003, p. 385) observed, the Supreme Court has allowed states to impose severe restrictions on mens rea: one cited example was the total exclusion of evidence on voluntary intoxication (see *Montana v. Egelhoff*, 1996). In contrast, Melton et al. (1997) provided a substantively different perspective: merely 13 states categorically rejecting mens rea testimony while 27 states expressly allowed it in some instances. Providing legal citations, Marlowe, Lambert, and Thompson (1999) presented detailed information on mens rea and voluntary intoxication. As discussed below, they report that 20 states permit such testimony on all offenses, and additional 18 on specific-intent offenses. Attorneys will need to research the admissibility in their jurisdiction of mens rea testimony.

A potential misconception is that expert evidence on mens rea and criminal culpability invariably favors the defense. As a novel approach, the prosecution might also consider the merits of presenting expert testimony on criminal culpability. From this perspective, several issues must be considered:

1. *What is the likelihood of an outright acquittal?* Even with unrebutted expert evidence, we surmise that the likelihood of a not-guilty verdict is extremely low. For example, most specific-intent crimes have general-intent alternatives available as lesser-included offenses (see Marlow et al., 1999). Assuming these other elements of the lesser-included offense are proven, the defendant will still be convicted.
2. *What is the likelihood such testimony may assist the prosecution?* Consider for the moment a very sympathetic defendant. Expert evidence underscoring the intentional and knowing actions of the defendant may be a useful countermeasure in securing a conviction.

The remainder of this section is organized into four components. First, levels of criminal culpability are considered with an emphasis on "purpose" and "knowledge." The next two components examine issues of culpability associated with specific clinical conditions: automatism and wife-battering syndrome. Finally, the verdict option of guilty-but-mentally-ill (GBMI) is operationalized.

CRIMINAL CULPABILITY

The influential Model Penal Code (American Law Institute, 1962) articulates four levels of criminal culpability. It represents a significant departure from the reasonable-person standard (Finkel & Slobogin, 1995, p. 448). Instead, the Model Penal Code provides that the defendant's *own* perceptions and reasoning are considered. This crucial distinction between reasonable-person and defendant-based standards for forensic assessment must be underscored. In general, forensic clinicians lack expertise in the normative analyses required for a reasonable-person standard. Such analyses must consider what can be generally inferred from the actions of ordinary, unimpaired individuals. In contrast, forensic clinicians often have considerable expertise that can be applied to the defendant-based standard. For example, many forensic clinicians are highly experienced in evaluating the effects of psychotic thinking on a defendant's cognitive abilities. The key points of this discussion are summarized: forensic clinicians should

- *generally avoid testifying about the reasonable-person standard, but*
- *selectively testify about the defendant-based standard.*

Attorneys must educate their experts about the two domains of direct relevance to criminal culpability. First, forensic clinicians must be informed regarding the standard to be employed: reasonable-person versus defendant-based. Second, they should be advised regarding the levels of culpability relevant to their particular referrals. Third, forensic clinicians should be notified about any restrictions on their conclusions and testimony. According to Melton et al. (1997), these restrictions may include (1) requisite evidence of a severe mental disease or defect and (2) application to only specified crimes, such as intentional homicide or so-called specific-intent crimes.

In jurisdictions potentially allowing such testimony, attorneys must also determine which cases may warrant expert consultation on criminal culpability. In the large majority of cases, attorneys may conclude that the role for forensic clinicians in establishing criminal culpability is far too limited to be useful. In occasional cases, they may conclude that such consultations are warranted. Where ambiguity exists (i.e., the standards or culpability levels), attorneys must advise forensic clinicians about this ambiguity and apprize them of which options they wish to have evaluated. In general, decisions to consider evidence on criminal culpability will take into account the merits of the case, the openness of the trial judge to allowing such testimony, and appeal considerations.

Purpose and Knowledge

Melton et al. (1997, p. 205) provide a valuable distinction in their analysis of the Model Penal Code: purpose and knowledge focus on the defendant's mental state (i.e., defendant-based standard) while negligence is normatively defined (i.e., reasonable-person standard). Recklessness falls in an indeterminate category between the two standards. In adopting this important distinction, we focus on operationalizing *purpose* and *knowledge*.

Purpose?

1. Did the defendant accomplish his or her conscious (intended) goals?
2. Did a severe mental disease or defect impair the defendant's ability to perceive his or her goals as unlawful?
3. Can this impaired ability be corroborated by others or documented in other aspects of the defendant's contemporaneous functioning?

Knowledge?

4. Was the defendant consciously aware of his or her actions and their immediate consequences?
5. Did a severe mental disease or defect impair the defendant's ability to recognize his or her actions as unlawful?

6. Can this impaired ability be corroborated by others or documented in other aspects of the defendant's contemporaneous functioning?

With these operationalizations, failure to meet the *purpose* and *knowledge* components requires a marked impairment of cognitive abilities at the time of the offense. As a result of these impairments, defendants lack criminal culpability only if they fail to recognize the unlawfulness of their goals or actions. The courts are rightly concerned that some defendants may inappropriately assert or even malinger these impairments. Therefore, two safeguards must be considered: First, is this impairment based on a well-established mental disease or defect? Second, can the impairment be verified by others or observed in other aspects of defendants' functioning?

Recklessness and Negligence

Forensic clinicians will rarely be asked to address the recklessness of the defendant's conduct with reference to criminal culpability. In hindsight analysis, recklessness is often raised only when the defendant was wrong about the likelihood of dire consequences. However, the issue is not whether the defendant *did* exercise good judgment but whether the defendant *could* exercise such judgment. Assuming the defendant generally exercises good judgment, the formidable task is to establish how the specific circumstances at the time of the offense might render him or her incapable of such judgment at the time of the offense. One common reason is self-induced states, such as intoxication (see Intoxication section).

Attorneys must be alert for specious reasoning in recklessness determinations. Such reasoning might be implicitly based on the mislogic: "The defendant's actions were 'out of character;' therefore, a loss of judgment regarding recklessness explains his or her conduct." This reasoning is based on a false premise. Rarely occurring events (e.g., murder and other violent crime) do not inform us regarding the character or personality of the defendant. Conversely, most career criminals are lawful most of the time. Clearly, the "out-of-character" argument is not persuasive.

Determinations of recklessness may have a solid foundation if they are based on severe mood disorders. Occasionally, a defendant with a well-established manic episode will not weigh the harmful consequences of his or her behavior. The impaired judgment can be clearly documented and linked to the severity of the manic episode. For instance, the defendant evidences an obvious pattern of impaired judgment that increases with the severity of the manic episode. The forensic clinician can document how symptoms contributed to defendant's gross misappraisal of risk; such symptoms include elevated mood, grandiosity, and thought racing. Like manic episodes, severe depression can occasionally impair judgment and prevent a normally prudent person from considering the potential risks associated with his or her behavior. Because severe depression typically leads to decreased activity and social withdrawal, recklessness leading to criminal charges is almost never observed.

Criminal negligence, as previously noted, is based entirely on a normative analysis of what reasonable persons might do under similar circumstances. Forensic clinicians typically lack the expertise and research data to opine on a reasonable-person standard. Therefore, we recommend that forensic clinicians do not consult on the negligence component of criminal culpability.

Intoxication

Voluntary intoxication often plays a significant role in affecting defendants' judgment at the time of the offense. However, the presence of severe intoxication *per se* is uninformative. Melton et al. (1997) observed that some defendants may use intoxicants to facilitate their commission of the offense (e.g., bolster courage). Moreover, a far-sighted defendant may recognize the possibility of apprehension and use intoxication as a partial excuse to the planned offense (e.g., charges stemming from date rape). Therefore, forensic clinicians must grapple with the defendant's motivations for intoxication and how these motivations may affect criminal culpability.

Marlowe et al. (1999) authored a seminal article on voluntary intoxication and the possible negation of mens rea. They provide a valuable analysis of the Supreme Court's decision in *Montana v. Egelhoff* (1996) in which a plurality opinion rejected the notion that defendants have the constitutional right to present evidence of intoxication to negate mens rea. Importantly, Marlowe et al. observed that other states did not enact similar legislation in the several years following the *Egelhoff* decision. On the contrary, they found that most states continue to allow such testimony. Only 12 states completely bar such expert testimony. Of the remaining states, comparable numbers allow mens rea evidence for (1) all crimes including general intent (20 states) and (2) specific-intent crimes only (18 states[1]). Criminal attorneys will need to familiarize forensic clinicians with current statutes and case law.

Nearly all jurisdictions all expert evidence on involuntary intoxication as it relates to criminal culpability. Involuntary intoxication extends beyond those rare instances when a criminal defendant was forced by others to ingest an intoxicant. According to Goldstein et al. (2003), other examples include untoward effects of prescribed medication and the unknowing

---

[1] In three states, mens rea is limited to murder charges.

ingestion of an intoxicant. More controversial are the infrequent cases of pathological intoxication whereby small amounts of alcohol cause profound cognitive and behavioral changes (Melton et al., 1997; Rogers & Mitchell, 1991); a critical issue is the predictability of the defendant's pathological intoxication. If the defendant could foresee the possibility of pathological intoxication based on prior history, then the defendant exercises some level of voluntariness (e.g., recklessness) by ingesting intoxicants.

AUTOMATISM

Melton et al. (1997) reported that automatism is rarely used and rarely successful as a defense. It requires that the defendant engage in criminal conduct during a state of unconsciousness. The critical challenge is establishing retrospectively whether the defendant was unconscious at the time of the offense. For example, a somnabulistic defendant must awaken only after the defense is committed. If wakeful prior to the offense, then automatism does not apply. In the absence of witnesses, the establishment of automatism is a highly inferential process. Defense attorneys are likely to encounter skepticism (Roberts & Wagstaff, 1996); likewise, the "convenience" of a single exculpatory factor may stretch the credibility of judges and juries.

Rogers and Shuman (2000a) present a conceptual overview of automatism in relationship to criminal conduct. Fenwick (1990) describes different subtypes of automatism. Two subtypes are potentially germane to criminal cases: somnabulism and epileptoid automatism. They are described individually in the next two enumerated paragraphs.

1. *Somnabulism*. Sleepwalking disorder or somnabulism is described by DSM-IV-TR (APA, 2000) as a sleep state in which the patient is unresponsive to others, difficult to rouse, and amnestic to the episode. Fenwick (1990) noted that somnabulistic behavior is typically of low complexity (e.g., walking) and often routinized (i.e., similar activity). Fenwick (1987) observed that somnabulism rarely has an adult onset and typically occurs in the first two hours of sleep. For purposes of forensic evaluations, critical issues include (1) amnesia, (2) initial onset during childhood or adolescence, (3) characteristic behavior (complexity and similar pattern), and (4) and no efforts at concealment.

2. *Epileptoid Automatism*. Delgardo-Esceuta et al. (1981) conducted a World Health Organization study of epilepsy and violence involving 5400 epileptics. They found that violence almost never occurred (.0035 prevalence rate) and was very brief, averaging 29 seconds.

The aggression was not goal-directed and typically involved unfocused violence. For purposes of forensic evaluations, Fenwick (1990) described the following: (1) no premeditation, (2) amnesia for the offense with prior memory intact, (3) confusion and disorientation, and (4) no efforts at concealment.

Automatism is also possible during a post-concussional state. Following a traumatic brain injury, an individual may become very confused and disorientated. Such persons may not be aware of their actions for the immediate period following the brain trauma. Automatism secondary to brain trauma is rarely applicable to forensic cases. A rare exception may occur when a brain-injured car driver becomes markedly confused and leave the scene of an automobile accident. In such rare cases, neuropsychological and neurological consults are essential.

Theoretically, the automatism defense could be raised on the basis of hypoglycemia or substance abuse. Low blood sugar in diabetes and other medical conditions can produce confusion but is rarely associated with unconscious yet purposeful behavior. Voluntary ingestion of alcohol or drugs (see previous section, *Intoxication*) most often produces blackouts rather than unconscious behavior. In both instances, the person typically exercises some control over a foreseeable event either in regulating sugar levels or deliberately entering an intoxicated state.

BATTERED WOMAN SYNDROME

Walker's (1979) pioneering book on the battered woman syndrome attempted to broaden a pattern of behavior preceding the offense as relevant to self-defense. This broadening has profound implications. Defendants are not evaluated on the immediate circumstances surrounding the offense but on a pattern of behavior extending months, if not years into the past.

The battered woman syndrome (Walker, 1984) posited specific responses to spousal abuse including learned helplessness, low self-esteem, hypervigilance, impaired functioning, and strong negative affect (e.g., fear, terror, anger, and rage). In roughly two-thirds of battering cases, these cardinal characteristics reflect responses to a cycle of abuse (tension building, abuse, and contrition) perpetuated by the batterer.

A syndrome is an intercorrelated group of symptoms which remain consistent across time (Cloninger, Martin, Guze, & Clayton, 1985). Important conceptual issues can be raised on whether battered woman syndrome qualifies as a syndrome. To qualify, its symptoms and cardinal characteristics must be reliably measured. Of critical importance, the interrelationships of these symptoms and cardinal characteristics must be empirically demonstrated. For example, are aspects of learned helplessness correlated with hypervigilance? Conceptually, it could be argued that these cardinal characteristics might be *inversely* related: with profound helplessness why exercise hypervigilance?

Morse (1998) delineated further problems in considering whether battered woman syndrome should be considered a syndrome. He observed the absence of clear classification rules for establishing these assorted characteristics as a syndrome, including which if any symptoms are required. Without the rudiments of inclusion criteria, the reliable appraisal of any syndrome cannot be accurately determined.

The following paragraphs selectively consider the empirical basis for the battered woman syndrome. They rely predominantly on Follingstad's (2003) scholarly analysis.

1. *Battering.* Follingstad (2003) provided an insightful analysis of battering that is directly relevant to clinical operationalization. She observes a fundamental lack of consensus on what constitutes battering. Walker's (1979) original conceptualization was all-inclusive, allowing nonphysical forms of abuse (e.g., browbeating) to be considered. According to Follingstad, two decades of writing and research has failed to establish what level of physical and/or psychological abuse constitutes the necessary foundation for battered woman syndrome. By itself, this lack of consensus imperils the scientific basis of this putative syndrome.

2. *Learned Helplessness.* Follingstad (2003) found that the clinical research did *not* support the hypothesized relationship of learned helplessness to battered women. Rather than passively accepting their fates, many battered women increased their efforts to find a constructive solution.

3. *Depression and Psychological Impairment.* Follingstad (2003) concluded that battered women tend to exhibit depression and overall distress. However, such general responses to extreme stress are very common. As such, they provide no validation for the hypothesized syndrome specific to battered women.

4. *Interpersonal Disturbance.* Follingstad (2003) found that the majority of studies did *not* support this predicted characteristic.

In summary, the hypothesized woman battered syndrome lacks the scientific foundation to be considered as a syndrome. Moreover, its predicted relations have generally failed to materialize. If rigorously examined, we doubt that this hypothesized syndrome would meet the *Daubert* criteria for admissibility. In particular, the potential error rates are unknowable, given the lack of consensus on what constitutes (1) battering as the necessary precondition, and (2) the requisite inclusion criteria for establishing the subsequent syndrome.

Guilty-but-Mentally-Ill (GBMI) Verdict

The GBMI standard, first promulgated in 1975 by the Michigan legislature, sought to curtail the number of insanity acquittals. Despite widespread criticism, the Michigan-based GBMI standard gained momentum during the 1980s. In addition, several other states embraced the concept of a GBMI verdict but changed the substantive criteria from that which they apply to their insanity defense. In particular, New Mexico, Pennsylvania, and South Carolina maintained the *M'Naghten* standard for their insanity defense but implement the American Law Institute (ALI) language for its GBMI verdict. In these states, forensic clinicians are referred to Chapter 7 for the clinical operationalization of the following criteria: mental disease or defect, substantial impairment, appreciate criminality, and conformity of conduct.

Steadman et al. (1993) studied whether the Michigan-based GBMI verdict had achieved its legislative intent in reducing the number of insanity pleas and acquittals. They conducted systematic comparisons in four GBMI states: Michigan, Illinois, Pennsylvania, and Georgia. Steadman et al. concluded that GBMI did not produce the desired effect; rates of insanity pleas and acquittals remained comparable after the passage of GBMI legislation.

The remainder of this section seeks to operationalize the Michigan-based standard, which has served as a template for the majority of GBMI states. As previously noted, triers of fact must first determine that the defendant does not meet the insanity standard. Subsequently, they must determine whether the defendant is mentally disordered. Relying on Michigan Mental Health Code, a mental disorder is defined as "a substantial disorder of thought or mood which significantly impairs judgment, behavior, capacity to recognize reality, or ability to cope with the ordinary demands of life" (Mich Comp Ann 330.1400a). The GBMI standard is composed of three operative concepts (see Rogers & Shuman, 2000a) requiring that the defendant (1) does not warrant a NGRI verdict, (2) has a substantial disorder involving thought or mood, and (3) has significant impairment in one or more general domains. The latter two issues will be addressed in next paragraphs.

Substantial disorder. This categorization is intended to exclude minor clinical conditions that do not substantively affect thought or mood. It is best conceptualized in terms of the severity of mood and psychotic symptoms (Rogers & Shuman, 2000a). Clearly, symptoms in the moderate to severe range would qualify as "substantial."

Significant impairment. This categorization attempts to eliminate individual cases where the disorder causes distress but not impairment in day-to-day functioning. Importantly, this impairment must be generally observed and not limited to the criminal offense. The disorder must cause impairment in one or more important domains of functioning: judgment, behavior, reality testing, or the ordinary demands of everyday life. These domains are outlined:

1. "Judgment" refers to the defendant's ability to identify critical issues, consider alternatives, and make reasoned choices.
2. "Behavior" refers to any significant behavioral disturbance that results from a mental disorder. Common examples include extreme suspiciousness associated with a paranoid disorder and marked social withdrawal associated with major depression.
3. "Reality testing" refers to the defendant's ability to perceive and comprehend his or her environment in a consensually validated manner. Impaired reality testing typically results from psychotic symptoms.
4. "Cope with the ordinary demands of life" refers to the defendant's capacity for self-care in meeting his or her day-to-day needs. This capacity requires the ability to engage in purposeful, goal-oriented behavior.

In summary, GBMI determinations are based on three general components plus the systematic evaluation of four specific domains. In cases where defendants may meet the GBMI criteria, forensic clinicians may wish to offer a detailed description of treatment needs and recommendations. While only advisory, a well-articulated and practical treatment plan may influence correctional staff in selecting the appropriate facility for a particular defendant.

CLINICAL METHODS RELEVANT TO ASSESSMENTS OF CRIMINAL RESPONSIBILITY

Clinical methods will vary substantially by the specific psycholegal issues related to criminal responsibility. Common across these evaluations, however, is the pressing need to standardize clinical data relevant to the presence and severity of Axis I symptoms. Toward this objective, the SADS (see Chapter 7) is recommended for the retrospective assessment of key Axis I symptoms and ascertaining their severity.

The following sections will focus on specific issues of criminal culpability. Specialized forensic measures are having limited relevance beyond issues of malingering and GBMI determinations. Therefore, we address how clinical methods can be applied to issues of criminal responsibility.

CRIMINAL CULPABILITY

Forensic psychologists and psychiatrists have considerable experience and expertise at retrospectively assessing cognitive abilities in relationship to criminal conduct. Evaluations of criminal culpability, while substantively different, parallel insanity evaluations. In assessing criminal culpability, the principal constructs are *purpose* and *knowing*. Occasionally, the construct of *recklessness* can be addressed when based on a well-established disorder with documented misappraisals of risk (e.g., a severe manic episode). Forensic clinicians will need guidance from referring attorneys on which construct(s) they should address for particular referrals.

Purpose in the context of criminal culpability entails the defendant's intended (conscious) goals for his or her conduct. As previously noted, the crux of the issue is whether a severe mental disorder or defect impaired the defendant's ability to recognize the unlawfulness of his or actions. Extrapolating from Rogers and Shuman's (2000a; see Chapter 7) discussion of motivation and wrongfulness, forensic clinicians should consider the following issues in evaluating purposefulness:

1. Regarding the offense, what was the defendant's *stated* goals?
2. Did these stated goals explicitly or implicitly recognize the unlawfulness of his or her conduct?
3. What alternative goals may have been achieved by his or her conduct?
4. What is the relationship between the defendant's diagnoses and goals (stated or alternative)?
5. Based on the clinical and legal data, which goals (stated or alternative) are supported?
6. Is there evidence that the defendant was *aware* of his or her actions were unlawful?
7. What were the defendant's expectations of the legal system?

Forensic clinicians should actively seek confirming and disconfirming data for each hypothesized goal. Assuming the defendant's stated goal did not recognize unlawfulness, alternative goals can often be generated. Specifically, what was achieved by the criminal conduct? Based on collateral sources, what else may have the defendant wanted to achieve? To inform clinical decision-making, forensic clinicians should assemble the relevant data for and against each hypothesized goal.

The singular contribution of forensic psychologists and psychiatrists is their expertise in understanding diagnoses, such as Axis I disorders, and their likely effect on a particular defendant's cognitive abilities. Therefore, confirming and disconfirming data must present clearly how the defendant's diagnoses and concomitant impairment relates to each hypothesized goal. In many instances, the greatest contribution of forensic clinicians may be the elucidation of mental disorders and the clarification of their likely effects on the defendant's functioning at the time of the offense.

The integral component of *knowing* is simply the recognition that the alleged conduct was unlawful. This component parallels the wrongfulness prong of several insanity standards but categorically excludes moral wrongfulness. On the basis of their expertise, forensic clinicians will generally limit their consultations to cases involving a severe mental disorder or defect. They will address whether the defendant's impaired apprehension of his or her circumstances compromised the *knowing* of unlawful actions.

For specialized assessment of criminal culpability, some forensic clinicians may find that the R-CRAS (Rogers, 1984) provides systematic ratings that are germane to purpose and knowing. R-CRAS items include elements of the criminal behavior (e.g., level of activity and degree of focus) and awareness of criminality. Obviously, the decision models cannot be applied to these elements of criminal culpability.

The *recklessness* component of criminal culpability combines both defendant-based and reasonable-person standards. As such, we recommend that forensic clinicians limit their consultations to well-defined cases where the relationship of the mental disorder to misappraisal of risk can be amply documented. Severe manic episodes occasionally provide compelling evidence of grossly impaired risk appraisals. For instance, a manic defendant may engage in a range of noncriminal behaviors (e.g., buying sprees and inappropriate social contact) that demonstrate compromised abilities at risk appraisals. We recommend the use of the SADS for current and retrospective assessments of manic episodes and the severity of disordered behavior related to risk misappraisals.

INTOXICATION

The use of voluntary intoxication to negate elements of criminal culpability is very challenging for forensic clinicians. With severe alcohol or drug use, many defendants experience "blackouts" where they fail to register the memories at the time of the offense (Rogers & Mitchell, 1991). With severe substance abuse, Campbell and Hodgins (1993) found that the great majority (86%) experienced blackouts. Contrary to earlier ideas, blackouts are also common among young persons who engage in severe episodes of severe episodes of drinking (Jennsion & Johnson, 1994).

Blackouts should not be confused with unconsciousness or a dissociated state. It is very common for severely intoxicated persons to function adequately at the time of the intoxication but fail to register their memories. Attorneys should be alert for forensic clinicians who draw improper inferences. *Blackouts, by themselves, provide no evidence germane to criminal culpability.*

The defendant's incapacity to recall important details from a past intoxication severely constrains forensic clinicians' ability to assess accurately issues of criminal culpability (for a general overview Chapter 5, Warrantless Searches). Witnesses' accounts can sometimes be helpful; however, a potential problem is the level of sobriety exhibited by these witnesses. Inferences from the defendant's actions are speculative and should be discouraged. In some instances, forensic clinicians may suspect that intentionality was impaired yet lack the clinical data to support this conclusion.

Specialized laboratory measures are available to evaluate the defendant's level of intoxication. Importantly, these measures evaluate physiological but not behavioral changes. Criminal cases have been observed in which the defendant has very high laboratory values yet appears to be functioning normally (see Rogers & Mitchell, 1991). Because issues of intoxication are raised frequently in sentencing, coverage of these specialized measures will be found in Chapter 9, *Sentencing Recommendations and Capital Issues.*

AUTOMATISM

Forensic psychology and psychiatry have not developed specialized measures of the assessment of automatistic behavior. Forensic clinicians must evaluate which subtypes of automatism would potentially apply in a particular forensic case; Table 8-1 outlines the key clinical and forensic issues. The least credible case occurs when the defendant has (1) no pattern or history of automatistic episodes, (2) lacks cardinal characteristics of the purported subtype, (3) engages in suspicious behavior, such as concealment, and (4) has other motivations for the offense. The convenience of a de novo episode that conveniently explains the criminal activity, while remotely possible, may strain the credibility of the judge or jury. In contrast, the most credible case occurs when a documented history can be

TABLE 8-1. CLINICAL CHARACTERISTICS AND FORENSIC ISSUES IN THE EVALUATION
OF COMMON AUTOMATISM SUBTYPES

Somnabulism

Clinical Characteristics
- Verifiable onset during childhood or adolescence?
- Similar pattern of low-complexity activity?
- Unresponsive to others during episode?

Forensic Issues
- Amnestic to the episode?
- No attempts at concealment?
- Other motivations for the offense are not supported?

Epileptoid Automatism

Clinical Characteristics
- Confusion and disorientation during the episode?
- Amnesia for the episode but not prior to the episode?
- Supported by neurological data that is consistent with epilepsy?

Forensic Issues
- No premeditation or planning prior to the episode?
- Evidence of past aggression during earlier episodes?
- No attempts at concealment?
- Other motivations for the offense are not supported?
- No voluntary use of substances (e.g., alcohol) known by the defendant to increase the likelihood of epileptoid automatism?

established that is highly consistent with the automatism subtype. In addition, no support can be reasonably mustered for other motivations, and the defendant did not engage in any behavior to minimize detection or avoid arrest.

BATTERED WOMAN SYNDROME

The battered woman syndrome, as previously discussed, lacks clarity in defining its boundaries and has fundamental problems with its construct and criterion-based validation. Specifically, many of its predicted relations are either unproved or disproved. However, the law appears to have outdistanced science in many jurisdictions in determining the admissibility of battered woman syndrome. Defense attorneys are faced with an important tactical decision: Should they seek expert testimony about this controversial syndrome? Potential considerations include (1) the severity and frequency of the spouse's violence, (2) characterization of the defendant as a sympathetic "victim," and (3) availability of alternative trial strategies.

Forensic clinicians may wonder what role, if any, they can professionally and ethically perform in these controversial cases. Two potential roles can be considered. First, forensic clinicians can provide rebuttal testimony when defense experts exceed empirical knowledge and offer unbuttressed opinions. Such testimony could address *Daubert* issues related to the general acceptance and error rates. Second, forensic clinicians could consider whether testimony on direct is *ever* warranted in even the most egregious cases. While we have grave reservations, an argument could be made that testimony in egregious cases could be justified with the following stipulation: *The forensic clinician is proactive in his or her report and subsequent testimony regarding about the limitations of the syndrome and their assessment methods.* For psychologists, this ethical requirement (APA, 2002) is covered by Ethical Standards 9.01(b) and 9.06 that require an open acknowledgment of limitations in both assessment methods and conclusions. For forensic psychiatrists (American Academy of Psychiatry and Law, 1995), Ethical Standard IV, *Honesty and Striving for Objectivity*, requires that psychiatrists should not withhold potentially damaging information.

Few clinical methods have been systematically utilized for assessing battered woman syndrome. Dutton (1999) discussed the use of the Psychological Maltreatment of Women Inventory (PMWI; Tolman, 1995) and the revised Conflict Tactics Scale (CTS-2; Straus, Hamby, Boney-McCoy, & Sugarman, 1996) in assessing battered women. We do not recommend that either measure be used in forensic practice based on their obvious content:

1. The PMWI is composed of 58 inquiries that are rated according to the frequency of their occurrence during the last 6 months. Items are "face-valid" (i.e., the purpose of these inquiries is obvious) and address the spouse's threats, abuse, and mistreatment of the spouse. The PMWI was developed as a *research* scale (see http://www-personal.umich.edu/~rtolman/index.html) and is readily available on the Internet. As a research scale, it does not need to meet the stringent requirements put forth by APA and other professional organizations.

2. The Revised CTS (CTS-2; Straus et al., 1996) attempted to correct problems found with the original CTS including insufficient item coverage and the obvious ordering of items from socially acceptable to blatantly unacceptable. The CTS-2 has 39 items that are organized into five scales of varying length (6–12 items): Physical Assault, Psychological Aggression, Negotiation, Injury, and Sexual Coercion. Although good to excellent alphas are reported; highly

correlated items have substantially inflated these estimates.[2] We do not recommend the CTS-2 because of its face validity and easy access on the Internet.

Dutton (1992) proposed several measures to facilitate data collection in wife-battering cases. These measures lack extensive validation and have been criticized for their incomplete coverage (Follingstad, 2003). In summary, specialized measures for the battered woman syndrome are highly vulnerable to manipulation, given their face-valid content. No scales have been developed to assess whether defendant using this defense have provided self-serving information. Beyond problems with deliberate manipulation, psychometric issues related to reliability and validity remain to be resolved.

As an important distinction, the diagnosis of posttraumatic stress disorder is well-established with sophisticated methods for its assessment (see Rogers, 2001). Such methods include (1) the Anxiety Disorders Interview Schedule for *DSM-IV* (ADIS-IV; Brown, DiNardo, & Barlow, 1995) and (2) the Clinician-Administered PTSD Scale for *DSM-IV* (CAPS; Blake et al., 1998). The ADIS-IV is a structured interview that assessing both PTSD and other anxiety disorder; it provides considerable detail about each anxiety disorder and its effects on day-to-day functioning. In contrast, the CAPS is a focused interview that provides highly reliable information on PTSD and its three clusters (i.e., intrusive, avoidant, and arousal). Strong support is found for its construct validity using confirmatory factor analysis. Beyond structured interviews, the PAI is a well-validated multiscale inventory that offers clinical data on (1) response styles including malingering and (2) anxiety including traumatic anxiety. In conclusion, forensic clinicians may wish to avoid the battered woman syndrome and offer testimony based on the established diagnosis of PTSD and the specialized measures for its evaluation.

GUILTY-BUT-MENTALLY-ILL (GBMI)

As noted in Chapter 7, the SADS is especially useful in assessing retrospectively the presence and severity of Axis I symptoms. Its systematic appraisal should prove useful for establishing a "substantial disorder" and documenting domains of "significant impairment." Regarding the latter, its strengths lie in the evaluation of reality testing and behavioral disturbances with less attention to judgment and impairment of day-to-day functioning.

---

[2]The most egregious example is the Injury scale for which the average item–scale correlation is .83.

The R-CRAS (Rogers, 1984; Rogers & Sewell, 1999) has four specific items that parallel the Michigan-based GBMI standard. These provide a systematic means to evaluate these relevant domains of impairment; they evidence marked differences for reality testing, behavior, and judgment when comparing clinically evaluated GBMI and insane defendants. Beyond the GBMI items, the R-CRAS also offers a test item on socially responsible behavior that is likely germane to the capacity to cope with ordinary demands. As an important consideration, GBMI items on the R-CRAS have content validity; however, their criterion-related validity has yet to be tested.

Trial and General Cross-Examination Issues

A challenge for defense counsel is the public's open skepticism for concepts that excuse criminal or deviant behavior. Alicke (2000) described the process of "blame-validation" whereby individuals are likely to ascribe responsibility and blame to a person who evokes negative emotions. The implication of willfulness must be subdued if defenses involving criminal culpability are to succeed.

Beyond the insanity defense, issues of criminal culpability often lack an empirically based theory and research-based methods. As a result, the greatest danger for criminal attorneys is that forensic clinicians will not ground their opinion in the *legal-empirical-forensic* model (see Chapter 1). Especially in unfamiliar territory, the largest temptation for experts is "commonsensical analysis." Instead of carefully formulating a conclusory opinion based on empirical knowledge and validated forensic measures, the forensic clinician adopts a commonsensical perspective. Importantly, a commonsensical analysis is not an expert opinion and should be vigorously assailed.

Biased Experts

Experts may be allowed to testify on issues of criminal responsibility for which the empirical data and forensic methods are not well established. In such instances, attorneys shoulder an onerous responsibility to ensure that such testimony relies on the available knowledge rather than self-serving speculation. Especially with novel defenses that are not grounded in solid research and validated measures, experts are vulnerable to "confirmatory biases." Confirmatory biases can occur when the expert unconsciously adopts the fact pattern or theory presented by the retaining attorney. Take for example the attempt to introduce evidence of the defendant's intoxication in response to being accuse in a date rape. An expert adopting a defense theory might see heavy drinking as compromising the defendant's judgment about the victim's consent. An expert adopting a prosecution theory might see the heavy drinking as a planned activity by the defendant to reduce the victim's ability to refuse sexual relations. One model for cross-examination is requiring forensic clinicians to articulate clearly the different possible motivations for the alleged criminal conduct.

A key issue for cross-examination is uncovering the expert's reasoning behind his or her opinions. Is it simply confirmatory bias with the expert echoing the ideas of the attorney? Did the expert have strongly held preconceived notions that shaped his or her testimony? One hallmark of the biased expert is one who did not actively consider different options. Pursuing only one hypothesis is akin to voting in a one-candidate election: the outcome is virtually assured.

Strong evidence of biased experts is often found in court reports. Attorneys should be especially alert for the following: *All the reported clinical data supports the position espoused by the retaining attorney.* Even in clear-cut cases, a few details are neutral or even contrary to any expert opinion. Chapter 3 provides additional data about the practice of *cherry-picking* by biased experts.

COMPETING HYPOTHESES

Forensic clinicians should genuinely consider alternative explanations in reaching their opinions (Shuman & Greenberg, 2003). Specialty guidelines for forensic psychologists formally adopted by the American Psychology-Law Society and the American Board of Forensic Psychology (see Committee on Ethical Guidelines for Forensic Psychologists, 1991), require that rival hypotheses be actively evaluated in reaching forensic conclusions. While not explicitly addressed, ethical standards for forensic psychiatrists emphasized completeness and objectivity (American Academy of Psychiatry and Law, 1995). Objectivity is difficult to achieve if competing hypotheses are not actively considered.

One potential approach to rival hypotheses is presented in Box 8-1. This illustrative questioning recognizes that forensic clinicians are often reluctant to acknowledge competing explanations for the defendant's conduct. Therefore, the sections A (psychologists) and B (psychiatrists) address forensic clinicians' professional and ethical responsibilities to evaluate different explanations for the defendant's criminal actions. The general goals of these questions are threefold: (1) uncover obvious bias (e.g., experts who will not even consider other alternatives), (2) reveal inadequacies in the experts' reasoning (e.g., "overlooking" data contrary to their opinions), and (3) educate the trier-of-fact about alternative explanations.

Box 8-1   Sample Cross-Examination Questions for Novel Defenses Based on the Foundation of Opinions and Rival Opinions

A. Setting the Stage: Psychologists
   1. [if not a member] *Are you a member of the American Academy of Psychiatry and Law?* [also known as Division 41 of the American Psychological Association] ... *Isn't it true that the American Academy of Psychiatry and Law provides rigorous standards for ethical practice? ... Is part of your <u>unwillingness</u> to join the American Psychology-Law Society and attempt to <u>avoid</u> these rigorous standards?*
   2. [all psychologists] *Are you knowledgeable about these specialty guidelines for forensic psychologists officially adopted by both the American Psychology-Law Society and the American Board of Forensic Psychologists?*
   3. *Are you aware of Ethical Guideline 6-C that explicitly requires you to consider "rival hypotheses?"*
   4. [irrespective of the response] *Please read to the* [select: jury/judge] *the highlighted subsection of the specialty guidelines* [Download from the American Psychology-Law Society web site, "Links"; the URL at the time of publication was http://www.unl.edu/ap-ls/foren.pdf; highlight Section 6-C]
   5. [if not explicitly stated] *Doctor, please turn your report and read to the court those sections that clearly addresses this issue.*
   6. [may suggest that rival hypotheses were considered but not reported] *When were you planning on telling the Court the "whole truth" that other hypotheses are possible?*
   7. *Isn't it true, doctor, that the Ethical Guideline 7-D requires you to present information to the court in a fair and unbiased manner? ... Would you consider your complete omission of rival hypotheses to be your best effort?*
B. Setting the Stage: Psychiatrists
   1. *Are you a member of the American Academy of Psychiatry and Law? ... Isn't it true that the American Academy of Psychiatry and Law provides professional standards for ethical practice? ...* [if not a member] *Is part of your <u>unwillingness</u> to join the American Academy of Psychiatry and Law and attempt to <u>avoid</u> these professional standards?*
   2. *Doesn't Ethical Principle IV require "Honesty and a Striving for Objectivity?"* [Check American Academy of Psychiatry and Law web site; the URL at the time of publication was http://www.forensic-psych.com/articles/artEthics.html; highlight Principle IV] ... *Referring to the official commentary, please read the highlighted material to the court:*

> He communicates the honesty and striving for objectivity of his work and the soundness of his clinical opinion by distinguishing, to the extent possible, between verified and unverified information as well as between clinical "facts," "inferences," and "impressions."

   3. *In assessing the "soundness of your clinical opinion" what rival hypotheses were considered?*

(*Continued*)

4. [if appropriate] *In promoting objectivity, where are these rival hypotheses presented in your psychiatric report?*

5. *Isn't it true, doctor, that the same commentary indicates the following:* "The impression that a psychiatrist in a forensic situation might distort his opinion in the service of the party which retained him is especially detrimental to the profession and must be assiduously avoided." ... *Would you really consider your complete omission of any rival hypotheses as avoiding this impression of being a partisan or biased expert?*

C. Rival Hypotheses

1. *What are <u>all</u> the possible motivations for why the defendant committed the criminal acts? Let me list them on this display ... Any others? ... Is this a complete list?*

2. [if appropriate] *In reading* [his/her] *report, you are aware that Dr. __, a forensic expert, described __ motivation? ... Was it simply selective memory that caused you to "forget" this?*

3. [if missing] *What about __ motivation? Isn't it <u>possible</u> that the defendant was motivated by this?*

4. *Doctor, please listen closely and be responsive to my question. Let's take __ possible motivation,*[1] *what data from the defendant's history would support this hypothesis?* [Write these down on a 2nd display; your goal is to minimize obfuscation.]

5. [if tries to "scramble" the response; e.g., adding negatives] *Excuse me, doctor; I am asking a very clear and specific question. "Let's take __ possible motivation, what data from the defendant's history would <u>support</u> this hypothesis?"*

6. [The attorney should be prepared to be pleasantly[2] persistent; this may take some time. Many experts will resist the idea that their thinking and opinions can and should be closely scrutinized.]

7. [If the forensic clinician appears arrogant, please refer to Box 3-2, *Self-Absorbed Expert*].

8. *Please list for me the various psychological and psychiatric evaluations. What clinical data from these evaluations support the hypothesis that the defendant was motivated by __?* [same possible motivation as used in #3] [Again, list supportive data on a display.]

9. [if stays with his/her own report] *Are you aware that you are avoiding the reports from Doctors __ and __? ...* [if unprepared] *So you only came to Court to <u>sell</u> your own point of view and not to help us find the truth in this case?*

---

[1] The attorney should prepare with his or her expert the possible motivations in each case with supportive data from the defendant's history and forensic evaluations.
[2] A danger is that the attorney may appear angry and demanding; this would nullify one goal of the cross-examination, namely to expose to the jury an uncooperative and biased expert.

As a practical matter, we advise that attorneys list on flip chart or other displays for each of the rival hypotheses. This writing can reduce verbosity and increase comprehension. It also makes it very clear to the Court if the expert is attempting to evade inquiries into alternative explanations.

Consider for the moment a hypothetical case of murder. Various motivations for the murder might include the following: (1) a discharge of negative affect, such as feelings of rage and impotence, (2) a business-related event, such as eliminating competition or fulfilling a contract, (3) peer approval, such as gaining respect or gang status, (4) sensation-seeking, such as an extreme escalation of thrill-seeking behavior, (5) a psychotically motivated solution, such as stopping the persecutions, and (6) self-defense. In preparation for cross-examination, attorneys and their experts should generate a comprehensive list of possible motivations and compile any support data. An expert's credibility will likely be eroded if he or she did not even consider some alternative motivations for the offense in question.

FLAWED REASONING

Experts are often reluctant, if not resistant, to sharing the logic and reasoning that undergirds their opinions. Attorneys are likely to have their own cross-examination style for exposing unbuttressed opinions and flawed reasoning. Section C of Box 8-1 provides only starting points for this process. As one possibility, attorneys may wish to divide the questions by specific domains. For instance, Box 8-1 Section C considers the defendant's history (i.e., Inquiry #4) separate from current evaluations (i.e., Inquiry #8). The goal is to concretization: the more specific the questioning, the more likely the expert will be compelled to delineate his or her reasoning.

Occasionally, experts will not have seriously considered other alternatives in reaching their conclusions about criminal culpability. Their uncertainty may be expressed in their language (e.g., excessive use of qualifiers) or their speech (e.g., excessive hesitations or "drifting-off" responses). One possibility is to point this out to the trier-of-fact through questioning. Possible examples include the following:

1. *I noticed you hesitating in your response. Is this something you have questions or reservations about?*
2. *Your voice began to drift off. Is this something you wonder about?*
3. *I noticed you are using a lot of words like __ and __ [e.g., "likely," "probably," "consistent with"] ... Would it be fair to say that you answer to this question is somewhat qualified? ... What makes you less certain about this answer than other answers you have given?*

Cross-examination should explicitly address the expert's reasoning in reaching his or her conclusions about culpability. Especially with controversial issues (e.g., intoxication defense and battered woman syndrome), the attorney should insist of knowing the step-by-step process of reaching each conclusion. A critical issue is whether the expert used a "hypothesis-testing" approach. Specifically, did he or she take the most appealing hypothesis and attempt to prove its validity? Surprisingly common, this seeking to prove the most appealing hypothesis (i.e., confirmatory bias) is a fundamental departure from objectivity (see previous discussion).

We suspect that most experts will not acknowledge the lack of objectivity inherent in selective hypothesis testing.[3] Instead, attorneys may wish to expose the expert's limitations without asking for any capitulation. The type of questioning will vary substantially with each particular case. A few illustrative questions follow:

1. *What was your initial formulation after being introduced to the case by Attorney __? [if "no idea"] . . . There was nothing that introduction that struck you as salient? . . . Were you paying attention?*
2. *After the initial formulation, how did you proceed?*
3. *What data did you collect that supported this initial formulation? . . . Challenged it?*
4. *What modifications did you make in the initial formulation? . . . Why?*
5. *At what point did you reach your final conclusions? . . . Please take us step-by-step through the process.*

Specific Issues of Criminal Culpability

For specific issues, attorneys should refer to the relevant subsections that address Clinical Operationalization and Clinical Methods. With the assistance of their own expert, questions can easily be formulated that address limitations in theory, empirical knowledge (i.e., science), and validated methods (i.e., practice). However, such cross-examination must be used selectively. When effective, it is likely to affect *all* experts, not just those with an opposing view.

The purpose of this section is to present highly salient issues that could be addressed during cross-examination. Obviously, the expert's own training and professional experience for specific issues of criminal culpability becomes very relevant. In many instances, the expert will never have testified on infrequently raised issues such as mens rea and automatism. In other instances, the expert may have developed a niche and frequently be asked to testify for intoxication or battered-woman cases. In all cases,

---

[3]Please note that a simultaneous evaluation of competing hypotheses is very different; it would minimize the likelihood of subjectivity and confirmatory biases influencing the outcome.

experts' training, professional experience, and track records (referrals and testimony) can be explored.

1. *Mens Rea*

   An expert that testifies, implicitly or explicitly, to the reasonable-person standard is likely overstepping his or her expertise. Negligence, and to a certain extent, recklessness, rely on the reasonable-person standard. Some criminal attorneys will pursue this matter indirectly. Illustrative questions might include the following:

   - *How was the defendant's intent* [chose: different from/similar to] *other persons charged with __? . . . In making that important judgment, please tell the Court what the intent is like for most persons charged with __?*
   - *Isn't it true, doctor, that you were just guessing about this?* [likely a negative response] *. . . Are you aware of any research that specifically addresses this point? . . . Please tell us what specialized knowledge you possess about most persons charged with this offense that would permit you to offer opinion testimony.* [Some persistence will likely be needed.]

   Forensic clinicians may have sufficient expertise to provide testimony on defendant-based issues of mens rea (see *Purpose and Knowledge* subsection). Attorneys should look for a documented history of severe mental disorder, clear evidence of impairment in different domains, and corroboration of this disorder and its concomitant impairment. Potential limitations for any of these areas should be strenuously questioned. Of particular concern to the prosecution are response styles. Specific considerations include (1) self-serving statements about intent issues (e.g., purpose and knowing) and (2) malingering of the mental disorder that forms the basis of the mens rea defense.

2. *Intoxication*

   Occasionally, experts testify that voluntary intoxication played a preponderant role in impairing a defendant's capacity to form intent. In doing so, these experts face formidable tasks in (1) assessing the role of intoxication and intent, and (2) offering credible testimony. In many cases, the defendant's blackouts prevent any direct assessment of intent. Unless the defendant's verbalizations were heard and remembered by believable (i.e., unintoxicated and disinterested) witnesses, critical data for making these determinations are simply unavailable. Because of these formidable tasks, specific cross-examination strategies greatly favor the prosecution. Knowing this, defense attorneys should take into account the credibility of their experts whose testimony might often be characterized as "going out of a limb."

Forensic clinicians linking voluntary intoxication to intent are vulnerable on cross-examination. Many do not have specialized training in alcohol and other intoxicants, including tolerance, cross-tolerance, and drug interactions. These deficiencies can easily be exposed with the assistance of a rebuttal expert. If an expert is unable to even articulate the potentiating effects of drug interactions that are relevant to the case, then his or her basic expertise is in question. As noted in the *Intoxication* subsection of Clinical Methods, blackouts are much more common then once believed. Cross-examination, perhaps bolstered by rebuttal testimony, should make clear to the Court that blackouts are (1) reported by significant numbers of college students, (2) common among sane defendants (17.3%; Rogers & Shuman, 2000), and (3) documented in most persons with severe substance abuse.

Cross-examination can also address the expert's reasoning on the putative link between voluntary intoxication and intent. If this is the *first time* that intoxication lead to criminal acts, then expert must address the "coincidence" and "convenience" of this single exculpatory occurrence. If this *pattern* of criminal acts, then the expert must address the defendant's knowledge that his or her intoxication may lead to criminal conduct. Such knowledge may vitiate the arguments maintaining the defendant's complete lack of intent.

3. *Automatism*

As previously noted, automatism is seldom used and rarely successful (Melton et al., 1997). Unlike the intoxication defense, automatism may be caused by a range of physical conditions and mental disorders. Forensic clinicians must have expertise specific to the type of automatism being evaluated. For example, most psychologists and psychiatrists have only a basic understanding of hypoglycemia and are often ill-prepared to identify its physiological signs, various etiologies, and behavioral correlates in empirically based detail. Similarly, specific expertise is required to evaluate epilepsy and post-concussional states. Therefore, an early component of cross-examination is a vigorous inquiry into the expert's qualifications and the admissibility of his or her testimony.

Automatism, based on a *chronic* clinical condition (e.g., epilepsy, hypoglycemia, and somnabulism) is rarely a satisfactory explanation for any "goal-oriented" criminal behavior.[4] The critical issue that must be actively pursued in cross-examination is simply, "Why now?" For example, a person with diabetes will likely have hundreds of hypoglycemic experiences and yet never have previously engaged in felonious conduct. *Why now?* Attorneys may wish to pursue the obvious. If hypoglycemia *caused* the criminal acts, then these acts should be repetitive and form a definable pattern. Moreover, the forensic expert should be able to demonstrate this clinically by videotaping the defendant during periods of low blood sugar.

Expert testimony is vulnerable when it attempts to explain that complex, purposeful behavior was "unconscious." For lay persons, the concepts of *unconscious* and *purposeful* appear contradictory. Cross-examination questions may highlight this apparent contradiction. In addition, many persons are uncomfortable with the notion that the unconscious separate entity that can elude criminal culpability. Illustrative cross-examination is presented in Box 8-2. Questions in Section A examine the potential arbitrariness of labeling some behaviors as conscious and others as unconscious. By closing scrutinizing the defendant's sequence of the behaviors prior to, during, and following the offense, many experts will have difficulty discriminating unconscious from conscious behaviors.

Box 8-2   SAMPLE CROSS-EXAMINATION FOR "UNCONSCIOUS BEHAVIOR" ASSOCIATED WITH AUTOMATISM

    A. Arbitrariness in Establishing Conscious and Unconscious Behavior
        1. *Was the defendant's __ [a specific action earlier that day; e.g., having a drink before going to bed] conscious or unconscious? . . . How do you know?*
        2. *What about __ [another specific action] conscious or unconscious? . . . How do you know that?*
        3. [Continue to ask questions about very specific actions for before, during, and after the criminal behavior]
    B. Implications of Unconscious Criminal Behavior
        4. *Who was in charge during__? [the criminal act]*
        5. *If the defendant wasn't responsible, who is? . . .*
        6. *With an unconscious like that, you make the defendant appear like a ticking time bomb, isn't that correct?*
        7. *If you are accurate, [he/she] could act violently and claim that it was [his/her] unconscious, isn't that correct?* [likely to disagree] *. . . Doesn't your testimony today give [him/her] a "get-out-of-jail-free" card for future crimes?*

---

[4] In contrast, automatism resulting in acts of omission (e.g., negligence) is much more compelling. For example, a parent in an automatistic state may not adequately monitor the safety of his or her child.

A potential strength of this approach is that experts may look self-serving by attributing all *criminal* behavior to the *unconscious*, and most *noncriminal* behavior to the consciousness. In these cases, the attorney may wish to point out this pattern:

1. *Doctor, I wonder if you noticed an interesting pattern in your testimony today?*
2. *It seems like everything that could get the defendant in trouble just happen to be unconscious, isn't that correct?* ... [if quibbles] *Let's prove me wrong. Name several things the defendant did, that* [he/she] *knew was criminal at the time of the offense.*

Testimony in support of automatism must overcome a major hurdle, especially with jurors. Even if they accept the expert's explanation of unconscious criminal behavior, they are likely to have serious reservations about minor convictions or outright acquittals. Section B of Box 8-2 helps to underscore these concerns in questioning whether (1) the defendant is a "ticking bomb" and (2) the current testimony is akin to a "get-out-of-jail-free" card.

Cross-examination on automatism may also address the difficult diagnostic issue of attempting to differentiate automatism from psychogenic amnesia. In both instances, the defendant is unlikely to have memories of his or her criminal conduct. However, a defendant with psychogenic amnesia is likely to have been substantially aware of his or her conduct at the time of the offense. Sample cross-examination questions are provided:

1. *Was committing* ___ [criminal offense] *traumatic for the defendant?* ... [if a negative or neutral response] *If it wasn't traumatic, wouldn't that suggest that the defendant was a callous, calculating individual that wasn't bothered by [his/her] criminal actions?* ... *Isn't that type of callousness indicative of criminal psychopaths?*
2. [if "traumatic"] *What is psychogenic amnesia?* ... *Isn't is true that a person with psychogenic amnesia is aware of his or her conduct at the time of the traumatic event but blocked these memories later?*
3. *What specific <u>psychological tests</u> do we have to establish the difference between psychogenic amnesia and automatism?* [none]
4. *What specific <u>laboratory tests</u> do we have to establish the difference between psychogenic amnesia and automatism?* [none]
5. *What specific parts of the Mini-Mental State Examination (MMSE) establish the difference between psychogenic amnesia and automatism?* [none]
6. *In the absence of any validated measures, isn't it true that you have no scientifically-based methods of distinguishing the two?* ... *And it was your*

earlier testimony that psychogenic amnesia would likely indicate that the defendant was aware of [his/her] criminal acts at the time, isn't that correct?

Some attorneys will want to develop a theme as part of their cross-examination on automatism. One such theme is *denial of responsibility*. For example, a defendant may have (1) denied any knowledge of the crime, (2) admitted knowledge but no major involvement, and (3) claimed automatism. Cross-examination questions can emphasize this theme with multiple questions about various denials during the police investigation. This theme can be explicitly addressed:

1. *Doctor, doesn't it seem that we have a theme here in denying responsibility?*
2. *At first, the defendant denied any involvement, isn't that correct?*
3. *Then [he/she] admitted to being involved but said it wasn't [him/her] because of unconsciousness, correct? . . . Isn't the automatism excuse simply another attempt to deny responsibility?*

Battered Woman Syndrome

Follingstad (2003) concluded in her penetrating analysis that battered woman syndrome had reached its apex and is gradually decreasing in importance. Attorneys may still be confronted with cases where this syndrome is raised. Cross-examination can be used to expose the fundamental weaknesses of this syndrome on both theoretical and empirical grounds. Attorneys should have no difficulty in the development of cross-examination strategies. The following paragraphs illustrate two approaches.

Cross-examination can underscore a core problem: the basic lack of consensus in defining the syndrome. After more than 25 years, experts still do not agree about what constitutes battered woman syndrome. Without this consensus, clinical research is stymied. Illustrative questions for cross-examination are presented:

1. *Isn't is true that the ideas about battered woman syndrome were first espoused by Dr. Walker in 1979? . . . Had she published any original research on domestic violence prior to this time? [if "no" or "unsure"] So as far as you know, this was her first attempt at studying domestic violence?*
2. *Did Dr. Walker have any personal or social agenda in promoting her ideas about battered woman syndrome? . . . [likely to respond negatively] Why did she systematically exclude men? . . . In all honesty, can't men be psychologically or even physically abused by their spouses?*

3. *Isn't is true that Dr. Walker believed that* <u>any</u> *psychological behavior which could be construed as coercive would qualify as battered woman syndrome as long as it was repeated more than once?* [should be an affirmative response] ... *Do you take issue with Dr. Walker on this point? ... Wouldn't most women have experienced a few acts of coercion during their marriages?*
4. *With spousal murder, you would testify to excuse women but not men, isn't that correct?*

The battered woman syndrome is also vulnerable to cross-examination because specialized measures are both poorly validated and easily manipulated. No psychological measures have been systematically tested on women with and without battered woman syndrome. A rigorous test would be to compare battered women with the syndrome to other women with nonspousal trauma. In the absence of rigorous comparisons, forensic clinicians have no knowledge whether their findings are specific to the battered woman syndrome or generic to trauma.

Questionnaires intended for anonymous research have been blithely used in forensic evaluations. A potentially effective cross-examination strategy is to secure copies of these research measures, which are readily available on the Internet. Forensic clinicians can be closely queried about these obvious questions (e.g., slapping and beating) and how any defendant could easily fake responses indicative of battered woman syndrome. This strategy is only useful in cases where collateral data does not corroborate but possibly contradicts the defendant's claims. The thrust of this strategy is to expose the weaknesses of these methods that are tantamount to a self-diagnosis of battered woman syndrome.

Guilty-But-Mentally-Ill (GBMI) Verdict

Attorneys are likely to be sharply divided by their respective roles (prosecution and defense) on the merits of the GBMI verdict. Prosecutors may see this as a useful compromise that holds the defendant accountable yet provides the defendant necessary treatment. Defense attorneys are likely to view the GBMI as a subterfuge that misleads jurors into believing that it may be an appropriate compromise verdict. In reality, the GBMI verdict is not a compromise.

The same sentencing options as a guilty verdict can be imposed, including the death penalty (Dickinson, 1984; *Ward v. Sternes*, 334 F.3d 696, 701 n1 [7th Cir., 2003]). Treatment is often not forthcoming and is often equally available to inmates with guilty and GBMI verdicts.

The GBMI option is only considered in relationship to the insanity defense with the NGRI verdict. Clinically, the GBMI and NGRI verdicts can be conceptualized as competing hypotheses. Attorneys may want to focus on these competing hypotheses in formulating their cross-examination. In addition, they should find strategies used insanity cases (see Chapter 7) are also applicable to GBMI verdicts. Several ideas specific to GBMI cases are presented in the subsequent paragraphs.

The prosecution may wish to emphasize a consensus-building approach to cross-examination. In many cases of criminal responsibility, experts on both sides are in general agreements on several key issues but differ on their opinions regarding insanity. As a hypothetical example, consider the case of a psychotic defendant for whom the defense expert concluded was likely insane. In attempting to convince the jury about the GBMI verdict, the prosecutor might adapt the following format:

1. *Every expert in this case agrees that the defendant is mentally disordered, isn't that correct?*
2. *Every expert also agrees that it impairs* __ [e.g., reality testing], *isn't that correct? ... Every expert also agrees about* __ [e.g., primary symptoms, such as delusions], *isn't that correct?*
3. *Wouldn't it be fair to say that there is sharp disagreement about* __ [prong of insanity] *between you and other experts?*
4. *Logically, doctor, should we trust the consensus of experts more than the sharp disagreement?*
5. *And that consensus on* __ [e.g., the disorder] *and* __ [e.g., an element of GBMI] *is consistent with the Guilty-but-mentally-ill verdict, isn't that correct? ...* [optional] *Would you fault anyone for going with the consensus rather than stepping into a controversy?*

One defense goal for cross-examination is to "telegraph" to the jury that GBMI is not a compromise and that most GBMI prisoners receive *no* special services and are simply housed in the general population. In general, jurors are not privy to information regarding the consequences of their verdicts. However, cross-examination questions may spur jurors to consider the possible consequences of their decision-making. One possibility is to question the forensic clinician about his or her "expertise" in GBMI determinations:

1. *How often have you conducted forensic evaluations in which you concluded the defendant was "guilty-but-mentally-ill?" ... How accurate were you in making these determinations?* [likely to be vague] *...Do you have any follow-up data at all about your accuracy?*

2. [not likely to know] *Wouldn't this be relatively easy to evaluate? . . . You would simply have to conduct a follow-up evaluation at the state prison, isn't that correct?* [if adds forensic hospital] *. . . Would you be surprised to learn that none of the patients at __ [forensic hospital] have a "guilty-but-mentally-ill" verdict?*

Cross-examination may also evaluate the expert's decision-making process. Some experts are inherently skeptical of the insanity defense and rarely opine that the defendant meets one or more prongs of the insanity defense. While such experts are not categorically opposed to insanity, the amount of information needed before they are convinced is simply unattainable in most cases. Defense attorneys may wish to question the expert directly about his or her understanding of the insanity and GBMI standards. Illustrative questions are provided:

1. *How hard is it for you to believe that a __ [e.g., "psychotic" or "markedly depressed"] defendant could be insane? . . . Does it take a lot to convince you?* [if yes] *. . . In all fairness, do you think your skepticism has ever affected your impartiality?*
2. *Do some cases fall between a "guilty-but-mentally-ill" conviction and an insane verdict? . . . Please give us an example from your own practice . . .* [if given] *What was the name of the defendant in that case? . . . Did you testify for defense or the prosecution?*
3. *What is your understanding of the GBMI verdict? . . . How does it differ from insanity? . . . Recognizing that your words may have a profound effect on the defendant's life, are you willing to openly admit that you might be wrong in this case?* [if obfuscates] *. . . That was some fancy talking; my question remains, "Are you willing to openly admit that you might be wrong in this case?*

SUMMARY

Forensic research and concomitant theory have largely neglected important issues of criminal culpability. As a result, forensic clinicians are often at a disadvantage, given the absence of programmatic studies and specialized measures to tackle complex psycholegal issues. A major purpose of this chapter was to provide an overview of far-ranging legal issues and clinical-forensic methods. While cross-examination strategies underscore the current deficiencies, we hope that further work on theory, research, and practice will advance forensic psychology and psychiatry on issues of criminal culpability.

9

Sentencing Recommendations and Capital Issues

Two different models (indeterminate and determinate sentencing) bracket the range of approaches that characterize the sentencing of offenders, who have been convicted of noncapital offenses in U.S. courts. *Indeterminate sentencing* provides the sentencing court with a broad range of permissible dispositions (e.g., probation to a maximum period of imprisonment) that can be tailored to the circumstances of the defendant and the crime. This model offers wide-ranging opportunities to explore the relevance of mental health issues to the appropriate disposition. In contrast, *determinate sentencing* provides the court with a limited range of punishments with sentencing guidelines for a particular crime (e.g., 18–25 months of incarceration). This model offers only limited opportunities for mental health issues to justify a departure from a narrow range of punishments. Within indeterminate and determinate sentencing models, extensive variations occur from jurisdiction to jurisdiction. Between indeterminate and determinate sentencing models, a myriad of approaches exist. Although many jurisdictions have adopted either a determinate or indeterminate model, many others have adopted a hybrid system combining selected aspects of both models (e.g., creating a presumptive sentence but permitting a variance by the sentencing court based on a host of individual circumstances).

The sentencing of offenders convicted of a capital offense is a distinct category with its own jurisprudence that extends beyond the determinate and indeterminate models used for noncapital crimes. Supreme Court decisions have carved out an evolving "death penalty" jurisprudence. Two paramount features of the jurisprudence affecting the role of forensic clinicians have emerged. First, the Court has required (*Furman v. Georgia*, 1972) structured, individualized determinations to guide the decision maker's exercise of discretion to impose capital punishment. In order to ensure that the appropriate punishment is imposed, the Court has required that the sentencing process permit consideration of the defendant's character and record as well as the circumstances of the offense (*Lockett v. Ohio*, 1978). To implement this guided discretion states have recognized the opportunity to address both relevant mitigating and aggravating circumstances. As an example of the latter, forensic clinicians are often asked to address future risk of violent behavior either because this is an explicit aggravating factor (Colorado, 2003; Idaho, 2004; Oklahoma, 2004; Oregon, 2003; Texas, 2004; Virginia, 2004; Washington, 2004) or because it is it is an inherent issue in criminal sentencing (*Skipper v. South Carolina, 1986*). Second, the Court in *Atkins v. Virginia* (2002) banned the capital punishment of a mentally retarded offender and in *Tennard v. Dretke* (2004) required the opportunity for the defendant to present evidence of low intelligence to mitigate against the imposition of capital punishment. Forensic clinicians have much to offer in these aspects of capital-sentencing proceedings.

Forensic clinicians may also assist the sentencing court in determining how different dispositions would further or frustrate the goals of punishment as they are incorporated in the law of the sentencing jurisdiction. These goals (see *Ewing v. California*, 2003) may include restraint (i.e., community safety), rehabilitation (i.e., treatment), retribution (i.e., just deserts), and deterrence (i.e., both general and specific). The procedural mechanisms that govern input into sentencing decisions vary across jurisdictions. While juries play an important role in capital sentencing, judges are responsible for sentencing in most states for noncapital cases. Six states have juries regularly involved in noncapital sentencing: Arkansas, Kentucky, Missouri, Oklahoma, Texas, and Virginia.

Recent Supreme Court decisions have limited sentencing enhancements in both state and federal courts. In state cases of *Blakely v. Washington* (124 S. Ct. 2531 [2004]) and *Apprendi v. New Jersey*, (530 U.S. 466 [2000]), the Supreme Court has held that any fact other than the fact of the prior conviction, used to enhance punishment beyond the prescribed statutory maximum, must be presented to and proved to a jury beyond a reasonable doubt. In *United States v. Booker* and *United States v. Fanfan*, 2005 US LEXIS 628 (2005), the Court addressed these same concerns with federal judicial enhancement of sentences under the federal sentencing guidelines based on facts that had not been found by the jury, according to the beyond a reasonable doubt standard of persuasion. The Court addressed the issue in two separate 5-4 majority opinions. In the Court's first opinion in its consolidated decision in *Booker* and *Fanfan*, the Court concluded that a federal judge's imposition of a sentence violates the defendant's Sixth Amendment right to trial by jury if it does not rest on (1) facts found to exist by a jury applying the reasonable doubt standard of persuasion or (2) a defendant's guilty plea. In its second opinion, the Court determined that the mandatory premise of the guidelines was incompatible with a constitutional jury trial requirement and relegated their sentencing ranges to advisory status. According to this portion of the opinion, federal judges are required to consider the guidelines' ranges, but are free to take other statutory concerns into account (e.g., seriousness of the offense, just punishment, deterrence, public protection, provision of needed education, vocational training, and medical care 18 U.S.C. § 3553(a)(20 (main ed. and Supp. 2004)). It is expected that Congress will take up legislation to address federal sentencing in light of *Booker* and *Fanfan*.

Sentencing determinations are substantively as well as procedurally distinct from guilt determinations. Evidence that would not ordinarily be admissible on the determination of guilt (e.g., Fed. R. Evid. 404 regarding other similar crimes committed by the defendant) is ordinarily admissible at sentencing, where the rules of evidence do not typically apply (Fed. R. Evid. 1101(d)(3)). Thus, sentencing is ordinarily bifurcated from the issue of guilt.

Beyond testimony, sentencing reports may play an informal though instrumental role in the negotiation of some plea agreements. As outlined in subsequent sections, forensic clinicians must be aware of both formal and informal uses of their sentencing consultations.

RELEVANT LEGAL STANDARDS

This section on relevant legal standards is organized by type of sentencing (noncapital and capital) and general jurisdiction (federal and state). This review is intended to provide a conceptual understanding. Attorneys and forensic clinicians must develop a sophisticated knowledge of the particular standards relevant to their jurisdictions.

Noncapital Sentencing

Federal Standards

The federal sentencing guidelines, a determinate sentencing system for those convicted of federal crimes, were promulgated by the Sentencing Commissions created under the 1984 Sentencing Reform Act (18 U.S.C.S. 3551 et seq. (1982 ed., Supp. IV) and 28 U.S.C.S. 991–998 (1982 ed., Supp. IV)). An overriding purpose of these guidelines was to reduce discretion in sentencing decisions. The constitutionality of these guidelines was upheld by the Supreme Court (*Mistretta v. United States,* 1989). The Court's decision in *United States v. Booker* and *United States v. Fanfan* (2005) does not quarrel with the constitutionality authority of the guidelines, only the procedures for imposing a sentence in excess of the guidelines. In so doing, however, it has relegated the sentencing ranges in the guidelines to advisory status.

The guidelines established a schema, which required the sentence to fall within a narrow range. A grid determining this range was created by the sentencing commission incorporating the offense level and the offender's criminal history. Of special interest to forensic clinicians, a downward departure from that range prescribed by the guidelines (i.e., a reduced sentence) could be warranted, based on a defendant's significantly reduced mental capacity. According to Perlin and Gould (1995), the use of reduced mental capacity to justify a downward departure had two limitations. First, impairment arising from voluntary drug use is *not* considered if it contributed to the offense. Second, a reduced sentence is not allowed when a need to protect the public from violence is established.

The key construct in assessing whether a downward departure was justified is *significantly reduced mental capacity.* This occurs when the defendant "has a significantly impaired ability to (A) understand the wrongfulness of the behavior compromising the offense or to exercise the power of reason; or (B) control behavior that the defendant knows is wrongful" (*United States v. Nunemacher,* 2004, p. 690). Thus, to address these advisory concerns, in sentencing for federal crimes that do not involve violence, forensic clinicians should address both cognitive and volitional impairment. Volitionally, defendants have often sought reduced sentencing for financial crimes apparently caused by the defendant's problem gambling (*United States v. Sadolsky,* 2000; *United States v. Iaconetti,* 1999). Courts have been careful, however, to require a close causal nexus between the impairment and the commission of the offense to justify a downward departure in sentencing. In *Venezia v. United States* (1995), for example, the court rejected evidence of the defendant's compulsive gambling to justify a downward departure in his sentence for conspiracy to defraud the United States and to commit wire fraud because it found that he was able to "absorb information in the usual way and to exercise the power of reason" (p. 925). Similarly, the court in *United States v. Kim* (2004) rejected evidence of the defendant's childhood sexual abuse as not sufficiently causally connected to bank fraud to justify a downward departure.

State Standards

Determinate state sentencing systems also seek to limit discretion but allow a reduced sentence because of the defendant's mental state. For example, Minnesota's highly structured sentencing guidelines permit evidence of mental impairment as a mitigating factor when "the offender, because of physical or mental impairment, lacked substantial capacity for judgment when the offense was committed" (Minnesota Sentencing Guidelines II.D.2.a. [3]). Minnesota courts have interpreted this provision to *include* severe disorders, such as paranoia and schizophrenia (*State v. Wall*, 1984) and *exclude* emotional states, namely depressed, angry, and impulsive (*State v. Lee*, 1992).

States vary widely in their level of detail and types of criteria that should guide the exercise of discretion in indeterminate sentencing systems. Some states, like Ohio (2004), provide exhaustive detail. Coverage for aggravation includes the victim's injuries, the offender's motivation (e.g., prejudice based on race, ethnic background, gender, sexual orientation, or religion), and future risk assessment. Coverage for mitigation includes the victim's role in facilitating the offense, provocation, or other mitigating factors that may not constitute a defense. Other states (e.g., Arkansas, 2003) provide only brief descriptions of general issues, such as prior convictions, victim impact statements, relevant character evidence, and aggravating and mitigating circumstances.

CAPITAL SENTENCING

Estelle Warning

In *Estelle v. Smith* (1981), a capital murder case, the trial court appointed Dr. James Grigson, a psychiatrist, to examine the defendant Smith's competency to stand trial. Smith's lawyer was not informed and did not participate in this decision. Importantly, Smith was not informed of his right to refuse to incriminate himself in the examination. Found competent, Smith was subsequently convicted of capital murder. At the capital sentencing hearing, over the defendant's objection, Dr. Grigson was permitted to testify regarding Smith's future violence, a critical issue for imposing the death penalty in Texas. Smith was subsequently sentenced to death. The case ultimately reached the Supreme Court which found that the Fifth Amendment privilege against self-incrimination applied in a pretrial psychiatric examination and held that:

> A criminal defendant, who neither initiates a psychiatric evaluation nor attempts to introduce any psychiatric evidence, may not be compelled to respond to a psychiatrist if his statements can be used against him at a capital sentencing proceeding. Because respondent did not voluntarily consent to the pretrial psychiatric examination after being informed of his right to remain silent and the possible use of his statements, the State could not rely on what he said to Dr. Grigson to establish his future dangerousness. If, upon being adequately warned, respondent had indicated that he would not answer Dr. Grigson's questions, the validly ordered competency examination nevertheless could have proceeded upon the condition that the results would be applied solely for that purpose. In such circumstances, the proper conduct and use of competency and sanity examinations are not frustrated, but the State must make its case on future dangerousness in some other way. (pp. 468–469)

Based on *Estelle*, a prosecution or court-appointed expert is required to advise the defendant of his or her rights, if the examination will be used subsequently at a capital sentencing proceeding. The defendant must be warned about the right to remain silent and the potential uses of statements to this expert. This right is limited to capital sentencing proceedings and does not apply to other mental health issues such as raising an insanity defense (*Buchanan v. Kentucky*, 1987). Some forensic clinicians give this warning in any forensic examination involving a capital crime in the event they are subsequently asked to address capital sentencing. Moreover, professional ethics require that all clients, including pretrial defendants, be informed about the purpose and methods of their examinations.

Aggravating Factors in Capital Sentencing

Some states with capital punishment require the sentencing judge or jury to reach affirmative findings on specific statutory issues before the death penalty is imposed. In Texas (2004), for example, the trial court is required to conduct a separate sentencing hearing to consider aggravating and mitigating evidence to determine whether the defendant should be sentenced to death or life imprisonment. At the conclusion of the proceeding, the following issues are submitted to the sentencer:

1. whether there is a probability that the defendant would commit criminal acts of violence that would constitute a continuing threat to society; and

2. in cases in which the jury charge at the guilt or innocence stage permitted the jury to find the defendant guilty as a party under *Sections 7.01 and 7.02, Penal Code*, whether the defendant actually caused the death of the deceased or did not actually cause the death of the deceased but intended to kill the deceased or another or anticipated that a human life would be taken.

A unanimous, affirmative finding on these issues is required to impose a sentence of death rather than life imprisonment.

Oregon (2003) has enacted a similar approach to capital sentencing, providing no lists of potential aggravating or mitigating circumstances and instead posing specific questions to the jury, which also includes a finding on the risk of future violence. On the basis of these questions, the jury must consider the deliberateness of the defendant's conduct in causing death, future violence constituting a continued threat to society, and any provocation. Interestingly, Virginia (2004) adds an alternative to future violence, namely the depravity of the offense. Depravity requires that the "conduct in committing the offense was outrageously or wantonly vile, horrible or inhuman, in that it involved torture, depravity of mind or aggravated battery to the victim."

Many states do not require future violence as a precondition to the death sentence. Instead, they simply consider it to be one aggravating factor. In Colorado (2003), the jury for a capital sentencing is directed to consider whether "at least one aggravating factor has been proved; and . . . there are insufficient mitigating factors to outweigh the aggravating factor or factors that were proved." Like many states, Colorado provides an extensive list of aggravating factors that include (1) specific prior felony convictions, (2) killing of particular professionals (e.g., judges, police officers, and firefighters) or elected officials, (3) types of murder (child, pregnant woman, multiple deaths, and use of explosives), (4) murder combined with certain other offenses (e.g., kidnapping and contract to kill), and (5) attributes of the murderer and murder (e.g., heinous acts and extreme indifference). Mitigating factors are equally as extensive. They include (1) characteristics of the defendant (i.e., age), (2) psychological factors (e.g., emotional state and intoxication), (3) culpability (e.g., impaired cognitive or volitional abilities, moral justification, and duress), (4) characteristics of the offender's behavior (e.g., a subsidiary role and the foreseeability of death) and (5) crime-related issues (e.g., cooperation with the prosecution, lack of prior convictions, and lack of continued threat).

Psychological factors and issues related to culpability are especially relevant to forensic clinicians. Under the Washington (2004) statute, mental health professionals may be asked to consider psychological factors (e.g., mental retardation and "extreme mental disturbance") and issues of criminal culpability (e.g., duress or domination of another person; and cognitive or volitional impairment). Regarding the latter, the statute uses similar language to the ALI standard of insanity: "Whether, at the time of the murder, the capacity of the defendant to appreciate the wrongfulness of his or her conduct or to conform his or her conduct to the requirements of law was substantially impaired as a result of mental disease or defect." This parallel to the ALI standard is fairly common. In California, the basis for impairment was expanded to include substance abuse, specifically, the "effects of intoxication."

An important yet ambiguous construct is "extreme mental disturbance." The state of Washington (2004) asks the jury, or the trial judge if a jury is waived, to consider: "Whether the murder was committed while the defendant was under the influence of extreme mental disturbance." (California, 2003; see also Florida, 2004) appears to have broadened this construct slightly by specifying an "extreme mental or emotional disturbance." In contrast, Colorado (2003) simply directs the jury to consider: "The emotional state of the defendant at the time the crime was committed."

Many states require that additional issues of criminal culpability be considered. Colorado directs the jury to consider the defendant's belief that the act was morally justified: "The good faith, although mistaken, belief by the defendant that circumstances existed which constituted a moral justification for the defendant's conduct." Mitigation could be conceptualized on a continuum from frank delusions to strongly held misbeliefs. California (2004) adds further ambiguity in specifying that the "offense was committed under circumstances which the defendant was reasonably believed to be a moral justification or extenuation for his conduct." Does "reasonably" mean "firmly" or "rationally" in this context? In California, forensic clinicians may also be asked whether the defendant "reasonably believed" there was *extenuation* for his conduct.

Duress has numerous meanings in many legal contexts but generally refers to the use of force or coercion by a third party to undermine an actor's consensual conduct. In capital sentencing, states vary substantially in defining the necessary level of duress required for mitigation. In Washington (2004), the defendant merely need to act under duress. In Colorado (2003), "unusual and substantial" duress is required. In other states (e.g., California and Florida), a higher standard of "extreme" duress is mandated.

Constitutionally Required Mitigation

As the Supreme Court has consistently noted, qualitative differences in death and other penalties "requires consideration of the character and record of the individual offender and the circumstances of the particular offense as a constitutionally indispensable part of the process of inflicting the penalty of death" (*Woodson v. North Carolina*, 1976, p. 304). Accordingly, the Constitution requires that "the sentencer, in all but the rarest kind of capital case, not be precluded from considering, as a mitigating factor, any aspect of a defendant's character or record and any of the circumstances of the offense that the defendant proffers as a basis for a sentence less than death" (*Lockett v. Ohio*, 1978, p. 604) including among other things, family history and emotional disorder (*Eddings v. Oklahoma*, 1982).

Beyond statutorily required mitigating consideration, the Supreme Court has found that certain classes of mitigating evidence are constitutionally required. Regarding mental health issues, the Court in *Penry v. Lynaugh* (1989, p. 328) held that the defendant must be permitted to introduce evidence of his or her mental retardation. Moreover, the jury must be instructed regarding the role that this evidence may play in mitigation of punishment. The Court ruled "in the absence of instructions informing the jury that it could consider and give effect to the mitigating evidence of Penry's mental retardation and abused background by declining to impose the death penalty, we conclude that the jury was not provided with a vehicle for expressing its 'reasoned moral response' to that evidence in rendering its sentencing decision." Recently, in *Tennard v. Dretke* (2004, p. 2571), the Court extended the requirement that the defendant be permitted to introduce mitigating evidence from mental retardation to low intelligence:

> Nothing in our [*Penry*] opinion suggested that a mentally retarded individual must establish a nexus between her mental capacity and her crime before the Eighth Amendment prohibition on executing her is triggered. Equally, we cannot countenance the suggestion that low IQ evidence is not relevant mitigating evidence—and thus that the Penry question need not even be asked—unless the defendant also establishes a nexus to the crime.

Atkins and the Mentally Retarded

In *Atkins v. Virginia* (2002), the Court went beyond mitigation and prohibited the imposition of the death penalty on mentally retarded defendants. It held that executions of persons who are mentally retarded was a violation of the constitution's ban against cruel and unusual punishment. Recognizing the potential for controversies in delineating mental retardation, the Court (pp. 347–348) left this matter to the states:

> To the extent there is serious disagreement about the execution of mentally retarded offenders, it is in determining which offenders are in fact retarded. In this case, for instance, the Commonwealth of Virginia disputes that Atkins suffers from mental retardation. Not all people who claim to be mentally retarded will

be so impaired as to fall within the range of mentally retarded offenders about whom there is a national consensus. As was our approach in Ford v. Wainwright, with regard to insanity, "we leave to the States the task of developing appropriate ways to enforce the constitutional restriction upon its execution of sentences."

The Court offered little guidance about what constitutes "the range of mentally retarded offenders about whom there is a national consensus." (The Court's observation that "Not all people who claim to be mentally retarded will be so impaired as to fall within the range of mentally retarded offenders about whom there is a national consensus" implies that a post-*Atkins* residual role may yet remain for evidence of mental retardation to mitigate capital punishment under *Penry*). In Footnote 3 (p. 309), it provided some assistance by quoting the definitions of mental retardation used by national organizations, namely the American Association of Mental Retardation (AAMR) and the American Psychiatric Association (APA):

> The American Association of Mental Retardation (AAMR) defines mental retardation as follows: "Mental retardation refers to substantial limitations in present functioning. It is characterized by significantly subaverage intellectual functioning, existing concurrently with related limitations in two or more of the following applicable adaptive skill areas: communication, self-care, home living, social skills, community use, self-direction, health and safety, functional academics, leisure, and work. Mental retardation manifests before age 18." Mental Retardation: Definition, Classification, and Systems of Supports 5 (9th ed. 1992).

The American Psychiatric Association's definition is similar: "The essential feature of Mental Retardation is significantly subaverage general intellectual functioning (Criterion A) that is accompanied by significant limitations in adaptive functioning in at least two of the following skill areas: communication, self-care, home living, social/interpersonal skills, use of community resources, self-direction, functional academic skills, work, leisure, health, and safety (Criterion B). The onset must occur before age 18 years (Criterion C). Mental Retardation has many different etiologies and may be seen as a final common pathway of various pathological processes that affect the functioning of the central nervous system." American Psychiatric Association, Diagnostic and Statistical Manual of Mental Disorders 41 (4th ed. 2000). "Mild" mental retardation is typically used to describe people with an IQ level of 50–55 to approximately 70 Id., at 42–43.

Attorneys must ensure that forensic clinicians employ nationally accepted standards in diagnosing mental retardation. Fortunately, the two national organizations (AAMR and APA) have achieved a general consensus on the diagnosis of mental retardation. Currently, forensic clinicians involved in post-conviction *Atkins* challenges must address a difficult obstacle: How do you establish "adaptive functioning" for defendants who have spent years of death row?

Admissibility of Expert Testimony

The Court's decision in *Barefoot v. Estelle* (1983) concluded that the constitution did not prohibit a sentence of death supported by a psychiatrist's clinically based prediction of dangerous, lacking demonstrable scientific validity. Many who were disappointed by *Barefoot's* disdain for the necessity of a scientific foundation to support such a critical determination on an issue that had been the subject of a significant body of research were optimistic about the impact of *Daubert* on *Barefoot*. But, the Court's decision in *Daubert v. Merrell Dow Pharmaceuticals, Inc.* (1993) regarding the threshold for the admissibility of expert testimony in the federal courts was an interpretation of Fed. R. Evid. 702. The Federal Rules of Evidence are not applicable in sentencing proceedings (Fed. R. Evid. 1101 (d)(3)), because (1) evidence that would ordinarily be inadmissible at trial on the issue of guilt, such as character evidence, is precisely the type of evidence contemplated at sentencing, and (2) at least in federal court, the jury does not sentence (i.e., the rules of evidence are largely designed as a jury protection mechanism). The federal courts have recognized this evidentiary limitation and held that exclusion of expert testimony on *Daubert* grounds at sentencing is erroneous (e.g., *United States v. Hunter*, 1998; *United States v. Ferron*, 2004), as have some state courts that have evidence codes patterned after the federal rules (e.g., *Douglas v. Commonwealth*, 2001). Others states, such as Idaho (*State v. Creech*, 1983), Louisiana (*State v. Clark*, 1990), and Virginia (*Quintana v. Commonwealth*, 1982) apply their evidence rules at sentencing proceedings. However, even in jurisdictions in which the rules of evidence and cases interpreting them do not apply in sentencing proceedings, sentencing guidelines or other procedural rules governing sentencing generally impose their own reliability threshold permitting courts to rely only on information that "has sufficient indicia of reliability to support its probable accuracy" (USSG 6A1.3(a)). Beyond *Daubert* or its state counterpart, all expert testimony must be relevant in addressing the substantive legal criteria (e.g., does the defendant's diminished capacity explain the cause of the behavior leading to this offense to justify a downward departure).

OVERVIEW OF CLINICAL METHODS AND SENTENCING DETERMINATIONS

Noncapital and capital sentencing often differ fundamentally in their provision of definite criteria. As noted in *Relevant Legal Standards*, forensic clinicians are often guided by general principles (e.g., incapacitation or re-habilitation) rather than professional standards when consulting on non-capital cases. In clear contrast, capital sentencing typically provides spe-cific, if sometimes vaguely defined, criteria for aggravation and mitigation. Therefore, noncapital and capital sentencing are addressed separately.

CLINICAL APPLICATIONS TO NONCAPITAL CASES

Melton et al. (1997) observed that the sentencing phase can be charac-terized by flexibility and informality. An important purpose of sentencing hearings is to provide the court with whatever information it deems impor-tant without any restrictions imposed by legal protections. The hallmark of sentencing is flexibility in order to achieve the appropriate punishment. By its very nature, the flexibility typically results in a lack of standardized procedures.

How do experts respond to a lack of standards and formal structure? Research by Rogers, Gillis, Dickens, and Webster (1988) examined psy-chiatric opinions on issues relevant to sentencing, specifically treatability and prognosis. Using an extensive database on 1,238 mentally disordered offenders referred for inpatient forensic assessments, they attempted to discern what variables predicted recommendations to the criminal courts that could be used at sentencing. For outpatient recommendations,[1] the investigators reached the very troubling conclusion *"who conducts the eval-uation* is at least as important as *who is evaluated"* (p. 494). One plausible interpretation of this finding is that the absence of standards promotes personal biases.

An interesting question is whether judges have similarly divergent patterns with some seeking alternatives to incarceration while others choosing incapacitation through incarceration. Wooldredge and Gordon (1997) found that judges varied substantially in their willingness to con-sider alternatives to incarceration. Variables potentially affecting decisions to accept alternatives included the sentencing structure, the perceived over-crowding of state prisons, and judges' willingness to accept plea bargains. On the matter of state prisons, attorneys may wish to emphasize issues that further their causes: (1) the prosecution might emphasize the priority of prison cells for very serious offenders, and (2) the defense might draw at-tention to the vast overcrowding caused by the incarceration of nonviolent offenders.

---

[1] If followed, these recommendations will likely result in a release into the community with modest (e.g., weekly) treatment requirements.

A minority of states uses jurors for noncapital sentencing. One consideration in jury selection is whether perspective jurors favor rehabilitation versus incapacitation. Gerber and Englehardt-Greer (1996) found that persons with less education were more likely to emphasize retribution: 66% = less than high school; 59% = high school graduate; 49% = some college; and 39% = college graduate. Rehabilitation was *not* the top priority of most persons; even among college graduates only one-third ranked rehabilitation first. Interesting, positive attitudes toward the treatment of violent offenders were more commonly found (>40%) among African Americans and politically liberal persons. Positive attitudes were infrequently observed (<25%) among European Americans, gun owners, politically conservative persons, and those feeling unprotected by the criminal courts.

The next subsection addresses squarely the parameters of expertise and the concomitant problems when experts overreach their expertise. Subsequent subsections distill key issues involving relevant clinical constructs such as treatability and risk assessment. Within the context of sentencing, we focus on sex offenders and psychopaths.

Parameters of Expertise

In the absence of psycholegal criteria, sentencing in noncapital cases might cover the full gamut of possible predictors. These predictors could include (1) demographic variables such as gender and race, (2) criminological variables such as past arrests, (3) sociological variables such as socioeconomic status, and (4) psychological variables such as diagnoses and past treatment. With respect to sentencing, a very large segment of the professional literature is found in the disciplines of criminology and criminal justice. These disciplines dwarf the contributions of forensic psychology and psychiatry to sentencing predictions.

Attorneys and their experts should not dodge the fundamental question, "What are the parameters of psychological and psychiatric expertise in noncapital sentencing?" At the extreme, should forensic psychology or psychiatry be allowed to masquerade as experts in criminal justice? Let us begin with an examination of the legitimate roles for forensic psychology and psychiatry. These specialties have expert knowledge in forensic populations about mental disorders, psychopathology, and clinical constructs. Using this expert knowledge, forensic clinicians can describe defendants' psychological functioning, treatment needs, and multiaxial diagnoses. While relatively sparse, their research has examined selectively psychological variables as predictors of treatment compliance, treatment outcome, and prosocial adjustments for mentally disordered offenders.

Taken together, forensic psychology and psychiatry have legitimate roles in noncapital sentencing cases.

When do forensic psychology and psychiatry exceed their professional expertise? A clear example involves the exclusive use of demographic and criminological variables for use in risk assessment as it relates to noncapital sentencing. Experts in this instance are plainly not relying on their discipline. Forensic clinicians may try to defend their improper use of criminal-justice measures through specious arguments such as the following:

1. *Several psychologists have made prominent contributions to criminal-justice measures.* While definitely true, this observation does not justify conclusions or testimony based on these measures. Consider for a moment that several psychologists have also made prominent contributions to neurology and biology. Should we allow psychologists or psychiatrists to claim expertise in these disciplines as well?

2. *These criminal-justice measures have been described in "risk assessment" literature, an area about which psychologists have expertise.* Simply because they are described in the psychological literature does not make them "psychological measures." In clear instances (e.g., RRASOR and Static-99; see the subsequent review and Chapter 11), no psychological variables are employed.

As mandated by the official *Standards for educational and psychological testing* (AERA/APA/NCME, 1999), use of psychological measures should be confined to "areas of competence as demonstrated through education, supervised training, experience, and appropriate credentialing" (p. 131). Psychologists and psychiatrists are not educated, trained, or credentialed in criminal-justice measures. Forensic clinicians relying on criminal-justice measures overstep their expertise when using measures outside their recognized disciplines.

TREATABILITY

Within the criminological literature, Martinson (1974) published the highly influential review that concluded "nothing works" in correctional rehabilitation. Despite research (see Bonta & Cormier, 1999) directly challenging Martinson's conclusions, the spillover effects of the "nothing works" hypothesis have produced intense pessimism regarding offender rehabilitation. Attorneys should be aware that some forensic clinicians are likely believers in this now-disputed hypothesis. As officers of the court, both prosecution and defense should actively seek to eliminate any "expert" who operates from disputed hunches rather than specialized knowledge.

Rogers and Webster (1989) provided a conceptual framework for treatment as a sentencing alternative to incarceration. On the basis of two principles (treatment effectiveness and public safety), they proposed that treatment alternatives only be considered when treatment is effective and substantially reduces the likelihood of serious recidivism. The latter issue requires that the defendant's criminal activity be linked to his or her psychological impairment. Table 4-1 (p. 93) provides a valuable checklist of key issues that should be considered for treatment alternatives. It applies equally well to diversion and sentencing alternatives.

The Rogers and Webster model is based on an individualized approach that considers both treatment and risk. Forensic clinicians should supplement this model with empirical data on what variables (1) predict treatment success versus treatment failure, and (2) predict community safety versus serious recidivism. Attorneys should be aware that the data on these predictions is far from complete. However, this specialized knowledge may assist the court in understanding the general issues but with limited applicability to a particular defendant.

RISK ASSESSMENT

Volumes have been written about risk assessment with a primary focus on violent and nonviolent recidivism. This subsection provides a brief overview of conceptual issues. A further examination of risk assessment is found in subsequent subsections (i.e., "Sex Offenders" and "Antisocial Persons and Psychopaths") and also in Chapter 11.

We surmise that sentencing judges and, where applicable, juries are interested in two fundamental questions. These are outlined with commentaries:

1. *What type of risk is posed by this particular offender?*
   Attorneys can fully appreciate that the broader categories will inevitably include more offenders. As a hypothetical, the risk that offenders will use expletives is likely to approach 100%. But are overly inclusive categories helpful to the sentencing process? Does writing an obscene letter to a consenting adult pose a serious community threat? Sexual Violence Recidivism—20 (SVR-20; Boer et al., 1997) does exactly that when it considers any obscene letter to be "sexual violence." Attorneys will likely need assistance from their own experts in understanding what *types* of risk are being predicted.

Overly inclusive categories may indiscriminantly combine nonviolent and violent behaviors.

2. *What is the likelihood of risk posed by this particular offender?*
As noted by Melton et al. (1997), the Supreme Court has underscored the importance of individualized punishment in sentencing criminals. This individualization is poorly served when the risk assessment data are not relevant to the particular offender. Statistics used by risk assessment methods often obscure rather than clarify the risk posed by a particular offender. The most direct and forthright approach is to establish as a percentage the likelihood of this offender recidivating on specific crimes. Two matters must be considered: the *standard error of measurement* (SEm) and individual factors that might affect interpretation.

Attorneys often misunderstand *standard error of measurement*. Because scores are not perfectly accurate, the likely error in their measurement must be calculated. In most instances, attorneys can safely assume that the defendant's score will fall within 2 *standard errors of measurement*. To make this more concrete, consider one of the best validated measures of intelligence, specifically the Weschler Adult Intelligence Scale—Third Edition (WAIS-III; Weschler, 1997). With an IQ of 100, a defendant would be considered at the 50% in terms of intelligence. Taking into account two *standard errors of measurement* (i.e., 2×2.30 SEm), the IQ almost certainly falls between 95 and 105. Although this sounds small, the range in percentages exceeds 25% (i.e., 37th percentile for an IQ of 95 versus 63rd percentile for an IQ of 105). Such marked differences in standard errors of measurement may dramatically affect the interpretation of risk assessment results.

The importance of *standard errors of measurement* cannot be underestimated:

- If standard errors of measurement are *large*, then predictions based on the results are probably meaningless.
- If standard errors of measurement are *unreported*, then the measure violates the official test standards (i.e., Standard 2.2; AERA/APA/NCME, 1999) and should not be used.

Risk assessment measures tend to report data on the overall accuracy and neglect relevant data on a particular defendant. For individual defendants, the most relevant utility estimates are positive predictive power (PPP) and negative predictive power (NPP). Given a particular score on a risk assessment measure, PPP tells us the likelihood (percentage) that a particular defendant *meets* this condition (e.g., violent recidivism). NPP tells us the likelihood that a particular defendant *does not meet* this condition.

The next sections focus on types of offenders for whom sentencing issues are often salient: sex offenders and persons with antisocial personality disorder/psychopathy. Both issues of treatability and risk are considered.

TREATMENT AND RISKS WITH SEX OFFENDERS

A range of clinical interventions has been formulated to treat sex offenders and their specific paraphilias (Laws & O' Donohue, 1997). In most instances, these treatment interventions have not been rigorously tested in an experimental design. As a result, much of the treatment literature for sex offenders is more descriptive than rigorously experimental.

Treatment interventions can be categorized by treatment modality rather than by treatment effectiveness. Abel and Osborn (2003) describe a range of behavioral and cognitive-behavioral methods used to decrease deviant sexual arousal. These methods include olfactory aversion (e.g., pairing the deviant fantasy with the smelling of ammonia), covert sensitization (i.e., cognitive imagining with an emphasis on negative consequences), masturbatory satiation (e.g., methods of ensuring nonperformance to deviant stimuli), and aversive behavioral rehearsal (i.e., creating shame by receiving feedback from a small audience of nonprofessionals). As summarized by Bradford and Harris (2003), several pharmacological interventions are intended to reduce sexual interest and performance: hormonal agents, antiandrogen medication, and LHRH agonists.

Beyond deviant arousal, treatment may focus on cognitive distortions and victim empathy (Abel & Osborn, 2003). This brief summary illustrates (1) the complexity of treatment interventions for sex offenders and (2) the need for specialized training for those forensic clinicians conducting sentencing evaluations with this population.

Pray (2003) conducted a meta-analysis that combined 10 controlled studies on 1,619 sex offenders to examine the effectiveness of psychotherapeutic interventions. The good news is that treated offenders (17.3%) had lower recidivism than their untreated counterparts (22.0%). This 4.7% difference represents 21.4% (i.e., 4.7/22.0) decrease in recidivism as a result of treatment. The bad news is that no clinical variables were found that effectively distinguished between positive and negative treatment outcomes.

For other recent studies of sex offender treatment, Hanson, Broom, and Stephenson (2004) demonstrated virtually no effect when offenders were indiscriminantly placed into treatment, irrespective of their motivation or other clinical issues. In contrast, McGrath, Cumming, Livingston, and Hoke (2003) found a remarkable success for prison-based cognitive-behavioral program with minimal recidivism for treatment completers (5.4%) as compared to treatment dropouts (30.6%) or untreated offenders (30.0%). These studies illustrate two important points. First, sex offenders should be screened to select those motivated and amenable to treatment. Second, treatment success must consider both the motivation of the sex offender and the effectiveness of the treatment program.

Bradford (2000; Bradford & Harris, 2003) recommended a treatment algorithm based on the seriousness of the sexually deviant behavior: (1) *mild* refers "hands-off" (i.e., nonphysical) paraphilias with minimal victimization (e.g., exhibitionism), (2) *moderate* refers to either "hands-off" paraphilias with poor control over "hands-on" sexual urges or "hands-on" paraphilias with few victims (<3) and low victimization (i.e., fondling), (3) *severe* refers to "hand-on" paraphilias with greater victimization, typically penetration, and (4) *catastrophic* refers to "hands-on" paraphilias resulting in severe injury or death. Bradford recommended that pharmacological treatments take into account the severity of the paraphilias with a complete androgen suppression (i.e., similar to surgical castration) for the most severe cases.

Bradford's treatment algorithm is both useful and controversial. It highlights the need to consider both the type and severity of the paraphilias in establishing sex offender treatment programs. It is naive to offer a generic treatment program for sex offenders. It is equally naive for forensic clinicians to provide generic treatment recommendations. While controversial, highly intrusive interventions (i.e., chemical castration) can "treat" very severe paraphilias and reduce sexual recidivism to below 5% (Bradford & Harris, 2003). Likewise, research on surgical castration found very low levels of sexual recidivism despite 20–50% maintaining some level of sexual functioning for 5 years following the surgical procedure (Stone, Winslade, & Klugman, 2000).

Successful treatment of sex offenders depends on effective assessment methods. Self-report methods for sexual histories and current paraphiliac activities are highly vulnerable to denial and minimization (Sewell & Cruise, 1997). Penile plethysmography can directly measure the level of tumescence to deviant and nondeviant sexual arousal. As previously noted (Rogers & Shuman, 2000), methodological concerns hamper the accuracy of these methods. When used for treatment monitoring rather than trial evidence, penile plethysmography may be effective in assessing comparative arousal levels. However, deviant arousal levels should be substantial. Ward, McCormack, Hudson, and Polaschek (1997) observed that the reliability of the penile plethysmography is substantially improved when the examinee achieves at least a 75% erection to deviant stimuli. In contrast to the circumscribed applications of penile plethysmography, Abel's (1995) Screen lacks sufficient validity to be employed for either trial or treatment purposes (Rogers & Shuman, 2000).

Craig, Browne, and Stringer (2003) provide a comprehensive review of risk scales used in sexual recidivism. As they note, most risk scales focus exclusively on static factors and neglect dynamic factors in making their predictions. They found (see Table 2, p. 54) that several risk measures (e.g., the VRAG and SORAG) were (1) poorly correlated with sexual recidivism (i.e., $rs \leq .20$), and (2) appeared to better measures of nonsexual recidivism. Contrary to expectations several general actuarial scales performed slightly better: RRASOR (rs from .22 to .28) and the MnSOST (rs from .11 to .45). Of particular concern, risk scales may even demonstrate *negative* though small correlations with sexual recidivism, as illustrated by a Swedish study (Sjostedt & Langstrom, 2002) for the PCL-R ($r = -.12$) and SVR-20 Total ($r = -.10$). Risk scales for sexual offending are described and discussed in Chapter 11.

TREATMENT AND RISKS WITH PSYCHOPATHS

Cleckley's (1976) seminal work on psychopathy described core personality characteristics that were resistant to change. Importantly, Cleckley did not see psychopathy as necessarily linked with violence or serious crime. This link was made partly by happenstance. Hare developed the widely used Psychopathy Checklist—Revised (PCL-R, 1991, 2003) in his research with male career criminals in maximum security prisons. Not surprisingly, these participants evidenced marked levels of violent offenses and institutional infractions. Subsequently, the PCL-R has been used successfully with male inmate populations to identify high-risk groups.

An absolutely crucial distinction must be made between antisocial personality disorder and psychopathy. Forensic clinicians often mistakenly believe these represent the same diagnostic construct. For example, Stevens (1994) found that approximately two-thirds of professional staff in corrections erroneously equated antisocial personality disorder with psychopathy. To the contrary, the relationship is very asymmetrical. In corrections, the majority of inmates warrant antisocial personality disorder while only 15–25% are psychopaths (Hare, 2003). Attorneys must be very alert of forensic clinicians who may assume psychopathy simply based on an antisocial past.

Are psychopaths treatable? Clinical lore, poorly informed by early research, provides a resoundingly negative response. Therapeutic pessimism about the treatment of psychopathy continues to persist despite reviews that indicate this judgment to be both premature and inaccurate. An early review by Wong and Elek (1989) found the conclusions about psychopaths lacked firm empirical basis. More recently, Salekin (2002) conducted a meta-analysis of 42 investigations and concluded that psychopathy was treatable. Three salient findings about positive treatment outcome with adult psychopaths follow:

1. *Type of Classification.* Classifications by Cleckley's original criteria produced a much higher proportion of treatment success (88%) than did the PCL-R (57%).
2. *Type of treatment.* Cognitive-behavioral (62%) and psychodynamic (59%) were more successful than therapeutic communities (25%).
3. *Duration of treatment.* Long-term interventions (more than 12 months) produced very positive results (91%). Shorter programs were less successful: 61% for less than 6 months and 77% for 6–12 months.

As an important caveat, treatment successes were defined differently by individual researchers. Definitions varied from a lack of recidivism to decreased hostility and improved social relations. For the several investigations that focused solely on offenses/convictions, the weighted average was 51% for treatment success.[2]

DeSilva, Duggan, and McCarthy (2004) reviewed 10 treatment studies for psychopathic samples and noted the obvious limitations in the research: (1) use of different cut scores for the classification of psychopathy, (2) lack of control groups, and (3) treatment that did not address psychopathy. DeSilva and her colleagues cautioned against prematurely concluding that psychopaths were untreatable, especially since most investigations did not attempt to treat psychopathy per se.

Skeem, Monahan, and Mulvey (2002) systematically evaluated the effects of treatment on inpatients classified with psychopathy. They found that moderate levels of treatment (seven or more sessions in 10 weeks) resulted in markedly decreased levels of violence. These results are noteworthy because most participants had Axis I disorders sufficiently severe to require hospitalization and many also had comorbid disorders, such as substance abuse.

Most treatment programs do *not* focus specifically on psychopathy but address general clinical issues. This major oversight likely has dramatic effects on treatment outcomes. For example, Seto and Barbaree (1999) found that psychopaths that "graduated" from a sex offender treatment program

---

[2]This percentage is more than double what was found for nontreatment conditions (20%).

had higher recidivism than others. However, the treatment program attempted to treat paraphilias and ignore the psychopathy. As a medical analogy, this treatment approach would be similar to treating a patient's liver disease but deliberately ignoring the pulmonary disorder. Such short-sighted efforts are likely to produce negative results. A more logical alternative would be to treat the psychopathy directly. Salekin (2002) found one youth-based program that addressed the sensation-seeking component of psychopathy and produced very positive results. Unquestionably, clinical interventions should directly target core psychopathic features rather than neglecting them.

Psychopathy likely poses an increased risk of recidivism in offender populations. This global statement is *unhelpful* to forensic clinicians and criminal attorneys simply because it obscures important data and overlooks meaningful limitations. A more relevant approach would be to consider the following questions: Which psychopaths have demonstrably greater risks of recidivism? How much of an increased risk do they pose?

An obvious research bias is uncovered in forensic research on psychopathy and recidivism. Many studies focus on the "worst of the worst." Studies situated only in maximum security facilities or those overrepresented with career criminals are likely to produce negative results. Forensic clinicians must bear this in mind whenever they attempt to apply PCL-R results to an individual offender.

Criminal attorneys should closely question forensic clinicians if they attempt to overgeneralize PCL-R findings to marginally relevant cases. We outline four major limitations in using the PCL-R findings to assess risk in criminal cases:

1. *Gender.* Walters (2003) found only four PCL studies that addressed female offenders and outcome that combined institutional problems and recidivism. The results are modest (i.e., M rs $< .30$) and do *not* address the key issue of violent recidivism in correctional/forensic samples.
2. *Ethnicity and Cultural Issues.* Small differences are found between European American and African American *male* offenders on the PCL measures. The significance of this finding is open to question (see Rogers, 2001). Insufficient data are available on other ethnic groups. In addition, marked differences are observed between North American and European studies on levels of psychopathy. Several studies (see Rogers, 2001) found only a small percentage of European offenders ($\leq 8\%$) are classified as psychopaths, which is less than one-third of what is typically observed in North America.

3. *Axis I Disorders.* It is estimated that 10–40% of patients with Axis I disorders are also classified as psychopaths (Hill, Neumann, & Rogers, 2004). Research is divided over whether this comorbidity increases or decreases the risk for violent behavior.

4. *Treatment.* Salekin's (2002) comprehensive review indicated that treatment would likely decreased risk of problematic behavior including recidivism. Most research has not taken this important issue (technically, a moderator variable) into consideration. As an exception, Skeem et al. (2002) found that psychopaths with sufficient treatment had two-thirds fewer violent acts, at least in the short term. Therefore, risk estimates only apply to *untreated* psychopaths.

Dozens of studies have attempted to examine the relationship with psychopathy, as measured by PCL measures, and general and violent recidivism. Table 9-1 summarizes four separate meta-analyses which provide comprehensive though overlapping coverage of PCL measures and recidivism. Modest but positive results were achieved by Simourd, Bonta, Andrews, and Hoge (1990) on the original PCL; these results are of limited value because subsequent revisions are substantially different from the original PCL (see Rogers, 2001). In considering the most comprehensive review, Salekin, Leistico, and Rogers (2004) found only an average correlation of .24 (i.e., 5.8% shared variance) between PCL-R total scores and violent recidivism. In general, Factor 2 scores ($Mr = .34$; 11.6% shared variance) were superior to both Factor 1 and total PCL-R scores for violent recidivism. These results are difficult to interpret. Conceptually, Factor 1

TABLE 9-1. A SUMMARY OF META-ANALYSES FOR PCL MEASURES WITH GENERAL AND VIOLENT RECIDIVISM: EFFECT SIZES EXPRESSED AS CORRELATIONS

Study	# of studies	General Recidivism			Violent Recidivism		
		Factor 1	Factor 2	Total	Factor 1	Factor 2	Total
Simourd et al. (1990)[a]	14	—	—	.33	—	—	.33
Hemphill et al. (1998)	7	.13	.30	.27	.13	.18	.27
Walters (2003)	24	.14	.31	—	.18	.26	—
Salekin et al. (2004)	54	.15	.34	.23	.17	.34	.24

Note. Salekin et al. (1996) and Gendreau, Goggin, and Smith (2002) also performed meta-analyses but did not report correlations; instead they used Cohen's ds and ϕ coefficients, respectively.
[a] Both postdictive and predictive studies using the original PCL.

forms the core features of psychopathy; negligible correlations ($Mr = .17$; 2.9% shared variance) seem to indicate that this factor has little bearing on violent recidivism. Clinically, no cut scores have been established for Factor 2 alone; therefore, this result cannot be effectively used in forensic practice.

Forensic clinicians are likely to be divided in how they interpret these modest correlations. For predictive validity, some forensic clinicians will consider such modest correlations (i.e., account for less than 10% of the variance) as weak and insubstantial evidence. Other forensic clinicians are likely to adopt a relativistic perspective and conclude that these admittedly modest correlations are better than many of the alternatives.

Hart (1998), a co-author of the PCL:SV, offers a well-reasoned centrist position on the use of the PCL-R in violent risk assessment. He recommended that forensic clinicians use the PCL-R selectively to evaluate violent recidivism by applying the standard cut score (i.e., 30) plus the standard error of measurement (estimated between approximately 3.00 and 3.25; Hare, 2003). By applying these criteria, offenders with PCL-R scores of 33 or higher (i.e., $\geq$33) would be classified as "high risk." This centrist position appears reasonable in noncapital cases. However, criminal attorneys must bear in mind two caveats:

1. *Misclassifications.* One standard error of measurement still results in a significant percentage of misclassification (11–16% range[3]). These offenders are misclassified as "psychopaths" when they are actually "nonpsychopaths."
2. *False-positives.* The false-positive rate when assuming all psychopaths are violent probably falls in the 20–30% range (see Hemphill et al., 1998; Salekin, Rogers, & Sewell, 1996).

How do these caveats affect accuracy? At the high end, the correct classification would be .89 (i.e., 11% misclassification) × .80 future violence (i.e., 20% false-positives) = 71.2% accuracy. At the low end, the correct classification would be .84 (i.e., 16% misclassification) × .70 (i.e., 30% false-positives) = 58.8% accuracy. The purpose of these calculations is to stress the level of imprecision in both the classification of psychopathy and predictions of violent recidivism. Even adopting Hart's centrist position, forensic clinicians are likely to be wrong in 30–40% of the forensic cases.

---

[3]Nearly all the predictive research is based on the PCL-R (Hare, 1991) which has a SEM of 3.25. We calculated the percentages for a one-tailed distribution at 1 SEM and 1.23 SEM (i.e., 4/3.25).

This discussion of the PCL-R has focused on violent recidivism rather than recidivism in general. In most instances, we surmise that sentencing determinations are especially concerned about aggressive acts. However, the results (see Table 9-1) are very similar to general recidivism.

Attorneys and forensic clinicians will be tempted to simplify the relationship of psychopathy to both treatment and recidivism. These are complicated and interrelated issues. Most concerning is the nearly pervasive therapeutic pessimism that colors both treatment efforts and risk estimates. Regarding risk, forensic clinicians must first consider under what circumstances should PCL measures be used. When used, they must clarify for the courts two types of imprecision involving the classification of psychopathy and predictions of recidivism.

CLINICAL APPLICATIONS TO CAPITAL CASES

Forensic clinicians engaged in capital sentencing cases must address the relevant psycholegal issues and also grapple with their personal attitudes and emotions involving the death penalty. As described further in Chapter 10, Deitchman, Kennedy, and Beckman (1991) addressed a related issue involving the death penalty, namely competency to be executed. They found moral beliefs against the death penalty was the strongest reasons for nonparticipation. Forensic clinicians willing to participate in these evaluations differed from their colleagues in their positive views toward capital punishment and stronger beliefs in the defendant's personal responsibility for his or her crimes. In summary, moral beliefs for and against the death penalty, and attributions of personal responsibility appear to be key determinants of professional involvement.

Capital sentencing evaluations differ fundamentally from other sentencing determinations in terms of both constitutionally mandated requirements and the formal consideration of explicit criteria that typically involve aggravating and mitigating factors. Constitutionally, the Supreme Court has imposed two restrictions on capital sentencing that are directly relevant to forensic practice, specifically warnings and the exclusion of mentally retarded persons. First, *Estelle v. Smith* (1981) requires that the defendant be informed about the purpose of the forensic evaluation and voluntarily consent to his or her participation. Second, *Atkins v. Virginia* (2002) requires that forensic evaluations consider the defendant's intellectual capacities; execution of mentally retarded defendants is expressly prohibited. Beyond these specific issues, state and federal standards provide explicit, although not necessarily exhaustive, criteria for aggravating and mitigating factors to be considered in death penalty cases. In addition, Supreme Court decisions

(*Lockett* and *Eddings*) require that the defendant be allowed to present any mitigating evidence with individual consideration to both offender and the circumstances surrounding his or her crimes.

This section is organized into four major components. First, we examine two components (*Estelle* Warnings and *Atkins* Determinations) address constitutionally mandated requirements. The latter two components (Aggravating Factors and Mitigating Factors) consider the pertinent clinical-forensic issues, such as dangerousness, culpability, and extreme emotional disturbance. Each component summarizes the specialized knowledge and applicable methods that are essential to forensic consultations.

ESTELLE WARNINGS

The Supreme Court in *Estelle v. Smith* (1981) held that capital defendants are entitled to be warned of their 5th Amendment protections in mental health evaluations initiated by the court or the prosecution that are used against the defendant in capital sentencing determinations. The Court determined that the expert testimony based on the defendant's statements were inadmissible, "Because respondent did not voluntarily consent to the pretrial psychiatric examination after being informed of his right to remain silent and the possible use of his statements" (p. 468). In addition, the Court determined that the capital defendant had the 6th Amendment right to counsel. At this critical stage, it held that the "respondent was denied the assistance of his attorneys in making the significant decision of whether to submit to the examination and to what end the psychiatrist's findings could be employed" (p. 471).

For capital sentencing evaluations, a simple notification regarding the purpose of the evaluation appears *insufficient* to meet the *Estelle* requirements. Instead, *Estelle* requires that the defendant be informed about (1) his or her choice to participate, (2) possible consequences of his or her statements (e.g., evidence may be presented in court supporting the death penalty), and (3) his or her right to confer with counsel prior to the decision to participate.

Consultations involving *Estelle* warnings should generally parallel evaluations of waiver of *Miranda* warnings (see Chapter 5). Forensic clinicians should document the defendant's appreciation of his or her right to participate (i.e., right to remain silent), the possible consequences of participating (i.e., attendant risks), and right to legal counsel prior to making this decision. The likely effects of Axis I disorders and cognitive deficits must be systematically evaluated. Chapter 5 includes a thorough review clinical methods used in assessing waivers of 5th and 6th Amendment rights. Please note the absence of any specialized measures that are adequately validated to assess either *Miranda* issues (e.g., the GMI) or the *Estelle* prongs.

Estelle warnings appear more specific than Miranda warnings in their articulation of the possible uses of the defendant's statements. Under *Estelle*, the forensic clinician should explain the uses and risks of participating in capital sentencing evaluations. As starkly described in *Estelle v. Smith* (1981), the purpose of the evaluation is explicitly to "gather evidence necessary to decide whether, if convicted, he should be sentenced to death" (p. 467). A potential risk is that the defendant volunteers or otherwise presents information, which is instrumental in his or her death sentence.

In some jurisdictions, forensic clinicians appear polarized on capital sentencing consultations. Some experts testify almost exclusively on matters of mitigation for the defense; other experts testify almost exclusively on matters of aggravation for the prosecution. Although no court has found potential expert bias or prejudice to be required to be included in a warning, the obvious question arises: How can the defendant make an *intelligent* waiver in a capital sentencing evaluation without knowing the expert's track record? Specifically, knowledge that an expert is "execution-prone" and testifies in favor of the death penalty in the great majority of cases might logically override other considerations in deciding whether to participate in a particular capital sentencing evaluation. Defense counsel should take an active role in ensuring that defendants are aware of an expert's track record prior to participating in any consultation that may include capital sentencing. In addition, they may also consider appealing a generic warning as insufficient or expressly misleading.

Hypothetical or contingent *Estelle* warnings are sometimes given in capital cases in which a forensic clinician was not specifically asked to conduct a capital sentencing evaluation. In such cases, the forensic clinician may inform the defendant:

> I have not been asked to evaluate any sentencing issues, including the death penalty. I just wanted to make you aware of that this possibility could arise in the future. My purpose today is to evaluate ___ (e.g., competency to stand trial), but you should be aware that sentencing issues could be raised in the future.

Does this warning, even if it includes the *Estelle* prongs, allow the defendant to weigh his or her options? The possibility of a dire outcome at sometime in the future may obscure what is potentially a life and death decision. *Given the gravity of the decision, very serious problems are raised by the use of hypothetical or contingent Estelle warnings.* Many defendants are unlikely to consider seriously this decision and its potential consequences, when presented simply as a "future possibility." Two other issues also affect the defendant's decisional abilities: (1) his or her clinical status (i.e., pretrial evaluations typically indicate the presence of an Axis I disorder), and (2) extreme stress (i.e., the pending capital trial).

Defense attorneys can seek to preclude hypothetical or contingent *Estelle* warnings at the time pretrial evaluations are court-ordered. One option is to request that the order be very specific about the issue to be considered (e.g., competency to stand trial) and that the forensic clinician be ordered not to address any extraneous issues. Depending on the jurisdiction, this option may be preferable to more a direct approach, such as attempting to exclude pretrial experts from testifying at the capital sentencing phase.

Forensic clinicians should ascertain whether defendants have an adequate understanding of these rights prior to proceeding with capital sentencing evaluations. Clinically, a simple affirmation (e.g., "I understand them.") is inadequate. The defendant should be able to explain in his or her own words the three separate prongs (choice, risks, and right to counsel) as required by *Estelle*. As an example, the waiver of counsel must be voluntary, knowing, and intelligent.[4]

Atkins Exclusion

In *Atkins* the Supreme Court prohibited the execution of persons with mental retardation. The seemingly uncomplicated task for forensic psychologists is to establish the defendant's intellectual functioning and determine whether it qualifies for mental retardation. We conceptualize this as a two-step process.

The assessment of intellectual functioning requires the individual administration of an intelligence test. Given the grave consequences of this evaluation, forensic clinicians should use the best-validated intelligence test, namely the Weschler Adult Intelligence Scale—Third Edition (WAIS-III; Weschler, 1997). The Stanford-Binet-IV (Thorndike, Hagen, & Sattler, 1986) should *not* be used given the limited normative data on adult populations. More recently, the Stanford-Binet-V (Roid, 2003) was published. As present, we do not recommend its use because a recent PsycInfo search (December 12, 2004) revealed no adult research. At noted in the Court's opinion, IQs of approximately 70 or lower are typically required for the diagnosis of mental retardation. Taking into account one standard error of measurement (SEM = 2.30), most forensic clinicians will consider defendants with IQ of 73 or less in their determinations of mental retardation. While ensuring considerable accuracy, an estimated 15.9% of persons with

---

[4]In Footnote 16 (p. 471), the Court stated in *Atkins*, "Waivers of the assistance of counsel, however, 'must not only be voluntary, but must also constitute a knowing and intelligent relinquishment or abandonment of a known right or privilege...'"

mental retardation will be missed. *DSM-IV* (APA, 2000, pp. 41–42) took into account the SEM and concluded, "Thus, it is possible to diagnose Mental Retardation in individuals with IQs between 70 and 75 who exhibit significant deficits in adaptive behavior."

Prosecutors are understandably concerned when capital defendants exhibit a downward trend in their IQ scores. A distinct possibility is that the defendant is feigning in order to avoid capital punishment. In one extreme case, a male defendant had "lost" almost all his cognitive capacities including the ability to write his name. Needless to say, the jury was unimpressed by his marked decline in intellectual abilities. In addressing downward trends, forensic clinicians must consider at least three explanations:

1. *Comparability of IQ measures.* IQ tests are not always comparable across measures. Group-administered (i.e., paper-and-pencil) IQ tests, common in school settings, may provide inflated estimates of intellectual functioning. Different versions of the same test (WAIS-III vs. WAIS-R) may yield small but significant differences.
2. *Severe Stress.* Intelligence testing is designed to assess the person's capacities under optimum conditions. As noted in the WAIS-III administration manual (Wechsler, 1997), the examinee's mood, activity level, and cooperation can negatively affect accurate testing (see p. 32). Anxiety or other affective states can diminish the examinee's performance on IQ tests. It is difficult to imagine a defendant whose life may depend on the results of intellectual assessment not being affected by apprehension, anxiety, and possibly despair. Less than standard administration conditions, as often found in jails, may also contribute to the stress and decreased IQ scores.
3. *Malingering.* The defendant may be feigning cognitive impairment in an effort to be diagnosed as mentally retarded. Malingering should not be inferred from a downward trend in IQ scores. Instead, well-validated detections strategies (see Chapter 2) must be used for the classification of malingering.

The diagnosis of mental retardation has two additional requirements beyond impaired intellectual functioning: age of onset and significant limitations adaptive functioning. The age of onset must be before the age of 18. After this age, any acquired condition might be diagnosed as a dementia or Cognitive Disorder, NOS.

The most challenging component of diagnosing mental retardation is establishing "impairments in adaptive functioning" (APA, 2000, p. 49). These impairments should be concurrent with the diagnosis and, therefore, evident prior to the age of 18. The Supreme Court in *Atkins* underscored this point regarding the diagnosis of mental retardation, "significant limitations in adaptive skills...that *became manifest before age 18*" (p. 318; emphasis added).

DSM-IV provided an extended list of "impairments in adaptive functioning" that address broad, difficult-to-define, domains of human activities. This list of impairments is extensive in its length and scope. To warrant the diagnosis of mental retardation, concurrent deficits or impairments must be observed in at least two areas: (1) communication, (2) self-care, (3) home living, (4) social and interpersonal skills, (5) use of community resources, (6) self-direction, (7) functional academic skills, (8) work, (9) leisure, (10) health, and (11) safety.

Two measures are frequently used to assess adaptive functioning: the Vineland Adaptive Behavior Scales (VABS; Sparrow, Balla, Chicchetti, & Harrison, 1985) and the AAMR Adaptive Behavior Scale—Residential and Community, Second Edition (ABS-RC:2; Nihara, Leland, & Lambert, 1993). We offer key summaries.

VABS. The VABS assesses the capacity to perform daily activities in four domains: Communication, Daily Living Skills, Socialization, and Motor Skills. It is intended to measure social competence from childhood through the age of 19. Interrater reliability estimates vary from marginal to moderate for the individual domains (i.e., .62–.75; Sattler, 1989). The major limitations of the VAB are threefold:

1. Limits in interrater reliabilities coupled with large standard errors of measurement (3.2 to 8.2 for the four domains) restricts the confidence that can be placed in the accuracy of the VAB scores.
2. The VAB coverage addresses only 3 of the 11 areas required by *DSM-IV*.
3. The VAB is intended for *current* use with youth and adolescents. It should not be applied retrospectively to adults.

ABS-RC:2. The ABS-RC:2 was developed to assess areas of adaptive functioning as delineated by the American Association of Mental Retardation for children through young adults up to 21 years of age. Part I addresses 10 domains: Independent Functioning, Physical Development, Economic Activity, Language Development, Numbers and Time, Domestic Activity, Prevocational–Vocational Activity, Self-Direction, Responsibility, and Socialization. Part II addresses additional domains: Social Behavior, Conformity, Trustworthiness, Stereotyped, and Hyperactive Behavior, Sexual Behavior, Self-Abusive Behavior, and Social Engagement. Many items address very simple abilities (e.g., toilet use). Carey's (1998) review indicated good internal reliabilities for Parts I and II, although efforts to establish the stability of domains may be inflated by using the same rater for both periods. Although covering more domains, its limitations parallel the VAB:

1. Interrater reliabilities based on extensive daily contact. Its usefulness with consulting professionals, who have limited contact or only collateral sources of information, is not known.
2. The ABS-RC:2 has normative data that is focused on persons with mental retardation, many of whom had other disabilities. The meaning of its scores cannot be interpreted with reference to deficits from normal intelligence or adaptive functioning (Harrison, 1998).
3. The ABS-RC:2 does not address all the *DSM-IV* domains and leaves some (e.g., three items) insufficiently sampled.
4. The ABS-RC:2 is not intended for retrospective evaluations of adaptive functioning in adults.

In summary, the Supreme Court in *Atkins*, while leaving the state courts to define mental retardation, cited with approval the definitions put forth by the AAMR and American Psychiatric Association. In states where these definitions are followed, the age requirement for mental retardation must be considered: "significant limitations in adaptive skills ... that *became manifest before age 18*" (APA, 2000, p. 318; emphasis added). In light of their decision, the ABS-RC:2 appears to be relevant for the current assessment of adolescents and adults up to the age of 21. However, opinions should be expressed that take into account the interrater reliabilities and standard errors of measurement based on interrater reliabilities. Even then, forensic clinicians must undertake their own evaluation of the domains outlined in *DSM-IV* to ensure comprehensive coverage.

AGGRAVATING FACTORS

Eisenberg (2004) reviewed statutorily defined aggravating factors that are common in the United States. The majority of these factors address the specific circumstances of the homicide, such as (1) the killing of a person functioning in an official capacity (e.g., judicial officer, police officer, fire fighter, or correctional officer), (2) the purpose of the homicide (murder for hire or murder to escape), or other circumstances (felony murders or multiple murders). These aggravating factors involve evidence presented at trial. Issues of a psychological nature are rarely raised with respect to these clearly defined aggravating factors (Melton et al., 1997). A possible exception is whether the defendant *knowingly* killed a police officer, especially when that defendant was in a state of severe intoxication.

Depravity

Aggravating factors may also include relatively subjective judgments, such as the defendant's depravity in committing a heinous murder. Forensic clinicians lack expertise to address issues of depravity, which is not a mental health concept. Welner (2001) is attempting to develop a Depravity Scale, asking for input from a wide range of professionals in law, sciences, and education. As a survey, professionals were asked to categorize the depravity of specific behaviors. One fundamental problem is that the guiding examples vary dramatically in their content and severity for the same item (e.g., secluding a claustrophobic person to defiling a corpse). We submit that forensic clinicians have no specialized knowledge of such constructs as depravity and evil. At best, such survey data assess personal opinions unbuttressed by empirical data.

Continuing Violence: Predictors

Forensic clinicians in approximately eight states may be asked to address dangerousness and future violence as an aggravating factor in capital sentencing (Melton et al., 1997). As noted in the Legal Overview, future violence is the centerpiece of aggravation in Texas and Oregon whereby the determination is made whether the defendant constitutes a continuing threat to society.

Mental health and legal professionals often suffer from misconceptions regarding the rate of future violence among capital murderers. Although the level of violence is very low on death row, it could be argued that violence is minimized by (1) the threat of death and (2) special security precautions. These issues can be addressed by examining studies of capital murderers released from death row. Cunningham and Reidy (2002) presented seven studies composed of 931 former death row inmates. In calculating the rate of violence, the annual percentage is 1.67% for these capital offenders released from death row. This percentage is very low. However, forensic clinicians may be concerned whether the cumulative percentage might continue to increase over the decades. Four studies report cumulative percentages for periods of 10 years or more. For an average of 15.07 years, the cumulative percentage is 22.58%. Simply put, less than one in four former death row inmates committed any known assaultive behavior during a 15-year follow-up.

Overall risk of assaultive behavior requires further refinement. Cunningham and Reid (1999) analyzed data on federal inmate violence. They found that serious injuries (e.g., resulting in stitches, broken bones, concussion, or hospitalization) occurred in roughly 20% of the assaults.

Extrapolating to former death row inmates, the cumulative percentage of serious assaults from death row inmates plummets to 4.52%. This extrapolation may be justly criticized, given the differences between the incarcerated samples. Even if we assume the rate of serious violence for former death row inmates is 100% greater than federal inmates (i.e., 40% rather than 20%), the cumulative rate of violence over a 15-year period is still estimated at less than 10% (i.e., 22.58% × .40 = 9.03%).

These data are important in disputing the intuitively appealing idea of once violent, always violent. Base rates, by themselves, provide strong evidence that serious violence represents a low risk. Many forensic clinicians rely on some combination of diagnostic and risk-assessment data in making their determinations of "continuing threat" of criminal violence. We provide brief commentaries of the usefulness of these indicators.

Antisocial Personality Disorder (APD). Although approximately 75% of inmates warrant the diagnosis of APD (Cunningham & Reidy, 1999), relatively few have committed homicide or life-threatening violence. Therefore, APD is not an effective discriminator between violent and nonviolent offenders.

PCL-R Classified Psychopathy. Use of the PCL-R classification of psychopathy has raised several important concerns. Edens, Petrila, and Buffington-Vollum (2001) examined the usefulness of psychopathy in predicting physical violence within correctional settings. Predictive studies produced disappointing results for adult inmates. As noted by these investigators, correlations with physical violence were generally *below* .30, accounting for substantially less than 10% of the variance. An additional problem is the prejudicial description of psychopathy. According to Cunningham and Reid (2001, p. 479) descriptions of psychopathy are "so profoundly pejorative as to equate with a sentence of death."

Connell (2003) noted the recent case of *U.S. v. Willis Haynes* (PJM-98-0520) that produced affidavits from several highly recognized experts on risk assessment, which argued against the use of the PCL-R and HCR-20 in capital sentencing. It is especially noteworthy that Stephen Hart, a coauthor of the PCL-SV, provided one of these affidavits.[5] After the government expert withdrew, these affidavits were not needed as evidence.

---

[5]Hart (2000, p. 4, paragraph 18) concluded, "It is my opinion, which I hold with a reasonable degree of scientific certainty, that there is no direct scientific evidence that the PCL-R and HCR-20 are predictive of institutional violence in correctional offenders in the United States; and that the PCL-R and HCR-20 are not generally accepted within the scientific community of clinical-forensic psychologists for the purpose of predicting institutional violence in correctional offenders."

However, copies of the affidavits are available from the defense counsel, Lisa Greenman at lgreenman@starpower.net.

MMPI-2 Psychopathic Deviance (Pd) Scale. Despite its name, the Pd scale does not measure psychopathy but rather chronic delinquency. Its ability to predict prison infractions is disappointing (see Cunningham & Reidy, 1999).

MCMI-III Antisocial (6A) and Aggressive (6B) Scales. These scales do not provide adequate diagnostic data about either APD or sadistic personality. On the basis of Millon (1994), the sensitivity rates are 4.8% and 0.0%, respectively; the positive predictive power is less than 20%. In an attempt to improve these unacceptably low numbers, Millon, Davis, and Millon (1997) conducted more recent but smaller study. Unfortunately, this research was fatally flawed by criterion contamination (see Rogers, Salekin, & Sewell, 2000).

Continued Violence: Pattern Analysis

The Supreme Court in *Barefoot* upheld the constitutionality of admitting mental health experts' opinions about dangerousness in capital proceedings. The majority concluded that it is not "generally so unreliable that it should be ignored" (p. 898). Forensic psychologists and psychiatrists who are nevertheless inclined to offer an opinion about dangerousness in capital sentencing may see themselves in a professional limbo based on a lack of specialized knowledge regarding this type of violence prediction.

One option is an individualized behavior pattern analysis. For defendants with extensive histories and serious violence, it is possible to examine the patterns of violence. In a few instances, the defendant engages in repetitive violence irrespective of situational characteristics or the setting. The clearest case for "continuing threat" is a defendant who demonstrates physical violence while incarcerated, even when placed in maximum security (see Cunningham & Reidy, 2002). The key consideration is whether the defendant has *ever* achieved any significant period of nonviolence during his or her incarcerations. This type of behavior pattern analysis is stringent; very few violent offenders have the both chronicity and severity of physical aggression that continues unabated during their incarceration. Even in these cases, question remains whether this violence would be maintained if the defendant were housed in a super-maximum facility.

MITIGATING FACTORS

Consultations on mitigation of capital sentencing are far more complex than its aggravation counterpart. While mitigation can address the *absence* of continuing violence risk, forensic clinicians are confronted with a host of statutorily defined and individualized mitigating factors. They face formidable challenges in defining the parameters of relevant factors for a particular case and implementing a systematic assessment of these issues. Conceptually, statutorily defined mitigation is clearly delineated by criminal law and may have greater weight than individualized factors on sentencing decisions. In contrast, individualized mitigating factors encompass any relevant information about the defendant's background or the offense that may lessen the sentence.

Statutorily Defined Mitigating Factors

As reviewed in the Legal Overview, several themes emerge from statutorily defined mitigating factors including (1) diminished culpability or blameworthiness, (2) extenuating circumstances, and (3) crime-related issues. These themes will be examined separately with a brief review of relevant clinical methods.

The clearest examples of diminished culpability relate to the defendant's cognitive and volitional abilities. Chapters 7 and 8 describe in detail how these capacities can be conceptualized on a continuum for trial issues of insanity and intent. The same methodology may be applied cognitive and volitional abilities at the capital sentencing phase. For example, the R-CRAS (Rogers, 1984) may provide relevant information regarding these abilities at the time of the offense. Diagnostic data is also germane when it demonstrates substantial impairment in the defendant's thinking, emotions, and behavioral regulation. Unlike insanity determinations, intoxication may play a role in reducing cognitive and volitional abilities. For the capital sentencing, these abilities are best conceptualized on a continuum with any significant impairment being introduced as evidence.

The concept of "extreme mental disturbance" emphasizes the severity of the symptoms, syndrome or disorder. It is a general term applying to the defendant's psychological impairment at the time of the offense. One conceptualization of extreme mental disturbance would be as a "partial product rule." Under the now defunct *Durham* (1954) standard of insanity, a defendant was not responsible for his or her criminal behavior if it were a "product" of a mental disorder. As applied to capital sentencing, extreme mental disturbance could be conceptualized as follows:

1. *Product rule*: The crime would not have occurred except for the extreme mental disturbance.
2. *Partial-product rule*: The extreme mental disturbance significantly contributed to the commission of the crime.

The main advantage of this conceptualization is that juries can easily grasp the link between the psychological impairment and the criminal behavior. In addition, forensic clinicians have a clear conceptual basis for their testimony. They can examine the defendant's motivations (see Chapter 8) and determine to what extent, if any, the mental disorder contributed to the commission of the offense.

Forensic clinicians may go beyond the *product rule* and *partial-product rule* to examine the severity of the impairment per se. The SADS provides a systematic method for evaluating symptom severity at the time of the offense (see Chapter 7). In addition, forensic clinicians may rely on the *DSM-IV* Global Assessment Functioning (American Psychiatric Association, 2000) to provide a general estimate of overall impairment.

Extenuating circumstances may also reduce the defendant's blameworthiness. The defendant may have played a subsidiary role in the capital offense or may have been under the influence of a co-defendant. Diagnostically, personality disorders may assist in understanding deficits in interpersonal functioning. In particular, an examination of dependent personality disorder or prominent features may be useful in evaluating a passive or secondary role. Among Axis II interviews, the SIDP-IV should be strongly considered because of its low face validity (i.e., more challenging to manipulate) and validation with comorbid Axis I disorders.

Crime-related issues category is a catch-all category for statutorily defined mitigation involving defendant's cooperation and future risk. Issues may include the defendant's background (age and lack of criminal history) and low risk for future violence. Of these, forensic clinicians may be called to address the lack of violence. Risk assessment methods and their concomitant limitations were reviewed in earlier sections of this chapter.

Individualized Mitigating Factors

Supreme Court decisions require that the trial courts permit individualized mitigation for each defendant faced with capital sentencing. The cases of *Lockett* and *Eddings* directed the courts to allow all avenues of mitigation to be considered (Cunningham & Goldstein, 2003). Mitigation can also include the defendant's postarrest adjustment to jail (*Skipper v. South Carolina*, 1986). The defendant's ability to function without violence during extended periods of incarceration is relevant to determining the risks of future violence.

Connell (2003) advocated a psychobiographical approach to mitigation assessment. She recommended a chronological history beginning at birth that addresses "childhood, family composition, early schooling, family socioeconomic status, and family relationships" (pp. 330–331). Beyond the defendant, she advocated collateral interviews with childhood neighbors and teachers supplemented by more contemporaneous interviews. Other sources of data are an exhaustive review of records and standardized assessment data.

Cunningham and Reidy (2001) outlined many issues that could be considered in individualized mitigation evaluations. The more salient issues include

- intellectual limitations and learning disorders,
- mental disorders,
- brain injuries and neurological deficits,
- childhood maltreatment and abuse,
- childhood traumas,
- impaired or unstable family relationships, and
- negative community influences (e.g., violence and poverty).

Juries may be reluctant to consider social and environmental factors by themselves. The implicit logic is that many persons "rise above" their impoverished and traumatic backgrounds. Based on the stress-diathesis model, one alternative is to relate the defendant's social and environmental factors to his or her vulnerabilities. A common theme is the *cumulative effects* of cognitive, psychological, familial, and environmental factors. Through voire dire, defense counsel should know something of the jurors' backgrounds. It is imperative that jurors can relate to the trauma and privations and understand their effects on an already impaired defendant.

Cornell (2003) suggested that nearly all social and environmental data could be used for individualized mitigation. On one hand, the defendant's *failings* could be used to explain his or her current problems based on genetic influences and life circumstances. On the other, the defendant's *successes* could be used to rehabilitate his or her image as basically a good person who committed a bad act. We wonder how persuasive jurors would find this two-prong approach.

This exhaustive approach to mitigation often requires 60–100 hours of professional time (Cunningham & Reidy, 2001). Obtaining the necessary funds for this approach may be challenging in many jurisdictions. An alternative would be the identification of several major themes that are likely to have the greatest impact on the jury. As discussed in the next section, a potential danger of the exhaustive approach is the unintended consequences that jurors adopt the "damaged goods" argument. In deciding between the selective (i.e., three to four major themes) versus exhaustive approaches, defense attorneys must weigh how much of "horror and pain" the jury can tolerate and still have some empathy for the defendant. A potential danger of the exhaustive approach is that the jury will lose its sympathetic understanding and see the defendant in nonhuman terms. If the defendant is somehow perceived as a monstrosity, then the efforts at mitigation have backfired.

GENERAL CROSS-EXAMINATION ISSUES IN NON-CAPITAL SENTENCING

The very flexibility of noncapital sentencing militates against empirically based standardization of relevant issues. The two key issues for cross-examination for noncapital sentencing are treatment effectiveness and risk assessment.

TREATMENT EFFECTIVENESS

Chapter 4 provides a conceptual framework (see Table 4-1) and sample questions for direct (see Box 9-1) for examining treatment amenability of mentally disordered offenders. These matters can be easily applied to direct and cross-examination of treatment recommendations at the sentencing phase. Attorneys should realize that forensic clinicians are likely to be strongly divided on the usefulness of treatment interventions with sex offenders and psychopaths. Trial strategy and cross-examination must take this polarization into account. Therefore, these issues are examined separately.

BOX 9-1   TRAINING AND EXPERTISE WITH SEX OFFENDERS: ILLUSTRATIVE CROSS-EXAMINATION

Training

1. *Please describe for the court your* _formal_ *training in the evaluation of sex offenders? . . . How has* _your_ *ability to assess sex offenders been formally evaluated?*

2. *How many years have you devoted specifically to the treatment of sex offenders? . . .* [if any] *How many hours per week did you spend in direct delivery of sex offender treatment?*

3. *How many* _supervised_ *sentencing evaluations of sex offenders have you performed for the* _courts_? [Many forensic clinicians have had very little supervision] . . . [if any] *What were the names of your supervisors? . . . Lets consider* __ [first supervisor], *what was [his/her] training? . . . What years*

(Continued)

were the supervision? . . . How many cases were formally supervised? [Continue with other supervisors; the goal is a relaxed but very thorough review.]

4. [The goal is to look for uncertainties or outright retractions] *You appear* [choose: confused/uncertain/uncomfortable], *doctor; isn't it true that you overstated your credentials?*

Combating Undue Treatment Optimism

5. *Doctor, tell us what will likely happen if you are <u>wrong</u> in your professional opinion? . . .* [if unclear] *Well based on the current offense[s], what is likely to happen to the next victim?*

6. *Given that the majority of rape victims do not report, this perpetrator could sexual assault several more* [select: men/women/children], *without even an investigation, isn't that true?*

7. *By the way, doctor, did [he/she] tell you about all [his/her] <u>past</u> sexual victims? . . .* [no way of really knowing] *Based on national statistics, isn't it <u>probable</u> there were at least a few more rape victims in the past? . . . Maybe even a dozen more?*

8. [if community treatment] *How well does treatment work if the defendant just walks away from this facility?*

9. *How well does treatment work if the defendant just gives lipservice to your therapy but does really change?*

Combating Undue Treatment Pessimism

10. *Doctor, tell us about your own treatment successes with sex offenders? . . .* [if none] *How is your own lack of effectiveness coloring your opinions today?*

11. [if inexperienced] *How is your own lack of experience coloring your opinions today?*

12. *Doctor, are you even knowledgeable of behavioral and cognitive-behavioral methods for treating sex offenders? . . . What is covert sensitization? . . . Are <u>you</u> effective at applying this treatment method? . . . What is aversive behavioral rehearsal? . . . Are <u>you</u> effective at applying this treatment method? . . . What is masturbatory satiation? . . . Are <u>you</u> effective at applying this treatment method?*

13. *What medications are used to control or suppress deviant sexual urges?*

14. *Isn't it true that complete androgen suppression can be achieved? . . . What typically occurs to sex urges and behaviors when androgen is completely suppressed?*

Sex Offenders

Attorneys for both prosecution and defense should choose forensic clinicians with expertise in the assessment and treatment of sex offenders. Given the specialized assessment methods, most forensic clinicians will lack the knowledge and training to perform comprehensive assessments of paraphilias and other sexual deviations. Especially challenging is the assessment of denial and defensiveness, which are common to many sex offenders. For treatment purposes, laboratory procedures, such as penile plethysmography, may be warranted. Given the array of treatment methods, most forensic clinicians lack the specialized training and experience to understand which interventions are likely to be helpful with a particular offender. In this regard, the typology by Bradford and Harris (2003) is a useful beginning; a combination of pharmacological and psychological interventions is likely necessary at the severe and catastrophic levels. Psychological interventions alone may be sufficient at the mild level (i.e., "hands-off" paraphilias).

Cross-examination of forensic clinicians will often focus on their inexpertise and their lack of treatment success with sex offenders. Without in-depth knowledge and direct experience, forensic clinicians are susceptible to naive conclusions favoring either the prosecution or the defense. Box 9-1 provides illustrative cross-examination that stresses the lack of training and experience in the assessment and treatment of paraphilias. In case any expert attempts to exaggerate his or her professional experiences, it may be helpful to focus specifically on the number of supervised cases that were conducted for the court. By requesting the names of forensic supervisors, experts will become immediately aware that their estimates may be subjected to future verification.

The effectiveness of treatment for sex offenders may be a polarizing issue among forensic clinicians. As previously summarized, studies of sex offenders have produced mixed results. Not surprisingly, poor results are found when sex offenders are indiscriminantly placed in generic programs (see Hanson et al., 2000). When carefully selected, tailored interventions can be successful although some recidivism is still expected. Box 9-1 provides sample cross-examination for experts expressing either undue optimism or pessimism. Regarding the former, questions underscore the uncertainties about recidivism and the likelihood that the offense history may be more extensive than known. The inference is clear: a more extensive history of sexual offenses may predict a greater likelihood of sexual recidivism. For undue pessimism, the thrust of cross-examination is the expert's own limited clinical abilities in the treatment of sex offenders. The argument is simply that effective clinicians with sex offenders will evince less biased testimony.

Psychopaths

Forensic clinicians are often strongly biased against the treatment of psychopaths, on the basis of early research. In offering expert testimony, their *ad hominem* bias may cause them to disregard both positive and mixed treatment results. As with most disorders and syndromes, the most severe cases are typically the most problematic to treat. In testifying on treatment amenability, forensic clinicians sometimes do not distinguish (1) the rare but extreme cases from (2) the typical cases involving marginal levels of psychopathy.

In the cross-examination of forensic clinicians, attorneys should be aware of these biases against the treatment of psychopaths. A major concern is whether cross-examination will simply provide the forensic clinician with additional opportunities to reiterate his or her negative biases at they relate to a particular defendant. Such biases are likely to be believed because they are consistent with the jurors' attribution biases. One alternative is to limit cross-examination. Questions might be focused on whether forensic clinicians might candidly disagree on this issue and that the available outcome data has only limited relevance to this particular defendant.

Substance Abuse

Forensic clinicians are also divided on the best course of action with chronic substance abusers. Their attitudes toward substance abuse may influence their expert opinions much more than specifics about an individual offender. Pallone and Hennessy (2003) the remarkable divergences among professionals on whether to treat or punish substance abusers. Clinicians range from therapeutic nihilism and just deserts ("get tough") to treatment efforts devoted to mental health care and drug rehabilitation. Cross-examination can seek to disclose how strongly held views, if not outright biases, may limit the objectivity of expert testimony.

RISK ASSESSMENT

A formidable challenge for cross-examination is exposing the marked limitations of risk assessment in predicting recidivism for sex offenders. As summarized by Craig et al. (2003), sex risk measures with psychological variables have minuscule correlations (e.g., VRAG and SORAG) with sexual recidivism. These scales typically account for less than 5% of the shared variance. As a rough analogy for the judge or jury, this amount of variance is akin to listening to 5% music and 95% static.

For those knowledgeable in psychometrics, consider an example involving a validity coefficient of .20 (i.e., 4% of the variance). Its standard error of estimate is .98, which means that 98% of the observed variation in scores is likely to be simply due to chance (Anastasi, 1988).

Attorneys and their rebuttal experts must make clear that the risk-assessment industry promises far more than it delivers. As previously described in the *Risk Assessment* section, most risk assessment measures have substantial limitations that should be underscored on cross-examination or addressed by rebuttal testimony. In this section, we focus a critical "oversight," whether accidental or intentional: the confusion of sensitivity with positive predictive power. As noted below, each addresses a very different issue:

- *Sensitivity*: What proportion of recidivating sex offenders exceed the cut score?
- *Positive predictive power*: What is the likelihood that this particular sex offender will recidivate?

Jurors can easily be confused by forensic clinicians who may not be anxious to clarify the critical differences. Box 9-2 provides illustrative cross-examination for distinguishing sensitivity from positive predictive power. By using the simplest example (i.e., ability to see or "sighted"), jurors can easily see that *sensitivity does not answer the crucial question*. Specifically what is the likelihood (or percentage of the time) that a specific offender will recidivate? This crucial estimate requires positive predictive power, which is expediently omitted from most risk measures. The fact finder must understand that sensitivity does not measure the accuracy of the risk assessment measure when applied to an individual offender.

The overriding goal of cross-examining attorneys is to silence substandard testimony based on substandard measures. Risk assessment is rife with poorly validated measures that do not satisfy even the most basic requirements of test development. The goals of justice are stymied by sciolism masquerading as science.

TRIAL STRATEGIES AND CROSS-EXAMINATION ISSUES IN CAPITAL SENTENCING

Research on capital sentencing provides valuable insights into the misunderstandings and misconceptions of jurors. The first subsection addresses these misconceptions from the prosecutorial and defense perspectives. The second subsection provides an analysis of official position statements on the death penalty by the American Psychiatric Association and Society for the Psychological Study of Social Issues. The third subsection examines two models of capital sentencing and provides illustrative cross-examination.

Box 9-2   CLARIFYING THE DIFFERENCES BETWEEN SENSITIVITY
AND POSITIVE PREDICTIVE POWER (PPP) IN RISK ASSESSMENTS

1. *In the clearest terms possible could you tell the jury the difference between sensitivity and positive predictive power?*
2. *Isn't it true that a measure can have 100% sensitivity and extremely poor positive predictive power?*
3. *Can you help me educate the jury? ... Using a simple example; let's say my criterion is "ability to see" and my classification is "serious offenders." Wouldn't almost every serious offender have the "ability to see?" ... So my sensitivity rate would be almost 100% wouldn't it?*

   Write on the display–
   Left side: "Sensitivity: What percentage of serious criminals are sighted?" Right side: "Answer = about 99%"

4. *Isn't it also true, that serious criminals form a tiny-tiny percentage of all the persons who are "able to see?" ... So the positive predictive power is close to 0% isn't it?*

   Write on the display–
   Left side: Positive Predictive Power: What percentage of sighted persons are serious criminals?
   Right side: About 1%

5. *Going back to your testimony about __* [a specific risk-assessment measure], *you were only talking about sensitivity weren't you?*
6. *When you skipped over positive predictive power, is that you simply didn't know or you were trying to duck the bad news? ...* [likely to equivocate] *Really doctor, it is a simple question that deserves a straight answer: Didn't know or were you ducking bad news?*
7. [didn't know] *So __* [a specific risk-assessment measure] *could be like my "ability to see" test, good sensitivity and lousy positive predictive power? ...* [likely to disagree] *Please doctor, you already admitted you didn't really know, isn't that correct? ... Your honor, please instruct the witness to testify on accepted knowledge not unsubstantiated guesses.*
8. [ducking bad news] *Would it be accurate to describe you as a "hired gun?"* [continue with questions about being a biased expert]

APPLICATION OF PSYCHOLOGICAL KNOWLEDGE
TO COURTROOM STRATEGY

Attorneys may wish to consult with psychologists with expertise in capital cases as part of the voire dire process and formulation of trial strategy. These experts have specialized knowledge of social and normative influences on the trial process. They typically lack clinical expertise and cannot be used to evaluate mental health issues. This brief section simply highlights the potential use of such experts in implementing courtroom strategies.

Prosecutorial Perspective

Psychological data suggest that jurors may be influenced by aspects of the case that may evoke outrage and fear. For example, Butler and Moran (2002) found that prospective death-qualified jurors rated highly as aggravating circumstances: (1) cold, calculated, and premeditated crime and (2) heinous, atrocious, or cruel crime. These themes can be developed during the trial, including the use of expert testimony. Also rated highly were aspects of the crime (e.g., felony murder), the offender (e.g., a gang member), and especially a vulnerable victim (e.g., elderly or disabled). Beyond anger and outrage, prosecutors may also wish to consider emphasizing fear. Steiner, Bowers, and Sarat (1999) found that the possibility of murderers securing an early release was related to the death penalty. In an 11-state survey of 916 jurors from capital cases, 19.5% believed that murderers not receiving the death penalty would be released in *less than 10 years*. The theme that murderers might be free to kill again could also be underscored by the prosecution.

Fear and community safety provide strong motivation for jurors to vote for the death penalty. Even in states that provide the option of life without the possibility of parole, a lingering fear may persist that somehow this murderer could be eventually released. This lingering apprehension may increase jurors' perceptions of dangerousness and influence their decision-making for capital sentencing (O'Neil, Patry, & Penrod, 2004).

Defense Perspective

The defense appears to face significantly more challenges than the prosecution at the capital sentencing phase. Frank and Applegate (1998) found that many prospective jurors did not understand critical elements of sentencing instructions. The most egregious misunderstandings are outlined:

1. *Burden of proof.* 93.4% did not believe that the prosecution bore the burden of proof.
2. *Mitigating factors.* 69.0% did not understand that mitigating factors were possible reasons for not sentencing the defendant to death. Equally concerning, the same percentage of jurors (69.0%) believed that they could only use mitigating factors that were specifically mentioned in the judge's sentencing instructions. In contrast, comparatively few jurors (16.7%) misunderstood aggravating factors.
3. *Decision-making.* 43.4% believed that they should always vote for the death penalty if the aggravating factors outnumbered mitigating factors.

These misunderstandings may be highly consequential, affecting the jury decision-making at the recommended sentencing. This lack of understanding may lead jurors in capital sentencing to vote for death (Wiener et al., 2004).

The Steiner et al. (1999) study found that many capital jurors seriously underestimated the duration of imprisonment for murderers, including their mandatory minimums. Defense attorneys cannot directly disabuse jurors of this misinformation. They may wish to consider indirect approaches to providing the jury with information (e.g., expert testimony about the likelihood of released defendants' in their 50s committing further violent crimes). In addition, defense counsel may wish use voire dire to identify jurors less likely to underestimate the length of incarceration. Jurors that are more active in their community and trust the criminal justice system appear less likely murderers are released in less than 10 years. Questions about the overuse or underuse of the death penalty may also be helpful. As a related concern for defense counsel, prospective jurors with favorable attitudes toward the death penalty tend to be conviction-prone (Allen, Mabry, & MeKelton, 1998).

The Butler and Moran (2002) study found few mitigating factors that were rated strongly. Among those delineated under Florida statute, the defendant's capacity to conform, and his or her role as an accomplice were the best mitigations. Background variables such as being a teenager and lacking a criminal history had minor effects. The following types of non-statutory mitigation appeared ineffective: physical abuse as a child, service in the military, and substance abuse (alcohol or illegal drugs). Defense counsel are faced with formidable challenges in presenting credible mitigations that sufficiently offset the aggravating factors that have typically been proven at trial.

PROFESSIONAL INVOLVEMENT IN CAPITAL SENTENCING

Forensic psychiatrists are vulnerable to vigorous cross-examination for their participation in death penalty cases. In 2000, the American Psychiatric Association issued an official statement that advocated a moratorium on capital punishment. As documented by Fava (2001, p. 168), this official statement included the following:

> ...Whereas psychiatrists, due to their involvement and familiarity with the criminal justice system, have become increasingly aware of the weaknesses and deficiencies in the capital sentencing process including consideration in regard to the mentally ill and developmentally disabled, the American Psychiatric Association endorses the moratorium on capital punishment in the United States until jurisdiction seeking to reform the death penalty implement polices and procedures to assure that capital punishment, if used at all, is administered fairly and impartially in accord with the basic requirements of due process.

This official statement may be more effective in cross-examining forensic psychiatrists testifying for the prosecution than for the defense. Their testimony supporting the capital punishment of a particular defendant would appear to run directly contrary of the American Psychiatric Association's position. They could be assailed for using biased methods and going against their own national organization.

Forensic psychologists can also be attacked for their involvement in capital sentencing. The Society for the Psychological Study of Social Issues (SPSSI; Ellsworth, Haney, & Constanzo, 2001) issued an official position statement on the death penalty. While forensic psychologists are not likely to be members of the SPSSI, they can be questioned about the professional ethics of their participation using the conclusions in the SPSSI position statement to question their objectivity and credibility. Under Ethical Principle A, Beneficence and Nonmaleficence, psychologists must "seek to safeguard the welfare and rights of those with whom they interact professionally and other affected persons" (p. 1062). After downloading the SPSSI position statement (http://www.spssi.org/positionstatements.html), forensic psychologists can be questioned about their involvement in an inaccurate process (2nd point) that has racial biases (3rd point). Attorneys will immediately recognize that such questioning also serves to educate the jurors about frailties and potential biases in *their own decisional process.*

Forensic experts testifying for the prosecution must also be sensitized to the possibility of racial biases. While research suggests complex interactions including the socioeconomic status and demeanor of the defendant, race does appear to play a role in the outcome of capital cases (Free, 2002). Vigorous cross-examination may address the potential biases in the forensic evaluation and the subsequent testimony. When faced with repeated denials, the defense attorney may wish to pose the question: *How do you explain the racial disparities with many more African Americans condemned to death?* Whether answered or objected to, the goal is to plant this issue of racial bias in the jury's mind.

Legal Models and Cross-Examination

Prosecutorial Perspective

Prosecutors have three natural advantages at the capital sentencing phase. First, they have already proven to the jury beyond a reasonable doubt that the defendant committed the capital offense. As a corollary, they typically have proven that defendant and possibly his or her attorneys are untrustworthy in their noncredible version of the crime. Second, many aggravating factors are straightforward and easy to prove. Third, the defense attorneys carry the onerous burden of proving their efforts are not transparently self-serving (e.g., "say anything" to keep the defendant alive), thereby further eroding credibility.

One option for prosecutors is to emphasize the "damaged goods" argument. Within this framework, they are not likely to contest defense testimony about genetic and neuropsychological deficits. Instead, they argue that defendant was damaged at birth (genetics) or soon after (psychological trauma or brain injury). They assert that the defendant remains damaged and practically unfixable. They also observe that his or her behavior continues to deteriorate (e.g., from multiple assault to murder). They may wonder aloud that if this downward spiral were allowed to continue what would be the next steps: single murders, multiple murders or mass murders? Illustrative cross-examination questions are presented in Box 9-3.

An alternative in jurisdictions that do not offer "life without the possibility of parole" as a sentencing option is to capitalize on fear. As noted by Steiner et al. (1999), jurors substantially underestimate the amount of time that defendants receive. The combination of fear and prospective guilt

---

Box 9-3   ILLUSTRATIVE CROSS-EXAMINATION OF DEFENSE EXPERTS
AT CAPITAL SENTENCING

A. Damaged Goods
1. *Based on your testimony, isn't it true that __ [the defendant] was damaged during early childhood, possibly even at birth?*
2. *And this damage has continued for the last* [select: 10 years/15 years/__ years]*of [his/her] life hasn't it? . . . If anything, it seems to have gotten worse?*
3. *Isn't it true that prison often makes things worse for vulnerable defendants?*
4. *So we have a damaged* [select: man/woman]*who is likely to be more damaged, correct? . . . Let's be honest, nothing is going to fix [him/her] in prison?*
5. *Given that [he/she] is damaged and won't be fixed, what is the only way you can guarantee [his/her] loved ones that it won't happen again?*

B. Fear
6. *Are you afraid of __ [the defendant]? . . . [if hesitates or equivocates] You don't seem entirely comfortable answering that question. Tell us about your reservations.*
7. [if denies fear] *Knowing what you know today, would you be afraid if [he/she] moved into your neighborhood? . . . [if denies fear] Let's assume for a moment, you're just a working-class person, no fear at all having him next door?*
8. [optional; still denies fear] *You're safe, doctor; [he/she] is not coming out soon. Did you see him alone in his cell?* [if explains why it can't happen] *Don't worry, doctor; I wouldn't want to do that either.*

can be summarized in a simple question: "When he or she is eventually released, do you want the victims' blood on your hands?" One option is to address the expert's own qualms about a defendant that has committed particularly vicious offenses. Box 9-3 presents a few illustrative questions to underscore the likely apprehension felt by many jurors. Experts may have trouble responding to direct questions about their fears and apprehensions: Admitting to fear furthers the prosecution's case. Flat denials of fear may weaken the expert's credibility. Ambivalent responses emphasize the uncertainty experienced by most jurors.

Defense Perspective

True to their ethical canons, defense counsel are highly invested in keeping their clients alive. We have not data whether a *zealous* defense of a death penalty case can sometimes appear to jurors as a *desperate* defense. In light of the prosecution's strategy that often entails painting the defendant in highly negative terms, the defense must also use emotions as an attempt to persuade jurors to mitigate the sentence. One option is the expression of heart-felt feelings that acknowledge the different tragedies: (1) the current tragedies including the victims and their families and (2) the past tragedies in the defendant's upbringing and past trauma. The point is to reduce the anger felt toward the defendant and partly replace it with sadness. We must underscore that this approach has not been empirically tested.

Cross-examination must often grapple with two formidable issues that are often presented by prosecution experts: *dangerousness* and *special categorization* (e.g., psychopath). A third issue resides implicitly with the jurors, namely *attribution bias*. Attribution bias occurs in everyday situations when persons attribute others' wrongdoings to stable factors in their personalities (e.g., "evilness" or "sadistic tendencies"). It is likely to be greatly amplified in cases of convicted murderers who may appear unrepentant during the trial phase. Attribution bias at this point will likely result in jurors thinking the worst of the client. Take, for example, the defendant's demeanor. If he or she looks unconcerned, this can be viewed as indicating a cold-hearted and callous personality (or killer). If he or she looks contrite, this can be viewed as a "false front" and an example of a devious personality (or killer). One possible option is to address attribution bias indirectly via defense experts. Forensic clinicians can sometimes explain how the extreme stresses of trial can alter a defendant's emotions and demeanor. However, this approach has its own risks in calling further attention to the defendant's apparent unconcern for the suffering he or she has inflicted.

"Evaluations of dangerousness" were repackaged during the last decade as "risk assessments." Despite the new generation of risk-assessment measures, these scales often lack basic psychometric standards and produce significant errors. When using cut scores to classify an individual offender as "high risk" (dangerous), these risk-assessment measures are more often wrong than right. Forensic clinicians often conveniently sidestep these embarrassing data and talk instead about group classifications. Risk assessment is addressed in three earlier sections: *Parameters of Expertise*, *Risk Assessment*, and *Continuing Violence: Predictors*. Box 9-4 provides conceptual ideas and illustrative cross-examination for risk assessment per se.

BOX 9-4   ILLUSTRATIVE CROSS-EXAMINATION OF PROSECUTION EXPERTS
ON "CONTINUING THREAT"

A. Continuing Threat While on Death Row
   1. *Doctor, do you have any specialized knowledge of capital sentencing evaluations? ... You understand that I am talking about* specialized knowledge, *not just experience, correct?*
   2. *Isn't it true, that less than 10% of inmates* ever *act violently after being placed on death row? ... Isn't it also true, they stay on death row for 10 sometimes 20 years without acting violently? ...* [optional] *Isn't correct that the only real physical violence they experience is when they themselves are put to death?*
   3. *What makes you better than other experienced experts in capital sentencing evaluations? ... Are you better because you get paid more money? ...* [optional] *Are you better because you're a favorite with the prosecution?*
   4. *Doctor, I'd like you to put aside the fact that the prosecution has hired you to "get the job done." Isn't it true that 9 out of 10 death row inmates don't act violently?*
   5. *Would you go to a dentist with a record like that?* [likely puzzled] *...Would you go to a dentist that pulled out 9 good teeth before they got to the bad one?*
B. Addressing Objections to Low Base-Rates on Death Row
   6. [Objection: special security on death row] *What you are saying is that with sufficient security, you wouldn't be trying to get __* [the defendant] *killed today, is that correct? ... Have ever you visited a super-maximum facility? ... Isn't it true, doctor, they offer about the same level of security as death row?*
   7. [Objection: death row inmates are on "best" behavior] *Are you aware that the death penalty was previously ruled unconstitutional? ... Without the death sentence hanging over their heads, how many of inmates engaged in serious assaults?*
   8. *Would it surprise you to know that it is about 1% to 2% a year? ... Cumulatively, less than 10% in a 15-year period?* [may need a rebuttal expert on this point] *... In all fairness, doctor, that's not much of a continuing threat is it?*

Risk assessment creates special problems for capital sentencing cases because of limited generalizability to death row and other special-security facilities (Edens et al., 2001). However, jurors may be more convinced by focusing on inaccuracies. The rates of violence appear very low for both persons on death row and former death-row inmates.[6] One compelling conclusion is that experts testifying about "continued threats" are markedly inaccurate in their findings of dangerousness or "high risk." As presented in *Continuing Violence: Predictors*, relatively few (likely less than 10%) of former death-row inmates act out with serious violence when place in general populations of maximum security facilities. Box 9-4 presents illustrative cross-examination to address the very low base rates of violence for current and former death-row inmates. In possibly overcoming attribution bias, questions should be raised about biases for prosecution experts. Jurors must be pressed to question why experts would continue to testify for the prosecution when their overall accuracy is clearly inadequate. Is it the money? The role of an avenger? This use of attribution bias on the prosecution expert may lessen the damage to the defendant.

The second formidable challenge is the special categorization of defendant. If the defendant can be dehumanized as a heartless psychopath, then juries may have less trouble deciding to execute this "infra-human." Classic research by Bandura (1973) found violence (e.g., execution) is more acceptable if the "victim" can be categorized as less than human. Therefore, the forensic clinician's determination that the defendant is a psychopath should be vigorously countered. As previously noted, the standard error of measurement is often "ignored" by forensic clinicians. This is a critical issue. Hare (2003, Table 9.1, p. 164) reports percentiles for 5,408 North American male offenders. Using his data, cut scores make a dramatic difference:

1. *Cut score ≥30 (i.e., ignoring standard error of measurement)*: 15.7% of male offenders are psychopaths.
2. *Cut score ≥33 (i.e., one standard error of measurement)*: 5.8% of male offenders are psychopaths. As previously noted, Hart is a close colleague of Hare and recommends this cut score for risk assessment.
3. *Cut score ≥36 (i.e., two standard errors of measurement)*: 1.0% of male offenders are psychopaths. This stringent standard reduces false-positives to a small percentage, estimated at 2.3%.

The application of even one standard error of measurement greatly reduces the percentage of male offenders classified as psychopaths. With

---

[6]Importantly, these estimates are based on defendants released by general court actions and statutory changes; they do not include exonerated inmates.

Box 9-5   Illustrative Cross-Examination: Low Score Psychopath
(Total PCL-R of 30–32)

1. *Isn't it true that __ [the defendant] received a total score on the PCL-R of __ [30 to 32]?*
2. *Certainly, you aware that the standard error of measurement is between 3 and 3.25 for the total PCL-R score?*
3. *Did you even bother to apply the standard error of measurement in this case where a [man's/woman's] life is at stake?*
4. [if "no"] *Are you aware that this is a major violation of the official test standards? ... Will you do the "right thing" and report yourself to state licensing board for this serious lapse in professional practice in a life-and-death case?*
5. [if "yes" to #3] *I believe you took an oath to tell the whole truth, is that correct? ... Was this your idea to withhold key information from the jury?*
6. *Are you aware of the work by Dr. Stephen Hart, a close colleague of Robert Hare's and a co-author of the PCL:SV?*
7. *When he recommends that you use at least one standard error of measurement in classifying psychopaths to avoid errors, wouldn't it be prudent to follow his expertise?*
8. [claims to be unaware] *So you are not as knowledgeable about the PCL-R as you thought? ... Let's see how good you are at addition. If you were to take the minimum cut score of 30 and add 3, 1 standard error of measurement, what would be your new cut score? ... Can we at least agree that __ [the defendant] does not meet this classification of psychopathy?*

---

nearly two-thirds of psychopaths scoring in the 30–32 range, defense counsel can assail the expert's negligence in not reporting standard error of measurement and diminished confidence that the defendant is actually a psychopath. Box 9-5 provides illustrative cross-examination questions on psychopaths close to the threshold (Total PCL-R from 30 to 32). Please note that the first set of questions related to standard error of measurement can be applied across the full range of psychopathy.

Defense counsel in capital cases may need a consulting expert that assists in case development, trial strategies, and rebuttal options. In cases with compelling evidence of guilt, a primary focus for the entire trial may be sentence mitigation. Consulting experts may assist in all aspects of the trial without legitimate concerns about their own testimony.

SUMMARY

Noncapital sentencing, similar to pretrial diversions, carry a great potential to inform judges, and where applicable, sentencing juries. The flexibility of sentencing guidelines provides for individualized consideration of a particular offender and his or her crime. By the same token, this flexibility allows forensic clinicians to emphasize their own singular conceptualization of the case. This chapter attempts to outline very general boundaries for expert testimony on noncapital sentencing and provide clear summaries of empirically validated knowledge on potentially controversial issues, such as sex offenders and psychopaths.

Experts in capital sentencing cases attempt to assist juries and judges in making determinations with life and death consequences. Such cases demand the highest level of competence and practice from participating forensic clinicians. Likewise, trial attorneys will need to become well versed in psychological constructs as they may apply to a particular case. Less well known, but likely of equal importance, is the weighing of evidence and its emotional impact on juries that provide sentencing recommendations in capital cases. Consulting (nontestifying) experts may assist with overall conceptualization of capital cases in psychological terms, prior to and during sentencing phase.

10

Competency to be Executed and Other Post-Conviction Relief Issues

Courtroom proceedings in capital murder offenses often culminate in the public's mind with an acquittal, or conviction and imposition of the death penalty. However, post-conviction issues often take a center stage and may ultimately overshadow the original trial. Forensic clinicians are periodically consulted by criminal attorneys on the adequacy of psychological and psychiatric issues raised at trial. Moreover, the post-conviction phase raises new psycholegal issues that must be addressed.

This chapter features the question of competency to be executed that was given constitutional stature by the Supreme Court in *Ford v. Wainwright* (1986). *Ford* necessitates psychological and psychiatric involvement in another layer of post-conviction issues. Although the Court's opinion in *Ford* did not reach the question of the substantive standard for competence to be executed, a concurring opinion by Justice Powell did and it has by default become the constitutional floor for addressing this question.

Regarding other post-conviction issues, some mentally disordered death-row inmates want to take charge of their legal circumstances. In some cases, the inmate will ask to represent him- or herself during the appellate process but the right to represent oneself has been accorded different recognition on appeal than at trial. In other cases, death row inmates want to forgo the appellate process and be executed. At issue is the inmate's competence to make this momentous decision with irreversible consequences.

RELEVANT LEGAL STANDARDS

COMPETENCE TO BE EXECUTED

States that imposed capital punishment prior to 1986 recognized some statutory or case law limitation on the execution of mentally disordered inmates. Prior to *Ford v. Wainwright* (1986), however, the Supreme Court had not elevated these limitations to a constitutional stature. Ford, convicted of murder and sentenced to death by the state of Florida in 1974, began to experience paranoid delusions in 1982 and was subsequently diagnosed as Paranoid Schizophrenia by a defense expert. Invoking the extant Florida procedures for determining the competency of a condemned inmate, Ford was examined at a single 30-minute meeting by a panel of three psychiatrists appointed by the Governor. It reported to the Governor that Ford suffered from "psychosis with paranoia" but retained "enough cognitive functioning to understand the nature and the effects of the death penalty, and why it is to be imposed on him" (p. 404). Relying on this report, the Governor signed a death warrant for Ford's execution. Ford then filed a petition for habeas corpus that ultimately wound its way before the Unites States Supreme Court.

Tracing the common law roots of the ban against executing a prisoner who has lost his sanity, the opinion enumerated numerous reasons for this prohibition. Its analysis with citations removed is presented:

> As is often true of common-law principles . . . the reasons for the rule are less sure and less uniform than the rule itself. One explanation is that the execution of an insane person simply offends humanity . . . ; another, that it provides no example to others and thus contributes nothing to whatever deterrence value is intended to be served by capital punishment . . . Other commentators postulate religious underpinnings: that it is uncharitable to dispatch an offender "into another world, when he is not of a capacity to fit himself for it," . . . It is also said that execution serves no purpose in these cases because madness is its own punishment . . . More recent commentators opine that the community's quest for "retribution" — the need to offset a criminal act by a punishment of equivalent

> "moral quality"—is not served by execution of an insane person, which has a "lesser value" than that of the crime for which he is to be punished . . . Unanimity of rationale, therefore, we do not find. "But whatever the reason of the law is, it is plain the law is so." . . . We know of virtually no authority condoning the execution of the insane at English common law. (pp. 407–408)

Relying on this common law foundation and the fact that no state permitted execution of the insane, a majority of the Justices concluded that the Eighth Amendment's ban on cruel and unusual punishment proscribed the execution of the insane:

> Faced with such widespread evidence of a restriction upon sovereign power, this Court is compelled to conclude that the Eighth Amendment prohibits a State from carrying out a sentence of death upon a prisoner who is insane. Whether its aim be to protect the condemned from fear and pain without comfort of understanding, or to protect the dignity of society itself from the barbarity of exacting mindless vengeance, the restriction finds enforcement in the Eighth Amendment. (pp. 409–410)

In a footnote (p. 410, Note 2), the opinion reported that the majority of states have statutes that suspend execution for those convicts who meet the legal test for incompetence, while others have adopted the common law rule by judicial decision or provide more discretionary statutory procedures. Only four states have no specific procedures but have not repudiated the common law rule. But at no point did a majority of the Court address the substantive standard for competence to be executed compelled by its recognition of the Eight Amendment's ban on execution of the insane.

The meaning of insanity in this context was, however, addressed in a concurring opinion by Justice Powell joined only by Justice O'Connor. This concurring opinion notes that the ancient prohibition on executing the insane was grounded in different rationales that do not yield a single answer to define the mental awareness that the Eight Amendment mandates precede an execution.

> On the one hand, some authorities contended that the prohibition against executing the insane was justified as a way of preserving the defendant's ability to make arguments on his own behalf . . . Other authorities suggest, however, that the prohibition derives from more straightforward humanitarian concerns. (pp. 419–420)

Concluding that modern criminal procedure, with the right to appointed counsel and extensive review of convictions and sentences, reduces the merit of the first argument, Powell reasoned that the humanitarian rationale remained the most vital argument against execution of the insane. This rationale then gave rise to the substantive standard his concurring opinion concludes should apply to address the standard for competence to be executed:

> The more general concern of the common law—that executions of the insane are simply cruel—retains its vitality. It is as true today as when Coke lived that most men and women value the opportunity to prepare, mentally and spiritually, for their death. Moreover, today as at common law, one of the death penalty's critical justifications, its retributive force, depends on the defendant's awareness of the penalty's existence and purpose. Thus, it remains true that executions of the insane both impose a uniquely cruel penalty and are inconsistent with one of the chief purposes of executions generally. For precisely these reasons, Florida requires the Governor to stay executions of those who "d[o] not have the mental capacity to understand the nature of the death penalty and why it was imposed" on them ... A number of States have more rigorous standards, n3 but none disputes the need to require that those who are executed know the fact of their impending execution and the reason for it.
>
> Such a standard appropriately defines the kind of mental deficiency that should trigger the Eighth Amendment prohibition. If the defendant perceives the connection between his crime and his punishment, the retributive goal of the criminal law is satisfied. And only if the defendant is aware that his death is approaching can he prepare himself for his passing. Accordingly, I would hold that the Eighth Amendment forbids the execution only of those who are unaware of the punishment they are about to suffer and why they are to suffer it. (pp. 421–422)

The substantive test articulated in Justice Powell's concurring opinion—"that the Eighth Amendment forbids the execution only of those who are unaware of the punishment they are about to suffer and why they are to suffer it"—addresses the convicted defendant's cognitive capacity to perceive the connection between the crime and punishment to give effect to the penalty's retributive force. Concluding that it is "unlikely indeed that a defendant today could go to his death with knowledge of undiscovered trial error that might set him free" (p. 420), Powell's concurring opinion rejects the premise for a test for competence to be executed centered on the condemned inmate's functional ability to assist counsel at this stage of the proceedings (i.e., an assistance prong). The basis of this opinion was a belief in the accuracy of the system in which the defendant's capacity to assist with "undiscovered trial errors" was largely irrelevant. Of course, Powell could not have anticipated recent developments in which concerns over the accuracy of the capital cases lead to (1) a moratorium and blanket commutation in Illinois, (2) a moratorium in Maryland, and (3) state investigations in Arizona and Nebraska (Lanier & Acker, 2004).

Powell acknowledged that several states have chosen a test for competence to be executed, which includes the ability to assist counsel in his own defense. He noted that states are free to require more than the constitutional minimum.

The cognitive standard articulated in Justice Powell's opinion requiring awareness of the punishment they are about to suffer and why they are about to suffer it, appears to have been implicitly adopted by the Court in *Penry v. Lynaugh* (1989, p. 333):

> The common law prohibition against punishing "idiots" for their crimes suggests that it may indeed be "cruel and unusual" punishment to execute persons who are profoundly or severely retarded and wholly lacking the capacity to appreciate the wrongfulness of their actions . . . [U]nder Ford v. Wainwright, 477 U.S. 399 (1986), someone who is "unaware of the punishment they are about to suffer and why they are to suffer it" cannot be executed. Id., at 422 (Powell, J., concurring in part and concurring in judgment).

The test advanced in Powell's concurrence in *Ford* has also been accepted as the substantive standard in several federal courts (*Rector v. Lockhart*, 1990; *Shaw v. Armontrouten*, 1990). Some federal courts have isolated its requirements into two elements: (1) "whether the petitioner understands that he is to be punished by execution" and (2) "whether the petitioner understands why he is being punished" (*Rector v. Clark*, 1991, p. 572). However, most courts and commentators treat Powell's test as a single prong approach. Most states that authorize capital punishment have not clarified *Ford*'s standard, although a minority of states have sought to do so (Harding, 1994). Clarification of the standard has taken two forms. Some states that have chosen to utilize only the cognitive standard addressed in Justice Powell's concurring opinion attempt to flesh out this standard. Other states have exceeded the constitutional minimum and addressed the condemned inmate's functional ability to assist counsel at this stage of the proceedings.

As an example of the first approach, Florida has clarified the relevant standard for competence to be executed, but has not added any criteria beyond the test described in Justice Powell's concurrence. Florida explicitly requires that the prisoner possess "the mental capacity to understand the fact of the impending execution and the reason for it" (Fla. R. Crim. P. 3.811 2004). Likewise, the Arizona statute (Ariz. Rev. Stat. § 13-4021 [2004]) also clarifies that it adopts the Powell standard, but goes no further:

> As used in this article, "mentally incompetent to be executed" means that due to a mental disease or defect a person who is sentenced to death is presently unaware that he is to be punished for the crime of murder or that he is unaware that the impending punishment for that crime is death.

Similarly, statutory law in Georgia (Ga. Code Ann. § 17-10-60 [2004]), Kentucky (Ky. Rev. Stat. § 431.213 [2004]), New York (NY CLS Correct. § 656 [2004]), and Wyoming (Wyo. Stat. Ann. § 7-13-901[2004]) adopts but does not expand the test articulated in Justice Powell's concurrence. Case law in Arkansas (*Rector v. Clinton*, 1992), Tennessee (*Heck Van Tran v. State,* 1999), and Texas (*Ex parte Jordan*, 1988) has also clarified that the test described in Powell's concurrence applies to their respective state.

The South Carolina Supreme Court decision in *Singleton v. State* (1993) provides a good example of an augmented approach exceeding the constitutional minimum. It provides both cognitive and assistance prongs:

> [W]e announce the appropriate test in South Carolina as a two-prong analysis. The first prong is the cognitive prong which can be defined as: whether a convicted defendant can understand the nature of the proceedings, what he or she was tried for, the reason for the punishment, or the nature of the punishment. The second prong is the assistance prong which can be defined as: whether the convicted defendant possesses sufficient capacity or ability to rationally communicate with counsel. (p. 58)

Other states have required both cognitive and assistance prongs. In Mississippi (Miss. Code Ann. § 99-19-57(2) [2004]), the emphasis addresses the understanding and disclosing relevant information, "a sufficient understanding to know any fact which might exist which would make his punishment unjust or unlawful and the intelligence requisite to convey such information to his attorneys or the court."

Criminal Justice Mental Health Standards of the American Bar Association (ABA, 1989) recommended an assistance prong (Standard 7-5.6, p. 290): "the convict lacks sufficient ability to recognize or understand any fact which might exist which would make the punishment unjust or unlawful, or lacks the ability to convey such information to counsel or the court." According to Brodsky, Zapf, and Boccaccini (2001), eight states have adopted language similar to ABA assistance prong.

COMPETENCE TO WAIVE THE RIGHT TO ATTACK A CONVICTION AND SENTENCE

A competent defendant may waive the right to attack his or her conviction and sentence. The critical psycholegal question is the defendant's competence to make this decision. A defendant's decision to abandon all appeals and accept execution may appear to be irrational. However, competence turns on the defendant's decision-making capacity and not the decision per se. The Supreme Court succinctly described the test that governs this issue in *Rees v. Peyton* (1966), directing that when the issue is raised the court determine whether the defendant has:

> the capacity to appreciate his position and make a rational choice with respect to continuing or abandoning further litigation or on the other hand whether he is suffering from a mental disease, disorder, or defect which may substantially affect his capacity in the premises. (p. 314)

The Supreme Court did not apply the *Rees* test, but remanded the case to the District Court to do so; therefore, the *Rees* decision provides no further guidance on the application of this test. A much-cited decision of the Fifth Circuit Court of Appeals in *Rumbaugh v. Procunier* (1985) does provide more explicit guidance in the application of *Rees*.

The *Rumbaugh* case involved a defendant convicted of capital murder in Texas and sentenced to death. His conviction was reversed by the Texas Court of Criminal Appeals on evidentiary grounds, retried and resentenced to death that was affirmed by the Texas Court of Criminal Appeals, who thereafter directed his court-appointed counsel to take no further steps to attack his conviction or sentence. In a bizarre series of events, Rumbaugh's parents filed a next friend application for habeas corpus to halt the execution and in the hearing that followed, Rumbaugh "pulled a homemade knife-like weapon from his pocket and advanced on the deputy U.S. Marshall, shouting 'Shoot!' The Marshall was forced to shoot Rumbaugh. After life-saving measures were taken, over Charles Rumbaugh's demands that no attempts be made to save his life, and he was removed by ambulance to the hospital, the hearing continued" (p. 397). The District Court then concluded that Rumbaugh was competent to waive his right to attack his conviction and Rumbaugh's parents appealed to the Fifth Circuit Court of Appeals which affirmed the lower court's findings. In a decision that operationalizes *Rees*, Court of Appeals laid out the relevant questions and the consequences of the answers to those questions:

> [*Rees*] requires the answer to three questions:
>
> 1. Is the person suffering from a mental disease or defect?
> 2. If the person is suffering from a mental disease or defect, does that disease or defect prevent him from understanding his legal position and the options available to him?
> 3. If the person is suffering from a mental disease or defect which does not prevent him from understanding his legal position and the options available to him, does that disease or defect, nevertheless, prevent him from making a rational choice among his options?
>
> If the answer to the first question is no, the court need go no further, the person is competent. If both the first and second questions are answered in the affirmative, the person is incompetent and the third question need not be addressed. If the first question is answered yes and the second is answered no, the third question is determinative; if yes, the person is incompetent, if no, the person is competent. (pp. 398–399)

Finding that Rumbaugh suffered from a mental disease that affected his volitional but not his cognitive capacity to forgo further attacks on his conviction and sentence and no case law to guide it, the Court of Appeals treated the matter as a question of fact on which the District Court's findings would be accepted unless shown to be clearly erroneous. In a dissenting opinion, Judge Goldberg attacked the test articulated by the Supreme Court in *Rees* as well as its application by the Court of Appeals in this case. Judge Goldberg pointed out that *Rees* requires a determination of the defendant's capacity to make a rational decision but contains no definition of rationality, a term that is contentious in contemporary philosophy.

> Under *Rees*, a person *either* is capable of rational choice *or* has a mental disease that "substantially affects his capacity in the premises," but he cannot have *both* conditions. If *Rees* were read to require only an inquiry into the person's ability to reason *logically*, without an inquiry into the person's autonomy, then both conditions would be possible. Yet a person can be both logical and have a mental disease that "substantially affects his capacity in the premises," i.e., that affects what the person in an ultimate sense desires. (p. 404)

Although Judge Goldberg's dissent presents a thoughtful critique of *Rees*, it has not persuaded the Supreme Court to reexamine *Rees*, or other courts to vary its application. Indeed, the majority opinion in *Rumbaugh* appears to have shaped the way in which the lower federal courts have applied *Rees*. For example, citing *Rumbaugh* in *Lonchar v. Zant* (1993, p. 641), the Eleventh Circuit Court of Appeals stated that *Rees* "involves a determination of (1) whether that person suffers from a mental disease, disorder, or defect; (2) whether a mental disease, disorder, or defect prevents that person from understanding his legal position and the options available to him; and (3) whether a mental disease, disorder, or defect prevents that person from making a rational choice among his options."

In another decision (*Whitmore v Arkansas*, 1990, p. 153), the Supreme Court affirmed an Arkansas Supreme Court finding that the defendant was competent to waive his appeal because he had "the capacity to understand the choice between life and death and to knowingly and intelligently waive any and all rights to appeal his sentence." Although *Whitmore* did not explicitly modify *Rees* and addresses a technically different question (i.e., the standing of a third party to intervene in the proceedings), several states have read *Whitmore* as an augmentation of the *Rees'* requirements. Ohio, for example, heightens the decisional competence required to waive the right to further appeals by combining *Rees* and *Whitmore*:

> Thus, in our view, a defendant "has capacity to appreciate his position," Rees, supra, if he understands the choice between life and death, see Franz v. State (1988), 296 Ark. 181, 189, 754 S.W.2d 839, 843; State v. Dodd (1992), 120 Wash. 2d 1, 23, 838 P.2d 86, 97, and he fully comprehends the ramifications of his decision to waive further legal proceedings, see Cole v. State (1985), 101 Nev. 585, 588, 707 P.2d 545, 547. And a defendant has the capacity to "make a rational choice with

respect to continuing or abandoning further litigation," Rees, supra, if he can make a voluntary, knowing, and intelligent decision, Franz, supra, at 189-190, 754 S.W.2d at 844; Dodd, supra, at 23, 838 P.2d at 97; and he has the "ability to reason logically," i.e., to choose "means which relate logically to his ends," see State v. Bailey (Del.Super.1986), 519 A.2d 132, 137–138 (*State v. Berry*, 1997, p. 1101; See also *State v. Torrence*, 1994; *State v. Dodd*, 1992).

Guardianship and Incompetent Defendants

Defense counsel are occasionally faced with severely impaired defendants who appear incompetent to make basic decisions about major aspects of their life including their legal cases. Their compromised cognitive abilities may affect their decisions and the awareness of their consequences (Moye, 2003). In a number of unreported decisions, attorneys have been successful at having matters of guardianship be considered at the post-conviction phase. For example, *Larry Gene Bell v. State of South Carolina* (Case No. 96-CF-41-0138), the defense counsel used guardianship to protect the rights of a psychotic defendant on death row. As a more recent example, the Court ordered for *In Re Jon Scott Dunkle* (California Supreme Court Case No. S 014200) that habeas counsel be appointed as Mr. Dunkle's guardian for specific purposes. In addition to considering the *Rees* and *Rumbaugh* standards, defense counsel will need to make an initial determination whether (1) the defendant lacks basic decisional capacities, and (2) this impairment warrants further evaluation regarding general or specific guardianship (Melton et al., 1997).

COMPETENCY TO WAIVE

In *Faretta v. California* (1975), the Supreme Court decided that the constitutional guarantee of assistance by counsel before a state can convict and imprison a defendant also encompasses the "constitutional right to proceed without counsel when he voluntarily and intelligently elects to do so" (p. 807). In *Martinez v. Court of Appeal* (2000), the Court held that its decision in *Faretta* only applies at trial. Because there is no constitutional right of self-representation on appeal, the question of a voluntary and intelligent waiver of the right to counsel under the federal constitution recognized in *Faretta* is not an issue on appeal requiring psychological or psychiatric assistance.

The Supreme Court decision in *Martinez* emphasized that the states themselves could provide for a right to self-representation on appeal under state law. In Texas, for example, although there is no state constitutional or statutory right to self-representation on appeal, Texas courts "review requests for self-representation in appeals from criminal convictions on a case-by-case basis, considering the best interests of the appellant, the State, and the administration of justice" (*Crawford v. State*, 2004, p. 417). In practice, however, the state courts are unlikely to permit self-representation in cases where the appellee's competency is in question (personal communication, Gary Hart, October 28, 2004). Therefore, capacity to proceed *pro se* is unlikely to become a post-conviction issue.

CLINICAL AND FORENSIC APPLICATIONS TO COMPETENCY TO BE EXECUTED

NOTIFICATION

Heilbrun (1987) noted that forensic clinicians have an ethical obligation to notify the defendant regarding the purpose and the nature of the evaluation. Defendants have typically met with their appellate attorneys and have been informed regarding its purpose. Whether the defendant understands this information is largely dependent on their level of functioning. Nonetheless, forensic clinicians have their own ethical responsibilities of communicating to the defendant in understandable terms their purpose in conducting a competency-to-be-executed examination. A potentially controversial issue is the expert's disclosure of his or her agency in this consultation. Should the defendant know whether the expert has been retained by prosecution or the defense? Given the gravity of circumstances, we recommend that forensic clinicians clarify their role in competency-to-be-executed examinations; for example, "I have been retained by the state to ... "

The focus is typically on notification rather than informed consent because most defendants may not have the formal choice to decline the evaluation. In practice, however, the defendant may simply refuse to participate by remaining silent. Forensic clinicians should clarify prior to their evaluations whether consent issues applied. Obviously, a significant risk is that defendants incompetent to be executed are also likely to be incompetent to consent.

COGNITIVE PRONG

Ebert (2001) developed a model for competency to be executed that operationalizes the cognitive prong and provided additional ratings of impairment. Of his 12 criteria, four appear especially relevant to the cognitive prong: (1) ability to understand the concept of punishment, (2) awareness of the pending execution, (3) understand the reason for his or her execution, and (4) basic knowledge of execution itself (e.g., lethal injection). Ebert (2001) provides a sample inquiries for addressing these criteria.

Brodsky, Zapf, and Boccacini (1999) provide three domains in the form of a checklist. They involve understanding of the crime, understanding the punishment, and an appreciation of its personal importance. For each domain, they recommend questions that ask the defendant to explain his or her thinking. For example, the defendant is asked to what it means to be executed and what it means to be dead. The idea is to go beyond simple, possibly rote, responses and examine the defendant's understanding.

Slobogin (2000) offered an insightful analysis of the cognitive prong that goes beyond the simple factual understanding (e.g., "I killed therefore I am being executed."). He observed that defendants are likely incompetent if they do not attach any significance to their own execution. Slobogin argued that the defendant must have some emotional appreciation regarding the retributive nature of the punishment and its personal importance to the defendant. In a Texas case (*Kelsey Patterson v. Gary Johnson, Director Texas Department of Criminal Justice, Institutional Division*, 4:98-CV-156 PNB), Patterson understood he had been convicted of murdering of two women and had been sentenced to death. However, he was grossly delusional about the criminal justice system and believed his punishment was directly the result "hell pledges" and a conspiracy by the trial judge and defense counsel to destroy him. Because of his delusional and markedly disorganized thinking, the nexus between his execution and the murders was severely impaired. In light of *Ford*, Patterson did not appear to have any rational appreciation of punishment and could not come to terms with why he must suffer it.

Zapf, Boccaccini, and Brodsky (2003) provided an extensive checklist for competency-to-be-executed evaluations that addresses the defendant's emotional appreciation of the execution and its retributive purpose. Representative issues are outlined:

- Perceived justice of the conviction;
- The defendant's understanding of the reasons for his or her execution;
- Appreciation of the personal importance of this punishment to the defendant;
- Irrational beliefs about invulnerability and the execution;
- Inappropriate affect about his or her execution.

These issues should be addressed in forensic assessments of the cognitive prong.

Two different assessment models have been proposed for evaluating the cognitive prong. Ebert (2001) advocated a comprehensive assessment that includes an exhaustive record review and a battery of test measures. In direct contrast, Brodsky, Zapf, and Boccacini (1999, 2001) recommended a more focused assessment of functional abilities. Assuming finality without the opportunity for further assessment, we recommend a thorough, although not necessarily exhaustive, evaluation. We have outlined the key *cognitive* issues:

1. *Time perspective.* The evaluation should focus on the defendant's current and recent functioning. Structured interviews and history can examine closely the defendant's level of functioning for the last 12 months. Childhood history and early treatment interventions are likely to be of secondary importance.
2. *Standardization.* The quality of competency evaluations can be substantially improved by systematic appraisals. These appraisals usually combine structured interviews with a multiscale inventory. In case of markedly impaired cognitive functioning, formal testing for intelligence and neuropsychological impairment is clearly indicated.
3. *Operationalized issues.* We recommend that forensic clinicians develop specific inquiries to address each component of the competency-to-be-executed standard. Before the evaluation, the goal is to have prepared at least several relevant questions for each component. This set of questions can be asked on more than one occasion to test the defendant's understanding. Ebert (2001) and Brodsky et al. (1999) offer sample questions.
4. *Malingering.* In cases where substantial impairment is observed, we recommend a formal assessment of malingering. Even when the defendant appears to be responding genuinely, the forensic clinician must be prepared to address the subjective impressions by another expert. On this point, the *Ford* case is instructive: only one of six experts concluded that Ford was malingering, yet the Judge accepted that opinion (Brodsky et al., 2001).

What level of understanding is required to meet the cognitive prong of the *Ford* standard? Are affirmative responses to direct questions ("Were you convicted of the murder of __ and __?" [yes] "Will you be executed for these murders? [yes]) be sufficient for the cognitive prong? What about the psychotic or retarded defendant who with repeated promptings can relate his or her convictions and sentence? In this instance, the defendant is only aware of the cognitive prong when focused and prompted. These examples are insufficient. Powell's concurrence in *Ford* is unambiguous, "And only if the defendant is aware that his death is approaching can he prepare himself for his passing." The statement requires an ongoing and internalized understanding of the pending execution. To fulfill the *Ford* requirement, forensic clinicians must determine the following standard: *Does the defendant have an ongoing and internalized understanding of the cognitive prong?*

ASSISTANCE PRONG

The assistance prong, where applicable, is much more complex than its cognitive counterpart. For example, the ABA standard involves extensive personal memory, discerning judgment, and the capacity to relate meaningfully to counsel. The key language of the standard is as follows: "the convict lacks sufficient ability to recognize or understand any fact which might exist which would make the punishment unjust or unlawful, or lacks the ability to convey such information to counsel or the court" (ABA, 1989, p. 290). Of critical importance is the breadth provided by this standard. Conclusive evidence is not necessary; simply the *possibility* (i.e., any fact which *might* exist) is sufficient. Because mitigation in capital sentencing is not limited in its scope, the possibility of an *unjust* sentence should be widely construed. These issues that must be considered are (1) memory impairment, (2) discerning judgment, and (3) capacity to communicate with counsel.

Memory impairment. Defendants with severe memory impairment are unlikely to recall and therefore recognize relevant information. Major problems may include amnesia for the time of the offense or even blackouts (see Chapter 8). In addition, persons with dementia (see Chapter 5) may lack the capacity to remember significant periods in their lives. These periods could possibly include trauma or other devastating experiences that would potentially mitigate the death sentence. Memory problems can also be exacerbated by the severe stresses and extended periods of social isolation found on many death rows (Arrigo & Tasca, 1999).

Discerning judgments. Chapter 9 outlines the complex array of statutorily defined and individualized mitigating factors. The defendant must be able to determine which personal and contextual variables would be helpful to defense counsel. Of course, this process is much more straightforward when defense attorneys systematically probe for relevant information.

Communicate with counsel. The component of the ABA competency-to-be-executed standard is closely related to the consult-with-counsel prong of competency to stand trial. However, it is less stringent. To communicate with counsel, the defendant must have sufficient verbal skills and the ability to recognize the defense counsel as the individual in charge of his or her appeals. Clinical issues can include incoherence, formal thought disorders or paranoid delusions. These clinical issues can be assessed by the SADS or another Axis I interviews. In addition, elements of "communicate with counsel" can be assessed via the ECST-R (see Chapter 6) Consult with Counsel scale.

Some defendants lack the capacity to communicate relevantly with anyone including their attorneys. In an Oklahoma case, the consulting psychologist[1] observed that the defendant manifested disorganized speech with clear derailment. Examples include that he was "fit to stand as a man not a criminal" ... "had been gassed, don't care" ... "willing to go back to the sky-Judas, 9–55 chapter." His impairment resulted from low intellectual functioning coupled with a diagnosis of schizophrenia.

Brodsky et al. (1999) provided a brief summary of useful questions that can assist in "communication with counsel" for states that use the ABA language and "ability to assist counsel" in other jurisdictions, such as South Carolina and Washington. In these latter states, the assistance prong is more broadly construed. The defendant should actively participate with his or her appellate attorney in making decisions regarding the appellate process. Questions include awareness of the appeal process, the attorney's objectives in filing these appeals, and any information the defendant has withheld from his attorney. Zapf et al. (2003) presented an extensive outline of these issues.

PROFESSIONAL ISSUES

Defining the Referral Issue

Forensic clinicians are faced with a critical decision on how narrowly or broadly they conceptualize the referral issue. Should they only address the most narrowly defined standard? Heilbrun and McClaren (1988) argue that forensic clinicians should take a broad perspective in their examinations of competency-to-be-executed, because of the lack of empirical data on this legal issue and vagueness of the standards. They reasoned that the court can always disregard any elements peripheral to this determination. Where the legal standard is vague, narrowly defined consultations run undesirable risk of omitting potentially relevant information. A simple option to broadening the issue is to request a detailed referral that outlines the various issues to be considered. A more expansive alternative is to

---

[1] A forensic report by Richard Rogers dated May 16, 2001. For confidentiality reasons, identifying information is withheld.

evaluate both cognitive and assistance prongs in every competency-to-be-executed evaluation.

Ethical Considerations

Forensic clinicians are likely to be strongly divided regarding the ethics and propriety of conducting competency-to-be-executed examinations. This brief section highlights the key issues. Forensic clinicians involved in such determinations have a professional responsibility to examine these ethical issues as well as their own moral scruples. In a penetrating analysis of Bonnie (1990) found no ethical issues inherent in competency-to-be-executed evaluations. He argued that there is no qualitative difference between capital sentencing and competency-to-be-executed consultations. Given the emotional impact of competency-to-be-executed evaluations, experts should refrain from such consultations if they cannot maintain their objectivity. On this point, Brodsky et al. (2001) note the "pull for affiliation" when defense counsel implore experts to save the inmate's life.

A core issue for many forensic clinicians is whether their participation is facilitating the death of a condemned inmate. As a practical matter, raising the issue of competency-to-be-executed *delays* rather than *expedites* the execution. It seeks to protect the inmates from being unfairly executed. The issue becomes far more complicated in those very few cases involving *restoration* of competency. In these rare cases, the practical result of testimony may result in expediting execution. Because experts involved in the determination of incompetency are also likely to be called for the restoration of competency, they must grapple with the issue prior to involvement in competency-to-be-executed evaluations.

Many forensic clinicians have ethical considerations about any involvement in the treatment of incompetent inmates (Appelbaum, 1986). The American Medical Association (1992) has deemed any participation in executions to be unethical. However, we argue that the professional roles of evaluation and treatment should remain entirely separate in competency-to-be-executed cases.

CLINICAL AND FORENSIC APPLICATIONS TO COMPETENCE TO WAIVE APPEALS

Forensic clinicians may be asked to evaluate a defendant's ability to make autonomous decisions in waiving his or her right to attack the conviction and sentence. Based on the *Rees* test, the critical question is whether the defendant is able to "make a rational choice with respect to continuing or abandoning further litigation." As noted in the Legal Standards, Fifth Circuit Court of Appeals further operationalized the *Rees* test in *Rumbaugh* case. Three determinations must be made:

1. Does the defendant a mental disease or defect?
2. If yes to #1, does it prevent him or her from understanding the particular legal position and available options?
3. If yes to #1, does it prevent him or her from making a rational choice among his or her options?

Fifth Circuit Court of Appeals imposed an algorithm on the *Rees* test in which #3 is only considered if #2 is not met. Because forensic clinicians will not be aware of this determination at the time on their consultation, they should address both #2 and #3 if the defendant has the requisite mental disease or defect.

Zapf et al. (2003) provided a helpful outline of the issues that should be considered in assessing the legal position and available options. The relevant issues are bulleted:

• awareness of execution date or likely date;
• status of current appeals;
• actual substance of appeals;
• objectives of the appeals;
• how appeals are processed and assessed.

We would add two considerations to Zapf et al.: (1) the availability of future appeals and (2) the expected time frame for each appeal. These issues should be addressed in every case where the defendant's capacity to waive appeals is in question. Forensic clinicians can appreciate the considerable cognitive abilities required to evaluate the different types of appeal. Comprehension of these different types of appeal is essential knowledge of the "available options."

RATIONAL ABILITIES

Bonnie (1990) provided an excellent framework for evaluating the defendant's rational choice to waive all current and further appeals. Listed below are a sampling of potentially rational arguments: The condemned prisoner

1. may feel "that the sentence of death is justly deserved and should be imposed and executed" (p. 73)

2. may prefer death to "known pains of perpetual imprisonment" (p. 73)
3. may want to exercise control over his or her fate (p. 74)

Irrational choices may reflect psychotic or otherwise severely impaired thinking. Delusions about the execution may grossly impair the decisional abilities. In above-cited *Bell* case, the defendant thought he was Jesus and saw his execution as "gateway to throne of God." His willingness to die was an opportunity to be reunited with his heavenly father. Irrational thinking can also result from major depression with severe hopelessness, worthless, extreme discouragement, and intense desire to die. The challenge for forensic clinicians is that some dysphoria, hopelessness, and discouragement may reflect *realistic* perceptions of the defendant's current circumstances. A SADS evaluation of the depression may be very useful in determining its severity. Still, the forensic clinicians face the formidable task of appraising how much depressed thinking and judgment vastly exceeds the defendant's circumstances.

Some irrational decisions involving the waiver of all appeals are not based principally on a mental disease or defect. In a post-conviction status hearing (Kenneth D. Thomas, Cause # F86 85457M), the defendant was under the gross misperception that his withdrawal of appeals would invite the trial judge to reconsider the merits of the case and likely result in a not-guilty verdict. This misbelief was not delusional; irregularities in the case had already results in two reversals and two retrials. When the trial judge became aware of this gross misperception, he confronted the defendant, who with great consternation asked that his appeals be reinstated.

Decisions to forgo all appeals are often multi-determined. In *State of Texas v. Robert R. Atworth* (Cause No. F96-00613-JH), the defendant asked that all appeals be ended and that an execution date be set. His motivations appeared to be anger, control, and resignation. He was angry that his attempts to contact his 8-year-old daughter were unsuccessful. He had learned from his estranged wife that his daughter wanted no contact with him. He expressed anger at himself for being on death row, his wife for contributing to his daughter's disinterest, and even his daughter for forsaking him. He desired some sense of control over his existence and preferred the certainty of an execution date to the uncertainties of further appeals and delays. Finally, he was resigned to what he considered to be the inevitable outcome. He believed that execution was only a matter of time. While part of his decision may have been irrational (e.g., "getting back" at his wife and daughter), he did not have the requisite mental disease or defect.

Determinations of rational decision-making involve the ability to consider and weigh the relevant options. Chapter 6, *Clinical Issues*, addresses different components of the decisional process (see also Chapter 5 on intelligent waivers). Two perspectives should be considered in evaluating rational decision-making for waiver-of-appeals determinations:

1. *Is the reasoning ability grossly impaired?* This gross impairment may be based on psychotic beliefs about the current circumstances or the meaning of the defendant's death. For example, a defendant in Oklahoma believed his death had far-reaching religious significance in signaling the spiritual ascendancy of African Americans and total annihilation of other races.[2] Cases with grossly impaired reasoning are the clearest for forensic determinations.
2. *Is the conclusion based on highly illogical reasoning?* In the absence of grossly impaired reasoning, defendants may evidence a highly illogical conclusion unsupported by either facts or commonsense. In a previously mentioned *Thomas* case, the defendant firmly believed the judge would reconsider his case and change the verdict. He reasoned that further appeals were delaying his eventual acquittal. On the basis of a completely false premise and buoyed naive optimism, he was convinced in the soundness of his judgment. Obviously not delusional, he was able to recognize his momentous error and rectify it.

In the second instance, *highly illogical thinking*, the forensic clinician may believe that the defendant is making an obviously wrong decision in forgoing all appeals. Forensic clinicians must avoid the facile conclusion that a "wrong" decision can be equated with impaired reasoning. The correctness of the decision is not at issue. What is at issue at issue is the defendant's capacity to recognize the alternatives and understand the consequences associated with each alternative. In deciding, the defendant must be able to articulate how his or her decision achieves or may achieve the desired objective.

The forensic assessment of reasoning ability should take into account both grossly impaired reasoning and highly illogical thinking. Because gross impairment is likely based on psychotic symptoms and other forms of severe psychopathology, the use of Axis I interviews is especially helpful. For cases of highly illogical thinking, extended clinical interviews are recommended that carefully document following: (1) the defendant's goals, (2) articulated alternatives, (3) denied alternatives (e.g., refusal to acknowledge clemency petitions), (4) likely consequences of each alternative, and

---

[2]A forensic report by Richard Rogers dated April 27, 2002. For confidentiality reasons, identifying information is withheld.

(5) the defendant's reasoning. These decisions are likely affected by emotions as well as reasoning. However, the defining issue is highly illogical thinking that does not adequately consider the alternatives and the likelihood of success.

Some forensic clinicians may wish to examine cognitive abilities, including verbal intelligence as part of their evaluations of reasoning ability. However, general measures of problem-solving ability are only peripherally related to the defendant's reasoning about his or her life decisions. A defendant may appear unimpaired on the Comprehension subtest of the WAIS-III, yet demonstrate markedly illogical thinking about his or her own circumstances and pending execution. In contrast, the defendant may evidence moderate impairment on these measures and be sufficiently rational to make highly consequential decisions about his or her life. Cognitive assessment may be useful when the defendant has borderline intellectual functioning or marked deficits (e.g., dementia) that may affect their decisional abilities. In these instances, reasoning ability is affected by the general level of cognitive functioning. One option is the Reynolds Intellectual Assessment Scales (Reynolds & Kamphaus, 2003), a brief intellectual measure that has a specific Verbal Reasoning subtest.

COMPETENCE TO WAIVE COUNSEL ON APPEAL

On the basis of the Supreme Court decision in *Martinez* defendants do not have a constitutional right to self-representation. It is possible that individual states will allow *pro se* appeals. In such cases, forensic clinicians should rely on the clinical issues and methods reviewed in Chapter 6, *Competency to Stand Trial*. At stake is whether this decision is *knowing* and *voluntary*. Importantly, CST measures will have only marginal relevance in capturing the issues germane to the appeal process.

GENERAL CROSS-EXAMINATION ISSUES

Deitchman et al. (1991), briefly mentioned in Chapter 9, surveyed 222 forensic examiners from Florida on their views of competency-to-be-executed. They found that willingness to participate in competency-to-be-executed evaluations were moderately predicted by two variables: favorable views of capital punishment and personal attributions of criminal responsibility. The differences between groups were not great. However, attorneys may wish to question forensic clinicians about their general views of capital punishment and criminal responsibility and whether these views

---

Box 10-1   Personal Attitudes and Competency-to-be-Executed
Evaluations

1. *Doctor, what is your personal view of the appeal process in capital cases?
   ... [if needed] Too long? Too short?*
2. *Would you like to personally participate in the execution of this defendant?*
3. [looks uncomfortable at #2] *You seem a bit squeamish about the execution.
   How does this affect your objectivity? ... Isn't it true you are involved in
   [his/her] execution one way or another? ... Tell us the truth, would you like
   to see [him/her] die?*
4. [looks impassive at #2] *It doesn't seem like that idea bothers you very much,
   does it? ... Are you just cold-hearted or are you silently pleased about the
   execution? ... Tell us the truth, wouldn't you like to see [him/her] die?*
5. [defense expert] *What do you think of experts that always testify for the
   prosecution on competency-to-be executed? ... Wouldn't it be fair to say, that
   you are biased in the opposite direction?*
6. [prosecution expert] *What do you think of experts that always testify for
   the defense on competency-to-be executed? ... Wouldn't it be fair to say, that
   you are biased in the opposite direction?*

---

would influence the outcome of the case. Jury research strongly suggests
that views of the death penalty do influence verdicts and sentencing. It
is likely that this influence extends further to competency-to-be-executed
determinations.

Forensic clinicians often experience strong emotions about their involvement in competency-to-be-executed determinations. While any involvement in a capital case may affect its outcome, competency-to-be-
executed is the closest type of professional participation. Depending on
the outcome of these proceedings, defendant may be executed in several
days. Box 10-1 contains a brief sampling of questions designed to elicit
the expert's emotions that may be influencing his or her testimony. Such
questions can be supplemented with case-specific information (e.g., the
rape and murder of a young child). This cross-examination strategy is to
unsettle the expert emotionally and thereby diminish the effectiveness of
his or her testimony. In addition, experts are often more willing to identify
biases in other experts. The last two questions attempt to elicit these biases
and apply them to the testifying expert.

Attorneys should realize that clinical decision-making typically takes
into account the nature and magnitude of these risks. For example, a wrong
decision in the management of a suicidal patient is far more serious that a
clinical decision about the treatment of generalized anxiety. Forensic clinicians are not immune to magnitude of wrong decisions. Box 10-2 provides illustrative cross-examination regarding the consequences of clinical

---

Box 10-2   CLINICAL DECISION-MAKING AND ITS POTENTIALLY BIASING EFFECTS ON COMPETENCY-TO-BE-EXECUTED DETERMINATIONS

1. *Is clinical judgment something abstract or does it take into account the potential consequences of a wrong decision?*
2. *So if you had two patients, one mildly anxious and one actively suicidal, in which case would you work hardest to avoid a mistake? . . . Take extra precautions? . . . Be more conservative in your clinical judgment?*
3. *Now in competency-to-be-executed evaluations, you can make basically two wrong decisions: you can say the defendant is <u>competent</u> and be wrong or you can say the defendant is <u>incompetent</u> and be wrong—isn't that correct?* [may quibble] . . . *Come on, doctor, we all make mistakes don't we? . . . You're not trying to act smarter than rest of us, are you?*

Prosecution expert:

4. *Which type of error has <u>irreversible</u> consequences?* [if quibbles] . . . *If your testimony helps to execute an incompetent defendant, you can't take it back, can you?*
5. *Honestly, doctor, how can you live with yourself if your mistake stopped this* [select: man/woman] *a chance to come to terms with [his/her] death and have what Justice Powell calls the "comfort of understanding?"*
6. *Would you want to be responsible for an incompetent person being executed? . . . What safeguards did you build into your evaluation?*

Defense expert:

7. *Honestly doctor, isn't your evaluation biased and unobjective? . . . Did you look just as hard for reasons to this defendant might be competent and should finally receive [his/her] sentence?*
8. [if yes to #7] *Share with us, doctor, just one single finding that supports [his/her] being competent.*
9. [if nothing to #8] *How can you say you were <u>fair and balanced</u> if you could not find <u>one bit</u> of information supporting [his/her] competency?*
10. *What are your moral principles about the sanctity of life? . . . Did you just put them up on a shelf during the few hours you spent evaluating the defendant? . . . How did they bias your conclusions?*

---

errors. Prosecution experts run the risk of appearing to be callous and seeking death. In contrast, their defense counterparts may appear driven by emotions and moral principles.

Cross-examination is likely to be crucial in marginal cases in which the defendant's capacity is short-lived. As described in *Cognitive Prong* subsection, some defendants can be prompted to give "correct" responses about their offense and the pending execution. However, their ability to remember and apply this information to their own lives is markedly impaired. Defense counsel through cross-examination and rebuttal experts will need to attack the transient nature of this "understanding." In light of Powell's concurrence in *Ford*, this information must be available to the defendant to enable his or her preparation for their pending execution. Commonsensically, this preparation cannot be achieved in several hours or even days. Moreover, the defendant is not prepared if his or her compromised cognitive abilities prevent this understanding from continuing until the time of execution.

For competency-to-waive appeals, attorneys must be alert for experts providing "bottom-line" testimony that infers competency or incompetency. The *Rees* test with the *Rumbaugh* criteria present a detailed approach to these waiver decisions. One option is for the attorney to develop a demonstrative display with different options (all remaining appeals, evidentiary issues, clemency, and waiver of appeals) listed. For each option, the attorney can probe whether the expert examined this alternative in depth. Questions can concentrate on the meaning and objective of each alternative:

- *Appeals.* The expert should have questioned the defendant about the substance and goals of any remaining appeals. The expert should have ascertained whether the defendant understands the different purposes that can be served by each appeal: (a) indefinite delay of sentencing and (b) overturn the conviction or sentencing. While highly variable, the expert should have a good understanding of the defendant's expectations of the time involved for each appeal. This time perspective may have a significant effect on the defendant's decision.
- *Evidentiary issues.* The expert should have explored the possibility of new evidence (e.g., DNA testing or the recanting of an eyewitness) and its potential effects on the defendant's decision.
- *Clemency.* The expert should have questioned the defendant about the clemency process and his or her expectations of success.
- *Waiver of appeals.* The expert should have questioned the defendant closely about waiver decision and his or her goals.

Attorneys must attack cursory evaluations by bottom-line experts, who often spend only an hour or so with the defendant. Simplistic conclusions deserve vigorous cross-examinations. One example is extrapolating for a diagnostic conclusion (e.g., a psychotic defendant) to the legal standard (e.g., *Rees* criteria). By methodically questioning the expert, the insufficiency of the consultation should be exposed. To standardize the cross-examination further, attorneys may wish to use the Zapf et al. (2003) outline as a basis for cross-examination.

SUMMARY

Most forensic psychologists and psychiatrists have little training and expertise in post-conviction issues. While specialized measures (i.e., forensic assessment instruments) are not yet available, considerable knowledge is available to forensic clinicians for assessing cognitive capacities as required by competency-to-be-executed proceedings. Where applicable, the assistance prong of competency-to-be-exceeuted generally parallels the rational understanding and consult-with-counsel components of the *Dusky* standard. For competency to waive further appeals, the *Rees* test with the *Rumbaugh* criteria provide a clear outline for forensic clinicians. Such consultations typically require standardized assessments supplemented by extensive case-specific inquiries.

11

Sexual Predator Determinations

Public revulsion at luridly violent accounts of sexual recidivism spurred the recent passage sexually violent predator commitment (SVP) statutes. In response to a public outcry, Washington passed the first SVP statute of the modern era following the rape, castration, and strangulation of a 7-year-old boy. These acts were committed by a notorious sex offender recently discharged from prison after serving the maximum term authorized for the crime for which he had been convicted (Lieb, 2003). Unlike earlier laws for the commitment of sexual psychopaths that emphasized treatment (Janus, 2000), this recent batch of SVP statutes was primarily intended to ensure community safety through incapacitation. As examined in *Legal Standards* section, legislators resorted to specialized civil procedures to extend the periods of confinement for convicted sex offenders who had fully served their meted punishment.

Forensic clinicians have readily embraced SVP determinations, despite ambiguities in the standards and the appreciable absence of empirical data (Jackson, Rogers, & Shuman, 2004). While the research lag is unavoidable with new legislation, hurried extrapolations from the general risk-assessment literature are unlikely to represent good science or good practice. We are concerned about this predicament for two reasons. First, more than 1,000 persons had been committed as SVP detainees[1] by 2001 (Fitch & Hammen, 2003). The error rate for these commitments is unknown. Second, initial research is understandably expedient, relying on easily obtained information and nonspecific predictors. At this early stage in SVP knowledge, the stopgap measures of today can be adopted as the established practices of tomorrow.

Despite their reliance on civil law, SVP statutes are likely to be addressed by criminal attorneys working with incarcerated populations. Therefore, we have subsumed SVP determinations within a text on criminal forensic issues. In setting the stage, the next section begins with an overview of the early legislation.

RELEVANT LEGAL STANDARDS

Legal Background

The first round of legislation addressing civil commitment of dangerous sex offenders reached the United States Supreme Court in *Minnesota ex rel. Pearsons v. Probate Court* (1940, p. 273) which challenged a Minnesota statue addressing "persons who, by an habitual course of misconduct in sexual matters, have evidenced an utter lack of power to control their sexual impulses and who, as a result, are likely to attack or otherwise inflict injury, loss, pain or other evil on the objects of their uncontrolled and uncontrollable desire." Like other specialized commitment statutes of this era for sex offenders, the Minnesota law was intended to provide treatment to sex offenders in lieu of incarceration. Pearson appeal questioned the legislation on due process and equal protection grounds challenging the state's approach to group classification because the group the state selected for treatment was part of a larger class of persons with psychopathic personalities not selected for treatment by the legislation. The United States Supreme Court upheld the legislation and the state's authority to identify and control a class of dangerous persons. Although their authority to enact such legislation was upheld on constitutional grounds, most states that had enacted such laws ultimately repealed them or they fell into disuse when the treatment provided proved to be ineffective (Fitch & Hammen, 2003).

---

[1] As noted by Schopp (2001), SVP commitments are very different other forms of commitment where the designation of "patients" could be accurately applied. Because the overriding purpose of SVP commitments is confinement, the term "detainees" is accurate.

The most recent round of Supreme Court decisions addressing the state's authority to confine sexually violent predators arose from legislation enacted in the 1990s in Washington and Kansas to address the commitment of offenders nearing the expiration of their criminal sentence for sexually violent acts, whose mental condition did not meet their state's civil commitment statute's definition of mental illness or disorder, and who were regarded as likely to commit acts of sexual violence upon their release (*Kansas v. Hendricks*, 1997). To address the risks of sexual violence posed by these persons, Washington and Kansas, among other states, created separate civil commitment criteria targeting individuals who had (1) completed the maximum term of criminal confinement for sexually violent acts, (2) still posed a high risk of sexual predation, but (3) did not meet traditional civil commitment criteria.

The Kansas SVP commitment statute targeted individuals who suffer from a "mental abnormality" or personality disorder; it did not require the diagnosis of a mental disorder. The act explained that for these purposes a "mental abnormality" is to be understood to be a "congenital or acquired condition affecting the emotional or volitional capacity which predisposes the person to commit sexually violent offenses in a degree constituting such person a menace to the health and safety of others" (p. 352). The purpose of the Act, as explained by the legislature and quoted by the Court (p. 351), was to address:

> "[A] small but extremely dangerous group of sexually violent predators exist who do not have a mental disease or defect that renders them appropriate for involuntary treatment pursuant to the [general involuntary civil commitment statute]. . . . In contrast to persons appropriate for civil commitment under the [general involuntary civil commitment statute], sexually violent predators generally have antisocial personality features which are unamenable to existing mental illness treatment modalities and those features render them likely to engage in sexually violent behavior. The legislature further finds that sexually violent predators' likelihood of engaging in repeat acts of predatory sexual violence is high. The existing involuntary commitment procedure . . . is inadequate to address the risk these sexually violent predators pose to society. The legislature further finds that the prognosis for rehabilitating sexually violent predators in a prison setting is poor, the treatment needs of this population are very long term and the treatment modalities for this population are very different than the traditional treatment modalities for people appropriate for commitment under the [general involuntary civil commitment statute]." Kan. Stat. Ann. § 59-29a01 (1994)

Individuals committed under the Kansas SVP act may be confined indefinitely, until their mental abnormality or personality disorder has changed so that it is safe for them to be at large.

CONSTITUTIONAL CHALLENGES TO SVP LAWS

Defendants mounted a series of constitutional challenges to SVP legislation that eventually made their way to the United States Supreme Court. Two challenges were considered in *Kansas v. Hendricks* (1997). Because these laws targeted persons who had completed their criminal sentence for past sexually violent crimes, one challenge asserted that this type of commitment violated the constitutional ban on double jeopardy and ex post facto punishment. Concluding that these commitment laws were civil in nature, the Court rejected this challenge. Because the laws targeted categories of individuals with "mental abnormality" who did not meet traditional diagnostic criteria for mental disorders, a second challenge asserted that this legislation violated due process. Noting that the legislature's authority to protect its citizens was not restricted to categories prescribed by any private organization, the Court also rejected this challenge.

The next Supreme Court decision regarding commitment of sexually violent predators (*Seling v. Young*, 2001) arose from the Washington legislation, from which the Kansas law upheld in *Kansas v. Hendricks* (1997) was patterned. Challenging the conditions under which he was confined, Young argued that regardless of the legislature's intent, in practice the legislation resulted in criminal confinement, necessitating double jeopardy and ex post facto challenges rejected in *Hendricks*. The Court similarly rejected this challenge maintaining that changes in the state's implementation affected Young's right to care and treatment under the legislation but not its constitutional characterization.

The third chapter in recent Supreme Court sexually violent predator commitment jurisprudence arose from a challenge to implementation of the Kansas legislation (*Kansas v. Crane*, 2002). Crane challenged his SVP commitment in Kansas asserting that he had not been found to be "volitionally impaired." He argued that *Hendricks'* recognition of a constitutional basis to confine dangerous individuals outside of the criminal justice or traditional civil commitment system rested, in part, on proof that person is dangerous and unable to control his or her behavior. The Court agreed with Crane and concluded that, while confinement did not require a complete lack of control, it does require the presence of a mental abnormality or personality disorder that makes it difficult, if not impossible, for the dangerous person to control his or her behavior.

COMPONENTS OF SVP STANDARDS

Currently 15 states have specialized SVP commitments: Arizona, California, Florida, Illinois, Iowa, Kansas, Massachusetts, Minnesota,

Missouri, North Dakota, New Jersey, South Carolina, Virginia, Washington, and Wisconsin (Fitch & Hammen, 2003). Washington's statute, the first of this era, from which the Kansas statute addressed in *Henricks* was taken, has served as a closely followed model for legislation in other states. Sexually violent predators, subject to commitment under the act include "a person who has been convicted of or charged with a crime of sexual violence" and who suffers from a mental abnormality or personality disorder which makes the person likely to engage in predatory acts of sexual violence" (Washington, 2004 § 71.09.020 (16)). This definition has two main components: sexual offending and a requisite mental condition.

Sexual Offense

First, the Washington SVP statute requires that the person subject to commitment have a criminal history manifested by a conviction for or the pendency of a charge of a crime of sexual violence ("a person who has been convicted of or charged with a crime of sexual violence'). Those offenses which satisfy the requirement of a crime of sexual violence include forcible and statutory rape, indecent liberties against a child under 14 occasioned by force, and other offenses found to be sexually motivated (Washington, 2004, § 71.09.020 (15)).

Most state SVP commitment schemes have followed Washington's criminal history requirement with some variations. California established a more stringent standard; it requires the conviction of an offense against at least two victims. In contrast, both Minnesota and North Dakota have no specific criminal charge or conviction requirement but require unspecified proof of similar misconduct (Fitch & Hammen, 2003).

Mental Condition

The second component of Washington SVP act requires that the person's mental state or condition make it likely that he or she will engage in predatory acts of sexual violence ("who suffers from a mental abnormality or personality disorder which makes the person likely to engage in predatory acts of sexual violence"). Although there is no definition provided for personality disorder, mental abnormality is defined statutorily (Washington, 2004, § 71.09.020 (8)) to include "a congenital or acquired condition affecting the emotional or volitional capacity which predisposes the person to the commission of criminal sexual acts."

This definition was designed to satisfy the legislative intent and does not take into account the nosology and diagnoses currently used in mental health practice (Zonana, Bonnie, & Hoge, 2003). It poses obvious clinical problems in the absence of recognized mental disorders.

This argument was advanced by *Hendricks* and rejected by the Court:

> Hendricks . . . argues that our earlier cases dictate a finding of "mental illness" as a prerequisite for civil commitment . . . that a "mental abnormality" is not equivalent to a "mental illness" because it is a term coined by the Kansas Legislature, rather than by the psychiatric community. Contrary to Hendricks' assertion, the term "mental illness" is devoid of any talismanic significance. Not only do "psychiatrists disagree widely and frequently on what constitutes mental illness . . . Indeed, we have never required State legislatures to adopt any particular nomenclature in drafting civil commitment statutes. Rather, we have traditionally left to legislators the task of defining terms of a medical nature that have legal significance . . . As a consequence, the States have, over the years, developed numerous specialized terms to define mental health concepts. Often, those definitions do not fit precisely with the definitions employed by the medical community. (pp. 358–359)

Every SVP commitment act requires the presence of a particular mental condition. Most states follow the Washington act and require a personality disorder or "mental abnormality." According to Lieb (2003), the remaining states either specify a mental disorder (Arizona, California, Illinois, Wisconsin) or offer their own broad definitions. Two broad definitions include (1) sexual psychopathic personality or sexual personality or other mental disorder or dysfunction (i.e., Minnesota), and (2) a congenital or acquired condition manifested by sexual, personality, or mental disorder (i.e., North Dakota).

The Washington act describes the necessary probability by which the mental condition affects the risk of sexual violence as that "which makes the person likely to engage in predatory acts of sexual violence." This phrase, clarified by *In re Crane* (2000, p. 288), "means the person's propensity to commit acts of sexual violence is of such a degree as to pose a menace to the health and safety of others." Most other states follow the Washington act's "likely to engage" requirement. Lieb (2003) outlined the different variations used in other states. For example, Missouri appears to be the clearest of states in adopting a 51% likelihood criterion: "more likely than not to engage in sexual violence if not confined" (Mo. Rev. Stat. §§ 632.480 [2004]). Other states (see Lieb, 2003) are less specific in their defining terms: (1) Illinois requires "substantially probable that the person will engage in acts of sexual violence" (725 Ill Comp. Stat. 207/15 [2004]), and (2) Virginia states "likely to commit sexually violent offense that person constitutes menace to heath and safety" (Va. Code Ann. §§ 37.1-70.1 [2004]).

The term "likely" is not given greater statutory definition in the applicable states. In particular, the courts have rejected its translation into a statistical probability (*Commonwealth v. Boucher*, 2002). Rather, it is understood by to mean "highly probable" (*In re Wilber W.*, 2002) or "a serious and well-founded risk" (*People v. Superior Court [Ghilotti]*, 2002).

SVP and Specialized Assessment Methods

Expert opinions about future dangerousness, based on clinical observations and personal experience, have generally been admitted in SVP cases without much threshold scrutiny beyond the expert's qualifications (*People v. Bolton*, 2003). In contrast, the use of specialized assessment methods to determine which persons present a high risk of re-offending for sexual crimes has frequently been challenged on *Frye/Daubert* grounds. Some courts (*People v. Ward*, 1999; *State ex rel. Romley v. Fields*, 2001) have summarily rejected such challenges to admissibility, concluding that identification of mental abnormality and prediction of future dangerousness is not novel scientific evidence subject to such threshold scrutiny. Other courts (e.g., *In re R.S.*, 2002, p. 221) categorically concluded that "actuarial risk assessment instruments may be admissible in evidence in a civil commitment proceeding under the SVPA when such tools are used in the formation of the basis for a testifying expert's opinion concerning the future dangerousness of a sex offender." Similarly, the court in *State v. Holtz* (2002) opined that it is not an abuse of discretion to permit an expert to offer an opinion relying on actuarial instruments. In contrast to these blanket decisions, other courts have more carefully scrutinized actuarial risk assessment instruments.

A Florida appellate court in *Collier v. State* (2003) applied that state's *Frye* test to exclude the state's expert's reliance on the SVR-20 to establish the likelihood of re-offending. Its reasoning (pp. 945–946) was straightforward: "... because the only evidence proffered at the Frye hearing was the testimony of Dr. Bursten, without additional support from case law or other sources to demonstrate the acceptability of SVR-20. Additionally, even if an expert's testimony alone were sufficient to establish Frye admissibility, Bursten's testimony still would not have met the State's burden because he admitted that the SVR-20 remained in a somewhat experimental phase and that some in the psychological science community questioned its use."

Recent Illinois appellate court opinions (*People v. Taylor*, 2002; *In re Detention of Hargett*, 2003) determined that the Minnesota Sex Offender Screening Tool (MnSOST), Minnesota Sex Offender Screening Tool—Revised (MnSOST-R), Rapid Risk Assessment of Sexual Offense (RRASOR), and Static-99 fail that state's *Frye* test for admissibility of scientific evidence because they were still experimental instruments whose validity had not been demonstrated by research presented in peer reviewed publications.

The pattern of admissibility requirements for SVP risk assessments is uneven from state to state and within the borders of the same state. Trial judges have broad discretion (see Chapter 3) in the admissibility of evidence. Attorneys should be prepared to address *Daubert* and *Fry* standards on expert testimony and scientific methods. Their experts should be prepared to present the science that supports their risk assessment methods for its initial admissibility and subsequent persuasibility.

CLINICAL OPERATIONALIZATION AND FORENSIC METHODS FOR SVP DETERMINATIONS

A recent survey of trial judges (Bumby & Maddox, 1999) underscored how their beliefs and perceptions might play an influential role in SVP determinations. Nearly half (47.6%) of trial judges believed that psychologists and psychiatrists could correctly identify the typical profile for sex offenders. A substantial minority (21.4%) expressed the belief that all sex offenders were mentally ill. In addition, the judges appeared indecisive about the benefits of treatment. While most (90.5%) felt it could potentially reduce recidivism, nearly one-third (31.7%) believed there was no currently effective treatment. Finally, an appreciable minority (17.0%) believed that the indefinite SVP confinement was unconstitutional. In light of these beliefs (Bumby & Maddox, 1999), we recommend that criminal attorneys become aware of individual judges and their beliefs about SVPs and SVP determinations. Misbeliefs about accuracy of profiling or the pervasiveness of mental disorders could be directly targeted through expert testimony.

SYNDROMAL EVIDENCE FOR SVP

Forensic research must determine first and foremost whether SVP actually exists as a *clinical entity* or *syndrome*. A *syndrome* is an established pattern of correlated symptoms that remain stable over time and have clinical significance. If SVP were validated as a syndrome, forensic clinicians would be able to demonstrate their specialized knowledge and provide directly relevant predictions to the courts. Conversely, the absence of a syndrome would leave forensic clinicians with a conceptual mismatch. They would be in the uncomfortable position of proffering predictions that were *not* based on the SVP requirements.

SVP statutes and case law appear to assume that the following are conceptually relevant and clinically predictive: (1) past sexually harmful conduct, (2) mental abnormality or disorder, and (3) decreased volitional control, resulting the mental abnormality or disorder. The key empirical question is the following: Does a definable group of sex offenders exist for whom these variables are theoretically linked and empirically useful? If empirically demonstrable, SVP could be established as syndrome.

An insightful analysis (Wood, Grossman, & Fichtner, 2000) found no constellation of symptoms that was common to persons designated as sexual psychopaths. We are unable to find any similar research specifically related to SVP. To establish SVP as a syndrome, definable types of mental abnormality would need to be linked to diminished volitional abilities. This diminished volitional ability would need to be (1) a stable characteristic that is demonstrable across extended time periods, likely years, and (2) a focused pattern of sexual violence. Regarding its stability, diminished volitional abilities must logically extend from the last conviction and period of incarceration into the indefinite future. We are not aware of any programmatic research on defining types and subtypes of mental abnormalities that are linked to diminished volitional abilities. Moreover, we are not aware of any longitudinal research on specific patterns of diminished volitional abilities that are demonstrable over years and specifically related to sexually violent behavior. In the complete absence of such data, we can only conclude that SVP has not yet been established as a clinical syndrome.

Forensic clinicians must be forthright with the courts that SVP is not an established syndrome. Their testimony should explicitly reflect their lack of specialized knowledge on SVP as a clinical entity. As with all psycholegal issues, experts should candidly acknowledge the limits of their competence.

COMPONENTS OF THE SVP STANDARDS

The following subsections systematically address the different components of SVP legislation. The conceptualization of "sexually harmful conduct" is critically important because this construct is used as a potential predictor (i.e., past conviction or behavior) and the outcome (i.e., future conduct). The two other relevant constructs are (1) mental disorder or abnormality and (2) diminished volitional abilities. These three concepts are evaluated individually with a discussion of relevant clinical methods.

Sexually Harmful Conduct

Washington defines the harmful conduct required under its SVP law as follows:

(15) "Sexually violent offense" means an act committed on, before, or after July 1, 1990, that is: (a) An act defined in Title 9A RCW as rape in the first degree, rape in the second degree by forcible compulsion, rape of a child in the first or second degree, statutory rape in the first or second degree, indecent liberties by forcible compulsion, indecent liberties against a child under age fourteen, incest against a child under age fourteen, or child molestation in the first or second degree; (b) a felony offense in effect at any time prior to July 1, 1990, that is comparable to a sexually violent offense as defined in (a) of this subsection, or any federal or out-of-state conviction for a felony offense that under the laws of this state would be a sexually violent offense as defined in this subsection; (c) an act of murder in the first or second degree, assault in the first or second degree, assault of a child in the first or second degree, kidnaping in the first or second degree, burglary in the first degree, residential burglary, or unlawful imprisonment, which act, either at the time of sentencing for the offense or subsequently during civil commitment proceedings pursuant to this chapter, has been determined beyond a reasonable doubt to have been sexually motivated, as that term is defined in RCW 9.94A.030; or (d) an act as described in chapter 9A.28 RCW, that is an attempt, criminal solicitation, or criminal conspiracy to commit one of the felonies designated in (a), (b), or (c) of this subsection. (16) "Sexually violent predator means any person who has been convicted of or charged with a crime of sexual violence and who suffers from a mental abnormality or personality disorder which makes the person likely to engage in predatory acts of sexual violence if not confined in a secure facility."

Lieb (2003) found that most states specify acts of "sexual violence" although the nature of this violence (e.g., severely physical, physical, or psychological) remains open to debate and controversy. As the template for other states, Washington intended the SVP statute to be used for a circumscribed group of serious sex offenders that are "likely to engage in predatory acts of sexual violence" (Washington Revised Code 7 1.09.020(1)). The addition of the term *"predatory"* implies an active pursuing rather than an impulsively opportunistic act. Pragmatically, Washington State Association of Prosecuting Attorneys recommends limiting SVP cases to those sex offenders with demonstrable patterns (typically 3 or more) of prior predatory acts for whom other legal alternatives have been exhausted (see Fitch & Hammen, 2003, p. 31).

Clinically, Doren (1998) argued that nonphysical sexual offenses (e.g., exhibitionism and obscene phone calls) typically fall outside SVP definitions as they relate to sexual misconduct. The more challenging issue is whether any form of physical sexual contact, ipso facto, constitutes sexual violence. While obviously coercive, would *any* unwanted touching of genitalia qualify under SVP standards? Clearly, the age of the victim would likely play a role in this determination. One option under statutes that are not as explicit as Washington's is to consider convictions for certain violent crimes, such as rape and deviant sexual assault; however, other crimes (e.g., kidnaping) may be sexually motivated and may also be considered (Zonana & Norko, 1999).

Each state is responsible for establishing its own standards for what constitutes sexually harmful behavior. In the case of Michael Crane, that eventually reached the Supreme Court on volitional issues, the trial court adopted a very broad standard for past sexual misconduct. Crane's criminal history was comparatively benign with two convictions for indecent exposure and one conviction for aggravated sexual battery stemming from a physical assault and threatened rape (Sarkar, 2003). Arguably, this broadened criterion becomes virtually a "nonstandard" because the vast majority of sex offenders would be readily included.

Forensic clinicians are responsible for checking SVP appellate cases that apply to their jurisdictions for defining "sexually harmful conduct." In some instances, appellate cases establish only the basic parameters of what might be considered. Unless explicitly mandated, forensic clinicians must still determine whether the defendant's particular actions qualify as sexually harmful conduct. In the absence of clear guidelines, we recommend that forensic clinicians clearly operationalize their definition of *sexually harmful conduct* for the courts. With most forms of violence, experts should specify the level of physical aggression and consequent injuries. This specification is especially important for the outcome. As a professional standard, we recommend the following: *All SVP predictions of sexually harmful behavior should include explicit statements regarding the likely level of physical violence (including "none") and likely level of physical injury.*

Practitioner-based overviews (Conroy, 2003; Hanson, 2003; Lacoursiere, 2003) of SVP evaluations pay relatively little attention to this core construct of *sexually harmful conduct*. Without delineating the degree of sexual harm, courts may be seriously misled about *severity* of the predicted violence. Importantly, this level of *sexually harmful conduct* cannot be inferred from psychological measures. As an extreme example, consider the Sexual Violence Recidivism—20 (SVR-20; Boer et al., 1997). Does a high score necessarily indicate any form of sexual violence? The answer is simply "no." On the basis of its validation, persons writing obscene letters were categorized as "violent" offenders.

Clinical assessment of *sexually harmful conduct* relies heavily on clinical interview and collateral data. Two key points include the level of aggression and degree of injury. We recommend that inquiries be embedded in a comprehensive sexual history. Borrowing from interrogation techniques (Inbau et al., 2000), some forensic clinicians may attempt to normalize deviant sexual behavior as method of eliciting more information. Our preference is to discuss these issues in a matter-of-fact, emotionally neutral tone.

This latter approach minimizes the risk that forensic clinicians engage in deceptive practices.

Mental Disorder and Mental Abnormality

Statutory requirements for the necessary clinical condition can be categorized into three general groups: (1) mental disorder, (2) mental abnormality, and (3) mental abnormality or personality disorder (Lieb, 2003). A *mental disorder* typically reflects an Axis I or Axis II diagnosis and is the best defined of the three alternatives. A *mental abnormality* is a broadly construed and ill-defined term that is replete with ambiguity. The final option augments the second alternative with the narrower choice of a *personality disorder*, presumably focused on diagnosable Axis II disorders.

The American Psychiatric Association was sharply critical of SVP in formulating "what purports to be a clinical condition without regard to science or clinical knowledge" (Zonana, Bonnie, & Hoge, 2003, p. 135). Zonana et al. (2003, p. 143) argued in their commentary on the *Hendricks* decision, "Legislatures should not have the prerogative to invent mental or emotional categories that are needed to justify involuntary treatment." From our perspective, it may be less an invention than an exercise in ambiguity.

What type of mental disorder would potentially meet the SVP standards? Lacoursiere (2003) argued that paraphilias such as pedophilia would be the most likely candidate. He also listed bipolar disorders, dementias, personality disorders, and substance abuse disorders. Cornwell (2003) included paraphilias, personality disorders, and impulse control disorders. Forensic clinicians must consider a range of diagnoses in addressing the SVP standard. *No diagnosis can be automatically equated with the SVP standard*. To illustrate this point, pedophilia can be diagnosed in persons who have always controlled their deviant sexual impulses. According to the American Psychiatric Association (2000, p. 572), pedophilia can be diagnosed based only on urges that have been strictly controlled.

Mental abnormalities could be defined according to either normative or pathological perspectives. Normatively, any marked deviation from the average could be construed as a mental abnormality. From this perspective, a person with a markedly *low* score on a test of mental abilities (e.g., poor spatial abilities) could be defined as a mental abnormality. By the same token, a markedly *high* score (e.g., superior spatial abilities) would also represent a mental abnormality. The reasoning in *Hendricks* does not support the normative perspective.[2] This point should not be overlooked: *Forensic*

---

[2]To do so, "mental abnormalities" would logically embrace persons with superior adjustment or abilities.

clinicians should avoid using a normative analysis: low scores or high scores on psychological measures should not be used to establish a mental abnormality.

A pathological perspective would require that the mental abnormality would cause significant impairment in psychological functioning. What would constitute such impairment? One model (derived from GBMI; see Chapter 8) involves one or more important domains: judgment, behavior, reality testing, or the ordinary demands of everyday life. The advantage of this model is that it has been well-articulated and subjected to clinical-forensic research (e.g., R-CRAS research; Rogers, 1984). Arguably, the domains of judgment and behavior may be implicated in with a subset of sex offenders. Additionally, significant impairments of reality testing and the ordinary demands of everyday life are typically associated with well-defined Axis I disorders.

The personality component of mental abnormalities emphasizes both chronicity and impairment. According to Melton et al. (1997), the legislative history of the Washington statute was intended to address persons with antisocial personality features. Arguments have been presented that psychopathy, a personality syndrome found in only a subset of persons with antisocial personality disorder should be a focus on interest (Schopp & Slain, 2000). However, two critical issues must be considered:

- *Chronicity?* First, the data are sketchy on the chronicity of both antisocial personality disorder and psychopathy. In community studies, nearly one-third of cases originally diagnosed with antisocial personality disorder no longer qualify when reevaluated after and an interval of 6–12 months (Rogers, 2001). This point is paramount. Many forensic clinicians are unaware that both antisocial personality disorder and conduct disorder lack substantial evidence of diagnostic stability. Data are also very limited on the chronicity of psychopathy.
- *Impairment?* Forensic clinicians must be careful not to leap to facile conclusions that simply equate psychopathy and antisocial personality disorder with impairment. Research on "successful" psychopaths or persons with antisocial personality disorder has yet to be conducted, although it is possible to speculate that some have accomplished (noncriminal) careers in business and politics. Of course, a forensic clinician might naively postulate that failures to meet societal expectations are *de facto* impairments. This perspective ignores entirely the choicefulness of such defendants.

Many criminal attorneys will see the irony of categorically excluding antisocial personality traits from any consideration of insanity in those states using the ALI standard (see Chapter 7) but potentially embracing identical traits for SVP standards. ALI formulations recognize that most criminal activities are chosen acts, not indicative of compulsions or otherwise impaired conduct.

Clinical methods for evaluating Axis I and Axis II disorders have been well developed and well validated. As noted in previous chapters, structured interviews provide the most systematic data from which forensic clinicians can establish reliable diagnoses and an accurate recording of key symptoms. These measures should also be used to assess critical symptoms and traits that could potentially comprise mental abnormalities. The following structured interviews are recommended:

1. For Axis I symptoms and diagnoses, the SADS provides the best information about the *severity* of symptomatology and any resulting disorders. Other choices include the SCID-IV (First, Spitzer, Williams, & Gibbon, 1997) without the use screening items and possibly the DIS (Robins, Marcus, Reich, et al., 1996).

2. For Axis II traits and diagnoses, the SIDP-IV provides the best information about the pervasiveness of traits and any resulting disorders. Other choices include the IPDE and the SCID-II (see Chapter 4).

Volitional Impairment and Future Risk

Criminal attorneys should be watchful for forensic clinicians that provide the courts with flawed reports and resulting testimony. As noted by Sarkar (2003), the Court in *Crane* held that "the severity of the disorder distinguishes mentally disordered SVPs from 'the dangerous but typical recidivist'" (p. 247 citing footnote 3, p. 5 of the decision). Note that dangerousness by itself is insufficient. In *Crane*, the Court ruled that the SVP standard required a substantial loss of volitional impairment. The majority opinion recognized that volitional impairment "will not be demonstrable with mathematical precision. It is enough to say that there must be proof of serious difficulty in controlling behavior" (p. 413).

The assessment of volitional impairment has been the subject of intense controversy following Hinckley's insanity acquittal. Nonetheless, most of our specialized knowledge of volitionality is based on forensic research involving the assessment of criminal responsibility. As outlined in Chapter 7, the crux of this issue appears directly related to the defendant's capacity to control his or her criminal conduct. In looking at past offenses, did he or she evidence a capacity to choose whether to conduct the sexual acts? Analogous to the "police-at-elbow" rule (see Chapter 7), clear evidence of impaired volitional abilities would be the sex offender whose repetitive conduct occurred irrespective of the consequences. As an example, a known male pedophile within a small community groped an unsuspecting child in front of her playmates. His capacity to stop or even delay his sexually gratifying behavior was severely impaired.

Sexual deviations differ fundamentally from the volitional impairment found with most insanity evaluations on two basic dimensions. First, the SVP law's requirement regarding the loss of behavioral control may be less complete than required by the volitional prong of the ALI rule. This matter is not completely resolved: SVP cases necessitate a "serious difficulty in controlling behavior" (Crane, 2002, p. 413), while the ALI standard demands that the defendant "lacks substantial capacity ... to conform his conduct" (ALI, 1962). Second and more importantly, the standard for SVP laws typically include sexual deviations that are repetitive across time, while the decision of a defendant under the ALI standard does not.

There are not yet forensic guidelines for the SVP assessment of impaired volitional abilities. In its absence, we have developed a basic but not exhaustive outline of the critical issues. As a *minimum* standard, all SVP evaluations should address explicitly the following four issues:

1. *Lack of Choicefulness.* Did the defendant exercise choices? Evidence of planning or rational decisions would support his or her capacity to choose. Importantly, impulsiveness does not negate volition (Sarkar, 2003); a defendant can engage in impulsive, although poorly informed, choices. Instead, forensic clinicians should consider the *driven* nature of SVP conduct and whether it affected the defendant's choicefulness. Evidence of a *driven* conduct is sometimes expressed by the defendant's *disregard for personal consequences*.

2. *Disregard for Personal Consequences.* When engaging in the sex offenses, did the defendant attempt to reduce the negative consequences to him- or herself? Efforts to reduce arrest might include attempts to (1) reduce the likelihood of the victim reporting the crime (e.g., intimidation or ingratiation), (2) minimize the physical evidence (e.g., finger prints and DNA), and (3) decrease the possibility of recognition (e.g., disguises or limiting the victim's view). In contrast, some defendants commit sexual offenses without any regard for the personal consequences. The probability of their arrests and convictions is virtually assured. This disregard for personal consequence may be indirect evidence of *driven* behavior.

3. *Incapacity for Delay.* Was the defendant able to delay sexual gratification via sex offenses for extended periods of time (e.g., months or years)? It is difficult to make the argument that the defendant has

impaired volitional abilities if he or she is able to exercise behavioral control over sexual deviations for indefinite periods. However, the matter of opportunity must also be considered; an institutionalized pedophile may simply not have the opportunity to engage in child molestation. Therefore, forensic clinicians must evaluate the defendant's ability to delay deviant sexual gratification. An example of incapacity would be a sex offender who (1) spent several hours each day seeking opportunities and (2) acted on these opportunities in majority of instances.

4. *Chronicity.* Does the defendant's deviant behavior constitute an enduring characteristic or stable trait? From an impairment perspective, one or several isolated incidents would appear insufficient to establish the impairment component of a mental disorder or mental abnormality.[3] Optimally, forensic clinicians should be able to identify the onset and course of the mental disorder or mental disability. Among sex offenders in particular, an early onset and a discernible pattern of sexual deviation are characteristically found.

In addressing these four issues, forensic clinicians must engage in an individualized assessment of volitional impairment and future risk. As outlined below, risk assessment instruments based simply on *actuarial methods* or *structured clinical judgments* are plainly inadequate to address this relationship. Clearly, the task facing forensic clinicians is much more challenging than merely calculating the number of risk factors, irrespective of volitional abilities and assigning a probability value.

Forensic clinicians must conduct comprehensive evaluations of Axis I and Axis II disorders that are supplemented with an assessment of syndromes and other prominent mental abnormalities. In assessing the relationship between volitional impairment and future risk, three discrete steps must be examined. As outlined in Table 11-1, volitional impairment must be first considered. If established, then two links are vital: With reference to *past and current functioning*, does the volitional impairment arise directly from a mental disorder or abnormality? With reference to *future functioning*, does the volitional impairment directly predict sexual recidivism?

Reviews of risk assessment measures as they relate to SVP evaluations (Conroy, 2003; Harris, Rice, & Quinsey, 1998; Rosell, 2004) reveal a profound oversight. Risk assessment measures do not take into account the array of mental disorders or other clinical conditions that could lead to impaired volitional abilities. In particular, actuarial measures often entirely

---

[3]As a parallel, several isolated experiences with illicit drugs do not establish a sufficient pattern for a substance abuse disorder.

TABLE 11-1. A CHECKLIST FOR VOLITIONAL IMPAIRMENT ARISING FROM A CLINICAL CONDITION AND FUTURE RISK OF SEXUAL RECIDIVISM

Step 1: Is there volitional impairment?
❐ Evidence that the defendant lacked choicefulness?
❐ Evidence that the defendant had no regard for his or her personal consequences?
❐ Evidence that the defendant had an incapacity to delay his or her sexual deviations?
❐ Evidence that the defendant's sexual deviations formed a discernible and stable pattern?

Step 2: Did the volitional impairment result directly from a clinical condition (mental disorder or mental disability)?
❐ Evidence of delusions specifically associated with sexual deviations?
❐ Evidence of command hallucinations specifically associated with sexual deviations?
❐ Evidence of manic-based behavior with severely impaired judgment?
❐ Evidence of severe compulsions arising from an obsessive-compulsive disorder?
❐ Evidence of severely dissociated behavior?
❐ Evidence of dementia or other severe cognitive disorder?
❐ Evidence of uncontrollable impulses associated with severe paraphilias?

Step 3: Does the volitional impairment result directly in a risk of sexual recidivism?
❐ Evidence of a clearly demonstrable pattern with exacerbations in the clinical condition (e.g., manic episode) directly linked to sexual recidivism?
❐ Evidence that deterioration in volitional abilities directly results in sexual recidivism?

neglect any consideration whatsoever of mental disorders or mental abnormality. In contrast, structured clinical judgment typically addresses a few clinical issues but give short shrift to a host of potentially relevant disorders, syndromes, and clinical conditions.

Risk assessment measures entirely overlook the clinically complex issues of assessing volitional abilities in relationship to the mental disorder or mental ability. They also fail to make an empirical link from the disorder/abnormality to the impaired volitional abilities to risk of sexual recidivism. In summary, risk assessment measure fail to establish the critical links required by SVP statutes:

Clinical condition (mental disorder or mental abnormality) → *impaired volitional abilities* → *increased risk of sexual recidivism.*

Criminal attorneys should be aware that many forensic clinicians use popularized risk assessment measures in SVP evaluations, despite their obvious inappropriateness. Commonly used risk assessment measures will be summarized in the next section, *General Cross-Examination Issues.* Attorneys will need to be familiar with these measures in their efforts to discredit expert testimony that falsely presents such data as relevant to SVP standards.

Putting aside all the objections to risk assessment measures, it could be argued that their effectiveness at determining sexual recidivism should be sufficient to determine their scientific admissibility. Even from this circumscribed perspective, the data appear insufficient. Barabaree, Seto, Langton, and Peacock (2001) tested six risk assessment measures. Correlations with sexual recidivism were very modest: .11 for the VRAG, .14 for the MnSOST-R, .17 for the SORAG, .18 for the Static-99, and .26 for the RRASOR (see Appendix H for full names). These correlations generally account for less than 5% of the variance. In addition, their effectiveness (i.e., PPP) and error rates (i.e., 1-PPP) at classifying individual sex offenders are not reported.

Hanson and Bussiere (1998) conducted a meta-analysis of 61 studies to examine the effectiveness of other indices in predicting sexual recidivism. Penile plethysmography was ineffective at predicting adult rape (unweighted median $r = 0.00$; weighted median $r = 0.05$) but modestly effective at child molesting (unweighted median $r = 0.20$; weighted median $r = 0.32$). Interestingly, the diagnosis of antisocial personality disorder performed poorly at predicting sex recidivism (unweighted median $r = 0.17$; weighted median $r = 0.14$). Prior sex offenses varied significantly with the type of victim. A related child victim produced *negative* correlations (unweighted median $r = -0.12$; weighted median $r = -0.11$), whereas a stranger victim (age not specified) resulted in *positive* correlations (unweighted median $r = 0.22$; weighted median $r = 0.15$). Substance abuse appeared to be virtually unrelated to sexual recidivism (unweighted median $r = 0.07$; weighted median $r = 0.04$). These findings, with the assistance of a consulting expert, may be very useful in rebutting clinical speculations about predictors of sexual recidivism.

GENERAL CROSS-EXAMINATION ISSUES

Competent testimony can be provided in extreme SVP cases where a severe disorder or other clinical condition can be directly linked to the defendant's impaired volitional abilities that result in a clearly documented and indisputable pattern of sexually deviant behavior. However, most SVP cases are far more ambiguous. Both defense counsel and prosecutors have a professional responsibility not to "mislead the judge and jury by artifice of law and fact" (*The Florida Bar v. Schaub*, 1993, p. 204), which includes making knowingly false statements about expert testimony.

Many forensic clinicians do not have a sophisticated understanding the SVP criteria and their legal bases (Jackson, 2003). Attorneys have a professional responsibility to ensure that a correct understanding of the SVP statute for their particular state and an overall understanding of the relevant appellate cases including the Supreme Court's findings in *Hendricks* and *Crane*. In addition, forensic clinicians must have specialized clinical knowledge regarding the assessment of sex offenders in general and the SVP evaluations in particular.

Expert Qualifications

Attorneys should not take for granted that forensic clinicians are qualified by their professional training and education to be involved in SVP cases and provide expert testimony. As *minimal* professional standards, forensic clinicians should meet the following criteria prior to any SVP consultations:

1. A minimum of 1 year post-doctoral experience in the forensic assessment of sex offenders. This requirement could be met by several years of part-time experience.
2. A working knowledge of SVP standards including the relevant state statute and appellate cases.
3. Expertise on the psychometric properties of risk assessment measures and other specialized methods. This expertise includes a sophisticated knowledge of their respective strengths and limitations.

Attorneys should be especially concerned about newly developed SVP programs in which clinicians are "learning on the job." We advise that attorneys closely examine the qualifications of each forensic clinician. We are troubled by the plethora of weekend workshops designed to "train" clinicians in risk assessment.

Limitations and Potential Biases in SVP Consultations

The lack of consensus on the meaning of such ambiguous constructs as "mental abnormality" and "impaired volitional abilities" is a fundamental problem for SVP cases (Tucker & Brakel, 2003). In cross-examination, criminal attorneys may wish to stress the inexactitude of these constructs and their vulnerability to the expert's preconceived notions. Box 11-1 offers illustrative cross-examination for exposing the conceptual weaknesses of SVP constructs and the obvious lack of consensus among forensic clinicians.

A specific concern for cross-examination is that the forensic clinician may simply attempt to equate a "low" or "deviant" score on a psychological measure with a mental abnormality. If this *normative* analysis is allowed, then virtually all persons including sex offenders are liable to qualify. Attorneys must be prepared to address this matter forcefully. As a possible example, #6 in Box 11-1 provides sample questions. The point is to illustrate that "deviations from average" are pervasive and cannot meaningfully inform SVP determinations.

Box 11-1   Illustrative Cross-Examination Questions on Sexually
Violent Predator Cases: Professional Understanding and
Specialized Knowledge

1. *Doctor, is your testimony today based on a correct understanding of the Sexually Violent Predator statute and your specialized knowledge of clinical and legal issues as they relate to this statute?* [if equivocates about specialized knowledge, pursue this issue...without relevant expertise, opinion testimony may be circumscribed]

2. *Are you aware of any Supreme Court cases that would guide you in conducting a sexually violent predator evaluation?* [If quibbles about this being a legal matter]...*As a forensic* [select: psychologist/psychiatrist], *what sources do you rely on for your specialized knowledge?* [if educated by others] ... *What sources did they rely on in educating you?* ... [if appropriate] *So you relied on the Supreme Court cases but weren't qualified to read them, is that correct?*

3. *Would you agree with me that you can't be an expert if you don't know what you are talking about?*

4. [mental disorder or mental abnormality] *When the Sexually Violent Predator statute refers to __* [use precise language], *what is professional understanding of this term? ... Is this professional understanding based on specialized knowledge? ... What is its sources?*

5. [if mental abnormality] *How does the American Psychiatric Association define "mental abnormality" in its official DSM book?* [it doesn't] ... *What is the official definition of a "mental disability" by the American Psychological Association?* [none] *Can you cite even one officially-sanctioned definition of "mental abnormality" by a national professional organization? ... Any authoritative sources recognized by profession? ... Isn't is true, doctor, that you are flying by the seat of your pants when it comes to something so basic as defining a "mental abnormality?"*

6. [very optional] *Isn't one definition of a "mental abnormality" something that is markedly different from average? ... Would this be called a "normative analysis" of "mental abnormality?" ... I know you are modest, but wouldn't you consider yourself to be a person of superior intelligence? ... Isn't that far higher than average? ... In the lack of any professional consensus about what constitutes a "mental abnormality" we don't really know if your superior intelligence would qualify do we?* [likely to quibble; patiently ask about national professional standards and underscore the level of professional ignorance] ... *Please don't get defensive, what are the national standards that define "mental abnormality?* [Etc.]

7. [volitional impairment] *Doctor, what is your professional understanding of volitional impairment? ... Would the an "inability to choose" be a key component of volitional impairment? ... How would you define an "inability to choose?" ... Thank you. And how would define the opposite, a "capacity to choose?"*

8. *As an attorney, I can choose whether to ask you any further questions or not, isn't that correct? ... What would this "capacity to choose" say about my volitional abilities?*

(Continued)

9. *If a defendant were able to control [his/her] criminal activity for months or even years, what would that say about their volitional abilities?* [likely to respond ambiguously] . . . *Doctor, don't we all have wild impulses that we keep under control?* [if "yes"] . . . *What would be an example of one of your wild impulses?* [if appropriate] . . . *Let's say as a hypothetical that you may have acted on this impulse several times in the past, would that necessarily mean that you have a volitional impairment as you sit here today? . . . Why not?*

10. [use only for symptoms *not* addressed in the forensic report] *Would it be correct that psychotic symptoms such as command hallucinations or delusions could lead to volitional impairment? . . . What about manic symptoms such as impaired judgment? And severe compulsions related to anxiety disorders? . . . What about periods of dissociation as found in fugue states, could they lead to volitional impairment? . . . What about severe cognitive problems, such as dementias? . . . Or impulse-control disorders such as pyromania?*

11. *Where in your report to you address command hallucinations?* [continue through relevant questions]

12. *Isn't it ethically required that you report all-important findings, not just those your attorney likes? . . . Isn't the presence or absence of command hallucinations relevant to volitional abilities? . . . What stopped you from being objective and putting this relevant information in your report that* [select: helps/hurts] *the defendant?*

Many SVP evaluations are narrowly focused and do not consider the possible relationships between clinical conditions (mental disorders or mental disabilities) and volitional impairment. Illustrative questions (see #10 and #11) are intended to highlight the inadequacies and possible biases found in some SVP consultations. The matter of bias is occasionally transparent. What other explanation can be offered if an expert only addresses a few clinical conditions (e.g., specific paraphilias) but intentionally disregards of host of other conditions (e.g., psychotic and manic symptoms)?

We suspect but cannot demonstrate empirically that some forensic clinicians engage in backward reasoning. They begin with the conclusion (e.g., "likely recidivator") and then selectively seek evidence to prove this conclusion. This serious problem is known as a "confirmatory bias." The problem for cross-examination is that forensic clinicians are unlikely to acknowledge confirmatory bias, given its implications for the persuasiveness of their testimony. One option on cross-examination is a methodical step-by-step review of the SVP determination. After this review, the attorney may attempt to uncover confirmatory bias. Take for example a forensic clinician with a strong prosecutorial perspective. Some possible strategies include

- *What would be alternative explanations for __* [negative conclusion]? For instance, a male defendant may have acknowledged past problems in controlling his sexual behavior. Instead of summarily concluding that this is evidence of "impaired volitional abilities," an alternative explanation is that the defendant is both gaining insight into his past misconduct and accepting responsibility for his actions.

• *What are the* _protective_ *factors that should be considered in this case?* Risk assessment encompasses both risk (variables that *increase* the likelihood of recidivism) and protective (variables that *decrease* the likelihood of recidivism) factors (Rogers, 2000). Focusing only on the risk factors may well produce a highly biased report. Some experts may not even be aware of potentially relevant *protective* factors (see also Chapter 9).

• *Isn't it true you focused only on* _static_ *factors and virtually ignored* _dynamic_ *factors?* The exclusive or nearly exclusive use of static factors may reflect a strong prosecutorial bias. The defendant can never change his or her gender or criminal past (e.g., age of first arrest). A predominant focus on static factors is tantamount to a "natural-life" SVP commitment.

SVP consultations with confirmatory biases may be overly focused and not even address the breadth of relevant clinical-forensic issues. A defense expert may incautiously conclude that an SVP finding is unwarranted because a male defendant's paraphilias did not "compel" his sexual misconduct. As outlined in Table 11-1, many other clinical conditions may contribute to volitional impairment. Each SVP report should be scrutinized for evidence of a one-sided presentation.

Misuse of Risk-Assessment Measures

Chapter 9 provides a useful distinction between criminal-justice measures and psychological measures. Criminal-justice measures (e.g., Static-99 and RRASOR) have no psychological variables and are beyond the scope of training and credentialing for psychologists and psychiatrists. Therefore, the use of such measures should be attacked on cross-examination as exceeding the experts' specialized knowledge.

A pivotal issue for cross-examination is the mismatch between SVP standards and risk-assessment measures. Because of this disparity, the following observation must be underscored: *Risk assessment methods do not address the relevant components of SVP standards.* Appendix H includes a reproducible table that summarizes the limitations of using risk assessment measures in SVP cases. Four key points must be emphasized:

1. All the reviewed risk assessment measures have "no" or "very limited coverage" of mental conditions (i.e., disorders including personality disorders and mental abnormalities). We have operationally defined "very limited coverage" as *missing more than 95%* of the possible mental conditions.
2. Risk assessment measures do not address volitional impairment. With one very minor exception (MnSOST-R), they simply ignore any systematic appraisal of volitional abilities.
3. Risk assessment measures categorically neglect the *Crane* requirement that volitional impairment arises from the mental condition (see "nexus" column in Appendix H).
4. Most risk assessment measures do not adequately define or provide research on sexual violence. In many instances, violent recidivism is nonspecific and includes non-sexual violence; these predictions are inappropriate to SVP cases. In other instances, it includes nonviolent offenses (e.g., obscene letters) in its overly broad categorization of sexual violence; these predictions are also inappropriate to SVP cases.

The SVP riddle for criminal attorneys: What does not measure the requisite mental condition, ignores volitional abilities, and offers inadequate predictions about sexual violence? The answer is clearly "risk assessment measures." Appendix H presents with summary data that may be helpful for cross-examination. Some attorneys may wish to make a demonstrative display so that the triers of fact can actually visualize the inapplicability of specific risk assessment methods for SVP determinations. Absent perjured testimony, the inescapable conclusion is that the "heart" of SVP evaluations (i.e., full range of clinical conditions, impaired volitional abilities, and the relationship of impaired volition to sexual recidivism) *simply cannot be evaluated* with the current risk assessment measures.

Box 11-2 outlines cross-examination strategies that are common to most risk assessment measures. Attorneys should be warned that the proliferation of such measures is likely to continue unabated; however, these basic strategies are likely to remain applicable. To remain current, attorneys should perform Internet searches and consult with their own experts.

A very common problem is that most risk assessment measures were developed in Canada, thereby creating two basic limitations: (1) cultural differences including markedly lower rates of sexual assault, and (2) a minority representation that is strikingly discrepant from the populations of the African Americans and Hispanic Americans found in the United States. Some forensic clinicians may try to gloss over these fundamental differences. Box 11-2 suggests some ideas to expose misleading testimony.

Box 11-2 Illustrative Cross-Examination Questions on
Sexually Violent Predator Cases and Risk Assessment Measures

Components of the Sexually Violent Predator statutes need to be addressed first; see Box 11-1. Attorneys need to be aware that Risk Assessment Measures are proliferating often with modest validation. Box 11-2 is intended to provide a conceptual overview with sample questions.

A. Cross-Cultural Applicability

1. *Doctor, are you sensitive to ethnic and cultural issues? . . . Would you be the kind of expert that says–if it works for Whites then it must work for Blacks?*

2. *Isn't it true that different cultures may respond differently? . . . That results from one culture can't be indiscriminately applied to another?*

3. *When were you planning to let the Court know that* __ **[select: HCR-20, RRASOR, SORAG, SVR-20, or VRAG]** *was primarily developed and validated in Canada?*

4. *In all honesty, doctor, aren't there dramatic differences in patterns of sex offenses between Canada and the United States? . . . Are you aware that Americans commit about 10 times more sex offenses when you control for differences in population? . . . That's a huge difference isn't it?*

5. *Isn't it also true that Canada does* not *have a statute similar in content to Sexually Violent Predator? . . . So you are not trying to mislead the Court that* __ **[select: HCR-20, RRASOR, SORAG, SVR-20, or VRAG]** *was developed to assess sexually violent predator, are you?*

6. *Isn't it a fact that the Canadians couldn't really test any measure on the Sexually Violent Predator statute, because it* doesn't even exist *in Canada?*

7. [These questions can be repeated for each Canadian measure used.]

B. Mental Disorder [Use only if applicable to your jurisdiction]

8. *Are you aware the Sexually Violent Predator statute requires that risk of sexual recidivism be based on a mental disorder? . . . Isn't it true that* __ [measure] *does not formally assess DSM-IV mental disorders? . . . [if quibbles] Or,* any formal diagnosis *of mental disorders?*

9. *Which personality disorders were specifically* tested *in the validation of* __ [measure]? . . . *Which personality disorders were specifically* omitted *in the validation of* __ [measure]? [if appropriate] . . . *What* standardized *tools did you use to* systematically *evaluate the defendant for each of the 10 personality disorders?*

10. *Doesn't this come down to a bunch of guesses based on untested assumptions? . . . You haven't formally tested all the personality disorders on* __ [measure], *have you? . . . [when appropriate] You have already admitted to not using standardized tools in assessing the defendant's personality disorders, isn't that correct? . . . Shouldn't the Court know all the shortcomings of* __ [measure] *when it comes to mental disorders? . . . Forget whose paying for your testimony today and tell the Court about all these shortcomings.*

C. Mental Abnormality [Use only if applicable to your jurisdiction]

11. *How many items are scored on* __ [measure]?

12. *Are you aware the Sexually Violent Predator statute requires that risk of sexual recidivism be based on a mental abnormality? . . . What is the*

(Continued)

official definition of a mental disorder? [see also Box 11-1, #2 through #6]

13. *Could severe symptoms possibly qualify as mental abnormalities? . . . Based on your knowledge of DSM-IV, isn't there hundreds of symptoms for Axis I disorders alone? . . . And more than 100 additional symptoms for Axis II disorders? . . . Are mental abnormalities limited to severe symptoms? . . . Isn't it possible there are hundreds of other mental abnormalities not even covered by diagnostic symptoms?*

14. *Let's be honest, doctor– even if every item of ___ [measure] address mental abnormalities, you would cover less than 1% of the possible mental abnormalities, isn't that correct? . . . In all honesty, you would miss more than 99% of possible mental abnormalities, isn't that right? . . . How did you let this critical piece of information be "glossed over" when you were testifying to the <u>whole truth</u> on direct examination?*

15. *If the measure doesn't take into account most mental abnormalities, how can it possibly be accurate for those defendants with these abnormalities?* [critical point; may need restressing]

D. Impaired Volitional Abilities

16. *Are you aware the Supreme Court requires that the defendant must show a lack of volitional impairment before the Sexually Violent Predator statute should be applied?* [likely objection]

17. *Are you aware that the Sexually Violent Predator statute does not apply to all sex offenders? . . . Isn't it true that it only applies to sex offenders with impaired volitional abilities?*

18. *Isn't is also true that ___ [measure] does <u>not</u> assess impaired volitional abilities? . . .* [if quibbles] *Tell us, doctor, which specific items assess impaired volitional abilities? . . .* [many risk assessment measures are available online; when available, print the list of items] *. . . Do you recognize these items from ___ [measure]? . . . Let's go through them one at a time, does this item, "___," directly assess impaired volitional abilities?* [repeat as necessary]

19. *When were you going to get around to telling this Court that ___ [measure], does not address a key component of the Sexually Violent Predator standard? . . . Don't you think the Court deserves to know that ___ [measure] is not relevant to the Sexually Violent Predator standard?*

[The key issue is found in *Crane*: "It is enough to say that there must be proof of serious difficulty in controlling behavior. And this, when viewed in light of such features of the case as the nature of the psychiatric diagnosis, and the severity of the mental abnormality itself, must be sufficient to distinguish the dangerous sexual offender whose serious mental illness, abnormality, or disorder subjects him to civil commitment from the dangerous but typical recidivist convicted in an ordinary criminal case."]

20. *Does ___ [measure] even bother to distinguish recidivism based on impaired volitional abilities from other types of recidivism?* [no] *. . . Then we have no idea whether these results apply to the Sexually Violent Predator statute isn't that true? . . . Therefore, we cannot assume these results have <u>any</u> weight in deciding a Sexually Violent Predator case, isn't that true, doctor?*

As previously discussed, risk assessment measures do not adequately assess clinical conditions (mental disorder or mental disability) that are a requisite condition for SVP determinations. Most actuarial measures (e.g., RRASOR and Static-99) simply ignore clinical conditions in their exclusive use of demographic and criminological variables. Completely lacking the requisite condition (mental disorder or mental disability), these measures are clearly irrelevant to SVP determinations. Other risk assessment measures utilize "structured clinical judgment"; these measures provide inadequate coverage of the specific Axis I and Axis II disorders. Box 11-2 provides a general framework for uncovering these weaknesses.

Simply put, risk assessment measures do not even *attempt* to evaluate impaired volitional abilities. Box 11-2 is intended as a starting point. Attorneys will need to prepare in consultation with their own experts, rigorous cross-examination on this pivotal issue. As articulated in *Crane*, mentally disordered defendants with impaired volitional abilities must be distinguished "from the dangerous but typical recidivist" (p. 413). A major thrust of cross-examination should be distinguishing between the two:

1. *What predictions does __ [measure] provide for the "dangerous but typical recidivist" who commits sexual assaults?*
2. *What separate predictions does __ [measure] provide for the sex offender with impaired volitional abilities?*

Currently, risk assessment measures are based on #1 and *not* on #2. We recommend that attorneys be fully prepared to address obfuscations and equivocations. Experts may be reluctant to make concessions strike to the heart of the matter and may weaken both their conclusions and credibility.

Research on the Mn-SOST-R (Epperson, Kaul, Huot, Goldman, & Alexander, 2003) illustrates several important points. First, the requisite mental condition and concomitant volitional impairment were not addressed. Second, alpha coefficients and standard errors of measurements were simply not reported. Third, the research underscored the importance of cross-validation. Initial results yielded much lower estimates on cross-validation (see Epperson et al., 2003, Table 6, p. 42): Risk Level 2 from 31 to 19%; Risk Level 3 from 61 to 52%; Refer (i.e., the highest risk) from 92 to 54%.

Psychological measures must meet explicit test standards that were officially adopted by the American Psychological Association, the American Educational Research Association, and the National Council on Measurement in Education. The *Standards for educational and psychological testing* (AERA/APA/NCME, 1999) officially articulate these requirements. Reliability cannot be assumed but must be demonstrated. With the help of a consulting expert, the attorney can often expose basic failings in the validation of risk assessment measures. Importantly, these standards cannot be circumvented by changing the name (i.e., test, scale, instrument, or measure).[4]

Box 11-2 illustrates the limitation of risk assessment measures in addressing the requisite mental condition. Whether a mental disorder, personality disorder, or mental abnormality, risk assessment measures are not equal to the task. It also provides sample questions for underscoring the inapplicability of risk assessment measures to the evaluation of volitional impairment. The goal is extract concession after concession from the expert regarding the fundamental weaknesses of his or her methods. Continued attempts to defend risk assessment measure for either the mental condition or impaired volition should further damage the expert's credibility.

Cross-examining attorneys will likely need a consulting expert to address the psychometric deficiencies of risk assessment measures. Some risk assessment measure are composed of several scales or subscales. When items are combined into a scale for clinical interpretation, those items should "hang together" and be measuring the same concept. If they do not, then the scale lacks internal consistency. *Alpha* is the most commonly used statistic, although others are occasionally applied. The most common approach is to calculate alpha coefficients. Here are sample cross-examination questions:

1. *What is an alpha coefficient?* [poorly trained clinicians may not know]
2. *Why is alpha critical to the validation of any scale?* ... [if applicable] *Isn't it true that the authors of _ [measure] did even not bother to report alphas?*

Both science and sound clinical practice requires that results are reproducible and do not vary dramatically based on the individual evaluator. *Interrater reliability* measures the degree of agreement across experts for the same time period. Sample questions include the following:

3. *What is interrater reliability? ... Why is interrater reliability critical to the validation of any scale?*
4. [if applicable] *Isn't it true that the authors of _ [measure] did not bother to report estimates of interrater reliability?*

---

[4]As noted in Chapter 5, the *Standards* (p. 3) affirm the following, "The applicability of the Standards to an evaluation device or method is not altered by the label applied to it (e.g., test, assessment, scale, inventory)."

No measurements are perfectly accurate. Even with well-validated measures, possibility of some error must taken into account when measuring complex constructs. For this purpose, the official test standards (AERA/APA/NCME, 1999) require that "standard errors of measurement" be documented for items and scales. They provide essential data on the reliability of individual scores (Anastasi, 1988). When standard errors of measurement are either missing or large, then the accuracy of our predictions is compromised. Consider the following questions with all risk assessment measures.

5. *What is the standard error of measurement? . . . Why is the standard error of measurement critical to the validation of any scale?*
6. *Isn't it true that the authors of __ [measure] did not bother to report the standard error of measurement?* [true for most risk assessment measures, but *not* the PCL-R]

Several risk assessment measures have specific weaknesses that should be explored through cross-examination (see Box 11-3). For example, the primary validation of the VRAG included patients involuntarily administered hallucinogens (e.g., LSD) and forced to participate in nude

---

Box 11-3   ILLUSTRATIVE CROSS-EXAMINATION QUESTIONS FOR SPECIFIC
                RISK ASSESSMENT MEASURES

RRASOR and Static-99

1. *What are the different items assessed by [RRASOR/Static-99]? . . . Are these items found routinely in police records? . . .*
2. *These are simple variables, correct? . . . Anyone with a high school education and a bit of practice be able collect these variables, isn't that correct?*
3. *Once they are collected, all you do is add them up, isn't that so? . . . Then you look at a table that tells you the level of risk? . . . [if relevant] Anyone on the jury could count these variables and look at a table, isn't that right?*
4. *How much did you charge for collecting these simple variables and adding them up?* [may underestimate] *. . . So how many minutes did it take?*
5. *Isn't it true that you didn't need to be a highly-paid forensic* [select: psychologist/psychiatrist] *to collect and count these simple variables? . . . Are you trying to make this look a validated test simply to justify your charges?*
6. [One option is to move to exclude this testimony as not being based on specialized psychological or psychiatric knowledge.]
7. *Doctor, do you believe it is possible for criminals to change over time? . . . Using only static variables, isn't it true this measure does not take into account the possibility of change? . . . Isn't it a biased measure that never provides the best defendant with even the possibility of positive change? . . . Isn't it also a biased measure that never provides the worst defendant with even the possibility of negative change?*

(*Continued*)

VRAG

Validation (also applies to the SORAG)

1. *Doctor, was the VRAG validated in Canada at the Oak Ridge Division, is that correct?*

2. *Are you aware that many of the patients in the VRAG's validation were part of therapeutic community program?*

3. *Anything about the therapeutic community program that might worry you about whether we can generalize its results to modern facilities in the United States?*

4. *So, the fact that patients at this hospital were being routinely treated with LSD wouldn't bother you?*

5. *Has the use of nude marathons ever been an accepted treatment for psychotic patients?*

6. *What about the use of the Total Encounter Capsule forcing patients to stay in a small, bare, windowless room and participate in group therapy for up to 11 days . . . is that accepted treatment for psychotic patients?*

7. *Judged by modern American standards, wasn't this treatment at Oak Ridge grossly inadequate and unethical?*

VRAG Scoring

8. *On the VRAG scoring, you would see my client as less dangerous if he had* <u>killed</u> *a woman rather than* <u>simply injuring</u> *her, isn't that correct? . . . Isn't this science gone mad?*

9. *On the VRAG scoring, you would penalize the defendant more for injuring a woman than a man, isn't that correct? . . . Wasn't the VRAG developed mostly by men? . . . Do you think they have something against women?*

HCR-20 and SVR-20

1. *The [HCR-20/SVR-20] is a structured clinical guide, isn't that correct? . . . Its items were "based on a review of the scientific and professional literature" on sexual violence, correct?* [The quote is from the test promotional material.]

2. *Do these items form several scales? . . . What are the names of these scales? . . . How do the items on __ scale correlate with each other?* [This information is unavailable] *. . . So you don't know for sure whether they are highly correlated or not? . . . If they are* <u>highly</u> *correlated, how would that invalidate the scale? . . . If they are uncorrelated, how would that invalidate the scale? . . . If they are* <u>negatively</u> *correlated, how would that invalidate the scale? . . . Do you feel entirely comfortable, doctor, using a measure that may well be invalid?*

3. *Do you believe that you are a fair and impartial expert? . . . I would like you to review the items on the [HCR-20/SVR-20] . . . In all honesty, doctor, aren't they all gunning for the defendant–trying to make [him/her] look violent?* [likely to quibble] *Can you point out a couple items that make [him/her] look to safe? . . . How can you be impartial and use an obviously biased measure?*

4. *Does the fact that the decision model has not been validated cause you any concern?*

marathons. Triers of fact can draw their own conclusions about the adequacy of treatment and the confidence that should be placed in subsequent research. Box 11-3 is intended in highlight specific weaknesses of particular risk assessment measures. More importantly, Box 11-3 should persuade criminal attorneys and their experts to examine all risk assessment measures for flagrant deficiencies in their development and validation. As observed by Ryan (2002), judges are dismayed by VRAG scoring that gives defendants *credit* for murder and penalizes them for simple assault.

A specific problem with structured clinical guides (e.g., HCR-20 and SVR-20) occurs when forensic clinicians pretend that they are empirically sound measures. These guides can be used to organize clinical material analogous to a checklist format. However, the crucial line is crossed when forensic clinicians either quantify scores or create scales. At that moment, the structured clinical guide becomes a "test," according to the official standards, that must be psychometrically validated. A particular problem with the HCR-20 and SVR-20 is that their variables were gleaned from the professional literature with no formal investigation of their multicollinearity or empirical support. Both item redundancy (e.g., high intercorrelations) and clinical folklore (e.g., intuitive but invalid variables) may contribute to consequential but unknown inaccuracies.

SUMMARY

Jackson et al. (2004) conducted the first experimental study to systematically assess the accuracy of forensic clinicians when provided with standardized clinical data. On the basis of outcome data, they found that forensic psychologists were inaccurate nearly two-thirds (64%) of the time at identifying cases with sexually violent recidivism. Surprisingly, the inaccuracy for practicing forensic psychologists was *greater* than graduate students who lacked their training and experience. Finally, their confidence in their prediction of sexual violence was slightly <u>higher</u> in cases where they were *inaccurate*. As one study using four case vignettes, this research is far from conclusive. Nevertheless, it raises disturbing and fundamental questions about expertise of forensic clinicians. These critical questions remain unanswered.

As noted in the introduction, the rapid emergence of SVP standards exerted considerable pressure on forensic clinicians to conduct SVP evaluations before the development of specialized knowledge and measures. These exigencies often led to compromises that threaten the integrity of forensic psychology and psychiatry. While the American Psychological Association has remained conspicuously silent, the American

Psychiatric Association has played an active role in underscoring pervasive problems in both conceptualization and methodology for SVP determinations.

This chapter has underscored the complexities of SVP evaluations and the compelling need for forensic clinicians to develop a sophisticated understanding of SVP standards and appellate interpretations of their components. In addition, forensic clinicians must develop expertise regarding sex offenders, paraphilias, and other sexual deviations. Knowledge of risk assessment methods and their general inapplicability to SVP determinations is vital. In the end, attorneys are also responsible for the integrity of the criminal justice system. They must ensure that experts do not substitute expediency for excellence and that each component of SVP standards is competently evaluated.

12

Integration: Themes in Criminal Forensic Practice

The purpose of this brief chapter is to address overarching themes in forensic psychology and psychiatry that apply to assessment of criminal law issues. Beyond theory, these overarching themes have direct relevance to forensic practice. We combine general issues from the Foundations of Practice with the forensic science and practice as they relate to specific psycholegal standards arising from criminal law. This integrative chapter further prepares criminal attorneys and forensic psychologists and psychiatrists by broadening the discussion across the existing methods, knowledge, and standards.

SCIENCE AND SKILL IN CLINICAL FORENSIC PRACTICE

Chapter 1 introduces the *legal-empirical-forensic* model that forms the foundation for the modern practice of forensic psychology and psychiatry. Focusing for the moment on the element of empirically validated methods, the pivotal question asked in Chapter 1 is, *"How do you know what you claim to know?"* The last eight chapters chronicle the notable successes and remaining challenges for forensic practice in establishing empirically based knowledge. Without empirically based knowledge built on scientific methodology, experts lose their claim to expertise.

Empirically based knowledge, once derived, cannot be magically employed to criminal defendants. It must be systematically and transparently applied in each case. Forensic clinicians should not be allowed to hide behind vague and unverifiable justifications for their conclusions under the guise of "clinical judgment." Without clear and understandable reasoning based on clinical data, the denotation of "clinical judgment" provides no assurance that an opinion is empirically based. With clear and understandable reasoning and data, this term is unnecessary. Attorneys have a responsibility to ensure that vague and unverifiable justifications are not accepted as valid conclusions based on specialized knowledge.

A major theme of this book is the proficient application of standardized methods for evaluating legally relevant multiaxial diagnoses and psycholegal issues. We maintain that standardization is the bedrock of empirically based knowledge. Without standardization, diagnoses and forensic conclusions are vulnerable to imprecision and error.

DIAGNOSES AND FORENSIC PRACTICE

The bedrock of forensic practice is the accurate assessment of legally relevant diagnoses, syndromes, and symptoms. Without accurate and reliable assessment, the entire enterprise is vulnerable to subjectivity and bias. Accurate assessment forms the necessary basis for more specialized evaluations of psycholegal issues.

A common question raised in earlier chapters is whether crucial opinions about legal standards should rely *entirely* on unstandardized diagnoses and unsystematic appraisal of symptoms. The next three subsections consider the accuracy and admissibility of unstandardized diagnoses, standardized diagnoses, and extrapolated diagnoses.

Unstandardized Diagnoses

Many forensic clinicians are likely to bristle at the notion that unstandardized diagnoses are often inaccurate. However, recent research suggests that mental health diagnoses are rife with significant inaccuracies. These inaccuracies include both *missed diagnoses* and *misdiagnoses* (Rogers, 2003a). *Missed diagnoses* occur when clinicians fail to diagnose a mental disorder that is present in the patient. In contrast, *misdiagnoses* occur when clinicians inaccurately diagnose a mental disorder that is not present in

TABLE 12-1. INACCURACIES IN UNSTANDARDIZED DIAGNOSES: MAJOR DEPRESSION AND SCHIZOPHRENIA

Study	Sample	Major Depression (%)		Schizophrenia (%)	
		Missed diagnoses	Misdiagnoses	Missed diagnoses	Misdiagnoses
Primary Care Settings					
Tiemens et al. (1999)	713	60	52	NS	NS
Lowe et al. (2004)	288	60	54	NS	NS
Schwenk et al. (1996)	92	65	NS	NS	NS
Christensen et al. (2003)	701	54	48	NS	NS
Mental Health Settings					
Shear et al. (2000)	164	54	28	NS[a]	NS[b]
Basco et al. (2000)[c]	200	50	24	18	30
North et al. (1997)	130	61	22	31	47

Note. Unstandardized diagnoses were compared to independent evaluations using validated structured inteviews. NS = not studied.
[a] For 5 SCID-based psychotic diagnoses, 100% were missed diagnoses.
[b] For 5 SCID-based psychotic diagnoses, 100% were misdiagnoses.
[c] These percentages are likely to be overly positive; the study suffered from criterion contamination which typically inflates estimates of accurate diagnoses.

the patient. Both types of diagnostic errors have serious consequences for forensic consultations by introducing fundamental mistakes in the evaluative process and resulting conclusions.

In primary care settings, clinical research has focused extensively on uncomplicated diagnosis of major depression. This common diagnosis is a hit-or-miss proposition. The majority of patients with major depression go undiagnosed (see Table 12-1). When the diagnosis of major depression is rendered, the likelihood of it being accurate is about 50%. Other diagnoses reflect a similar pattern of accuracy (Christensen et al., 2003). However, these findings have only limited relevance to forensic practice. Often, forensic psychologists and psychiatrists rely on medical records to document earlier diagnoses and past episodes in their evaluation of criminal defendants. The majority of these mental health diagnoses are rendered by health care professionals. Therefore, forensic clinicians must scrutinize records for evidence of diagnostic inclusion criteria. Otherwise, the ready acceptance of past diagnoses may introduce more errors than accuracies.

Mental health professionals using unstandardized assessments were more accurate than primary care professionals in the diagnosis of major depression (see Table 12-1) and other nonpsychotic disorders. Nonetheless, the percentage of missed diagnoses for major depression still exceeded 50% (weighted $M = 54.2\%$). When major depression was diagnosed, mental health professionals achieved a moderate level of accuracy but were still inaccurate in about one-fourth of the cases. For the diagnosis of schizophrenia, the percentage of diagnoses missed by mental health professionals decreased (weighted $M = 23.2\%$), but the percentage of misdiagnoses increased substantially (weighted $M = 36.7\%$). Importantly, a methodological flaw (i.e., criterion contamination) in the Basco et al. (2000) study probably results in an *underestimate* of these inaccuracies.

Standardized Diagnoses

Clinical researchers recognized in the 1970s in studies on the evaluation and treatment of mental disorders that diagnostic imprecisions were unacceptable. For close to three decades, extensive research has sought to standardize and validate structured interviews (Rogers, 1995, 2001). Structured interviews have systematized the diagnostic inquiries, clinical ratings, and diagnoses of both Axis I and Axis II disorders. Criminal attorneys often encounter forensic clinicians who have not stayed abreast of these important diagnostic advances during the last 25 years. Tradition and insularity are insufficient excuses for not providing the courts with the best-validated information (see Chapter 3).

Forensic clinicians systematically using structured interviews can standardize the diagnostic coverage and symptom appraisal. Their major advantages are enumerated in Appendix I. The two most salient advantages are increased reliability and increased accuracy:

- *Increased reliability.* Structured interviews can be tested and further refined to improve their reliability. A basic requirement of science and any empirically based assessment is that the results are reproducible. For example, structured interviews are routinely tested to ensure that different clinicians evaluating the same patient will yield similar results. Without the demonstrable reliability of structured interviews, diagnoses lack empirical validation. *An unstandardized interview yields unverifiable results.*
- *Increased accuracy.* Structured interviews ensure adequate to excellent coverage of relevant mental disorders. This coverage reduces the likelihood of *missed diagnoses.* In addition, structured interviews provide systematic ratings of symptoms and associated features. This standardization, often corresponding with DSM nosology, reduces the likelihood of *misdiagnoses.*

An additional advantage found with certain structured interviews is the reliable assessment of symptom severity. For most criminal-forensic

issues, the mere presence or absence of a symptom is helpful but insufficient. More helpful is systematic data that documents the severity of a
symptom regarding (1) its intensity (e.g., frequency and duration) and
(2) concomitant impairment (e.g., effects of goal-oriented behavior).

Extrapolated Diagnoses

Traditional psychological testing provides valuable information about
clinical correlates (e.g., descriptors of individual MMPI-2 scales) and patterns of psychopathology (e.g., MMPI-2 codetypes). However, these measures are not diagnostic tools. In the case of the MMPI-2, its potential usefulness as a diagnostic measure has not proved successful and has been largely
ignored by current research. Even automated interpretations, known for
their overinterpretation (see Rogers, 2003b), do not attempt to offer DSM
diagnoses. Instead, these interpretations simply list possible disorders that
require fuller evaluations.

One exception is the MCMI-III, which purports to provide diagnostic
data on Axis II disorders (see also Chapter 7). Rogers (2003b) outlined the
unacceptable error rates for the MCMI-III. Its false-positive rates of approximately 80% means that it misdiagnoses personality disorders about four
out of five times. More recent research attempting to improve MCMI-III
diagnostic classifications were fundamentally flawed.

Projective measures sometimes provide diagnostic data but their findings should not be mistaken for either a formal diagnosis or a systematic
appraisal of symptoms. As outlined in Appendix I, coverage of symptoms
and reliability of diagnoses are rarely addressed in research on projective
measures. At best, projective measures provide a general indicator regarding the likelihood of a few general disorders. They make no attempt to
provide broad diagnostic coverage or to assess reliably the presence or
severity of specific symptoms.

The Rorschach has several indexes including the Schizophrenia Index
(SCZI) and the Depression Index (DEPI) which provide general diagnostic
data but no specific disorders. For these indexes, Wiener (1998) concluded
the low scores on either index had *no* diagnostic significance because low
scores do not rule out these disorders. High scores suggest "schizophrenia spectrum disorder" (p. 151), which may include such diagnoses as
"schizophrenia, schizophreniform, and delusional disorder, and paranoid
and schizotypal personality disorder" (p. 152). Likewise, high scores on
DEPI may include a spectrum of diagnoses: "major depressive disorder,
dysthymia, bipolar disorder, cyclothymia, and borderline personality disorder" (p. 152). The Rorschach cannot be used to rule out or to establish
specific diagnoses.

Cross-Examination of Unstandardized and Extrapolated Diagnoses

This section addresses diagnostic evaluations that *exclude* standardized diagnoses. Most forensic assessments include traditional interviews and some input from psychological testing. Such practices are entirely acceptable. This section is focused on those forensic clinicians who rely *solely* on unstandardized and extrapolated diagnoses.

A major issue, touched in Chapter 3, is the traditional and insular practice of using only unstandardized diagnoses. In some instances, the choice to use unstandardized diagnoses is based on ignorance rather than an informed decision. Box 12-1 presents illustrative cross-examination that characterizes two general themes. First, the expert's ignorance of standard diagnostic measures can sometimes be brought to light. Some psychiatrists may attempt to dismiss their lack of knowledge by simply asserting that these measures fall within the psychologists' domain. This dismissal is disingenuous. The American Psychiatric Association (2000b) promoted the use of standardized measures through its authoritative text, *Handbook of Psychiatric Measures*. This text includes structured interviews and assessment measures for both adults and adolescents.

The second theme of Box 12-1 is to document the shortcomings of unstandardized interviews. The illustrative questions assume that the cross-examining attorney is not conversant with specific diagnostic issues. Therefore, the demonstrative display and disadvantages of unstandardized diagnoses should be self-evident to the fact finder. Questions about the shortcomings of unstandardized diagnoses are kept general to avoid extended technical discussions. The availability of a consulting expert could greatly enhance the depth and breadth of this cross-examination.

Extrapolated diagnoses are more difficult to cross-examine without extensive technical knowledge of specific psychological tests. One option is for the attorney to begin with the particular *DSM-IV* inclusion criteria for the relevant disorders. Using these criteria as a demonstrative display, the attorney can ask the expert to point to specific evidence for each symptoms. Unless the expert chooses to obfuscate the incompatibility of *DSM-IV* symptoms and test results, the expert will have to concede that test data do not yield *DSM-IV* diagnoses. When these diagnostic issues are pivotal to the case, rebuttal experts may offer the only reasonable alternative. However, these rebuttal experts should be questioned closely about their training and expertise. For example, some psychologists may be overly sympathetic to their colleagues despite strong empirical evidence that measures, such as the MCMI-III, have little diagnostic usefulness.

Box 12-1   ILLUSTRATIVE CROSS-EXAMINATION FOR DIAGNOSTIC
INADEQUACIES IN FORENSIC ASSESSMENTS

These questions are intended for experts that did not use any structured
interviews to establish Axis I and Axis II disorders

A. Overview and the SCID
  1. *Isn't it true you used clinical interviews to establish your diagnoses of
     the defendant?*
  2. [If brings in records, be prepared to questions about the range of
     diagnoses and accuracy of the diagnoses in the records using Ap-
     pendix I. For defendants with extensive mental health histories,
     these records are often a conflicting mess.]
  3. [if affirmative] *What is the name of the clinical interview that you
     administered? . . . Isn't it true that you didn't bother to give a validated
     clinical interview to the defendant?*
  4. [if psychiatrist] *Are you even aware that the American Psychiatric
     Association has published the SCID* [spell out] *based on more the 20
     years of research?*
  5. [if psychologist] *Are you even aware of the SCID* [spell out] *was
     published based on more the 20 years of research?*
  6. [all experts] *What does the SCID stand for?* [Structured Clinical In-
     terview of DSM-IV Disorders]
  7. [if seems less confident] *Which was published first the SCID or the
     SCID-II? . . . And what is the basic difference between the two measures?*
     [a naive expert may guess that they are different editions of the
     same measure; this a very grave error[1]] . . . *What you are saying
     is that they measure the same disorders, but one is a more recent edi-
     tion, is that correct? . . .* [if affirmative] *Are you aware, doctor, that
     you don't have even a basic understanding of the SCID or validated
     diagnostic interviews?* [Pretrial preparation: access the American
     Psychiatric Association website (http://www.appi.org/dsm.cfx)
     and print copies of the SCID and SCID-II descriptions. Use these
     materials to refute the expert's guesswork.]
B. The Expert's Knowledge
  8. *Doctor, let's see how knowledgeable you are about diagnostic issues.
     Please look at the following demonstrative display* [Appendix I], *can you
     tell the court what is meant by "coverage of symptoms"? . . . "Systematic
     inquiries about symptoms"?* [Continue through the list if the first
     column. This approach may build interest in the trier-of-fact about
     how the bad news (2nd column) will be addressed. It may also
     build apprehension in the expert.]
  9. *Please look at the 2nd column, doctor. You really have to admit its bad
     news, don't you?*
 10. [if quibbles] *Let me give you an analogy. Let's say you have a son who
     is seriously ill. If the doctors were using a method, like yours, that got
     this many "not possibles," would you be* <u>completely</u> *satisfied with their
     diagnoses? . . .* [still quibbles: ask incredulously] *. . . Your son might
     be dying and you'd still stand by your answer?*

[1] Correct answer: SCID measures Axis I disorders; SCID-II measures Axis II disorders, also known
as "personality disorders."

Specialized Forensic Measures and Forensic Practice

A fundamental issue is whether specialty training in forensic psychology and psychiatry affords the criminal courts any additional expertise than that found with most doctorally trained clinicians. Why should the criminal courts rely on *forensic* psychologists and psychiatrists with specialty training as experts? A cynical answer might simply be that these professionals are "battle-hardened" and able to easily withstand the rigors of aggressive cross-examination. A more enlightened response would take into account their advanced understanding of legal issues and empirically based knowledge on conceptual issues and forensic methods.

Application of the *legal-empirical-forensic* model requires a sound conceptualization of the legal and forensic issues involved with each psycholegal standard. Legal conceptualization, based on scholarship and law, is indispensable for forensic consultations. For example, forensic specialists should understand the *Dusky* standard and why it might best be conceptualized as a two or three prong test (see Chapter 6). The understanding of forensic issues defines the parameter of practices and incorporates both ethical and professional dimensions. However, the centerpiece of forensic specialties claim to expertise is their sophisticated use of empirically based knowledge.

Empirically based knowledge informs both theory and practice. For example, volitional capacity is conceptualized differently for insanity evaluations, warrantless searches, and capital sentencing. While each legal issue is understood in categorical terms (i.e., presence or absence), together they form a continuum of related standards of volitional capacity and impairment. Empirically tested theory provides a sound framework for forensic knowledge and decision-making. As a second example, models of risk assessment will yield dissimilar results depending on whether they embrace a balanced (risk and protective factors) versus an unbalanced (risk factors only) approach. Moreover, these risk assessment models are strongly influenced by their choice of static and dynamic predictors. Those models relying exclusively on static (i.e., unchangeable variables, such as gender and past crimes) predictors offer little hope to clinical interventions of any positive change. In contrast, models with both static and dynamic variables can potentially differentiate between poor and good treatment risks. Forensic psychologists and psychiatrists must be grounded in empirically tested theory so that they understand such issues (e.g., volitionality and risk) before rendering expert opinions in criminal cases.

The second component of empirically based knowledge is the development and application of empirically validated measures. Theory, by itself, cannot be meaningfully applied to specific standards with demonstrable reliability and validity. Moving from theory to practice, specialized measures provide the most rigorous approach to forensic evaluations.

Heilbrun, Rogers, and Otto (2002) make a useful distinction between forensic assessment instruments and forensically relevant instruments. A *forensic assessment instrument* directly evaluates a specific legal standard, both as a single construct and relevant components (often referred to as "prongs" in the legal literature). In contrast, a *forensically relevant instrument* addresses clinical constructs that are relevant to the legal standard. The crucial distinction is that forensically relevant instruments do not operationalize the legal standard or test it directly. As an example, malingering is a clinical issue that is central to most criminal forensic evaluations; however, it is not included in any legal standard. Thus, an instrument measuring malingering would be forensically relevant instrument, but not a forensic assessment instrument.

Forensic Assessment Instruments

Forensic assessment instruments were developed to assess competency to stand trial. CST measures have evolved during the last several decades from simple checklists to sophisticated measures with sound psychometric properties (see Chapter 6). In adding science to the forensic specialization, the use of a second-generation CST measure (ECST-R or MacCAT-CA) provides empirically based knowledge to the evaluations that is (1) relevant to the case, (2) standardized in its methodology, and validated for CST determinations. Their rigorously tested relevance to CST cases offers a significant advantage over clinical interviews and standard testing.

What inferences can be drawn when forensic clinicians do not use sophisticated CST measures in competency evaluations? Criminal attorneys should examine this question closely and weigh alternative inferences. We present three possible alternatives:

1. *Apprenticeship*. The forensic clinician lacks the breadth of formal training and education. Akin to an apprenticeship model, he or she learned from a senior clinician through observation and supervision. This model emphasizes an adherence to modeled practices rather than an open-minded inquiry into best-validated methods.
2. *Outdated Methods*. The forensic clinician has not kept current with advances in forensic assessment. A critical reevaluation of practices is need periodically by all forensic clinicians.
3. *Applicability*. A legitimate reason why a forensic clinician does not use sophisticated CST measures are their applicability in a

particular case. As a simple example, second-generation CST measures were not validated for defendants with moderate retardation. The forensic clinician should not use CST measures on populations for which they were not validated.

Beyond CST evaluations, forensic assessment instruments have focused on *Miranda* rights and criminal responsibility. These measures vary substantially in their development and validation (see Chapters 5 and 7). *Miranda* measures presently lack sufficient validity to be considered forensic assessment instruments. Regarding criminal responsibility, the MSE-Offense remains in its early stage of development, while the R-CRAS is a useful adjunct to insanity evaluations. Decisions on whether to use these measures are very different from CST evaluations.

Forensically Relevant Instruments

Forensically relevant instruments address *clinical* constructs that are relevant to legal standards. These instruments provide empirically validated measures for assessing issues that should not be overlooked by forensic clinicians. Measures of malingering and psychopathy must often be considered as fundamental components of forensic consultations. Some key points include

- The assessment of malingering is divided into several domains including feigned mental disorders and feigned cognitive impairments (see Chapter 2). Both specialized measures and specific scales from standardized testing have been developed and validated. Many scales have extensive validation with offender populations.
- The construct of psychopathy has been extensively validated with offender populations (see Chapter 9; see also Chapters 4 and 11). Its assessment via of semi-structured inverviews (e.g., the PCL-R) has demonstrated excellent reliability and construct validity.

Forensic clinicians should routinely use empirically validated measures for the assessment of malingering and psychopathy. This conclusion is warranted on two grounds: (1) sophistication of the empirically validated measures that standardize the assessment, and (2) the importance of these clinical determinations to the outcome of the forensic evaluations. Rogers and Shuman (2000) formulated the following standard for forensic practice: *"No determination of malingering should rest solely on traditional interviews"* (p. 94). This standard applies equally to the assessment of psychopathy: *All assessments of psychopathy should include standardized measures with extensive validation.*

Attorneys should be prepared to use both cross-examination and rebuttal experts to attack unsubstantiated opinions on malingering or psychopathy. Because of attribution bias, judges and jurors are likely to believe the worst about criminal defendants. Beliefs that exculpatory mental health claims are fraudulent (i.e., malingering) will likely obscure consideration of the defendant's clinical status during the trial and sentencing phases. Beliefs that the defendant is fundamentally bad or even evil (i.e., psychopathy) will likely foreclose consideration of any other motives for the offense at trial or any clinical interventions at sentencing. Attorneys may wish to allocate considerable resources to combating such unsubstantiated claims, which may have a poisoning effect on the fact finder.

Forensically relevant instruments have made strong advances during the last two decades. A crucial component of forensic expertise is a thorough knowledge of these measures and their forensic applications. With the assistance of consulting experts, criminal attorneys can become knowledgeable about these measures. The general strategy is twofold: (1) establish the "status of the specialty" with respect to forensically relevant instruments, and (2) demonstrate how the expert falls far short of this standard. Regarding the latter, the ideal outcome is that the fact finder is aware of the expert's *general ignorance* of forensically relevant instruments. From this context of general ignorance, his or her specific conclusions about a particular defendant may weigh accordingly.

FORENSIC PREDICTIONS AND CLASSIFICATIONS

TEMPORAL FRAMEWORK

The accuracy and completeness of forensic evaluations is dependent on the temporal framework addressed by the legal standard. There are three possible temporal frameworks: *current, retrospective,* and *prospective. Current* evaluations are the least demanding for accuracy and completeness because forensic clinicians are evaluating the defendant's contemporaneous functioning and level of impairment. Current evaluations are used with several criminal competencies (e.g., competency to stand trial and competency to be executed). When relying of empirically validated measures, these forensic assessments can often produce consistent and arguably accurate results. Current evaluations become more challenging for clinically unstable defendants, whose fluctuating capacities may alter the forensic conclusions.

Retrospective evaluations, such as insanity and criminal culpability, present forensic clinicians with a particular outcome (e.g., murder) and ask them to assemble the possible explanations for this particular outcome in a specific case. Competent forensic clinicians extensively gather standardized and collateral data as well as the defendant's own accounts. On the basis of comparative analyses, experts attempt to assess what was the predominant motivation for the criminal behavior. Accurate and complete determinations can be reached in cases where the data are strongly convergent.

Prospective evaluations (i.e., future predictions), such as bail and sentencing, attempt to assemble relevant predictors of what is typically rare occurrences (i.e., low base rates). The accuracy and completeness of future predictions are the most challenging because *they must rely on group data to predict an individual's highly atypical behavior.* By definition, the group data can never capture the complex individual and situational variables that contribute to a particular offender's crime. Therefore, attorneys should not be surprised when sophisticated researchers often produce unsatisfactory results. Poor results reflect on the nature of the task not the expertise of the researchers.

A simple but important distinction must be drawn for prospective evaluations based on past patterns. Specifically, highly repetitive failures must be differentiated from general cases:

- *Highly repetitive failures.* Our ability to predict problematic behavior is comparatively easy in cases of highly repetitive failures. For example, Klassen and O'Conner (1988) were able to predict violence in patients with extensive failures (≥ 10 arrests or ≥ 10 hospitalizations for aggressive behavior). One metric for highly repetitive failures is the defendant's inability to maintain any period of time (e.g., 12 months) *without* engaging in the problematic behavior.[1]
- *General cases.* The majority of cases involves limited past histories and significant periods without any known evidence of the problematic behavior. These cases pose greater challenges for accurate predictions. Attorneys and their consulting experts must be vigilant that research on highly repetitive failures is not misapplied to their general cases.

ACCURACY OF PREDICTIONS AND CLASSIFICATIONS

Many attorneys and forensic clinicians lack sufficient background regarding what constitutes *accuracy* in predictions and classifications.

---

[1]Obviously, the absence of opportunity (e.g., heterosexual rape in an all male facility) cannot be counted.

Different estimates are applied depending on the question (see Chapter 9). The law is idiographic (Haney, 1980); it wants to know what is the likelihood that this *particular* offender will engage in this *problematic* behavior. While all utility estimates are important, the most relevant estimate is positive predictive power. Chapter 9 (see Box 9-2) addresses the following issue: *When given a high score (i.e., above the established cut score), what is the likelihood this defendant will engage in problematic behavior?* If forensic clinicians attempt to obfuscate this issue, the cross-examining attorney will need a firm understanding of utility estimates to minimize misleading responses.

Experts are often asked to testify to a reasonable degree of psychological or medical certainty. This level of certainty should not be based on the "strength of our convictions" (Rogers and Shuman, 2000, p. 45). Rather, it should be based on solid clinical data, supported by the accuracy of the methods and the consistency of their findings.

For many predictions, extensive data are available to forensic clinicians and criminal attorneys. Unfortunately, technical language may intentionally or unintentionally confuse the fact finder. Irrespective of the intent, the result is likely to be the same: expert evidence is seriously misinterpreted by judges and juries.

Table 12-2 presents six levels of certainty that can be applied to clinical predictions and classifications. Measures lacking internal consistency and reliability will introduce unacceptable variability into predictions. Therefore, high values on these basic psychometric properties are essential. Of critical importance is the measure's ability to predict the likelihood of problematic behavior for a particular defendant (i.e., positive predictive power). Because cut scores (like all scores) are imprecise, estimates

TABLE 12-2. TESTIMONY TO A REASONABLE DEGREE OF PSYCHOLOGICAL OR MEDICAL CERTAINTY: LEVELS OF CERTAINTY

	Use of positive predictive power		Reliability estimates	
Levels of certainty	*Cut score*	*Cut Score—1SE$_M$*	*Alpha*	*Reliability*[a]
"excellent"	$\geq.90$	$\geq.80$	$\geq.80$	$\geq.90$
"robust"	.81–.89	.70–.79	$\geq.80$	$\geq.80$
"fair"	.70–.79	.60–.69	$\geq.80$	$\geq.80$
"marginal"	.60–.69	.51–.59	$\geq.80$	$\geq.80$
"substandard"	.50–.59	.40–.49	$\geq.70$	$\geq.70$
"very substandard"	<.50	<.40	<.70	<.70

Note. Level of certainty: the highest level that meets *all* criteria (i.e., across the four columns).
[a] Reliability coefficients will vary with the type of forensic measure and its indicated use. For current issues, interrater *r*s will likely be used. For predictions of future issues, test–retest *r*s are essential.

Box 12-2   ILLUSTRATIVE CROSS-EXAMINATION FOR DECONSTRUCTING
                              GLOBAL OPINIONS

Some experts offer verbose generalities when asked to provide the bases of their opinions. They resist all attempts to clarify their data and their reasoning.

A. The Kindly Forbearing Approach: The strategy is to provide ample opportunity for the expert to alienate the trier-of-fact by his or her evasiveness and prolixity. The general idea is "not to win," but to allow the expert to "lose." As an analogy, it may help to think of the expert as a headstrong child.

1. *What is the basis of your opinion about __? ... Thank you doctor, could you help me list the individual sources you relied on? ... I am sorry to interrupt, but I am trying to make write down the list as you go* [use flip chart], *could you just give me the major sources?*

2. [This may take some patience. Don't confront. Keep asking help.]

3. [many sources] *That is quite a list, doctor, any trouble keeping them all in mind?* [likely a negative response] ... *It may be harder for the rest of us, don't you agree?*

4. *Let's start with __* [an external source such as one hospitalization], *what would be three important findings? ...* [likely verbose and difficult to follow] ... *We don't need an explanation just yet. What are three important findings?* [Continue questions; remember you goal is allow the expert to irritate the jury by not answering simple questions simply.]

5. [more verbosity] *Your honor, we don't want to be here all day, could please instruct the witness to simply answer the question?*

B. Confrontational Approach: This strategy may be considered if the judge appears impatient or irritated with the expert. The general idea is for juries to become aware of the judge's negative impressions. The questions should be straightforward requiring only simple responses.

6. [long-winded convoluted response] *Doctor, do you even remember what the question was?* [likely affirmative] ... *So all you needed to tell us, was __* [e.g., "the defendant had hallucinations"]?

7. [long-winded convoluted response] *You don't have to try impressing us with how many sentences you can put together. What is your straight answer about __?*

8. [long-winded convoluted response; ask the court reporter to read back the question] *Doctor, do you want to try to give us a simple answer to a simple question?*

9. [long-winded convoluted response] *Are you aware that the judge has a full docket? ... And that your long-winded answers may keep all of us here for an extra day? ... By the way, how much are you getting paid for each day of testimony?*

10. [long-winded convoluted response] *Your honor, could you instruct the witness to be* respectful *to this court and* simply respond *to the questions?* [after several more long-winded convoluted responses] ... *Your honor, could you remind the witness to be responsive to the questions?*

of positive predictive power must take into account the standard error of measurement (SEM). Table 12-2 uses 1 SEM, which still introduces some error in the prediction. This point is illustrated in Chapter 9 by Hart's (1998) similar recommendation for the PCL-R.

Some forensic clinicians may argue that the levels of certainty put forth in Table 12-2 are too stringent. Attorneys may wish to counter this position with several inquiries on cross-examination:

1. *Looking at the third column* [Cut Score—1 SEM] *doesn't "excellent" certainty allows up to 20% errors? ...And knowing that about 16% of defendants will exceed one standard error of measurement means that the error rate could easily go up to 25% or higher doesn't it?*[2]
2. *Are you really complaining that simply asking you to be right 3 out of 4 times, is just too hard for you?*

Heilbrun (1992) proposed that reliability estimates should reach a minimum benchmark of .80 in order to ensure the consistency of measurement. This standard appears to be fair for most levels of certainty. However, those versed in statistics will quickly realize that .80 is less than optimal; at the threshold, it accounts for less than two-thirds of the variance (i.e., 64.0%). Therefore, we require for the highest level of certainty ("excellent") a minimum reliability of .90. This accounts for most of the variance (i.e., 81.0%).

What level of certainty is necessary to testify with a reasonable degree of psychological or medical certainty? We believe that more forensic clinicians will find "excellent" and "robust" levels of certainty to be sufficient to meet the *reasonable degree* criterion. Experts are likely to be conflicted over the admissibility of "fair" and especially "marginal" levels of certainty. "Substandard" and "very substandard" levels are likely to introduce more error than accuracy. For example, Cut Score—1 SEM for "substandard" is likely to wrong more than it is right.

With reliable measures, forensic clinicians may often increase the level of certainty by adding 1SEM to the established cut score. As described in Chapter 9, Hart (1998) recommended this identical modification for the highly reliable and well-validated PCL-R. This modification allows measures with only moderate effectiveness as expressed by positive predictive power to be used in forensic evaluations.

---

[2]Pretrial preparation on standard errors of measurement will likely be necessary with the consulting expert.

SCRUTINY AND SKEPTICISM AS WATCHWORDS FOR CRIMINAL ATTORNEYS

The adversarial nature of criminal trials is intended to expose the weaknesses of an opponent's evidence or arguments. Expert evidence is not excepted from this adversarial process. Although experts are guided by professional and ethical standards, their evidence in each criminal case must be examined and tested by opposing counsel. Two main tools of doing this are cross-examination and the use of their own experts. This crucible of the adversary system is best served by knowledgeable attorneys who are skeptical of all experts.

PAST PATTERNS OF TESTIFYING EXPERTS

We recommend that attorneys examine experts for the opposing side with attention to their backgrounds and past cases. For example, a well-known expert in capital-sentencing cases was found to be unethical and expelled from membership in the American Psychiatric Association "for arriving at a psychiatric diagnosis without first having examined the individuals in question, and for indicating, while testifying in court as an expert witness, that he could predict with 100 [percent] certainty that the individuals would engage in future violent acts." (American Psychiatric Association, 1995). Should not this expert's credibility be assailed in every capital-sentencing case by extended cross-examination about his unethical behavior? Should not this cross-examination elicit specific details of the ethical charges, the formal findings, and the outcome (i.e., the most severe ethical sanction, expulsion from the American Psychiatric Association)? Depending on other factors in the case, attorneys may wish to spend a significant portion of their time on cross-examination discrediting an expert based on his or her unethical and unprofessional conduct.

Scrutiny of past cases can often reveal startling similarities in the expert's conclusions. At times, the expert may use exact terminology in his or her reports or testimony. Via demonstrative displays, jurors can see exact wording and conclusions across a number of cases. Cross-examination may underscore this unsettling pattern:

1. *You seem to have gotten this testimony down pretty well, haven't you doctor?*
2. *Weren't these cases very different in their backgrounds with __ [e.g., a 50-year old man with an extensive substance abuse history], and __ [i.e., a very different background] and __ [i.e., the current*

case]? ... *Without trying to explain it away, these are different cases and same testimony, aren't they? ...* [optional] *It must be easier on you if you don't have to prepare new conclusions each time?*

Scrutiny of past cases can sometimes reveal divergent conclusions in cases with similar findings. In some instances, these apparent discrepancies are warranted. Still, we contend that the jury should understand the expert within a broader context (i.e., past patterns) rather than form an isolated perspective, such as one-time visitor to the courtroom. On occasion, attorneys may want to "follow the money" in explaining the divergent conclusions:

1. *In case* __ [a past case for the prosecution] *you were paid thousands of dollars for your opinion that [he/she] was a "continuing threat to society?"*
2. *In case* __ [a past case for the defense] *you were paid thousands of dollars for your opinion that [he/she] was <u>not</u> a "continuing threat to society?"*
3. [continue to alternate between prosecution and defense cases]
4. *Would it be fair to say, that we could have predicted your testimony today by simply knowing you were going to be called by the* [choose: prosecution/defense]?

This type of cross-examination may be unfair to those experts who do disagree with retaining attorneys and do not invariably testify in the direction of the money. Retaining attorneys should provide experts with an opportunity on redirect to explain their agreements and disagreements with open-ended questions.

EVASION OF ACCOUNTABILITY

Forensic clinicians may attempt to avoid a destructive cross-examination by refusing to detail the bases and reasoning undergirding their conclusions. A common evasion is for the forensic clinician to take refuge in his or her "global" opinion (see also the discussion of "clinical judgment" in Chapter 3). Global opinions are easily recognized when the expert continues to launch into complicated explanations when asked simple questions about the sources of clinical data. For example, experts that begin with intricate phrases such as a "bio-psycho-social model" are unlikely to be responsive to a specific source of data. Evasions of accountability may pose a serious threat to the adversarial process and its search for truth.

Attorneys have many options in their cross-examination of global-opinion experts. We have outlined two alternatives in Box 12-2: the "kindly forbearing" and "confrontational" approaches. The kindly forbearing approach is based on the general premise that jurors tend to disregard unlikable experts. As noted in the preliminary comment (see Box 12-2), the goal of this approach is for the expert to "lose" and not for the attorney to "win." What does the expert lose? If successful, the kindly forbearing approach will allow the jury to see that the expert accurately as unhelpful and evasive. Success is more likely to be achieved if the jury identifies with the attorney and his or her quest for straightforward answers to simple questions.

Some attorneys may prefer a confrontational approach to the global-opinion subterfuge. The danger is that the jury will see the forensic clinician as being "attacked" and overlook his or her evasions. We surmise that the confrontational approach may work best on long-winded and convoluted responses, because these answers may alienate both the judge and jury. If the judge becomes impatient with nonresponsive prolixity, then judge's negative impressions may affect the expert's persuasiveness. The risk is that the judge will become more exasperated with the cross-examination than the expert. We suggest that remaining attuned to the judge's perspective (e.g., full docket) and authority (e.g., remonstrating the expert) may assist in keeping the judge sympathetic to this type of cross-examination.

Skepticism of Expert Testimony

Attorneys should not blithely accept any witnesses' testimony, including experts. We submit that an attitude of skepticism may help cross-examining attorneys to remain observant and critical of experts. This chapter began with an affirmation of skepticism, "How do you know what you claim to know?" Attorneys should be skeptical of experts and their opinions. To maintain their vigilance, they keep in mind the following questions:

1. How does the expert know? Is his or her conclusion even knowable?
2. What would it take to change the expert's mind? Is all new information summarily discounted?
3. Is the expert aware of his or her fallibility?

Skepticism can be pursued as a fallback strategy of cross-examination when the prepared questions do not appear to be effective. Promotion of a skeptical attitude should not be confused with anger or confrontation. Instead, cross-examination can question directly without attempting to prove the expert wrong. A measure of success is achieved when the forensic clinician becomes more adamant in his or her position. Attorneys should be alert for responses in which the expert becomes his or her own authority. Jurors are likely to recognize similar responses in the exasperations of ineffectual parents (e.g., "Because I said so.").

Skepticism should not be confused with any blanket criticisms of forensic psychology and psychiatry. These specialties have made important advances in theory and practice during the last several decades. Rather, the skepticism is centered on this particular expert and his or her knowledge and competence as it applies to the case at hand. Does the expert understand the legal standard and its conceptual framework? Does he or she have expertise with the relevant forensic assessment instruments and forensically relevant instruments? Were the choices of clinical methods made out of professional ignorance or professional knowledge?

THE INTERDEPENDENCE OF LAW AND FORENSIC PRACTICE

The final theme of this book is the interdependence of criminal attorneys (both prosecution and defense attorneys) and forensic mental health specialists. As the preceding chapters illustrate, the legal standards address a broad range of criminal issues, such as competency to stand trial or to be executed, criminal responsibility, sentencing, and the waiver of a panoply of constitutional rights. With these standards, the defendant's mental state may be central to the legal determination and opinion testimony by mental health experts may be admissible, if not legally or practically required, to address the issue. Judges, prosecutors, or criminal defense attorneys, however, are not required to develop an advanced knowledge of forensic psychology and psychiatry. Their expertise is focused on law with only basic knowledge of the empirical and forensic components of the *legal-empirical-forensic model* employed by competent forensic mental health specialists. In contrast, competent forensic clinicians bring to bear only basic knowledge of the law along with their expertise in the empirical and forensic components. The interdependence of law and forensic practice is illustrated by their respective strengths and weaknesses exemplified by the *legal-empirical-forensic* model.

This interdependence is underscored by recent appellate decisions addressing the admissibility of expert testimony. *Daubert*, its federal court progeny and its state court counterparts, reflect recent systemic efforts to raise the level of threshold scrutiny for all experts. Attorneys need forensic clinicians for their understanding and expertise both to offer and to challenge psychological and psychiatric evidence. While often not legally mandated, use of expert testimony and consultation is often crucial to the outcome of cases involving mental health issues. Attorneys and experts must work together to examine the empirically established knowledge and the validity of forensic methods. Beyond admissibility, direct testimony and cross-examination must address the relevant psycholegal issues in a manner understandable to judge and juries. The interdependence of law and forensic practice is exemplified by the need to communicate clearly and persuasively. Expert testimony and nontestifying consulting experts are often crucial to the outcome of cases involving mental health issues. Criminal attorneys need forensic clinicians just as forensic clinicians need criminal attorneys.

Forensic psychologists and psychiatrists who testify in criminal trials are "invited guests" and do not get to set the rules that govern their appearances at trial. They have no independent authority; they may be required to or be prohibited from testifying in a trial at the direction of counsel or the court. Once called to testify, like all witnesses, they have no authority to provide information to the fact finder other than in response to the questions propounded by counsel or the court.

Experts interdependence on criminal attorneys is extensive; forensic clinicians rely on attorneys for their knowledge of relevant legal standards and subsequent case law. Forensic clinicians, who assess the wrong issues (e.g., criminal responsibility vs. competency to stand trial) or apply the wrong criteria (e.g., misapply the volitional prong in a jurisdiction that follows *M'Naghten*) do not assist the courts and may have their testimony excluded.

An acknowledgment of this mutual interdependence is the key to professional respect and effective cooperation. Beyond the adversarial rigors of criminal trials, attorneys and mental health professionals share common ground. Pragmatically, they need each other's expertise to perform their professional functions competently. Conceptually, they share a desire to serve justice.

CONCLUDING REMARKS

One major purpose of this text is to bridge the attitudinal and knowledge-based divisions between attorneys and forensic practitioners on mental health issues in criminal law. A second major purpose is to provide forensic clinicians with sound theory and current data within the *legal-empirical-forensic* model. A third goal is to equip criminal attorneys with the necessary tools for the direct and cross-examination of forensic experts. In light of these three goals, we would like to hear from you. We are envisioning a second book devoted to civil-forensic issues. We welcome feedback on what is helpful and what could be improved. Because cross-examination is a process of evolution and refinement, we also welcome brief transcripts that illustrate both successful and unsuccessful approaches to mental health issues. Depending on the needs of our readers, we may even assemble a professional text for both experts and attorneys that analyzes and illustrates different strategies for direct and cross-examination. Please address these comments to Dr. Rogers at rogersr@unt.edu. To ensure that your message is not inadvertently discarded, please put the title, *Fundamental of Forensic Practice*, in the subject line.

Appendix A

THE ACCURACY OF DSM INDICES OF MALINGERING*

Note: Although the study was conducted with DSM-III indices, these indices remain unchanged with DSM-IV-TR (American Psychiatric Association, 2000).

A SUMMARY OF THE ROGERS (1990) STUDY

An archival study examined the accuracy of DSM indices of malingering on forensic inpatients referred for court evaluations.

Two research assistants blind (masked) to the purpose of the study examined the comprehensive records of 113 randomly selected genuine inpatients and 24 probable malingerers.

---

*Specifically for use as court exhibits, copies of Appendices A through I are permitted for this explicit purpose.

RESEARCH QUESTION

How accurate is the *DSM-IV* indices at identifying potential malingerers?

DSM-IV benchmark: two or more indices (i.e., "any combination") should "strongly suspect" malingering.

RESULTS

- True positives ("hits") range from 13.6 to 20.1%.
- False positives ("misses") range from 79.9 to 86.4%.

CONCLUSION

Use of the *DSM-IV* indices are inaccurate at identifying potential malingerers more than four out of five times.

REFERENCE

Rogers, R. (1990). Models of feigned mental illness. *Professional Psychology: Research and Practice, 21*, 182–188.

Appendix B

SYSTEMATIC REVIEW OF STANDARDIZED MEASURES FOR FEIGNED MENTAL DISORDERS AND THEIR DETECTION STRATEGIES*

Detection strategy	Interview	SIRS	MMPI-2	PAI	MCMI-III	MPS
Rare symptoms	Unknown	Yes	Yes	Yes	No	Yes
Improbable symptoms	Unknown	Yes	No	No	Partial[a]	No
Erroneous stereotypes	Unknown	No	Yes	No	Partial[b]	No
Symptom combinations	Unknown	Yes	No	No	No	No
Unlikely patterns of psychopathology	Unknown	No	No	Yes	No	No
Subtle vs. obvious symptoms	Unknown	Yes	Yes	No	No	No
Symptom severity	Unknown	Yes	No	No	No	No
Symptom selectivity	Unknown	Yes	Partial[c]	No	No	No

[a] Based on the MCMI-III validity index which is not intended as a feigning scale but to assess carelessness or random responding.
[b] Based on items more frequently endorsed by 12 graduate students simulating their worst side with psychological impairment.
[c] Based on the MMPI-2 Lachar–Wrobel (LW) critical items that covers a broad range of serious symptoms.

*Specifically for use as court exhibits, copies of Appendices A through I are permitted for this explicit purpose.

Appendix C

SYSTEMATIC REVIEW OF STANDARDIZED MEASURES
FOR FEIGNED COGNITIVE IMPAIRMENT AND THEIR
DETECTION STRATEGIES*

	TOMM	VIP	PDRT	Rey-15	WMT	VSVT	CARB	DCT	NSI	TOCA
Detection strategy										
Floor effect	Yes	No	No	Yes	Yes	Yes	Yes	No	No	Yes
Symptom validity testing	Yes	Yes	Yes	No	Yes	Yes	Yes	No	No	Yes
Magnitude of error	No	No	No	No	No	No	No	No	No	Yes
Performance curve	No	Yes	No	No	Partial[a]	No	No	No	No	Yes
Violation of learning principles	Yes	No	No	No	Partial[b]	No	No	Yes	No	No
Consistency for comparable items	No	Yes	No	No	No	No	No	No	No	No

(*Continued*)

(Continued)

	TOMM	VIP	PDRT	Rey-15	WMT	VSVT	CARB	DCT	NSI	TOCA
Questionable detection strategies										
Forced choice testing	No	No	Yes	No	Yes	Yes	Yes	No	No	No
Psychological sequelae	No	No	No	No	No	No	No	No	Yes	No
Atypical presentation	No	No	No	No	No	No	No	No	Yes	No

Note. TOMM: Test of Malingered Memory; VIP: Validity Indicator Profile; PDRT: Portland Digit Recognition Test; Rey-15: Rey's 15-Item Test; WMT: Word Memory Test; VSVT: Victoria Symptom Validity Test; CARB: Computerized Assessment of Response Bias; DCT: Dot Counting Test; NSI: Neuropsychological Symptom Inventory; TOCA: Test of Cognitive Abilities.

[a] The WMT includes items with different gradients of difficulty, but performance curve is not used as a formal strategy.

[b] Several learning principles are included (e.g., recall vs. recognition; short vs. long retention; cued vs. uncued recall).

Appendix D

MMPI-2 META-ANALYSIS AND FEIGNED MENTAL DISORDERS: A SUMMARY OF ROGERS ET AL. (2003)*

SOURCE

Rogers, R., Sewell, K. W., Martin, M. A., & Vitacco, M. J. (2003). Detection of feigned mental disorders: A meta-analysis of the MMPI-2 and malingering. *Assessment, 10,* 160–177.

STUDY

65 malingering studies, 11 diagnostic studies, with a total of 4,151 patients vs. feigners

*Specifically for use as court exhibits, copies of Appendices A through I are permitted for this explicit purpose.

Strongest Results: The Fp Scale

- very large effect sizes,
- narrow range of cutting scores,
- effective with different diagnostic groups.

Concerns About the F Scale

Genuine patients with certain diagnoses score high on the F scale:

- $72T$ is the average for depression (standard deviation = 22),
- $80T$ is the average for schizophrenia (standard deviation = 23),
- $86T$ is the average for PTSD (standard deviation = 22), and
- no consensus on cut scores; they range from $61T$ to $128T$.

Concerns About the Fb Scale

Genuine patients with certain diagnoses score high on the Fb scale:

- $82T$ is the average for depression (standard deviation = 24),
- $79T$ is the average for schizophrenia (standard deviation = 24),
- $92T$ is the average for PTSD (standard deviation = 25),
- no consensus on cut scores; they range from 80T to an extrapolated 152T.

Appendix E

ULTIMATE OPINIONS: BANS AND
QUESTIONABLE PRACTICES*

Bans: Ultimate-opinion testimony can only be prohibited by law or professional ethics.

LEGAL PROHIBITIONS?

As noted in Chapter 3, federal courts and state courts in California prohibit ultimate-opinion testimony on the circumscribed issues insanity and criminal responsibility.

The vast majority of courts allow and may even encourage ultimate-opinion testimony.

*Specifically for use as court exhibits, copies of Appendices A through I are permitted for this explicit purpose.

Reproduced with permission from *Fundamentals of Forensic Practice:*
Mental Health and Criminal Law © 2005, all rights reserved.
Richard Rogers, Ph.D. and Daniel W. Shuman, J.D.

Ethical Prohibitions?

Specialty guidelines by the American Psychology Law Society and the American Academy of Forensic Psychiatrists do *not* consider ultimate-opinion testimony to be unethical.

Questionable practices: Ultimate-opinion testimony has been attacked as a substandard professional practice.

Criticized by Most Scholars?

Melton, Petrila, Poythress, and Slobogin (1997, p. 17) inaccurately claimed "near-unanimity among scholarly commentators" against ultimate opinions.

In reality, many scholars are not against ultimate opinions and several early proponents have since retracted their positions (Rogers & Shuman, 2000a).

Melton has set an example for rendering ultimate-opinions in his work on insanity evaluations (Rogers & Shuman, 2000b) and the legally based decisional capacities of adolescents seeking abortions (Rogers & Ewing, 2003).

Usurping the Role of the Factfinder?

Available research finds no evidence to support this hypothesis (Rogers & Shuman, 2000a).

Beyond the Expertise of Forensic Cinicians

Melton et al. (1997) attempt to discredit forensic clinicians in terms of their abilities to render conclusions[1] ("more art and intuition than science," p. 7) and integrity ("simple intellectual dishonesty," p. 12). Subsequent arguments against ultimate opinions flow these discrediting perceptions.

This book outlines the advances made in the specialized assessments of criminal forensic standards. Decisions about ultimate opinions should be made on a case-by-case basis and be informed by the clarity of clinical data and the sophistication of available assessment methods.

---

[1]Ironically, Melton et al.'s conclusion was based on outdated *DSM-II* era studies from the 1970s (see footnote 80, p. 648).

Appendix F

SUMMARY OF THE GRISSO'S (1998) *MIRANDA* INSTRUMENTS FOR USE WITH ADULT OFFENDERS*

Criteria	CMR	CMR-R	CMV	FRI
A. Reliability				
Standard error of measurement	Unknown	Unknown	Unknown	Unknown
Internal consistency	Unknown	Unknown	Unknown	Unknown
Interrater reliability	Unknown[a]	Unknown	Unknown[a]	Unknown[a]
Test–retest reliability	Unknown[b]	Unknown	Unknown	Unknown
B. Validity				
Content validity[c]	N.A.	N.A.	N.A.	Yes
Construct validity[d]	Limited	Limited	Limited	Limited
Concurrent validity[e]	Unknown	Unknown	Unknown	Unknown
Criterion-related validity	None	None	None	None

Note. N.A.: not applicable to current jurisdictions.
[a] On juveniles but not adults, good reliability was achieved *after* months of training with Dr. Grisso and the completion of 60–80 protocols. Forensic clinicians simply do not have the opportunity for this training.
[b] On juveniles but not adults, good test–retest reliability was reported after 2 *days*. However, most evaluations of adult *Miranda* cases require intervals of 1–6 *months*.
[c] The *Miranda* warning used in this research does not apply to other jurisdictions.
[d] Basic comparison is to global intelligence; other more relevant comparisons are missing.
[e] Concurrent validity requires a comparison to established *Miranda* measures; this could not be done.

*Specifically for use as court exhibits, copies of Appendices A through I are permitted for this explicit purpose.

Appendix G

THE MMPI-2 AND INSANITY EVALUATIONS:
A DESCRIPTIVE ANALYSIS*

Source

Rogers, R., & McKee, G. R. (1995). Use of the MMPI-2 in the assessment of criminal responsibility. In Y. S. Ben-Porath, J. R. Graham, G. C. N. Hall, R. D. Hirschman, & M. S. Zaragoza (Eds.), *Forensic applications of the MMPI-2* (pp. 103–126). Newbury Park, CA: Sage.

Samples

MMPI-2 profiles from pretrial forensic evaluations:

- 149 sane defendants with no Axis I diagnoses,
- 50 sane defendants with Axis I diagnoses,

*Specifically for use as court exhibits, copies of Appendices A through I are permitted for this explicit purpose.

- 21 insane defendants based on the M'Naghten criteria
- 25 insane defendants based on the ALI but not the M'Naghten criteria.[1]

KEY RESULTS

- Scale 2 (Depression): Sane with Axis I diagnoses had significantly higher scores than the M'Naghten-insane and a similar trend for the ALI-insane.
- Scale 6 (Paranoid): Sane with Axis I diagnoses had a trend toward higher scores than the two insane groups.
- Scale 8 (Schizophrenia): Sane with Axis I diagnoses had significantly higher scores than the M'Naghten-insane and a similar trend for the ALI-insane.

CONCLUSION

Clinical elevations on the MMPI-2 cannot be used to determine or otherwise indicate which defendants are likely to be evaluated as *sane* or *insane*.

---

[1] These defendants were judged to be GBMI under the South Carolina standard that uses the same language as the ALI insanity standard.

Appendix H

ANALYSIS OF RISK ASSESSMENT MEASURES: ARE THEY RELEVANT TO SEXUALLY VIOLENT PREDATOR (SVP) STANDARDS?*

| Measure | Mental condition | | Volitional abilities | | Sexual recidivism | |
	Disorder	Abnormality	Impaired volition	Nexus[a]	General	Violent
HCR-20	Very limited	Very limited	No	No	No	No
MnSOST-R	No	No	No[b]	No	Limited	No
PCL-R	No	Very limited	No	No	Limited	Very limited
PPG	No	No	No	No	Limited	Limited
RRASOR	No	No	No	No	Limited	Limited
SORAG	Very limited	Very limited	No	No	Yes	Yes
Static-99	No	No	No	No	Limited	Limited
SVR-20	Very limited	Very limited	No	No	No	Yes[c]
VRAG	Very limited	Very limited	No	No	Limited	Limited

Note. "Yes": It has sufficient data to address a substantial component of the SVP standard. "Limited": Prediction (Sexual recividism) is based on a small number of studies that do not systematically consider gender and ethnicity. "Very limited": Coverage (Mental condition and volitional abilities) misses more than 95% of these components. "Very Limited": Prediction (Sexual recividism) is based on a very small number of studies with modest predictive ability. "No": It has *no* or *negligible* data to address this component of the SVP standard.

Abbreviations: HCR-20: Historical Clinical Risk—20 (Webster, Douglas, Eaves, & Hart, 1997); MnSOST-R: Minnesota Sex Offender Screening Tool (Epperson et al., 2000); PPG: penile plethysmography; RRASOR: Rapid Risk Assessment of Sexual Offense Recidivism (Hanson, 1997); SORAG: Sex Offense Risk Appraisal Guide (Rice & Harris, 1997); SVR-20: Sexual Violence Recidivism—20 (Boer et al., 1997); VRAG: Violence Risk Appraisal Guide (Harris, Rice, & Quinsey, 1993).

[a] "Nexus" simply refers to whether the connection between volitional impairment and the mental condition has been established.

[b] Item #4 addresses whether sex offense occurred in a public place, which is possibly an indication of poor impulse control. Other facets of impaired volition are completely omitted.

[c] It includes nonviolent acts such as exhibitionism, obscene letters or phone calls, distribution of pornography, and voyeurism.

*Specifically for use as court exhibits, copies of Appendices A through I are permitted for this explicit purpose.

Appendix I

STANDARDS FOR DIAGNOSES IN FORENSIC
PRACTICE: A COMPARISON OF UNSTANDARDIZED,
STANDARDIZED, AND EXTRAPOLATED
DIAGNOSES*

KEY TERMS

- Unstandardized diagnoses: clinical and collateral interviews plus record review.
- Standardized diagnoses: empirically based structured interviews plus collateral interviews and record review.
- Extrapolated diagnoses: clinical correlates from psychological tests that are associated with broad diagnostic groups (e.g., all psychotic disorders).

*Specifically for use as court exhibits, copies of Appendices A through I are permitted for this explicit purpose.

Reproduced with permission from *Fundamentals of Forensic Practice: Mental Health and Criminal Law* © 2005, all rights reserved.
Richard Rogers, Ph.D. and Daniel W. Shuman, J.D.

A Systematic Comparison of Unstandardized, Standardized, and Extrapolated Diagnoses

Diagnostic issues	Unstandardized diagnoses	Standardized diagnoses	Extrapolated diagnoses
Coverage of symptoms	Idiosyncratic	Systematic	Very limited
Systematic inquiries about symptoms	Not possible	Integral component	Not possible
Systematic recording of symptoms	Not possible	Integral component	Very limited
Ratings of symptom severity	Not possible	Varies with measure	Not possible
Usefulness with different populations	Cannot be tested	Often demonstrated	Very limited
Reliability of symptoms	Not possible	Integral component	Rarely addressed
Reliability of diagnoses	Not possible	Integral component	Rarely addressed
Predictive research on outcome	Not possible	Varies with measure	Rarely addressed

References

Abel, G. G. (1995). *The comparison of the Abel Assessment with penile plethymography.* Unpublished manuscript, Behavioral Medicine Institute, Atlanta, GA.

Abel, G. G., & Osborn, C. A. (2003). Treatment of sex offenders. In R. Rosner (Ed.), *Principles and practice of forensic psychiatry* (2nd ed., pp. 705–716). London: Arnold.

Abrams, A. A. (2002). Assessing competency in criminal proceedings. In B. Van Dorstein (Ed.), *Forensic psychology from classroom to courtroom* (pp. 105–141). New York: Kluwer.

Adams v. United States ex rel. McCann, 317 U.S. (1942).

Alaska Stat. § 12.47.030 (2003).

Alicke, M. D. (2000). Culpable control and the psychology of blame. *Psychological Bulletin, 126,* 556–574.

Allen, L. M., Conder, R., Green, P., & Cox, D. R. (1997). *Computerized assessment of response bias.* Durham, NC: Cognisyst, Inc.

Allen, M., Mabry, E., & McKelton, D. M. (1998). Impact of juror attitudes about the death penalty or juror evaluations of guilt and punishment: A meta-analysis. *Law and Human Behavior, 22,* 715–731.

American Academy of Psychiatry and Law. (1991). *Ethical guidelines for the practice of forensic psychiatry.* Bloomington, CT: Author.

American Academy of Psychiatry and Law. (1995). *Ethical guidelines for the practice of forensic psychiatry.* Bloomington, CT: Author.

American Association of Mental Retardation. (1992). *Mental retardation: Definition, classification, and systems of support* (9th ed.). Washington: Author.

American Bar Association, Standing Committee on Association Standards for Criminal Justice. (1983). *Criminal justice and mental health standards, First draft.* Chicago: American Bar Association.

American Bar Association Criminal Justice and Mental Health Standards. (1989). *Criminal justice and mental health standards*. Project of the American Bar Association Criminal Justice Standards Committee, Washington, DC.

American Educational Research Association, American Psychological Association, and National Council on Measurement in Education (AERA/APA/NCME). (1999). *Standards for educational and psychological testing*. Washington, DC: American Educational Research Association.

American Law Institute, Model Penal Code, Forward (1962).

American Psychiatric Association. (1968). *Diagnostic and statistical manual of mental disorders* (2nd ed.). Washington, DC. Author.

American Psychiatric Association. (1983). American Psychiatric Association statement on the insanity defense. *American Journal of Psychiatry, 140*, 681–688.

American Psychiatric Association. (1995). News Release No. 95-25, July 20, 1995.

American Psychiatric Association. (2000a). *Diagnostic and statistical manual of mental disorders: Text revision* (4th ed.). Washington, DC: American Psychiatric Press.

American Psychiatric Association. (2000b). *Handbook of psychiatric measures*. Washington, DC: American Psychiatric Press.

American Psychological Association. (2002). Ethical standards and code of conduct. *American Psychologist, 57*(12), 1060–1073.

American University. (2000). *Drug court activity update: Summary*. Washington, DC: US Department of Justice, Office of Justice Programs, Drug Court Clearinghouse.

American University. (2003). *Implementation status of drug court programs*. Washington, DC: US Department of Justice, Office of Justice Programs, Drug Court Clearinghouse.

Anastasi, A. (1988). Psychological testing (6th ed.). New York: Macmillan.

Appelbaum, P. S. (1986). Competence to be executed: Another conundrum for mental health professionals. *Hospital and Community Psychiatry, 37*, 682–684.

Ariz. Rev. Stat. Ann. § 13-3961 (2003).

Ariz. Rev. Stat. § 13-4021 (2004).

Ariz. Rev. Stat. § 13-4507 (2004).

Arkansas. Code § 16-97-103 (2003).

Arrigo, B. A., & Tasca, J. J. (1999). Right to refuse treatment, competency to be executed, and therapeutic jurisprudence: Toward a systematic analysis. *Law and Psychology Review, 23*, 1–47.

Ashendorf, L., Constantinou, M., & McCaffrey, R. J. (2004). The effect of depression and anxiety on the TOMM in community-dwelling older adults. *Achives of Clinical Neuropsychology, 19*, 125–130.

Atkins v. Virginia, 536 U.S. 304 (2002).

Babcock, J. C., & Steiner, R. (1999). The relationship between treatment, incarceration, and recidivism of battering: A program evaluation of Seattle's coordinated community response to domestic violence. *Journal of Family Psychology, 13*, 46–59.

Bandura, A. (1973). *Aggression: A social learning analysis*. Englewood Cliffs, NJ: Prentice-Hall.

Barbaree, H. E., Seto, M. C., Langton, C. M., & Peacock, E. J. (2001). Evaluating the predictive accuracy of six risk assessment instruments for adult sex offenders. *Criminal Justice and Behavior, 28*, 490–521.

Basco, M. R., Bostic, J. Q., Davies, D., Rush, A. J., Witte, B., et al. (2000). Methods to improve diagnostic accuracy in a community mental health setting. *American Journal of Psychiatry, 157*, 1599–1605.

Bechtel v. State, 840 P.2d 1(Okla., 1992).

Becker, R. F. (1997). *Scientific evidence and expert testimony handbook*. Springfield, IL: C.C. Thomas.

Belenko, S. (2001). *Research on drug courts: A critical review, 2001 Update*. New York: National Center on Addiction and Substance Abuse at Columbia University. Retrieved November 20, 2003, from http://www.casacolumbia.org/absolutenm/articlefiles/researchondrug.pdf

Bender, S. D., & Rogers, R. (2004). Detection of cognitive feigning: Development of a multi-strategy assessment. *Archives of Clinical Neuropsychology, 19*, 49–60.

Bennett v. Commonwealth, 511 S.E.2d 439 (Va. App., 1999).

Bersoff, D. N., & Hofer, P. J. (2003). Legal issues in computerized psychological testing. In D. N. Bersoff (Ed.), *Ethical conflicts in psychology* (3rd ed., pp. 300–302). Washington, DC: American Psychological Association.

Binder, L. M. (1993). Assessment of malingering after mild head trauma with the Portland Digit Recognition Test. *Journal of Clinical and Experimental Neuropsychology, 15*, 170–182.

Binder, L. M., & Willis, S. C. (1991). Assessment of motivation after financially compensable minor head trauma. *Psychological Assessment: A Journal of Consulting and Clinical Psychology, 3*, 175–181.

Binks, P. G., Gouvier, W. D., & Waters, W. F. (1997). Malingering detection with the Dot Counting Test. *Archives of Clinical Neuropsychology, 12*(1), 41–46.

Blashfield, R. K. (1992, August). *Are there any prototypical patients with personality disorders?* Paper presented at the American Psychological Association convention, Washington, DC.

Blake, D. D., Weathers, F., Nagy, L. M., Kaloupek, D. G., Charney, D. S., & Keane, T. M. (1998). *Clinician-Administered PTSD Scale for DSM-IV*. Boston, MA: National Center for Posttraumatic Stress Disorder.

Boehnert, C. E. (1985). Psychological and demographic differences associated with individuals using the insanity defense. *Journal of Psychiatry and Law, 13*, 9–31.

Boer, D. P., Hart, S. D., Kropp, P. R., & Webster, C. D. (1997). *Manual for the Sexual Violence Risk—20*. Burnaby, BC: Mental Health, Law, & Policy Institute, Simon Fraser University.

Bonnie, R. J. (1990). Dilemmas in administering the death penalty. *Law and Human Behavior, 14*, 67–90.

Bonnie, R. J. (1992). The competence of criminal defendants: A theoretical reformulation. *Behavioral Sciences and the Law, 10*, 291–316.

Bonnie, R. J. (1993). The competence of criminal defendants: Beyond *Dusky* and *Drope*. *Miami Law Review, 47*, 539–601.

Bonnie, R. J., & Grisso, T. (2000). Adjudicative competence and youthful offenders. In T. Grisso & R. G. Schwartz (Eds.), *Youth on trial: A developmental perspective on juvenile justice* (pp. 73–103). Chicago: University of Chicago Press.

Bonnie, R. J., Hoge, S. K., Monahan, J., Poythress, N., Eisenberg, M., & Feucht-Haviar, T. (1997). The MacArthur adjudicative competence study: A comparison of criteria for assessing the competence of criminal defendants. *Journal of the American Academy of Psychiatry and Law, 25*, 249–259.

Bonta, J., & Cormier, R. B. (1999). Corrections research in Canada: Impressive progress and promising prospects. *Canadian Journal of Criminology, 41*, 235–247.

Borum, R. (2003). Not guilty by reason of insanity. In T. Grisso (Ed.), *Evaluating competencies: Forensic assessments and instruments* (2nd ed., pp. 193–227). New York: Kluwer Academic.

Borum, R., & Grisso, T. (1995). Psychological test use in criminal forensic evaluations. *Professional Psychology: Research and Practice, 26*, 465–473.

Boykin v. Alabama, 395 U.S. 238 (1969).

Bradford, J. (2000). The treatment of sexual deviation using a pharmacological approach. *Journal of Sex Research, 37*, 248–257.

Bradford, J., & Harris, V. L. (2003). Psychopharmacological treatment of sex offenders. In R. Rosner (Ed.), *Principles and practice of forensic psychiatry* (2nd ed., pp. 685–698). London: Arnold.

Brakel, S. J., Parry, J., & Weiner, B. A. (1985). *The mentally disabled and the law* (3rd ed.). Chicago: American Bar Foundation.

Brennan, L. M. (1998). Comment: Drug courts: A new beginning for nonviolent drug addicted offenders—An end to cruel and unusual punishment. *Hamline Law Review, 22*, 355–396.

Brigham, J. C., & Grisso, J. T. (2003). Forensic psychology. In D. K. Freedheim (Ed.), *History of psychology* (Vol. 1, pp. 391–411). New York: Wiley.

Brodsky, S. L. (1991) *Testifying in court: Guidelines and maxims for the expert witness.* Washington, DC: American Psychological Association.

Brodsky, S. L., Zapf, P. A., & Boccacini, M. T. (1999). Post-conviction relief: These assessments of competence for execution. In *Proceedings of the APA/ABA Conference for Psychologists and Lawyers on Psychological Expertise and Criminal Justice* (Vol. 2, pp. 189–201). Washington, DC: American Psychological Association.

Brodsky, S. L., Zapf, P. A., & Boccacini, M. T. (2001). The last competency: An examination of legal, ethical, and professional ambiguities regarding evaluations of competence for execution. *Journal of Forensic Psychology Practice, 1*, 1–25.

Brooks, A. D. (1974). *Law, psychiatry, and the mental health system.* Boston: Little, Brown.

Brown v. Mississippi, 297 U.S. 278 (1936).

Brown, T. A., DiNardo, P. A., & Barlow, D. H. (1995). *Anxiety Disorders Interview Schedule for DSM-IV (ADIS-IV).* Albany, NY: Center for Stress and Anxiety Disorders, State University of New York at Albany.

Buchanan, A. (2000). *Psychiatric aspects of justification, excuse, and mitigation.* London: Jessica Kingsley Publishers.

Buchanan v. Kentucky, 483 U.S. 402 (1987).

Buhrle v. State, 627 P.2d 1374 (Wyo. 1981).

Bumby, K. M., & Maddox, M. C. (1999). Judges knowledge about sex offenders, difficulties presiding over sexual offense cases, and opinions on sentencing, treatment, and legislation. *Sexual Abuse: A Journal of Research and Treatment, 11*, 305–315.

Burke, A. S. (2002). Rational actors, self-defense, and duress: Making sense, not syndromes, out of the battered woman. *North Carolina Law Review, 81*, 211–316.

Burket v. Angelone, 208 F.3d 172 (4th Cir., 2000).

Burns Ind. Code Ann. § 35-36-2-3 (2004).

Butcher, J. N., Dahlstrom, W. G., Graham, J. R., Tellegen, A., & Kaemmer, B. (1989). *Manual for the administration and scoring of the MMPI-2.* Minneapolis, MN: University of Minnesota Press.

Butler, B. M., & Moran, G. (2002). The role of death qualification in venirepersons' evaluations of aggravating and mitigating circumstances in capital cases. *Law and Human Behavior, 26*, 175–184.

Cal. Const., Art. I § 12 (2003).

Cal. Evid. Code § 1107 (2004).

Cal. Pen. Code § 29 (2003).

Cal. Pen. Code § 190.3 (2004).

Cal. Pen. Code § 1367 (2003).

Cal. Pen. Code § 1367 (2004).

Cal. Pen. Code § 1001.20 (2004).

Campbell, W. G., & Hodgins, D. C. (1993). Alcholic-related blackouts in a medical practice. *American Journal of Drug and Alcohol Abuse, 19*, 369–376.

Carey, K. T. (1998). Review of AAMR Adaptive Behavior Scale—Residential and Community, Second Edition. In J. C. Impara & B. S. Plake (Eds.), *The thirteenth mental measurements yearbook* [Electronic version]. Retrieved December 12, 2004, from the Buros Institute's *Test Reviews Online* website: http://www.unl.edu/buros.

Carter v. United States, 530 U.S. 255, 269 (2000).

Casey, P., & Rottman, D. (1999, July). Therapeutic jurisprudence and the emergence of problem-solving courts. *National Institute of Justice Journal*, 12–19.

Christensen, K. S., Toft, T., Frostholm, L., Ørnbøl, E., Fink, P., & Olesen, F. (2003). The FIP study: A randomized, controlled, trial of screening and recognition of psychiatric disorders. *British Journal of General Practice, 53*, 758–763.

Cirincione, C. (1996). Revisiting the insanity defense: Contested or consensus? *Bulletin of the American Academy of Psychiatry and the Law, 24*, 165–176.

Cleckley, H. (1976). *The mask of insanity* (4th ed.). St. Louis, MN: Mosby.

Cloninger, C. R., Marin, R. L., Guze, S. B., & Clayton, P. J. (1985). Diagnosis and prognosis in schizophrenia. *Archives of General Psychiatry, 42*, 15–25.

Cole v. State (1985).

Collier v. State, 857 So. 2d 943 (Fla. Dist. Ct. App., 2003).

Colorado v. Connelly, 479 U.S. 157 (1986).

Colorado v. Spring, 479 U.S. 564 (1987).

Colo. Rev. Stat. 16-8-114.5 (2003).

Colo. Rev. Stat. § 18-1.3-1201 (2003).

Constanzo, M. (2004). *Psychology applied to law*. Belmont, CA: Wadsworth/Thompson.

Committee on Ethical Guidelines for Forensic Psychologists. (1991). Speciality guidelines for forensic psychologists. *Law and Human Behavior, 15*, 655–665.

Commonwealth v. Boucher, 780 N.E.2d 47 (Mass., 2002).

Conn. Gen. Stat. § 53a-19 (2003).

Connell, M. A. (2003). A psychobiographical approach to sentence mitigation. *Journal of Psychiatry and Law, 31*, 319–354.

Conroy, M. A. (2003). Evaluation of sexual predators. In A. M. Goldstein (Ed.), *Comprehensive handbook of psychology: Forensic psychology* (Vol. 11, pp. 463–484). New York: Wiley.

Cooke, D. J., & Michie, C. (1997). An item response theory analysis of the Hare Psychopathy Checklist—Revised. *Psychological Assessment, 9*, 3–14.

Cooke, D. J., & Michie, C. (2001). Refining the concept of psychopathy: Towards a hierarchical model. *Psychological Assessment, 13*, 171–188.

Cooper v. Griffin, 455 F.2d 1142 (5th Cir., 1972).

Cooper v. Oklahoma, 517 U.S. 348 (1996).

Cornell, M. A. (2003). A psychobiographical approach for sentence mitigation. *Journal of Psychiatry and Law, 31*, 319–354.

Cornwell, J. K. (2003). Sex offenders and the Supreme Court: The significance and limits of *Kansas v. Hendricks*. In B. J. Winick & J. Q. LaFond (Eds.), *Protecting society from sexually dangerous offenders* (pp. 197–210). Washington, DC: American Psychological Association.

Cosden, M., Ellens, J. K., Schnell, J. L., Yamini-Diouf, Y., & Wolfe, M. M. (2003). Evaluation of a mental health treatment court with assertive community treatment. *Behavioral Sciences and the Law, 21*, 415–427.

Cowles v. State, 510 S.W.2d 608 (Tex. Crim. App., 1974).

Craig, L. A., Browne, K. D., & Stringer, I. (2003). Risk scales and factors predictive of sexual offense recidivism. *Trauma, Violence, and Abuse, 4*, 45–69.

Crawford v. State, 136 S.W.3d 417 (Tex.App. – Corpus Christi, 2004).

Culombe v. Connecticut, 367 U.S. 568 (1961).

Cunnien, A. J. (1997). Psychiatric and medical syndromes associated with deception. In R. Rogers (Ed.), *Clinical assessment of malingering and deception* (2nd ed., pp. 23–46). New York: Guilford Press.

Cunningham, M. D., & Goldstein, A. M. (2003). Sentencing determinations in death penalty cases. In A. M. Goldstein (Ed.), *Comprehensive handbook of psychology: Forensic psychology* (Vol. 11, pp. 407–436). New York: Wiley.

Cunningham, M., & Reidy, T. J. (1999). Don't confuse me with the facts: Common errors in violence risk assessment at capital sentencing. *Criminal Justice and Behavior, 26,* 20–43.

Cunningham, M., & Reidy, T. J. (2001). A matter of life or death: Special considerations and heightened practice standards in capital sentencing evaluations. *Behavioral Sciences and the Law, 19,* 473–490.

Cunningham, M., & Reidy, T. J. (2002). Violence risk assessment at federal capital sentencing. *Criminal Justice and Behavior, 29,* 512–537.

D'Silva, K., Duggan, C., & McCarthy, L. (2004). Does treatment really make psychopaths worse? A review of the evidence. *Journal of Personality Disorders, 18,* 163–177.

Daicoff, S., & Wexler, D. B. (2003). Therapeutic jurisprudence. In A. M. Goldstein (Ed.), *Handbook of psychology, Vol. 11: Forensic psychology* (pp. 561–580). New York: Wiley.

Dan-Cohen, M. (2000). The morality of criminal law: A symposium in honor of Professor Sandy Kadish: Basic values and the victim's state of mind. *California Law Review, 88,* 759–778.

Daubert v. Merrell Dow Pharmaceutical, Inc., 509 U.S. 579 (1993).

Davidson, H. A. (1965). *Forensic psychiatry* (2nd ed.). New York: Ronald Press.

Deitchman, M. A., Kennedy, W. A., & Beckman, J. C. (1991). Self-selection factors in the participation of mental health professionals in competency for execution evaluations. *Law and Human Behavior, 15,* 287–303.

Delgado-Escueta, A. V., Mattson, R. H., King, L., Goldensohn, E. S., Spiegel, H., et al. (1981). The nature of aggression during epileptic seizures. *New England Journal of Medicine, 305,* 711–716.

Dickinson, R. L. (1984). Indiana court condemns mentally ill man to die for murder. *Mental Health Reports, 8,* 1–2.

Dodge, K. A., Price, J. M., Bachorowski, J.-A., & Newman, J. P. (1990). Hostile attributional biases in severely aggressive adolescents. *Journal of Abnormal Psychology, 99,* 385–392.

Doren, D. M. (1998). Recidivism base rates, predictions of sex offender recidivism, and the "sexual predator" commitment laws. *Behavioral Sciences and the Law, 16,* 97–114.

Douglas v. Commonwealth, 83 S.W.3d 462 (Ky., 2001).

Dunn, G., Everitt, B., & Pickles, A. (1993). *Modeling covariances and latent variables using EQS.* London: Chapman and Hall.

Durham v. United States, 214 F.2d 862 (D.C. Cir., 1954).

Dusek v. State, 978 S.W.2d 129 (Tex. App., 1998).

Dusky v. United States, 362 U.S. 402 (1960).

Dutton, D. G. (1999). Profiles of abuse. In American Psychological Association, *Proceedings of Psychological Expertise and Criminal Justice* (Vol. 1, pp. 281–287). Washington, DC: Author.

Dutton, M. A. (1992). *Empowering and healing the battered woman.* New York: Springer.

Dutton, D. G., & Kropp, P. R. (2000). A review of domestic violence risk assessments. *Trauma, Violence, and Abuse, 1,* 171–181.

Dyer, F. J., & McCann, J. T. (2000). Millon clinical inventories: Research critical to their forensic application and Daubert criteria. *Law and Human Behavior, 24,* 487–498.

Ebert, B. (2001). Competency to be executed: A proposed instrument to evaluate an inmate's level of competency in light of the Eighth Amendment prohibition against the execution of the presently insane. *Law and Psychology Review, 25,* 29–57.

Eddings v. Oklahoma, 455 U.S. 104 (1982).

Edens, J. F., Petrila, J., & Buffington-Vollum, K. (2001). Psychopath and the death penalty: Can the Psychopathy Checklist Revised identify offenders who represent "a continuing threat to society"? *Journal of Psychiatry and Law, 29*, 433–481.

Edwards v. Arizona, 451 U.S. 477 (1981).

Eisenberg, J. R. (2004). *Law, psychology and death penalty litigation.* Sarasota: Professional Resources Press.

Ellsworth, P. C., Haney, C., & Constanzo, M. (2001). *Society for the Study of Social Issues (SPSSI) position statement on the death penalty.* Retrieved from www.spssi.org

Epperson, D. L., Kaul, J. D., & Hasselton, D. (1998, October). *Final report on the development of the Minnesota Sex Offender Screening Tool—Revised (MnSOST-R).* In Proceedings of the Research and Treatment Conference of the Association for the Treatment of Sexual Abusers, Vancouver, Canada.

Epperson, D. L., Kaul, J. D., Huot, S., Goldman, R., & Alexander, W. (2003). *Minnesota Sex Offender Screening Tool—Revised (MnSOST-R) technical paper: Development validation, and recommended risk level cut scores.* Retrieved December 20, 2004, from http://129.186.143.73/faculty/epperson/mnsost_download.htm

Epperson, D. L., Kaul, J. D., Huot, S., Hesselton, D., Alexander, W., et al. (2000). *Minnesota Sex Offender Screening Tool—Revised (MnSOST-R).* St. Paul, MN: Minnesota Dept. of Corrections. Retrieved December 20, 2004, from http://www.doc.state.mn.us

Erdberg, P. (1990). Rorschach assessment. In G. Goldstein & M. Hersen (Eds.), *Handbook of psychological assessment* (2nd ed., pp. 387–399). New York: Pergamon.

Escobedo v. Illinois, 378 U.S. 478 (1964).

Estelle v. Smith, 451 U.S. 454 (1981).

Everington, C., & Fulero, S. M. (1999). Competence to confess: Measuring understanding and suggestibility of defendants with mental retardation. *Mental Retardation, 37,* 212–220.

Everington, C., & Luckasson, R. (1992). *Manual for Competence Assessment for Standing Trial for Defendants with Mental Retardation: CAST-MR.* Worthington, OH: IDS Publishing.

Ewing, C. P. (1987). *Battered women who kill: Psychological self-defense as legal justification.* Lexington, MA: D.C. Heath.

Ewing, C. P. (2003). Expert testimony: Law and practice. In A. M. Goldstein (Ed.), *Comprehensive handbook of psychology: Forensic psychology* (Vol. 11, pp. 55–66). New York: Wiley.

Ewing v. California, 538 U.S. 11 (2003).

Ex parte Jordan, 758 S.W.2d 250 (Tex. Crim. App., 1988).

Faigman, D., & Wright, A. (1997). The battered woman syndrome in the age of science. *Arizona Law Review, 39,* 67–115.

Falk, P. J. (1996). Novel theories of criminal defense based upon the toxicity of the social environment: urban psychosis, television intoxication, and black rage. *North Carolina Law Review, 74,* 731–811.

Fare v. Michael C., 422 U.S. 707 (1979).

Faretta v. California, 422 U.S. 806 (1975).

Faust, D., Hart, K., & Guilmette, T. J. (1988). Pediatric malingering: The capacity of children to fake believable deficits of neuropsychological testing. *Journal of Consulting and Clinical Psychology, 56,* 578–582.

Faust, D., & Ziskin, J. (1988). The expert witness in psychology and psychiatry. *Science, 241,* 31–35.

Fava, G. A. (2001). Physicians, medical associations, and death penalty. *Psychotherapy and Psychosomatics, 70,* 168.

Fed R. Evid 404 (1975).

Fed R. Evid. 704 (1975).

Fed. R. 704(b) (1984).

Fed R. Evid 1101 (d) (3) (1975).

Federal Bureau of Investigation. (2002). *Crime in the United States—2002*. Washington, D.C.: U.S. Department of Justice. http://www.fbi.gov/ucr/cius_02/pdf/4sectionfour.pdf

Fenwick, P. (1987). Somnambulism and the law: A review. *Behavioral Science and the Law, 5*, 343–350.

Fenwick, P. (1990). Automatism, medicine and the law. *Psychological Medicine Monograph, 17* (whole).

Fingarette, H., & Hasse, A. F. (1979). *Mental disabilities and criminal responsibility*. Berkeley: University of California Press.

Finkel, N. J., Shaw, R., Bercaw, S., & Koch, J. (1985). Insanity defenses: From the jurors' perspective. *Law and Psychology Review, 9*, 77–92.

Finkel, N. J., & Slobogin, C. (1995). Insanity, justification, and culpability toward a unifying schema. *Law and Human Behavior, 19*, 447–464.

Finlay, W. M. L., & Lyons, E. (2001). Methodological issues in interviewing and using self-report questionnaires with people with mental retardation. *Psychological Assessment, 13*, 319–325.

First, M. B., Gibbon, M., Spitzer, R. L., Williams, J. B. W., & Benjamin, L. S. (1997). The Structured Clinical Interview for *DSM-IV* Axis II Personality Disorders (SCID-II). Washington, DC: American Psychiatric Press.

First, M. B., Spitzer, R. L., Williams, J. B. W., & Gibbon, M. (1997). *Structured Clinical Interview of DSM-IV Disorders (SCID)*. Washington, DC: American Psychiatric Association.

Fitch, W. L., & Hammen, D. A. (2003). The new generation of sex offender commitment laws: Which states have them and how do they work? In B. J. Winick & J. Q. LaFond (Eds.), *Protecting society from sexually dangerous offenders* (pp. 27–39). Washington, DC: American Psychological Association.

Fla. R. Crim P. 3.811 (2004).

Fla. Stat. Ann. § 916.12 (2002).

Fla. Stat. Ann. § 916.12 (2004).

Fla. Stat. § 921.141 (2004).

The Florida Bar v. Schaub, 618 So. 2d 202 (Fla., 1993).

Follingstad, D. R. (2003). Battered woman syndrome in the courts. In A. M. Goldstein (Ed.), *Comprehensive handbook of psychology: Forensic psychology* (Vol. 11, pp. 485–507). New York: Wiley.

Folstein, M. F., Folstein, S. E., & McHugh, P. R. (1975). Mini-mental state. A practical method of grading cognitive state of patients for the clinician. *Journal of Psychiatric Research, 12*, 189–198.

Ford v. Wainwright, 477 U.S. 399 (1986).

Foster v. State. (2000). Tex. App. LEXIS 8622 (Tex. App. Corpus Christi).

Frank, J., & Applegate, B. K. (1998). Assessing juror understanding of capital-sentencing instructions. *Crime and Delinquency, 44*, 412–433.

Franz v. State, 745 S.W.2d 839 (Ark. 1988).

Frederick, R. I., & Foster, H. G. (1997). *The validity indicator profile*. Minneapolis, MN: National Computer Systems.

Free, M. D., Jr. (2002). Race and pre-sentencing decisions in the United States: A summary and critique of the research. *Criminal Justice Review, 27*, 203–232.

Frumkin, B. (2000). Competency to waive Miranda rights: Clinical and legal issues. *Mental Health and Physical Disability Law Reporter, 24*, 326–331.

Frye v. United States, 293 F. 1013 (D.C. Cir., 1923).

Fulcher v. State, 633 P.2d 142 (Wyo., 1981).

Fulero, S. M., & Everington, C. (1995). Assessing competency to waive Miranda rights in defendants with mental retardation. *Law and Human Behavior, 19*, 533–543.

Fulero, S. M., & Finkel, N. J. Barring ultimate issue testimony: An "insane" rule? *Law and Human Behavior, 15,* 495–507.

Furman v. Georgia, 408 U.S. 238 (1972).

Ga. Code Ann. § 17-10-60 (2004).

Gacono, G. B., Meloy, J. R., Sheppard, K., Speth, E., & Roske, A. (1995). A clinical investigation of malingering and psychopathy in hospitalized NGRI patients. *Bulletin of the American Academy of Psychiatry and Law, 23,* 387–397.

Gee, M. M. (2003). Modern status of test of criminal responsibility-state cases. *American Law Reports (4th ed.), 9,* 526–543.

Gelder, B. C., Titus, J. B., & Dean, R. S. (2002). The efficacy of Neuropsychological Psychological Symptom Inventory in the differential diagnosis of medical, psychiatric, and malingering patients. *International Journal of Neuroscience, 112,* 1377–1392.

Gendreau, P., Goggin, C., & Smith, P. (2002). Is the PCL-R really the "unparalleled" measure of offender risk? A lesson in knowledge cumulation. *Criminal Justice and Behavior, 29,* 397–426.

General Electric Co. v. Joiner, 522 U.S. 136 (1997).

Georgia Code Ann. § 16-3-3 (2002).

Georgia O.C.G.A. § 17-2-4 (2002).

Gerber, J., & Englehardt-Greer, S. (1996). Just and painful: Attitudes toward sentencing criminals. In T. J. Flanagan & D. R. Longmire (Eds.), *Americans view crime and justice: A national public opinion survey* (pp. 62–74). Thousand Oaks, CA: Sage.

Godinez v. Moran, 509 U.S. 389 (1993).

Goldstein, A. S. (1967). *The insanity defense.* New Haven, CT: Yale University Press.

Goldstein, A. M. (Ed.). (2003a). *Comprehensive handbook of psychology: Forensic psychology.* New York: Wiley.

Goldstein, A. M. (2003b). Overview of forensic psychology. In A. M. Goldstein (Ed.), *Comprehensive handbook of psychology: Forensic psychology* (pp. 3–20). New York: Wiley.

Goldstein, A. M., Morse, S. J., & Shapiro, D. L. (2003). Evaluation of criminal responsibility. In A. M. Goldstein (Ed.), *Comprehensive handbook of psychology: Forensic psychology* (pp. 381–406). New York: Wiley.

Goodness, K. R., & Rogers, R. (1999, August). *Retrospective malingering detection: The validations of the R-SIRS and CT-SIRS.* Paper presented at the American Psychological Association Annual Convention, Boston.

Gothard, S., Rogers, R., & Sewell, K. W. (1995). Feigning incompetency to stand trial: An investigation of the GCCT. *Law and Human Behavior, 19,* 363–373.

Gov't of Virgin Islands v. Smith, 278 F.2d 169 (3rd Cir., 1960).

Green, W. P., Allen, L. M., III, & Astner, K. (1996). *The Word Memory Test.* Durham: CogniSyst.

Greenberg, S. A., Shuman, D. W., Meyer, R. G. (2004). Unmaking forensic diagnosis. *International Journal of Law and Psychiatry, 27,* 1–15.

Greene, R. L. (1997). Assessment of malingering and defensiveness on multiscale inventories. In R. Rogers (Ed.), *Clinical assessment of malingering and deception* (2nd ed., pp. 169–207). New York: Guilford.

Greenfield, D. P., Dougherty, E. J., Jackson, R. M., Podboy, J. W., & Zimmermann, M. L. (2001). Retrospective evaluation of Miranda reading levels and waiver competency. *American Journal of Forensic Psychology, 19,* 75–86.

Griffin, P. A., Steadman, H. J., & Petrila, J. (2002). The use of criminal charges and sanctions in Mental Health Courts. *Psychiatric Services, 53,* 1285–1289.

Griggs v. Commonwealth, 255 S.E.2d 475 (Va. 1979).

Grisso, T. (1981). *Juveniles' waiver of rights: Legal and psychological competence.* New York: Plenum.

Grisso, T. (1986). *Evaluating competencies: Forensic assessments and instruments.* New York: Plenum.

Grisso, T. (1987). Psychological assessments for legal decisions. In D. N. Weisstub (Ed.), *Law and mental health: International perspectives* (Vol. 3, pp. 125–157). New York: Pergamon.

Grisso, T. (1988). *Competency to stand trial evaluations: A manual for practice.* Sarasota, FL: Professional Resource Exchange.

Grisso, T. (1998). *Instruments for assessing understanding and appreciation of Miranda rights.* Sarasota, FL: Professional Resource Press.

Grisso, T. (2003a). Competence to stand trial. In T. Grisso (Ed.), *Evaluating competencies: Forensic assessments and instruments* (2nd ed., pp. 69–148). New York: Kluwer Academic.

Grisso, T. (2003b). *Evaluating competencies: Forensic assessments and instruments* (2nd ed.). New York: Kluwer Academic.

Gudjonsson, G. H. (1984). A new scale of interrogative suggestibility. *Personality and Individual Differences, 5,* 303–314.

Gudjonsson, G. H. (1990). The relationship of intellectual skills to suggestibility, compliance, and acquiescence. *Personality and Individual Differences, 11,* 227–231.

Gudjonsson, G. H. (1992). Interrogative suggestibility: Factor analysis of the Gudjonsson Suggestibility Scale (GSS 2). *Personality and Individual Differences, 13,* 479–481.

Gudjonsson, G. H. (2003). *The psychology of interrogations and confessions handbook.* London: Wiley.

Gutheil, T. G. (1998a). *The psychiatrist as expert witness.* Washington, DC: American Psychiatric Press.

Gutheil, T. G. (1998b). *The psychiatrist in court.* Washington, DC: American Psychiatric Press.

Haney, C. (1980). Psychology and legal change: On the limits of factual jurisprudence. *Law and Human Behavior, 4,* 147–200.

Hanson, R. K. (1997). *The development of a brief actuarial risk scale for sexual recidivism* (User report 1997-04). Ottawa: Department of the Solicitor General of Canada.

Hanson, R. K. (2003). Who is dangerous and when are they safe? Risk assessment with sexual offenders. In B. J. Winick & J. Q. LaFond (Eds.), *Protecting society from sexually dangerous offenders* (pp. 63–75). Washington, DC: American Psychological Association.

Hanson, R. K., Broom, I., & Stephenson, M. (2004). Evaluating community sex offender treatment programs: A 12-year follow-up of 724 offenders. *Canadian Journal of Behavioral Science, 36,* 87–96.

Hanson, R. K., & Bussiere, M. T. (1998). Predicting relapse: A meta-analysis of sexual offender recidivism studies. *Journal of Consulting and Clinical Psychology, 66,* 348–362.

Hanson, R. K. & Thornton, D. (1999). *Static-99: Improving actuarial risk assessments for sex offenders.* Solicitor General of Canada. Retrieved from www.sgc.gc.ca

Harding, R. M. (1994). "Endgame": Competency and the execution of condemned inmates— A proposal to satisfy the Eight Amendment's prohibition against infliction of cruel and unusual punishment. *St. Louis University Public Law Review, 14,* 105–151.

Hare, R. D. (1991). *Manual for the Hare Psychopathy Checklist—Revised.* Toronto: Multi-Health Systems.

Hare, R. D. (2003). *Manual for the Hare Psychopathy Checklist—Revised* (2nd ed.). Toronto: Multi-Health Systems.

Harris, G. T., Rice, M. E., & Quinsey, V. L. (1993). Violent recidivism of mentally disordered offenders: The development of a statistical prediction instrument. *Criminal Justice and Behavior, 20,* 315–335.

Harris, G. T., Rice, M. E., & Quinsey, V. L. (1998). Appraisal and management of risk in sexual aggressors: Implications for criminal justice policy. *Psychology, Public Policy, and Law, 4,* 73–115.

Harrison, P. L. (1998). Review of AAMR Adaptive Behavior Scale—Residential and Community, 2nd ed. In J. C. Impara & B. S. Plake (Eds.), *The thirteenth mental measurements yearbook* [Electronic version]. Retrieved December 12, 2004, from the Buros Institute's *Test Reviews Online* website http://www.unl.edu/buros

Hart, S. D. (1998). The role of psychopathy in assessing risk for violence: Conceptual and methodological issues. *Legal and Criminological Psychology, 3*, 121–137.

Hart, S. D. (2000). *Affidavits submitted in support of motion in limine to exclude expert testimony regarding the PCL-R and HCR-20 risk assessment instruments and the diagnosis of psychopathy.* In U.S. v. Willis Haynes. Unpublished document, Simon Fraser University, Vancouver.

Heal, L. W., & Sigelman, C. K. (1995). Response biases in interviews of individuals with limited mental ability. *Journal of Intellectual Disability Research, 39*, 331–340.

Heck Van Tran v. State, 6 S.W.3d 257 (Tenn., 1999).

Heilbrun, K. S. (1987). The assessment of competency for execution: An overview. *Behavioral Sciences and the Law, 5*, 383–396.

Heilbrun, K. S. (1992). The role of psychological testing in forensic assessment. *Law and Human Behavior, 16*, 257–272.

Heilbrun, K. S. (2001). *Principles of forensic mental health assessment.* New York: Kluwer.

Heilbrun, K. S., & McClaren, H. A. (1988). Assessment of competency to be executed: A guide to mental health professionals. *Bulletin of the American Academy of Psychiatry and Law, 16*, 205–216.

Heilbrun, K., Rogers, R., & Otto, R. K. (2002). Forensic assessment: Current status and future directions. In J. R. P. Ogloff (Ed.), *Taking psychology and law into the twenty-first century* (pp. 120–146). New York: Kluwer.

Helms, J. L. (2003). Analysis of Miranda reading levels across jurisdictions: Implications for evaluating waiver competency. *Journal of Forensic Psychology and Practice, 3*, 25–37.

Hemphill, J. F., Hare, R. D., & Wong, S. (1998). Psychopathy and recidivism: A review. *Legal and Criminological Psychology, 3*, 139–170.

Henderson v. Morgan, 426 U.S. 637 (1976).

Hill, C. D., Neumann, C. S., & Rogers, R. (2004). Confirmatory factor analysis of the Psychopathy Checklist: Screening Version (PCL:SV) in offenders with Axis I disorders. *Psychological Assessment, 16*, 90–95.

Hiscoke, U. L., Langstrom, N., Ottosson, H., & Grann, M. (2003). Self-reported personality traits and disorders (DSM-IV) and risk of criminal recidivism: A prospective study. *Journal of Personality Disorders, 17*, 293–305.

House of Lords. (1843). Daniel M'Naghten's case. Mews' Dig. i. 349; iv. 1112. S.C. 8 Scott N.R. 595; 1 C. and K. 130; 4 St. Tr. N.S. 847. Retrieved May 13, 2004, from http://www.llcc.cc.il.us/gtruitt/SCJ%20100%20Fall%202003%20Start%20Page/mnaghten%20case.htm.

Hubbard v. Haley, 317 F.3d 1245 (11th Cir., 2003).

Hudson v. Parker, 156 U.S. 277 (1895).

Ibn-Tamas v. United States, 407 A.2d 6264 (D.C., 1979).

Idaho Code § 18-207 (2003).

Idaho Code § 18-4001 (2003).

Idaho Code § 18-4002 (2003).

Idaho Code § 19-2515 (2004).

725 Ill. Comp. Stat.5/104-25 (2004).

725 Ill. Compiled Stat. Ann 5/113-4 (2004).

In re Crane, 7 P.3d 285 (Kan., 2000).

In re Detention of Hargett, 786 N.E.2d 557 (Ill. App., 2003).

In re R.S., 801 A.2d 219 (N.J., 2002).

In re Wilber W., 53 P.3d 1145 (Ariz. Ct. App., 2002).

Inbau, F. E., Reid, J. E., Buckley, J. P., & Jayne, B. C. (2001). *Criminal interrogation and confessions* (4th ed.). Gaithersberg, MD: Aspen.

Ind. Code Ann. § 35-36-3-3 (2004).

Insanity Defense Reform Act. (1984).

Iowa v. Tovar, 124 S. Ct. 1379 (2004).

Iowa Code § 812.5 (2003).

Jackson, R. L. (2003). *Contextualized risk assessment in clinical practice: Utility of actuarial, clinical and structured clinical approaches to predictions of violence.* Unpublished doctoral dissertation, University of North Texas.

Jackson v. Indiana, 406 U.S. 715 (1972).

Jackson, R. L., Rogers, R., & Shuman, D. W. (in press). The adequacy and accuracy of sexually violent predator evaluations: Contextualized risk assessment in clinical practice. *International Journal of Forensic Mental Health.*

Jackson, R. L., Rogers, R., & Sewell, K. W. (in press). Miller Forensic Assessment of Symptoms Test (MFAST): Forensic applications as a screen for feigned incompetence to stand trial. *Law and Human Behavior.*

Jackson, R. L., Rogers, R., & Shuman, D. W. (2004). *The adequacy and accuracy of sexually violent predator evaluations: Contextualized risk assessment in clinical practice.* Manuscript submitted for publication.

Janus, E. S. (2000). Sexual predator commitment laws: Lessons for law and the behavioral sciences. *Behavioral Sciences and the Law, 18,* 5–21.

Jenkins v. United States, 307 F.2d 637 (D.C. Cir., 1962).

Jennison, K. M., & Johnson, K. A. (1994). Drinking-induced blackouts among young adults: Results from a national longitudinal study. *International Journal of Addictions, 29,* 23–51.

Johnson, W. G., & Mullett, N. (1987). Georgia Court Competency Test-R. In M. Hersen & A. Bellack (Eds.), *Dictionary of behavioral assessment techniques.* New York: Pergamon.

Johnson v. Zerbst, 304 U.S. 458 (1938).

KRS § 504.120 (2003).

Kansas v. Crane, 534 U.S. 407 (2002).

Kansas v. Hendricks, 521 U.S. 346 (1997).

Kansas Statute Ann. § 22-3220 (2003).

Kansas Stat. Ann. § 59-29a01 (1994).

Kassin, S. M., & Kiechel, K. L. (1996). The social psychology of false confessions: Compliance, internalizations, and confabulation. *Psychological Science, 7,* 125–128.

Kentucky Rev. Stat. § 504.120 (2003).

Kinkade, P. T., Leone, M. C., & Welsh, W. N. (1995). "Tough" laws: Policymaker perceptions and commitment. *The Social Science Journal, 32,* 157–178.

Klassen, D., & O'Connor, W. (1988). A prospective study of predictors of violence in adult male mental patients. *Law and Human Behavior, 12,* 143–158.

Klein, M. H., Michels, J. L., & Kolden, G. G. (2001).Congruence or genuineness. *Psychotherapy: Theory, Research, Practice, Training, 38*(4), 396–400.

Koerner, H. H. (2002). The efficacy of forced treatment. *The Journal of Drug Issues, 32,*543–552.

Kohler v. State, 713 S.W.2d 141 (Tex. App. Corpus Christi, 1986).

Krauss, D. A., & Sales, B. D. (2003). Forensic psychology, public policy, and the law. In A. M. Goldstein (Ed.), *Comprehensive handbook of psychology: Forensic psychology* (Vol. 11, pp. 543–560). New York: Wiley.

Kumho Tire Co., Ltd. v. Carmichael, 526 U.S. 137 (1999).

Ky. Rev. Stat. § 431.213 (2004).

Lacoursiere, R. B. (2003). Evaluating offenders under a sexually violent predator law: The practical practice. In B. J. Winick & J. Q. LaFond (Eds.), *Protecting society from sexually dangerous offenders* (pp. 75–97). Washington, DC: American Psychological Association.

Lamb, R., & Bachrach, L. (2001). Some perspectives on deinstitutionalization. *Psychiatric Services, 52*, 1039–1045.

Lamb, R., & Weinberger, L. (1998). Persons with severe mental illness in jails and prisons: A review. *Psychiatric Services, 49*, 483–492.

Lanier, C. S., & Acker, J. R. (2004). Capital punishment, the moratorium movement, and empirical questions. *Psychology, Public Policy, and Law,* 577–617.

Laws, D. R., & O'Donohue, W. (Eds.). (1997). *Sexual deviance.* New York: Guilford.

Lazowski, L. E., Miller, F. G., Boye, M. W., & Miller, G. A. (1998). Efficacy of the Substance Abuse Subtle Screening Inventory—3 (SASSI-3) in identifying substance dependence disorders in clinical settings. *Journal of Personality Assessment, 71*, 114–128.

LeBlanc-Allman, R. J. (1990). Guilty but mentally ill: A poor prognosis. *South Carolina Law Review, 49*, 1095–1114.

Lee v. Wiman, 280 F.2d 257 (5th Cir., 1960).

Leland v Oregon, 343 US 790 (1952).

Lewis v. State, 27 S.E. 2d 659 (Ga., 1943).

Lewis v. State, 529 S.W.2d 550 (Tex. Crim. App., 1975).

Lezak, M. D. (1995). *Neuropsychological assessment* (3rd ed.). New York: Oxford.

Lieb, R. (2003). State policy perspectives on sexual predator laws. In B. J. Winick & J. Q. LaFond (Eds.), *Protecting society from sexually dangerous offenders* (pp. 41–59). Washington, DC: American Psychological Association.

Lipsett, P., Lelos, D., & McGarry, A. L. (1971). Competency for trial: A screening instrument. *American Journal of Psychiatry, 128*, 105–109.

Lockett v. Ohio, 438 U.S. 586 (1978).

Lonchar v. Zant, 978 F.2d 637 (11th Cir., 1993).

Loranger, A. W. (1999). *International Personality Disorder Examination (IPDE) manual.* Odessa, FL: Psychological Assessment Resources.

Low, P. W., Jeffries, J. C., Jr., & Bonnie, R. J. (1986). *The trial of John W. Hincklely, Jr.: A case study in the insanity defense.* Mineola, NY: Foundation Press.

Lowe, B., Spitzer, R. L., Gräfe, K., Kroenke, K., Quenter, A., et al. (2004). Comparative validity of three screening questionnaires for DSM-IV depressive disorders and physician's diagnoses. *Journal of Affective Disorders, 78*, 131–140.

Luskin, M. L. (2001). Who is diverted? Case selection for court-monitored mental health treatment. *Law and Policy, 23*, 217–236.

MCLS § 768.36 (2003).

M'Naghten, 8 Eng. Rep. 718 (1843).

Mapp v. Ohio, 367 U.S. 643 (1961).

Marlowe, D. B., Lambert, J. B., & Thompson, R. G. (1999). Voluntary intoxication and criminal responsibility. *Behavioral Sciences and the Law, 17*, 195–217.

Martinez v. Court of Appeal, 528 U.S. 152 (2000).

Martinez v. State, 16 S.W.3d 845 (Tex. App. Houston 1st Dist., 2000).

Martinson, R. (1974). What works? Questions and answers about prison reform. *Public Interest, 35*, 22–54.

Maryland Code Cts. & Jud. Proc. § 10-916 (2003).

Mass. Gen Laws ch. 123, § 15 (2003).

Matson, J. V. (1994). *Effective expert witnessing* (2nd ed.). Boca Raton, FL: Lewis Publishers.

McCann, J. T., & Dyer, F. J. (1996). *Forensic assessment with the Millon inventories.* New York: Guilford.

McClain v. State, 678 N.E.2d 104 (Ind., 1997).

McCray v. State, 591 So. 2d 108 (Ala. Crim. App., 1991).

McDonald v. United States, 312 F.2d 847 (D.C. Cir., 1962).

McGaha, A., Boothroyd, R. A., Poythress, N. G., Petrila, J., & Ort, R. G. (2002). Lessons from the Broward County Mental Health Court Evaluation. *Evaluation and Program Planning, 25,* 125–135.

McGarry, A. L., & Curran, W. J. (1973). *Competency to stand trial and mental illness.* Rockville, MD: National Institute of Mental Health.

McGrath, R. J., Cumming, G., Livingston, J. A., & Hoke, S. E. (2003). Outcome of a treatment program for adult sex offenders: From prison to community. *Journal of Interpersonal Violence, 18,* 3–17.

McQuiston, J. (1995). Jury Finds Ferguson Guilty of Slaying on the L.I.R.R. *N.Y. Times,* Feb. 17, 1995, at 1.

Md. Code Ann., Cts. & Jud. Proc. § 10-916 (2003).

Medina v. California, 505 U.S. 437 (1992).

Melton, G. B. (1999). Due care, not prohibition of expert opinions. *Clinical Psychology: Science and Practice, 6,* 335–338.

Melton, G. B., Petrila, J., Poythress, N. G., & Slobogin, C. (1987). *Psychological evaluations for the courts.* New York: Guilford.

Melton, G. B., Petrila, J., Poythress, N. G., & Slobogin, C. (1997). *Psychological evaluations for the courts* (2nd ed.). New York: Guilford.

Meza v. State. (2002). Tex. App. LEXIS 6171 (Tex. App. Corpus Christi).

Michigan Comp Ann 330.1400a (2003).

Miller, H. A. (2001). *MFAST: Miller Forensic Assessment of Symptoms Test professional manual.* Odessa, FL: Psychological Assessment Resources, Inc.

Miller, R. D. (2003). Criminal competence. In R. Rosner (Ed.), *Principles and practice of forensic psychiatry* (2nd ed., pp. 186–212). New York: Wiley.

Miller v. Dugger, 838 F.2d 1530 (11th Cir., 1988).

Mills v. State, 742 S.W.2d 831 (Tex. App. Dallas, 1987).

Millon, T. (1994). *The Millon Clinical Multiaxial Inventory—III manual.* Minneapolis, MN: National Computer Systems.

Millon, T., Davis, R., & Millon, C. (1997). *The Millon Clinical Multiaxial Inventory—III manual* (2nd ed.). Minneapolis, MN: National Computer Systems.

Mincey v. Arizona, 437 U.S. 385 (1978).

Minnesota ex rel. Pearson v. Probate Court, 309 U.S. 270 (1940).

Minnesota Sentencing Guidelines II.D.2.a.(3) (1990).

Miranda v. Arizona, 384 U.S. 436 (1966).

Miss. Code Ann. § 99-19-57(2) (2004).

Missouri (2004).

Mistretta v. United States, 488 U.S. 261 (1989).

Mo. Ann. Stat. § 563.033(1) (2004).

Model Penal Code, Forward (1962).

Moeller, F. G., & Dougherty, D. M. (2000). Impulsivity and substance abuse: What is the connection? *Addictive Disorders and Their Treatment, 1,* 3–10.

Monacella, K. G. (1997). Comment, supporting a defense of duress: The admissibility of battered woman syndrome. *Temple Law Review, 70,* 699–744.

Mont. Code Anno., § 46-14-102 (2002).

Mont. Code Anno., § 46-14-102 (2003).

Montana v. Egelhoff, 518 U.S. 537 (1966).

Moore v. Ballone, 658 F.2d 218 (4th Cir., 1981) 425, Ohio Rev. Code 2901.06 (2004).

Moran v. Burbine, 475 U.S. 412 (1986).

Morey, L. C. (1991). *Personality Assessment Inventory: Professional manual.* Tampa: Psychological Assessment Resources, Inc.

Morey, L. C. (1996). *An interpretive guide to the Personality Assessment Inventory (PAI).* Tampa: Psychological Assessment Resources, Inc.

Morris v. Slappy, 461 U.S. 1 (1983).

Morse, S. J. (1984). Undiminished confusion in diminished capacity. *Journal of Criminal Law and Criminology, 75*, 1–55.

Morse, S. J. (1998). Excusing and the new excuse defenses: A legal and conceptual view. *Crime and Justice, 23*, 329–403.

Mossman, D. (1995). Denouement of an execution competency case: Is *Perry* pyrrhic? *Bulletin of the American Academy of Psychiatry and the Law, 23*, 269–284.

Muench v. State, 210 N.W.2d 716 (Wis., 1973).

Moye, J. (2003). Guardianship and conservatorship. In T. Grisso (Ed.), *Evaluating competencies: Forensic assessments and instruments* (pp. 309–389; 2nd ed.). New York: Kluwer Academic.

Munetz, M. R., Grande, T. P., & Chambers, M. R. (2001). The incarceration of individuals with severe mental disorders. *Community Mental Health Journal, 37*, 361–372.

Naples, M., & Steadman, H. J. (2003). Can persons with co-occurring disorders and violent charges be successfully diverted? *International Journal of Forensic Mental Health, 2*, 137–142.

N.M. Stat. Ann. § 31-9-3 (2003).

Nicholson, R. A. (1999). Test review: Malingering Probability Scale. *American Psychology-Law Society News, 19*, 8–14.

Nihara, K., Leland, H., & Lambert, N. (1993). *AAMR Adaptive Behavior Scale—Residential and Community* (2nd ed.). Austin: Pro-Ed.

North, C. S., Pollio, D. E., Thompson, S. J., Ricci, D. A., Smith, E. M., & Spitznagel, E. L. (1997). A comparison of clinical and structured interview diagnoses in a homeless mental health clinic. *Community Mental Health Journal, 33*, 531–543.

Novaco, R. W. (1975). *Anger control: The development of experimental treatment.* Lexington, MA: Lexington Books.

Nusbaum, D. J. (2002). The craziest reform of them all: A critical analysis of the constitutional implications of "abolishing" the insanity defense. *Cornell Law Review 87*, 1509–1572.

NY CLS Correct § 656 (2004).

Oberlander, L. B., & Goldstein, N. E. (2001). A review and update on the practice of evaluating Miranda comprehension. *Behavioral Sciences and the Law, 19*, 453–471.

Oberlander, L. B., Goldstein, N. E., & Goldstein, A. M. (2003). Competence to confess. In Goldstein, A. (Ed), *Handbook of psychology. Vol. 11: Forensic psychology* (pp. 335–357). New York: Wiley.

Ogloff, J. R. P., Roberts, C. F., & Roesch, R. (1993). The insanity defense: Legal standards and clinical assessment. *Applied and Preventive Psychology, 2*, 163–178.

Ohio (2004).

Ohio Rev. Code Ann. § 2901.06(A) (2004).

Ohio Rev. Code § 2929.12 (2004).

21 Okl. St. § 152 (2004).

22 Okl. St. § 1175.5 (2004).

Okla Stat. Ann. tit 21, § 701.12(7) (2004).

O'Neill, K. M., Patry, M. W., & Penrod, S. D. (2004). Exploring the effects of attitudes toward the death penalty on capital sentencing verdicts. *Psychology, Public Policy, and Law, 10*, 443–470.

Or Rev. Stat. § 163.150(1)(b)(B) (2003).

Otto, R. K., Poythress, N. G., Nicholson, R. A., Edens, J. F., Monahan, J., et al.. (1998). Psychometric properties of the MacArthur Competence Assessment Tool—Criminal Adjudication. *Psychological Assessment, 10*, 435–443.

18 Pa. Cons. Stat. § 314 (2004).

50 Pa. Stat. Ann. § 7402 (2002).

Pa. Stat. Ann. § 7402 (2004).

Pallone, N. J., & Hennessy, J. J. (2003). To punish or to treat: Substance abuse within the context of oscillating attitudes toward correctional rehabilitation. *Journal of Offender Rehabilitation, 37*(3–4), 2003.

Palmer v. State, 857 S.W.2d 898 (Tex. App. Houston 1st Dist., 1993).

Pate v. Robinson, 383 U.S. 375 (1966).

Patterson v. Illinois, 487 U.S. 285 (1988).

Patterson v. New York, 432 U.S. 197 (1977).

Pennsylvania (2004).

Penry v. Johnson, 531 U.S. 1003 (2001).

Penry v. Lynaugh, 492 U.S. 302 (1989).

People v. Bolton, 800 N.E.2d 128 (Ill. App., 2003).

People v. Carpenter, 627 N.W.2d 276 (Mich., 2001).

People v. Edney, 350 N.E.2d 400 (N.Y., 1976).

People v. Ferguson, 670 NYS2d 327 (NY App. Div., 1998).

People v. Lines, 531 P. 793 (Cal., 1975).

People v. Schmidt, 110 N.E. 945 (N.Y., 1915).

People v. Superior Court (Ghilotti), 44 P.3d 949 (Cal., 2002).

People v. Taylor, 782 N.E.2d 920 (Ill. App., 2002).

People v. Ward, 71 Cal. App. 4th 368 (Cal. Ct. App., 1999).

People v. Wolff, 394 P.2d 959 (Cal. 1964).

Perlin, M. L. (1994). *The jurisprudence of the insanity defense.* Durham, NC: Carolina Academic Press.

Perlin, M. K., & Gould, K. K. (1995). Rashomon and the Criminal law: Mental disability and the Federal Sentencing Guidelines. *American Journal of Criminology and Law, 22*, 431–459.

Pfohl, B., Blum, N., & Zimmerman, M., (1995). *The Structured Interview for DSM-IV Personality: SIDP-IV.* Iowa City: University of Iowa.

Philipsborn, J. T. (2004). Searching for uniformity in adjudications of the accused's competence to assist and consult in capital cases. *Psychology, Public Policy, and Law, 10*, 417–442.

Poythress, N. G., Nicholson, R., Otto, R. K., Edens, J. F., Bonnie, R. J., Monahan, J., et al. (1999). *Professional manual for the MacArthur Competence Assessment Tool—Criminal Adjudication.* Odessa, FL: Psychological Assessment Resources.

Poythress, N., Melton, G. B., Petrila, J., & Slobogin, C. (2000). Commentary on "Mental Status at the Time of the Offense measure." *Journal of the American Academy of Psychiatry and Law, 28*, 29–32.

Pray, R. T. (2003). Sex offender therapy outcome: A meta-analysis. *Dissertation Abstracts International: Section B: The Sciences and Engineering, 63*(10-B), 4919.

Prosono, M. (2002). History of forensic psychiatry. In R. Rosner (Ed.), *Principles and practice of forensic psychiatry* (2nd ed., pp. 14–30). New York: Wiley.

Psychological Corporation. (2002). *Wechsler Individual Achievement Test* (2nd ed.). San Antonio: Author.

Quen, J. M. (1981). Anglo American concepts of criminal responsibility. In S. J. Hucker, C. D. Webster, & M. H. Ben-Aron (Eds.), *Mental disorder and criminal responsibility* (pp. 1–10). Toronto: Butterworth.

Quintana v. Commonwealth, 295 S.E.2d 643 (Va. 1982).

Rattan, G., Dean, R. S., & Rattan, A. I. (1989). *Neuropsychological Symptom Inventory*. Muncie: IN: Author.

Rector v. Clark, 923 F.2d 570 (8th Cir., 1991).

Rector v. Clinton, 823 S.W. 2d 829 (Ark., 1992).

Rector v. Lockhart, 727 F. Supp. 1285 (D. Ark., 1990).

Rees v. Peyton, 384 U.S. 312 (1966).

Resnick, P. J. (2003). Guidelines for courtroom testimony. In R. Rosner (Ed.), *Principles and practice of forensic psychiatry* (pp. 37–44). New York: Wiley.

Reynolds, C. R., & Kamphaus, R. W. (2003). *Reynolds Intellectual Assessment Scales*. Lutz, FL: Psychological Assessment Resources, Inc.

Reznek, L. (1997). *Evil or ill? Justifying the insanity defense*. New York: Rutledge.

Rhode Island v. Innis, 446 U.S. 291 (1980).

Rice, M. S., & Harris, G. T. (1997). Cross-validation and extension of the Violence Risk Appraisal Guide for child molesters and rapists. *Law and Human Behavior, 21*, 231–241.

Riggins v. Nevada, 504 U.S. 127 (1992).

Ring v. Arizona, 536 U.S. 584 (2002).

Roberts, K., & Wagstaff, G. F. (1996). The effects of beliefs and information about hypnosis on the legal defense of automatism through hypnosis. *Psychology, Crime, and Law, 2*, 259–268.

Robey, A. (1965). Criteria for competency to stand trial: A checklist for psychiatrists. *American Journal of Psychiatry, 122*, 616–623.

Robins, L. N., Marcus, S. C., Reich, W., et al. (1996). *Diagnostic Interview Schedule, Version IV*. St. Louis, MO: Washington School of Medicine.

Robitscher, J. B. (1966). *Pursuit of agreement: Psychiatry and the law*. Philadelphia: J. B. Lippincott.

Roesch, R., & Golding, S. L. (1980). *Competency to stand trial*. Chicago: University of Illinois Press.

Roesch, R., & Golding, S. L. (1988). Defining and assessing competency to stand trial. In I. B. Weiner & A. K. Hess (Eds.), *Handbook of forensic psychology* (pp. 378–394). New York: Wiley.

Rogers, R. (1984). *Rogers criminal responsibility assessment scales (RCRAS) and test manual*. Odessa, FL: Psychological Assessment Resources, Inc.

Rogers, R. (1986). *Conducting insanity evaluations* (1st ed.). New York: Van Nostrand Reinhold.

Rogers, R. (1987). The APA position on the insanity defense: Empiricism vs. emotionalism. *American Psychologist, 42*, 840–848.

Rogers, R. (1990). Models of feigned mental illness. *Professional Psychology: Research and Practice, 21*, 182–188.

Rogers, R. (1995). *Diagnostic and structured interviewing: A handbook for psychologists*. Odessa, FL: Psychological Assessment Resources, Inc.

Rogers, R. (Ed.). (1997). *Clinical assessment of malingering and deception* (2nd ed.). New York: Guilford.

Rogers, R. (2000). The uncritical acceptance of risk assessment in forensic practice. *Law and Human Behavior, 24*, 595–605.

Rogers, R. (2001). *Handbook of diagnostic and structured interviewing*. New York: Guilford Publications.

Rogers, R. (2002). Validating retrospective assessments: An overview of research models. In R. I. Simon & D. W. Shuman (Eds.), *Predicting the past: The retrospective assessment of mental states in civil and criminal litigation* (pp. 287–306). Washington, DC: American Psychiatric Press.

Rogers, R. (2003a). Standardizing DSM-IV diagnoses: The clinical applications of structured interviews. *Journal of Personality Assessment, 81*, 220–225.

Rogers, R. (2003b). The use and abuse of psychological tests in clinical and forensic practice: A focus on multiscale inventories. *Journal of Psychiatric Practice, 9*, 316–320.

Rogers, R. (2004). *Models of Miranda comprehension for representative warnings.* Grant from the National Science Foundation (NSF SES-0418057).

Rogers, R., & Bagby, R. M. (1992). Diversion of mentally disordered offenders: A legitimate role for clinicians? *Behavioral Sciences and Law, 10*, 407–418.

Rogers, R., Bagby, R. M., Crouch, M., & Cutler, B. (1990, March). *The insanity defense and ultimate opinion testimony.* Paper presented at the 1990 American Psychology-Law Society Midwinter Conference, Williamsburg, VA.

Rogers, R., Bagby, R. M., & Dickens, S. E. (1992). *Structured Interview of Reported Symptoms (SIRS) and professional manual.* Odessa, FL: Psychological Assessment Resources, Inc.

Rogers, R., & Bender, S. D. (2003). Evaluation of malingering and deception. In A. M. Goldstein (Ed.), *Comprehensive handbook of psychology: Forensic psychology* (Vol. 11, pp. 109–129). New York: Wiley.

Rogers, R., & Cruise, K. R. (2000). Malingering and deception among psychopaths. In C. B. Gacono (Ed.), *The clinical and forensic assessment of psychopathy: A practitioner's guide* (pp. 269–284). New York: LEA.

Rogers, R., Dion, K. L., & Lynett, E. (1992). Diagnostic validity of antisocial personality disorder: A prototypical analysis. *Law and Human Behavior, 16*, 677–689.

Rogers, R., Duncan, J. C., & Sewell, K. W. (1994). Prototypical analysis of antisocial personality disorder: DSM-IV and beyond. *Law and Human Behavior, 18*, 471–484.

Rogers, R., & Ewing, C. P. (1989). Proscribing ultimate opinions: A quick and cosmetic fix. *Law and Human Behavior, 13*, 357–374.

Rogers, R., & Ewing, C. P. (2003). The prohibition of ultimate opinions: A misguided enterprise. *Journal of Forensic Psychology Practice, 3*, 65–75.

Rogers, R., Gillis, J. R., Dickens, S. E., & Webster, C. D. (1988). The treatability of forensic patients: Are clinical judgments more than roulette? *Behavioral Sciences and the Law, 6*, 487–495.

Rogers, R., & Grandjean, N. R. (2000, March). *Competency measures and the Dusky standard: A conceptual mismatch?* Biennial convention of the American Psychology-Law Society, New Orleans.

Rogers, R., Grandjean, N. R., Tillbrook, C. E., Vitacco, M. J., & Sewell, K. W. (2001). Recent interview-based measures of competency to stand trial: A critical review augmented with research data. *Behavioral Sciences and the Law, 19*, 503–518.

Rogers, R., Harrell, E. H., & Liff, C. D. (1993). Feigning neuropsychological impairment: A critical review of methodological and clinical considerations. *Clinical Psychology Review, 13*, 255–274.

Rogers, R., Jackson, R. L., Sewell, K. W., & Salekin, K. L. (in press). Detection strategies for malingering: A confirmatory factor analysis of the SIRS. *Criminal Justice and Behavior.*

Rogers, R., Jackson, R. L., Sewell, K. W., & Harrison, K. S. (2004). An examination of the ECST-R as a screen for feigned incompetency to stand trial. *Psychological Assessment.*

Rogers, R., Jackson, R. L., Sewell, K. W., & Tillbrook, C. E. (2003a). *Assessing dimensions of competency to stand trial: Construct validation of the ECST-R.* Manuscript submitted for publication.

Rogers, R., Jackson, R. L., Sewell, K. W., Tillbrook, C. E., & Martin, M. A. (2003). Assessing dimensions of competency to stand trial: Construct validation of the ECST-R. *Assessment, 10*, 344–351.

Rogers, R., Jordan, M. J., & Harrison, K. S. (2004). A critical review of published competency-to-confess measures. *Law and Human Behavior, 28*, 707–718.

Rogers, R., & Kelly, K. S. (1997). Denial and misreporting of substance abuse. In R. Rogers (Ed.), *Clinical assessment of malingering and deception* (2nd ed., pp. 108–129). New York: Guilford.

Rogers, R., & McKee, G. R. (1995). Use of the MMPI-2 in the assessment of criminal responsibility. In Y. S. Ben-Porath, J. R. Graham, G. C. N. Hall, R. D. Hirschman, & M. S. Zaragoza (Eds.), *Forensic applications of the MMPI-2* (pp. 103–126). Newbury Park, CA: Sage.

Rogers, R., & Mitchell, C. N. (1991). *Mental health experts and the criminal courts: A handbook for lawyers and clinicians*. Toronto: Carswell.

Rogers, R., & Neumann, C. S. (2003). Conceptual issues and explanatory models of malingering. In P. W. Halligan, C. Bass, & D. A. Oakley (Eds.), *Malingering and illness deception: Clinical and theoretical perspectives* (pp. 71–82). Oxford, England: Oxford University Press.

Rogers, R., & Reinhardt, V. (1998). Conceptualization and assessment of secondary gain. In G. P. Koocher, J. C. Norcross, & S. S. Hill III (Eds.), *Psychologist's desk reference* (pp. 57–62). New York: Oxford University Press.

Rogers, R., Salekin, R. T., & Sewell, K. W. (1999). Validation of the Millon Multiaxial Inventory for Axis II disorders: Does it meet the *Daubert* standard? *Law and Human Behavior, 23,* 425–443.

Rogers, R., Salekin, R. T., & Sewell, K. W. (2000). The Millon Clinical Multiaxial Inventory: Separating rhetoric from reality. *Law and Human Behavior, 24,* 501–506.

Rogers, R., Salekin, R. T., Sewell, K. W., & Cruise, K. R. (2000). Prototypical analysis of antisocial personality disorder: A study of inmate samples. *Criminal Justice and Behavior, 27,* 216–233.

Rogers, R., Salekin, R. T., Sewell, K. W., Goldstein, A., & Leonard, K. (1998). A comparison of forensic and nonforensic malingerers: A prototypical analysis of explanatory models. *Law and Human Behavior, 22,* 353–367.

Rogers, R., & Sewell, K. W. (1999). The R-CRAS and insanity evaluations: A re-examination of construct validity. *Behavioral Sciences and the Law, 17,* 181–194.

Rogers, R., Sewell, K. W., Cruise, K. R., Wang, E. W., & Ustad, K. L. (1998). The PAI and feigning: A cautionary note on its use in forensic-correctional settings. *Assessment, 5,* 399–405.

Rogers, R., Sewell, K. W., Martin, M. A., & Vitacco, M. J. (2003). Detection of feigned mental disorders: A meta-analysis of the MMPI-2 and malingering. *Assessment, 10,* 160–177.

Rogers, R., Sewell, K. W., Morey, L. C., & Ustad, K. L. (1996). Detection of feigned mental disorders on the Personality Assessment Inventory: A discriminant analysis. *Journal of Personality Assessment, 67,* 629–640.

Rogers, R., & Shuman, D. W. (2000a). *Conducting insanity evaluations* (2nd ed.). New York: Guilford Publications.

Rogers, R., & Shuman, D. W. (2000b). The "Mental Status at the Time of the Offense" measure: Its validation and admissibility under Daubert. *Journal of the American Academy of Psychiatry and Law, 28,* 23–28.

Rogers, R., Tillbrook, C. E., & Sewell, K. W. (1998). *Evaluation of Competency to Stand Trial—Revised (ECST-R)*. Unpublished test, University of North Texas, Denton.

Rogers, R., Tillbrook, C. E., & Sewell, K. W. (2004). *Evaluation of Competency to Stand Trial—Revised (ECST-R) and professional manual*. Odessa, FL: Psychological Assessment Resources, Inc.

Rogers, R., & Webster, C. D. (1989). Assessing treatability in mentally disordered offenders. *Law and Human Behavior, 13,* 19–29.

Rogers, R., & Vitacco, M. J. (2002). Forensic assessment of malingering and related response styles. In B. Van Dorsten (Ed.), *Forensic psychology: From classroom to courtroom* (pp. 83–104). Boston: Kluwer Academic/Plenum Publishers.

Roid, G. (2003). Stanford–Binet Intelligence Scales, 5th edition. Itasca, IL: Riverside Publishing.

Rosch, E. (1973). On the internal structure of perceptual and semantic categories. In T. E. Moore (Ed.), *Cognitive development and the acquisition of language* (pp. 111–144). New York: Academic Press.

Rosch, E. (1978). Principles of categorization. In E. Rosch & B. B. Lloyd (Eds.), *Cognition and categorization* (pp. 27–48). Hillsdale, NJ: Erlbaum.

Rosell, L. (2004, March). *Actuarial instruments in SVP evaluations: Proceed with caution*. Paper presented that the American Psychology-Law Society Convention, Scottsdale.

Rosner, R. (Ed.). (2003). *Principles and practice of forensic psychiatry* (2nd ed.). London: Arnold.

Rumbaugh v. Procunier, 753 F.2d 395 (5th Cir., 1985).

Ryan, M. (2002, February). *Risk assessment*. Monterey Beach: California Association for Criminal Justice.

Salekin, R. T. (2002). Psychopathy and therapeutic pessimism: Clinical lore or clinical reality. *Clinical Psychology Review, 22*, 79–112.

Salekin, R. T., Leistico, A. R., & Rogers, R. (2004, August). *A review and meta-analysis of the PCL-R*. Paper presented at the American Psychological Association in Honolulu, Hawaii.

Salekin, R. T., Rogers, R., & Sewell, K. W. (1996). A review and meta-analysis of the Psychopathy Checklist and Psychopathy Checklist—Revised: Predictive validity of dangerousness. *Clinical Psychology: Science and Practice, 3*, 203–215.

Sallee v. State; 544 P.2d 902 (Okla. Crim. App., 1975).

Sarkar, S. P. (2003). From *Hendricks* to *Crane*: The sexually violent predator trilogy and the inchoate jurisprudence of the US Supreme Court. *Journal of the American Academy of Psychiatry and the Law, 31*, 242–248.

Sattler, J. M. (1989). Review of Vineland Adaptive Behavior Scales. In J. C. Conoley & J. J. Kramer (Eds.), *The tenth mental measurements yearbook* [Electronic version]. Retrieved December 12, 2004, from the Buros Institute's *Test Reviews Online* website http://www.unl.edu/buros

Saunders, D. G. (1994). Child custody decisions in families experiencing woman abuse. *Social Work, 39*, 51–59.

Schexnider v. State, 943 S.W.2d 194 (Tex. App. Beaumont, 1997).

Schneckloth v. Bustamonte, 412 U.S. 218 (1973).

Schoenberg, M. R., Dorr, D., & Morgan, C. D. (2003). The ability of the Millon Clinical Multiaxial Inventory—Third Edition to detect malingering. *Psychological Assessment, 15*, 198–204.

Schopp, R. F. (2001). *Competence, condemnation, and commitment: An integrated theory of mental health law*. Washington, DC: American Psychological Association.

Schopp, R. F., & Slain, A. J. (2000). Psychopathy, criminal responsibility, and civil commitment as a sexual predator. *Behavioral Sciences and the Law, 18*, 247–274.

Schraff v. State, 544 P.2d 834 (Alaska, 1975).

Schretlen, D. J. (1997). Dissimulation on the Rorschach and other projective measures. In R. Rogers (Ed.), *Clinical assessment of malingering and deception* (2nd ed., pp. 208–222). New York: Guilford.

Schretlen, D. J., Brandt, J., Krafft, L., & Van Gorp, W. G. (1991). Some caveats in using the Rey 15-Item Memory Test to detect malingered amnesia. *Psychological Assessment, 3*(4), 667–672.

Schuessler v. State, 719 S.W.2d 320 (Tex. Crim. App., 1986).

Schwenk, T. L., Coyne, J. C., & Fechner-Bates, S. (1996). Differences between detected an undetected patients in primary care and depressed psychiatric patients. *General Hospital Psychiatry, 18*, 407–415.

Seling v. Young, 521 U.S. 250 (2001).

Sell v United States, 539 U.S. 166 (2003).

Sellers v. State, 809 P.2d 676 (Okla. Crim. App., 1991).

Selzer, M. L. (1971). Michigan Alcoholism Screening Test: The quest for a new diagnostic instrument. *American Journal of Psychiatry, 127,* 1653–1658.

Serin, R., Barbaree, H., Seto, M., Malcolm, B., & Peacock, E. (1997). *A model for a clinically-informed risk assessment strategy for sex offenders.* Ottawa: Correctional Service Canada. Retrieved August 6, 2004, from http://www.cscscc.gc.ca/text/rsrch/reports/r56/ r56e_e.shtml

Seto, M. C., & Barbaree, H. E. (1999). Psychopathy, treatment behavior, and sex offender recidivism. *Journal of Interpersonal Violence, 14,* 1235–1248.

Sewell, K. W., & Cruise, K. R. (1997). Understanding and detecting dissimulation in sex offenders. In R. Rogers (Ed.), *Clinical assessment of malingering and deception* (2nd ed., pp. 328–350). New York: Guilford.

Shafer v. Bowersox, 329 F.3d 637 (8th Cir., 2003).

Shapiro, D. L. (1999). *Criminal responsibility evaluations: A manual for practice.* Sarasota, FL: Professional Resource Press.

Shaw v. Armontrout, 900 F.2d 123 (8th Cir., 1990).

Shear, M. K., Greeno, C., Kang, J., Ludewig, D., Frank, E. et al. (2000). Diagnosis of nonpsychotic patients in community clinics. *American Journal of Psychiatry, 157,* 581–587.

Shuman, D. W. (1996). *Psychiatric and psychological evidence* (2nd ed.). Colorado Springs: Shepherds/McGraw-Hill.

Shuman, D. W., Champagne, A., & Whitaker, E. (1996). Assessing the believability of expert witnesses: Science in the jurybox. *Jurimetrics, 37,* 23–31.

Shuman, D. W., & Greenberg, S. A. (2003). The expert witness, the adversary system, and the voice of reason: Reconciling impartiality and advocacy. *Professional Psychology: Research and Practice, 3,* 219–224.

Silver, E., Cirincione, C., & Steadman, H. J. (1994). Demythologizing inaccurate perceptions of the insanity defense. *Law and Human Behavior, 18,* 63–70.

Silverton, L., & Gruber, E. (1998). *The Malingering Probability Scale (MPS) manual.* Los Angeles: Western Psychological Services.

Simon, R. A. (1967). *The jury and the defense of insanity.* Boston: Little, Brown.

Simon, R. I., & Shuman, D. W. (1999). Conducting forensic examinations on the road: Are you practicing your profession without a license? *Journal of the American Academy of Psychiatry and Law, 27,* 75–82.

Simourd, D. J., Bonta, J., Andrews, D. A., & Hoge, R. D. (1990, May). *Criterion validity of assessments of psychopathy: A meta-analysis.* Paper presented at the meeting of the Canadian Psychological Association, Ottawa, Canada.

Singleton v. State, 437 S.E.2d 53 (S.C., 1993).

Sjostedt, G., & Langstrom, N. (2002). Assessment of risk for criminal recidivism among rapists: A comparison of four different measures. *Psychology, Crime, and Law, 8,* 25–40.

Skeem, J. L., Golding, S. L., Cohn, N. B., & Berge, G. (1998). Logic and reliability of evaluations of competence to stand trial. *Law and Human Behavior, 22,* 519–547.

Skeem, J. L., Monahan, J., & Mulvey, E. P. (2002). Psychopathy, treatment involvement, and subsequent violence among civil psychiatric patients. *Law and Human Behavior, 26,* 577–603.

Skinner, H. A. (1982). The Drug Abuse Screening Test. *Addictive Behaviors, 7,* 363–371.

Skipper v. South Carolina, 476 U.S. 1 (1986).

Slick, D. J., Hopp, G., Strauss, E., Hunter, M., & Pinch, D. (1994). Detecting dissimulation: Profiles of simulated malingerers, traumatic brain-injured individuals, and normal controls on a revised version of Hiscock and Hiscock's forced-choice memory test. *Journal of Clinical and Experimental Neuropsychology, 16*(3), 472–481.

Slick, D. J., Hopp, G., Strauss, E., & Spellacy, F. (1996). Victoria Symptom Validity Test: Efficiency for detecting feigned memory impairment and the relationship to neuropsychological tests and MMPI-2 validity scales. *Journal of Clinical and Experimental Neuropsychology, 18*(6), 911–922.

Slick, D., Hopp, G., Strauss, E., & Thompson, G. B. (1997). *Professional manual for the Victoria Symptom Validity Test.* Odessa, FL: Psychological Assessment Resources.

Slobogin, C. (2000). Mental illness and the death penalty. *MPDLR, 24,* 667–677.

Slobogin, C., Melton, G. B., & Showalter, C. R. (1984). The feasibility of a brief evaluation of mental state at the time of the offense. *Law and Human Behavior, 8,* 305–320.

Slosson, R. L., & Nicholson, C. L. (2002). *Slosson Oral Reading Test.* Wilmington, DE: Wide Range, Inc.

Smith, G. P. (1998). Test review: The Test of Memory Malingering. *American Psychology-Law Society News, 18,* 16–18, 29–30.

Smith v. Bowersox, 540 U.S. 893 (2002).

Smith v. McCormick, 914 F.2d 1153 (9th Cir., 1990).

S.C. Code Ann. § 17-24-20 (2003).

S.D. Codified Laws § 23A-7-2 (2003).

Sparrow, S. S., Balla, D. A., Chicchetti, D. V., & Harrison, P. L. (1985). *Vineland Adaptive Behavior Scales.* Circle Pines, MN: American Guidance Service.

Spitzer, R. L., & Endicott, J. (1978a). *Schedule of Affective Disorders and Schizophrenia* (3rd ed.). New York: Biometrics Research.

Spitzer, R. L., & Endicott, J. (1978b). *Schedule of Affective Disorders and Schizophrenia—Change Version.* New York: Biometrics Research.

Stack v. Boyle, 342 U.S. 1 (1951).

Stafford, K. P. (2003). Assessment of competence to stand trial. In A. M. Goldstein (Ed.), *Handbook of psychology. Vol. 11: Forensic psychology* (pp. 359–380). New York: Wiley.

State v. Bailey, 519 A.2d 132 (Del. Super. Ct., 1986) 434, USSG (1995).

State v. Berry, 686 N.E.2d 1097 (Ohio, 1997).

State v. Caddell, 215 S.E.2d 348 (N.C., 1975).

State v. Clark, 389 So. 2d 1335 (La., 1990).

State v. Cooey, 544 N.E.2d 895 (Ohio, 1989).

State v. Corely, 495 P.2d 470 (Ariz., 1972).

State v. Creech, 670 P.2d 463 (Idaho, 1983).

State v. Dodd, 424 P.2d 302 (Wash., 1967).

State v. Dodd, 838 P.2d 86 (Wash., 1992).

State ex rel. Romley v. Fields, 35 P.3d 82 (Ariz. Ct. App., 2001).

State v. Esser, 115 N.W.2d 505 (Wisc., 1962).

State v. Garrett, 391 S.W.2d 235 (Mo., 1965).

State v. Guatney, 299 N.W.2d 538 (Neb., 1980) (Krivosha, C.J., concurring).

State v. Hamlet, 944 P.2d 1026 (Wash., 1997).

State v. Hamrick, 236 S.E.2d 247 (W. Va., 1977).

State v. Harden, 480 P.2d 53 (Kan., 1971).

State v Herrera, 895 P.2d 359 (Utah, 1995).

State v. Hodges, 716 P.2d 563, 567 (Kan., 1986).

State v. Holtz, 653 N.W.2d 613 (Iowa Ct. App., 2002).

State v. Jones, 527 S.E.2d 700 (N.C. Ct. App., 2000).

State v. Kelly, 478 A.2d 364 (N.J., 1984a).

State v. Kelly, 685 P.2d 564 (Wash., 1984b).

State v. Korell, 690 P.2d 992 (Mont., 1984).

State v. Koss, 551 N.E.2d 970 (Ohio, 1990).

State v. Lamar, 698 P.2d 735 (Ariz. Ct. App., 1984).

State v. Lee, 491 N.W.2d 895 (Minn., 1992).

State v McClendon, 437 P2d 421 (Ariz., 1968).

State v. Mott, 931 P.2d 1046 (Ariz., 1997).

State v. Perry, 610 So.2d 746 (LA, 1992).

State v. Rees, 748 A.2d 976 (Me., 2000).

State v. Searcy, 798 P.2d 914 (Idaho, 1990).

State v. Thomas, 423 N.E.2d 137 (Ohio, 1981).

State v. Torrence, 451 S.E.2d 883 (S.C., 1994).

State v. Wall, 343 N.W.2d 22 (Minn., 1984).

State v. Williams, 252 S.E.2d 739 (N.C., 1979).

Steadman, H. J., Barbera, S. H., & Dennis, D. L. (1994). A national survey of jail mental health diversion programs. *Hospital and Community Psychiatry, 45,* 1109–1113.

Steadman, H. J., Corcozza, J. J., & Veysey, B. M. (1999). Comparing outcomes for diverted and nondiverted jail detainees with mental illnesses. *Law and Human Behavior, 23,* 615–627.

Steadman, H. J., McGreevy, M. A., Morrissey, J. P., Callahan, L. A., Robbins, P. C., & Cirincione, C. (1993). *Before and after Hinckley: Evaluating the insanity defense reform.* New York: Guilford.

Steadman, H. J., Morris, S. M., & Dennis, D. L. (1995). The diversion of mentally ill persons from jails to community-based services: A profile of programs. *American Journal of Public Health, 85,* 1630–1635.

Steen v. State, 69 S.W.2d 144 (Tex. Crim. App., 1934).

Steiner, B. D., Bowers, W. J., & Sarat, A. (1999). Folk knowledge as legal action: Death penalty judgments and the tenet of early release in a culture of mistrust and punitiveness. *Law and Society Review, 33,* 461–505.

Sterling, S., & Edelmann, R. J. (1998). Reactions of anger and anxiety-provoking events: Psychopathic and nonpsychopathic groups compared. *Journal of Clinical Psychology, 44,* 96–100.

Stevens, G. F. (1994). Prison clinicians' perceptions of antisocial personality disorders as a formal diagnosis. *Journal of Offender Rehabilitation, 20,* 159–185.

Stone, T. H., Winslade, W. J., & Klugman, C. M. (2000). Sex offenders, sentencing laws and pharmaceutical treatment: A prescription for failure. *Behavioral Sciences and the Law, 18,* 83–110.

Straus, M. A., Hamby, S. L., Boney-McCoy, S., & Sugarman, D. B. (1996). The Revised Conflict Tactics Scale (CTS-2): Development of preliminary psychometric data. *Journal of Family Issues, 17,* 283–316.

Teichner, G., & Wagner, M. T. (2004). The Test of Memory Malingering (TOMM): Normative data from cognitively intact, cognitively impaired, and elderly patients with dementia. *Archives of Clinical Neuropsychology, 19,* 455–464.

Tellegen, A., Ben-Porath, Y. S., McNulty, J. L., Arbisi, P. A., Graham, J. R., & Kaemmer, B. (2003). *The MMPI-2 restructured clinical (RC) scales: Development, validation and interpretation.* Minneapolis: University of Minnesota Press.

Tennard v. Dretke. (2004). WL 1402731.

Teplin, L. A. (Ed.). (1984). *Mental health and criminal justice.* Beverly Hills, CA: Sage.

Tex. Code Crim. Proc. Ann. Art. 37.071 (2004).

Tex. Code Crim. Proc. art. 46B.003 (2004).

Tex. Code Crim. Proc. art. 46B.073 (2004).

Tex. Code Crim. Proc. art. 46.02 (Vernon, 2002).

Texas § 19.02 (2004).

Tex. Penal Code Ann. § 8.01 (Vernon, 1994).

Tex. Penal Code § 19.04 (2004).

Tex. Penal Code § 19.05 (2004).

Tex. Penal Code Ann. § 6.03 (2004).

Tex. Penal Code Ann. § 8.01 (Vernon, 1994).

Tiemens, B. G., VonKorff, M., & Lin, E. H. B. (1999). Diagnosis of depression by primary care physicians versus a structured diagnostic interview. *General Hospital Psychiatry, 21,* 87–96.

Thompson v. State, 676 S.W.2d 173 (Tex. App. Houston 14th Dist., 1984).

Thompson, A. C. (2002). Access to justice: The social responsibility of lawyers: Courting disorder: Some thoughts on community courts. *Washington University Journal of Law and Policy, 10,* 63–99.

Thorndike, R. L., Hagen, E. P., & Sattler, J. M. (1986). *The Stanford–Binet Intelligence Scale,* 4th ed. Chicago: Riverside Publishing.

Tillbrook, C. E. (1997). *Validation of the Evaluation of Competency to Stand Trial (ECST) instrument: A preliminary assessment.* Unpublished Masters thesis, University of Alabama, Tuscaloosa.

Tolman, R. M. (1995). *Psychological Maltreatment of Women Inventory.* Unpublished research scale, University of Michigan. Retrieved December 21, 2004, from http://sitemaker.umich.edu/pmwi/files/pmwif.pdf

Tombaugh, T. N. (1996). *TOMM: The Test of Memory Malingering.* North Tonawanda, NY: MultiHealth Systems.

Tucker, D. E., & Brakel, S. J. (2003). Sexually violent predator laws. In R. Rosner (Ed.), *Principles and practice of forensic psychiatry* (2nd ed., pp. 717–723). London: Arnold.

18 U.S.C.A. § 4241 (2003).

18 U.S.C. § 3141 et seq. (1982 ed., Supp. III).

18 U.S.C. § 3551 et seq. (1982 ed., Supp. IV).

28 U.S.C.S. §§ 991-998 (1982 ed., Supp. IV).

USSG § 6A1.3.

United States v. $100,000 in United States Currency, 602 F Supp 712 (SDNY, 1985).

United States v. Bailey, 444 U.S. 394 (1980).

United State v. Barone, 968 F.2d 1378 (2nd Cir., 1992).

United States v Bartlett, 856 F2d 1071 (8th Cir., 1988).

United States v. Brawner, 471 F.2d 969 (D.C. Cir., 1972).

United States v. Byrd (1992).

United States v Cameron, 907 F2d 1051 (11th Cir., 1990).

United States v. Downs-Moses, 329 F.3d 253 (2nd Cir., 2003).

United States v. Dysart, 705 F.2d 1247 (10th Cir., 1983).

United States v. Elrod, 441 F.2d 353 (5th Cir., 1971).

United States v. Ferron, 357 F.3d 722 (7th Cir., 2004).

United States v. Garcia, 94 F.3d 57 (2nd Cir., 1996).

United States v. Gay, 774 F.2d 368, 377 (10th Cir., 1985).

United States v Gomes, 289 F.3d 71 (2nd Cir., 2002).

United States v. Hall, 565 F.2d 917 (5th Cir., 1978).

United States v. Holmes, 671 F. Supp. 120 (D. Conn., 1987).

United States v. Hunter, 145 F.3d 946 (7th Cir., 1998).

United States v. Iaconetti, 59 F. Supp. 2d 139 (D. Mass., 1999).

United States v. Kim, 313 F. Supp. 2d 295 (D.N.Y., 2004).

United States v Knott, 894 F2d 1119 (9th Cir., 1990) *cert den.* 498 US 873 (1990).

United States v. Marcello, 508 F. Supp. 586 (E.D. La., 1981).

United States v. Martin-Trigona, 767 F.2d 35 (2nd Cir., 1985), cert. denied, 474 U.S. 1061 (1986).

United States v. Matlock, 415 U.S. 164 (1974).

United States v. Newton, U.S. App. LEXIS 10343 (2nd Cir., 2004).

United States v. Nunemacher, 362 F.3d 682 (10th Cir., 2004).

United States v. Palmer, 203 F. 3rd 55, 60 (1st Cir., 2000).

United States v. Rambo, 789 F.2d 1289 (8th Cir., 1986).

United States v. Rezaq, 918 F. Supp. 463 (D.D.C., 1996).

United States v. Rojas-Martinez, 968 F.2d 415 (5th Cir., 1992).

United States v. Rosario-Diaz F.3d 54, 69 (1st Cir., 2000).

United States v. Ruiz, 536 U.S. 622, 153 L. Ed. 2d 586, 122 Ct. 2450 (2002).

United States v. Sadolsky, 234 F.3d 938 (6th Cir., 2000).

United States v. Sahhar, 56 F.3d 1026 (9th Cir., 1995).

United States v. Salava, 978 F.2d 320 (7th Cir., 1992).

United States v. Salerno, 481 U.S. 739 (1987).

United States v. Short, 790 F.2d 464, 469 (6th Cir., 1986).

United States v Villegas, 899 F2d 1324 (2nd Cir., 1990), *cert denied* 498 U.S. 991.

United States v. Watson, 423 U.S. 411 (1976).

United States v. Webster, 162 F.3d 308, 356-57 (5th Cir., 1998).

United States v. Wen Ho Lee, 79 F Supp 2d 1280 (D.N.M. 1999), aff'd 208 F.3d 288 (10th Cir., 2000).

United States v. Westcott, 83 F.3d 1354 (11th Cir., 1996).

United States v White, 766 F2d 22 (1st Cir., 1985).

United States v. Willis Haynes (PJM-98-0520) date of this unreported decision is not reported.

United States v. Yockel, 320 F.3d 818 (8th Cir., 2003).

United States Department of Justice. (2000). Emerging Judicial Strategies for the Mentally Ill in the Criminal Caseload: Mental Health Courts in Fort Lauderdale, Seattle, San Bernardino, and Anchorage. Retrieved from http://www.ncjrs.org/html/bja/mentalhealth/exec.html)

US Constitution, Amendments IV, V, VI.

Utah Code Ann. § 76-2-305 (2003).

Utah Code Ann. § 76-5-102 (2003a).

Utah Code Ann. § 76-5-103 (2003b).

Utah Code Ann. § 77-2-5 (2004).

Va. Code Ann. § 19.2-264.4 (2004).

Venezia v. United States, 884 F. Supp. 919 (D.N..J., 1995).

Viljoen, J. L., Roesch, R., & Zapf, P. A. (2002). An examination of the relationship between competency to stand trial, competency to waive, interrogation rights, and psychopathology. *Law and Human Behavior, 26*, 481–506.

Virgin Islands v. Charles, 72 F.3d 401 (3rd Cir., 1995).

Walker, L. E. (1979). *The battered woman.* New York: Harper & Row.

Walker, L. E. (1984). *The battered woman syndrome.* New York: Springer.

Walker, L. E., & Monahan, J. (1987). Social frameworks: A new use of social science in law. *Virginia Law Review, 73*, 559–598.

Walters, G. D. (2003). Predicting criminal justice outcomes with the Psychopathy Checklist and Lifestyle Criminal Screening Form: A meta-analytic comparison. *Behavioral Sciences and the Law, 21*, 83–88.

Walters v. Hubbard, 725 F.2d 381 (6th Cir., 1984), *cert denied* 469 U.S. 837 (1984).

Ward, C. H., Beck, A. T., Mendelson, M., Mock, J. E., & Erbaugh, J. K. (1962). The psychiatric nomenclature. *Archives of General Psychiatry, 7*, 198–205.

Ward v. Sternes, 334 F.3d 696, 701 n1 (7th Cir., 2003).

Ward, T., McCormack, J., Hudson, S. M., & Polaschek, D. (1997). Rape: Assessment and treatment. In D. R. Laws & W. O'Donohue (Eds.), *Sexual deviance: Theory, assessment, and treatment* (pp. 356–393). New York: Guilford.

Wash. Rev. Code Ann. § 10.95.070 (2004).

Wash. Rev. Code Ann. § 71.09.020 (2004).

Washington v. Harper, 493 U.S.210 (1990).

Watson v. DeTella, 122 F.3d 450 (7th Cir., 1997).

Watson, A., Hanrahan, P., Luchins, D., & Lurigio, A. (2001). Mental health courts and the complex issue of mentally ill offenders. *Psychiatric Services, 52*, 477–481.

Watt, M. J., & MacLean, W. E. (2003). Competency to be sentenced and executed. *Ethics and Behavior, 13*, 35–41.

Webster, C. D., Douglas, K. S., Eaves, D., & Hart, S. D. (1997). *HCR-20: Assessing risk for violence* (Version 2). Burnaby, BC: Mental Health, Law, and Policy Institute, Simon Fraser University.

Wechsler, D. (1997). *Weschler Adult Intelligence Scale—Third edition (WAIS-III)*. San Antonio, TX: Psychological Corporation.

Wechsler, D. (1999). *Wechsler Abbreviated Scale of Intelligence*. San Antonio, TX: Psychological Corporation.

Weinborn, M. Orr, T., Woods, S. P., Conover, E., & Feix, J. (2003). A validation of the Test of Memory Malingering in a forensic psychiatric setting. *Journal of Clinical and Experimental Neuropsychology, 25*, 979–990.

Weiner, I. B. (1995). Methodological considerations in Rorschach research. *Psychological Assessment, 7*, 330–337.

Weiner, I. B. (1997). Current status of the Rorschach inkblot method. *Journal of Personality Assessment, 68*, 5–19.

Welner, D. (2001). *The Depravity Scale*. Retrieved October 21, 2004, from http://www.depravityscale.org/.

Wettstein, R. M., Mulvey, E., & Rogers, R. (1991). Insanity defense standards: A prospective comparison. *American Journal of Psychiatry, 148*, 21–27.

Wettstein, R. M., Rogers, R., & Mulvey, E. (1986, October). *Insanity standards: A prospective comparison*. Paper presented at the American Academy of Psychiatry and Law, Philadelphia.

Wexler, D. B., & Winick, B. J. (1996). *Law in a therapeutic key: Developments in therapeutic jurisprudence*. Durham, NC: Carolina Academic Press.

Whitmore v. Arkansas, 495 U.S. 149 (1990).

Wiener, I. B. (1998). Rorschach differentiation of schizophrenia and affective disorder. In G. P. Koocher, J. C. Norcross, & S. S. Hill III (Eds.), *Psychologist's desk reference* (pp. 151–154). New York: Oxford University Press.

Wiener, R. L., Rogers, M., Winter, R., Hurt, L., Hackney, A., et al. (2004). Guided jury discretion in capital murder cases: The role of declarative and procedural knowledge. *Psychology, Public Policy, and Law, 10*, 516–576.

Wildman, R., Batchelor, E., Thompson, L., Nelson, F., Moore, J., Patterson, M., & deLaosa, M. (1979). The Georgia Court Competency Test. *Newsletter of the American Association of Correctional Psychologists, 2*, 4 (Abstract).

Williams, K. D., Bourgeois, M. J., & Croyle, R. T. (1993). The effects of stealing thunder in criminal and civil trials. *Law and Human Behavior, 17*, 597–609.

Wilkinson, G. S. (1993). *The Wide Range Achievement Test—3 administration manual*. Wilmington, DE: Wide Range.

Winkler, J. D., Kanouse, D. E., & Ware, J. E., Jr. (1982). Controlling for acquiescence response set in scale development. *Journal of Applied Psychology, 67*, 555–561.

Withrow v. Williams, 507 U.S. 680, 693, 123, L. Ed 2d 407, 113 S. Ct. 1745 (1993).

Wong, S., & Elek, D. (1989, August). *The treatment of psychopathy: A review.* Presented at the American Psychological Association Convention, New Orleans.

Wood, R. M., Grossman, L. S., & Fitchner, C. G. (2000). Psychological assessment, treatment, and outcome with sex offenders. *Behavioral Sciences and the Law, 18*, 23–41.

Woodson v. North Carolina, 428 U.S. 280 (1976).

Wooldredge, J., & Gordon, J. (1997). Predicting the estimated use of alternatives to incarceration. *Journal of Quantitative Criminology, 13*, 121–142.

Wortley, S., Fischer, B., & Webster, C. (2002). Vice lessons: A survey of prostitution offenders enrolled in the Toronto John School Division Program. *Canadian Journal of Criminology, 44*, 369–402.

Wrightsman, L. S., Greene, E., Nietzel, M. T., & Fortune, W. H. (2002). *Psychology and the Legal System* (5th ed.). Belmont, CA: Wadsworth.

Wrightsman, L. S., & Kassin, S. M. (1993). *Confessions in the courtroom.* Thousand Oaks, CA: Sage.

Wyo. Stat. Ann. § 7-11-302 (Michie, 2002).

Wyo. Stat. Ann. § 7-11-302 (2003).

Wyo. Stat. Ann. § 7-13-901 (2004).

Yarborough v. Alvarado, U.S. LEXIS 3843 (2004).

Zapf, P. A., Boccaccini, M. T., & Brodsky, S. L. (2003). Assessment of competency for execution: Professional guidelines and an evaluation checklist. *Behavioral Sciences and the Law, 21*, 103–120.

Zimmerman, M., & Mattia, J. I. (1999). Psychiatric diagnosis in clinical practice: Is comorbidity being missed? *Comprehensive Psychiatry, 40*, 182–191.

Ziskin, J. (1995). *Coping with psychological and psychiatric testimony* (Vols. 1—3, 5th ed.). Los Angeles, CA: Law and Psychology Press.

Zonana, H. V., Bonnie, R. J., & Hoge, S. K. (2003). In the wake of *Hendricks*: The treatment and restraint of sexually dangerous offenders viewed from the perspective of American psychiatry. In B. J. Winick & J. Q. LaFond (Eds.), *Protecting society from sexually dangerous offenders* (pp. 131–145). Washington, DC: American Psychological Association.

Zonana, H. V., & Norko, M. A. (1999). Sexual predators. *Psychiatric Clinics of North America, 22*, 109–127.

Name Index

Subject Index